Research Series on the Chinese Dream and China's Development Path

Drawing on a large body of empirical studies done over the last two decades, this Series provides its readers with in-depth analyses of the past and present and forecasts for the future course of China's development. It contains the latest research results made by members of the Chinese Academy of Social Sciences. This series is an invaluable companion to every researcher who is trying to gain a deeper understanding of the development model, path and experience unique to China. Thanks to the adoption of Socialism with Chinese characteristics, and the implementation of comprehensive reform and opening-up, China has made tremendous achievements in areas such as political reform, economic development, and social construction, and is making great strides towards the realization of the Chinese dream of national rejuvenation. In addition to presenting a detailed account of many of these achievements, the authors also discuss what lessons other countries can learn from China's experience.

More information about this series at http://www.springer.com/series/13571

Changhong Pei · Jianfeng Xu
Editors

Chinese Dream and Practice in Zhejiang – Economy

SSAP

Springer

Editors
Changhong Pei
Institute of Economics
Chinese Academy of Social Sciences
Beijing, China

Jianfeng Xu
Zhejiang Academy of Social Sciences
Hangzhou, China

Translated by Zheng Kaixiang

Published with support of Zhejiang People's Publishing House

ISSN 2363-6866 ISSN 2363-6874 (electronic)
Research Series on the Chinese Dream and China's Development Path
ISBN 978-981-13-7483-8 ISBN 978-981-13-7484-5 (eBook)
https://doi.org/10.1007/978-981-13-7484-5

Jointly published with Social Sciences Academic Press, Beijing, China
The print edition is not for sale in China Mainland. Customers from China Mainland please order the print book from: Social Sciences Academic Press.

Library of Congress Control Number: 2019935987

This Springer imprint is published by the registered company Springer Nature Singapore Pte Ltd.
The registered company address is: 152 Beach Road, #21-01/04 Gateway East, Singapore 189721, Singapore

Series Preface

Since China's reform and opening began in 1978, the country has come a long way on the path of Socialism with Chinese Characteristics, under the leadership of the Communist Party of China. Over thirty years of reform, efforts and sustained spectacular economic growth have turned China into the world's second-largest economy and wrought many profound changes in the Chinese society. These historically significant developments have been garnering increasing attention from scholars, governments, and the general public alike around the world since the 1990s, when the newest wave of China studies began to gather steam. Some of the hottest topics have included the so-called China miracle, Chinese phenomenon, Chinese experience, Chinese path, and the Chinese model. Homegrown researchers have soon followed suit. Already hugely productive, this vibrant field is putting out a large number of books each year, with Social Sciences Academic Press alone having published hundreds of titles on a wide range of subjects.

Because most of these books have been written and published in Chinese; however, readership has been limited outside China—even among many who study China—for whom English is still the lingua franca. This language barrier has been an impediment to efforts by academia, business communities, and policy-makers in other countries to form a thorough understanding of contemporary China, of what is distinct about China's past and present may mean not only for her future but also for the future of the world. The need to remove such an impediment is both real and urgent, and the *Research Series on the Chinese Dream and China's Development Path* is my answer to the call.

This series features some of the most notable achievements from the last 20 years by scholars in China in a variety of research topics related to reform and opening. They include both theoretical explorations and empirical studies and cover economy, society, politics, law, culture, and ecology; the six areas in which reform and opening policies have had the deepest impact and farthest-reaching consequences for the country. Authors for the series have also tried to articulate their visions of the "Chinese Dream" and how the country can realize it in these fields and beyond.

All of the editors and authors for the *Research Series on the Chinese Dream and China's Development Path* are both longtime students of reform and opening and recognized authorities in their respective academic fields. Their credentials and expertise lend credibility to these books, each of which has been subjected to a rigorous peer review process for inclusion in the series. As part of the Reform and Development Program under the State Administration of Press, Publication, Radio, Film, and Television of the People's Republic of China, the series is published by Springer, a Germany-based academic publisher of international repute, and distributed overseas. I am confident that it will help fill a lacuna in studies of China in the era of reform and opening.

Xie Shouguang

Contents

Chapter 1
Introduction: Zhejiang's Economic Development and the Chinese Dream

Jianfeng Xu

Zhejiang has witnessed sustained rapid economic development since its reform and opening up; in particular, since the beginning of the 21st century, the Zhejiang Provincial Party Committee and the Provincial Government have comprehensively, systematically summarized eight advantages of Zhejiang Province in development, and have put forward and thoroughly carried out eight measures for future development—the "Eight-Eight Strategies".[1] Afterwards, the successive governments of Zhejiang carried through one blueprint to consistently pursue development, implemented the strategy of making the people rich by starting businesses and of building a strong province through innovation, they worked toward the construction goal of becoming

[1] "Eight-Eight Strategies" means proceeding from Zhejiang's actual conditions to further give scope to eight advantages and push forward eight measures. First, further give play to the advantages of Zhejiang's institutions and mechanisms, actively promote the common development of the economy with different types of ownership while ensuring that public ownership remains dominant, continuously improve the system of a socialist market economy; second, further draw on the advantage of Zhejiang's location, proactively keep in line with Shanghai, actively engage in cooperation and communication with the Yangtze River Delta, constantly increase the level of opening up internally and externally; third, further leverage the advantages of the massive characteristic industries in Zhejiang, speed up the building of advanced manufacturing bases, take the path of new industrialization; fourth, further give play to Zhejiang's advantages in coordinated urban and rural development, quicken urban and rural integration; fifth, further utilize Zhejiang's ecological advantage, turn Zhejiang into an ecological province, build a green Zhejiang; sixth, further exploit the advantages of mountain and marine resources, energetically develop the marine economy, boost the leapfrog development of the underdeveloped areas, and make the development of the marine economy and the underdeveloped areas become the new economic growth point of Zhejiang Province; seventh, further utilize Zhejiang's environmental advantages, actively push forward main construction principally including five major ten-billion projects, practically strengthen legal construction, credit construction and improve the efficiency of organs; eighth, further leverage Zhejiang's humanistic advantage, actively rejuvenate the province through science, technology and talent, step up efforts to turn Zhejiang into a culturally strong province.

J. Xu (✉)
Zhejiang Academy of Social Sciences, Hangzhou, China

C. Pei and J. Xu (eds.), *Chinese Dream and Practice in Zhejiang – Economy*,
Research Series on the Chinese Dream and China's Development Path,
https://doi.org/10.1007/978-981-13-7484-5_1

affluent in material and rich in mind, by building a beautiful Zhejiang and creating a good life for its inhabitants, and they focused on transforming the economic developmental mode and acted in a down-to-earth manner, and they systematically carried forward a number of projects, such as "Four Changes and Three Famous Things", "Three Renovating and One Demolishing", and "The Governance for Five Kinds of Water"[2]; as a result, on the economic front, based on the original relatively high level, Zhejiang broke through the environmental constraints involving resources and factors, rapidly extricated itself from the adverse impact from the external environment including the global financial crisis, and ensured that its economic development would continue to be at the forefront nationwide.

Making the people rich and the country powerful is the core of the Chinese Dream, while sustainable economic development is the foundation for making the people rich and the country powerful. Zhejiang's development from a small economic province to a large economic province and then an economically strong province is precisely the best practice of the Chinese Dream in Zhejiang. Zhejiang's economic development offers excellent experience and inspirations for China to realize the dream of building an economically powerful country.

1.1 The Practice in Realizing the Dream of Turning Zhejiang into an Economically Strong Province

With entry into the 21st century, as domestic and foreign economic environments have changed, Zhejiang's economy has suffered from growing pains and has been subject to increasing resource and environmental constraints from factors such as land, labor, energy, and raw material, which have hindered the further development of Zhejiang's economy. In July, 2003, the Zhejiang Provincial Party Committee and the Provincial Government developed and implemented the "Eight-Eight Strategies", overcame new problems and new challenges in development and achieved rapid economic growth. In 2008, Zhejiang's per capita GDP exceeded USD 6,000, Zhejiang's economy became industrially developed, the people's living standard markedly improved, economic openness was increased in an all-round way and the capability of sustainable development was significantly enhanced.[3]

---

[2]"Four Changes and Three Famous Things" means "Vacating the cage to change birds," replacing the people with machines, optimizing space to save land, expanding the market through e-commerce, and cultivating well-known enterprises, famous products, and eminent experts; "Three Renovating and One Demolishing" means renovating old residential areas, old factory areas in urban areas and the villages in cities, demolishing illegal buildings; "The Governance for Five Kinds of Water" means treating sewage, controlling flooding, discharging the accumulated water, guaranteeing water supply, and saving water.

[3]See Xu Jianfeng, Zhejiang Has Economically Become Industrially Developed, *Zhejiang Academic Journal*, 2009(1).

1. The people's living standard was continuously improved

During the period from 2003 to 2014, Zhejiang's economic aggregate soared from 970,502 million yuan to 4,015,350 million yuan,[4] a 2.72-fold increase based on comparable prices. Although Zhejiang's economy was affected by SARS and the financial crisis, and was restricted by increasing factor resource and environmental protection pressure from the stages of economic development and great RMB appreciation and international economic slowdown in this period, Zhejiang's average annual economic growth rate still exceeded 12%, Zhejiang achieved sustained rapid growth; even in 2009 when Zhejiang suffered from a strong impact from the financial crisis, Zhejiang's economy still grew by 8.9%. Zhejiang's per capita GDP skyrocketed from 19,730 yuan in 2003 to 72,967 yuan in 2014; Zhejiang's per capita GDP in 2014 reached USD 11,878 based on the average exchange rate in 2014, five times the USD 2,380 in 2003. Zhejiang ranked No. 4 among provinces, autonomous regions, and municipalities directly under the Central Government nationwide in terms of per capita GDP, next only to Shanghai, Beijing, and Tianjin—three municipalities directly under the Central Government; Zhejiang was close to the level of a developed economy.

During the period from 2003 to 2014, the per capita disposable income of permanent urban residents and the per capita net income of permanent rural residents in Zhejiang increased from 13,180 yuan and 5,431 yuan to 40,393 yuan and 19,373 yuan, respectively, the living standard of urban and rural people greatly improved and the income gap between urban and rural residents narrowed to 2.09:1, and harmonious urban and rural development was maintained. The basic medical care, public health, the systems of public cultural and convenient services basically covered both urban and rural areas; the level of social assistance steadily increased; the construction of the housing security system continued to be strengthened; the life of urban and rural people greatly improved.

2. The capability for innovation improved significantly

Since 2003, new progress has been made in various programs of scientific and technological innovation in Zhejiang. According to the *2014 Annual Report of China's Regional Capability for Innovation*, Zhejiang Province ranked No. 5 nationwide in terms of regional capability for innovation, the same as that in 2003. According to the *2014 Annual Report on the Statistical Monitoring of Scientific and Technological Progress in China*, Zhejiang Province ranked No. 6 in the nationwide index of the level of comprehensive scientific and technological progress, up one place from 2003. The regional competitive advantage of new and hi-tech industries is taking shape in the areas around Hangzhou Bay, where many enterprises are transforming from extensive operations to intensive operations and from support based on low-cost labor to support based on scientific and technological innovation.

In 2003, Zhejiang's total expenditure in scientific and technological activities stood at 18.52 billion yuan, equivalent to 1.91% of the GDP. R&D expenditure

[4]According to the *Zhejiang Statistical Yearbook 2015*, all of them are based on the prices in the same year.

was 7776 million yuan, accounting for 0.80% of GDP. A total of 21,400 patent applications were accepted for handling and 14,400 patents were granted. There were 2750 invention patent applications accepted for handling and 398 invention patents were granted. The contracts concluded in the technology market amounted to 5.3 billion yuan. In 2014, Zhejiang's total expenditure in scientific and technological activities increased to 147 billion yuan, accounting for 3.66% of the GDP; R&D expenditure exceeded 93.9 billion yuan, accounting for 2.34% of the GDP. Fiscal input in science and technology was 20.8 billion yuan, up 8.4% over the previous year. Fiscal appropriation for science and technology made up 4.03% of fiscal expenditure. A total of 261,000 patent applications were accepted for handling and 189,000 patents were granted. In Zhejiang, there were 77 enterprise technology centers identified by the State and 6232 new and hi-tech enterprises were identified. There were 492 and 296 provincial-level innovative pilot enterprises and demonstration enterprises. The output value of new products from industrial enterprises above the designated size in Zhejiang Province reached 1.94 trillion yuan; the new product output value rate hit 29.2%, up 18.6 percentage points compared with 2003.[5]

3. The industrial structure was constantly upgraded

The structure of three industries changed greatly. During the period from 2003 to 2014, the growth of Zhejiang's service industry was faster than the growth of the GDP, the proportion of the service industry in the GDP increased to 47.9%, higher than that of the secondary industry (47.7%). The structure of the three industries was 7.4:52.5:40.1 in 2003 and 4.4:47.7:47.9 in 2014.[6] The ratios of the primary and secondary industries decreased by 3 percentage points and 4.8% points, respectively, while that of the tertiary industry increased by 7.8% points.

In 2014, the added value of Zhejiang's new and hi-tech industries reached 428.3 billion yuan, its proportion in the added value of industries above the designated size rose to 34.1%,[7] a dramatic increase compared with less than 10% in 2003.

In the tertiary industry, there was a great increase in the proportion of intermediary service sectors such as banking and finance, audit, accounting, consulting, educational, scientific and technological sectors and service sectors such as the transport sector. The information economy developed rapidly, it became a new bright spot in Zhejiang's economy; the business types in traditional commerce and trade and specialized markets changed rapidly; e-commerce developed quickly; online and offline transactions merged more rapidly, thus promoting the improvement in the industrial structure.

4. Industrial organization was continuously optimized

The massive economy resulting from the concentration of a large number of small and medium-sized enterprises in the same industry or industrial chain is a major charac-

[5]Data come from the *Zhejiang Statistical Yearbook 2015* and the Science Technology Department of Zhejiang Province.

[6]Data come from the *Zhejiang Statistical Yearbook 2015.*

[7]Data come from the *Zhejiang Statistical Yearbook 2015.*

teristic of Zhejiang's economy. However, as market competition increased, excessive competition, unscrupulous imitation, but a lack of innovation restricted the development and improvement of the massive economy. Since 2003, Zhejiang's enterprises have undergone constant competition and integration, the original industrial clusters have incessantly transformed, the number of industrial clusters has decreased to some extent, but the competitive capacity has improved greatly. With innovations in e-commerce and logistics, there was an improvement in the function of specialized markets in serving product display involving industrial clusters, and the exchange of technology and market information, and professional associations and chambers of commerce played an increasing role in enhancing information exchange, technical cooperation, and market coordination among members.

5. Internal and external openness was increased in an all-round way

Foreign trade reached a new height; the import and export trade showed a relatively balanced development; trade in services grew rapidly and the quality of foreign capital utilization improved. Zhejiang's import and export trade volume soared from USD 61.4 billion in 2003 to USD 355.05 billion in 2014,[8] representing a 4.78-fold increase. Trade in services grew at an average annual growth rate of above 20%, higher than the national growth rate and the rate of growth of Zhejiang's trade in goods in the same period. Tourism, building, transportation, and information are four pillar industries involving service exports in Zhejiang Province. The pace of "going global" has quickened, a new pattern of two-way interaction between "going global" and "bringing in", benign development has taken shape. Zhejiang merchants have become the most active entrepreneur groups nationwide; more than 6 million Zhejiang merchants have made investments and started businesses nationwide; 1.50 million Zhejiang people have started business overseas. Zhejiang merchants have initiated a wave of returning home to start a business, thus helping Zhejiang's economic transformation and upgrading.

6. A great stride was made in ecological economic construction

The notions that we must place equal emphasis on the "gold and silver mountains" and lucid water and lush mountains, and that lucid water and the lush mountains are the "gold and silver mountains" are deeply rooted among the people; ecological environmental protection has been intensified. With the construction of a resource-conserving society, Zhejiang made remarkable improvements in the output level per unit of land, energy, and water resources, Zhejiang reached the national advanced level in this regard. Zhejiang stood firm in the first echelon nationwide in terms of energy conservation and emission reduction. Staged achievements were made in transforming the developmental mode and the industrial structure.

7. There was harmonious urban and rural regional economic development

With urban–rural integration, construction of new socialist countryside and implementation of such special projects as "the city nurturing the countryside" and "the

---

[8]Data come from the *Zhejiang Statistical Yearbook 2015.*

industry nurturing the agriculture," Zhejiang's rural economy developed in a sustained way; the living standard of rural residents significantly improved; Zhejiang ranked No. 1 among provinces, autonomous regions, and municipalities directly under the Central Government nationwide in the income level of rural residents; the income gap between urban and rural residents was stable; the county economy with Zhejiang's characteristics served as the main carrier for promoting urban and rural development and narrowing the urban–rural gap.

8. The new-type urbanization was rapidly propelled

With the development of township enterprises and the rise of an urban economy, Zhejiang advanced from town development to urbanization as from the late 1990s. With great efforts for many years, Zhejiang's new-type urbanization was promoted in a people-oriented way by focusing on the people's livelihood to achieve intensive, harmonious, coordinated, and innovative development, and the urbanization level markedly increased. In 2014, Zhejiang's urbanization rate reached 64.87%, up 13.97 percentage points compared with 2001 and being 10.1 percentage points higher than the national average level of urbanization in 2014; a system of small, medium-sized, and large cities (towns) with a relatively rational layout and scientific structure and at a relatively high level took shape.

1.2 The Exploration and Deepening of the Constructive Philosophy of Turning Zhejiang into an Economically Strong Province

At the beginning of the 21st century, in response to the severe challenges posed on Zhejiang's economic development by the great changes in domestic and foreign factors, resources and environments, the Zhejiang Provincial Party Committee and the Provincial Government fully summarized the experience in Zhejiang's economic development since the reform and opening up, and identified eight advantages of Zhejiang and put forward eight famous measures according to the requirements of future economic development. Afterward, the successive provincial Party Committees and provincial governments thoroughly carried out the "Eight-Eight Strategies" in light of the changes in the environment of economic development, continuously intensified the structural reform, increased the openness, consolidated the original advantages, created new advantages, speeded up Zhejiang's economic transformation and upgrading to achieve sustainable economic development.

First, Comrade Xi Jinping expanded the philosophy of "two hands" and vowed to accelerate the structural reform on the basis of leveraging Zhejiang's advantages regarding institutions and mechanisms; second, he put forward the philosophy of "two birds"—"vacating the cage to change birds" and "achieving the rebirth of the phoenix amid fire" to more rapidly reshape and renew Zhejiang's industries; third, he proceeded from the changes in the ecological environment to develop the philosophy of "two mountains"—the "gold and silver mountains" which means economic development, and that of lucid water and lush mountains—and called for upholding the new notions that we must place equal emphasis on the "gold and silver mountains" and on lucid water and the lush mountains and that lucid water and lush mountains are the "gold and silver mountains," with a view to promoting harmonious economic and ecological development; fourth, he put forward and extended the idea of harmonious development, and he became the first to develop the strategies of the new-type urbanization and of building a strong province through marine economy in the light of the widening urban–rural gap and the regional gap in industrialization; finally, given the new changes in both domestic and foreign environments, Zhejiang constantly expanded the philosophy of opening up, moved from "bringing in and going global" to "going out of Zhejiang to develop Zhejiang" so as to better utilize domestic and foreign resources and markets, and engaged in all-round internal and external opening up rather than merely stressing external opening up.

1.2.1 The Development and Practice of the Reform Philosophy of "Two Hands"

During the period of the 10th Five-Year Plan, Comrade Xi Jinping, then Secretary of the Zhejiang Provincial Party Committee, creatively developed the philosophy of "two hands" in light of Zhejiang's economic characteristics—giving scope to the fundamental role of the market in resource allocation, realistically transforming the functions of the government as a hand, switching government functions to economic regulation, market supervision, social management, and public service, building a service-oriented, limited government under the rule of law, better utilizing, regularizing, and coordinating the relations between the "two hands".

1. Innovations in institutional and mechanism reforms were pushed forward

(1) Reforms of government institutions and the system of administrative approval. The reform of government institutions focused on transforming government functions, standardizing the setting of institutions, optimizing the organizational structure, improving the operating mechanism and the management mode, actively delegating administrative powers to the lower levels and creating a good environment for the development of the regional economy, especially the county economy. The reform of the system of administrative approval was promoted in a classified way according to the requirements of building a service-oriented government under the rule of law, so as to turn Zhejiang into the most efficient province with minimum items subject to examination and approval and the best investment environment nationwide.

(2) The reform involving market-oriented allocation of resources was actively promoted. First, a unified land market for urban and rural construction was established. The bidding, auction, and listing system for industrial land was improved,

and the reform involving the transfer of industrial land based on a different number of years was energetically piloted; changing the use property of homestead in various forms were actively and steadily adopted. Second, an effective mechanism for law-based open transfer of rural collective profit-oriented construction land was established; the mechanism of tidal flat reclamation and the comprehensive utilization of mild slopes of low mountains and hills was reformed, and saving and intensive utilization of land continued to be expanded. Third, intensified efforts were made in financial factor innovation and differentiated allocation of such resources as water and electricity, and the efficiency of resource and factor utilization was continuously improved.

(3) Pilot reforms were promoted in a systematic way. First, actions were taken to comprehensively, systematically, and steadily push forward the Yiwu Pilot Comprehensive International Trade Reform, the Wenzhou Comprehensive Financial Reform Experimental Area, the Lishui Pilot Rural Financial Reform, and the Haining Pilot Comprehensive Market-oriented Factor Allocation Reform. Second, remarkable effects were produced in reforms carried out in pilot provinces for the development of the marine economy, the circular economy, national technological innovation projects, transportation and logistics, and the reform of the cultural system.

2. The state-owned economy was invigorated and the advantages of state-owned enterprises were strengthened

When Comrade Xi Jinping served as the Secretary of the Zhejiang Provincial Party Committee, he developed the following thoughts and ideas about the invigoration of the state-owned economy: first, fully finishing the reform of state-owned and urban collective enterprises which focuses on reforming the property rights system and transforming employees' labor relations; improving the mechanism for the distribution of incentives within enterprises; strengthening enterprise management; further improving the corporate governance structure; establishing the modern enterprise systems. Second, building and improving a state-owned assets administration system under which powers are commensurate with obligations and responsibilities at the provincial and municipal levels, and the administration of assets is combined with the administration of personnel and affairs. Third, quickening the strategic adjustment in the layout of the state-owned economy, making the state-owned economy better and stronger. Combining the state-owned enterprise reform with actions designed to promote enterprise integration and increase the vitality of the enterprise; providing classified guidance for the existing state-owned enterprises, developing and growing a number of state-owned enterprises, optimizing and organizing a group of state-owned enterprises, shutting down and phasing out some state-owned enterprises. We should more rapidly cultivate a number of large internationally competitive enterprises and conglomerates in the key fields and advantageous industries. Fourth, boldly exploring various ways of realizing the state-owned economy. We should provide foreign and private capital with more access, vigorously developing the mixed ownership economy.[9]

With this philosophy in mind, the Zhejiang Provincial Party Committee and the Provincial Government focused on diversification of property rights and structural adjustment to systematically push forward the reform of the state-owned enterprises and concentrate state-owned capital on important industries, key enterprises, and main businesses.

(1) The reform of the property rights system and enterprise reorganization were promoted. First, steps were taken to enable strategic cooperation between provincial enterprises and the enterprises managed by the Central Government, between private enterprises and overseas enterprises, to actively press ahead with shareholding reform and listing; second, actions were taken to promote the reorganization and integration of provincial enterprises; third, enterprise management hierarchies were gradually reduced.
(2) The industrial structure was adjusted and optimized. First, the development of the main business was highlighted and emphasis was placed on cultivating six advantageous industries, including energy, transportation, commerce and trade, iron and steel, chemical engineering, and building. Second, "double-thousand projects" were carried out; the scale of operations or the assets of three groups involving products, transport, and energy exceeded 100 billion yuan. Third, the emerging industrial fields were continually developed, and new growth points, including marine economy and finance, were cultivated.
(3) Innovations were made in the developmental mode. First, active innovations were carried out in the control system. Second, efforts were made to innovate the platform of development. Third, innovations in the business model were boosted. Fourth, technical innovations were solidly promoted.
(4) The supervision service mode was improved. First, the supervision service mode was further ameliorated, and the efficiency of supervising and serving enterprises was enhanced; second, the system of institutional supervision was further improved; third, the supervision system became sounder.

In Zhejiang Province, with reforms and structural adjustments, the strength of state-owned enterprises was increased; the quality and efficiency of enterprise operations were continuously enhanced; the structure of state-owned enterprises was constantly optimized, and the position of state-owned enterprises in basic industries, including energy, transport, commerce, trade, and logistics, was consolidated; state-owned enterprises played an active role in increasing the government's fiscal and tax revenue, guaranteeing market supplies and production orders, and supporting major projects and the construction of people's livelihood. State-owned enterprises maintained a strong control over Zhejiang's national economy, they served as the pioneers in emerging industries, innovators in cutting-edge technologies, guardians

[9]Xi Jinping, Remaining Steadfast on Two Fronts, Creating New Advantages of Zhejiang in Developing the Economy with Different Types of Ownership, *Economic Times*, March 15, 2003.

in key fields, constructors in basic sectors, and supporters in the development of small and medium-sized enterprises.

1.2.2 The Exploitation of Mechanism Advantages and Revitalization of the Private Economy

The developed private economy is the characteristic and advantage of Zhejiang's economy. In the opinion of Comrade Xi Jinping, one of the important causes for driving Zhejiang to develop from a small province of resources into a large economic province since the reform and opening up is the rapid development of the private economy. Among the "Eight-Eight Strategies" developed by the Zhejiang Provincial Party Committee and the Provincial Government in 2003, the first strategy lies in further leveraging Zhejiang's advantages of its institutions and its mechanisms, and vigorously stimulating diverse forms of ownership to develop side by side, with public ownership remaining dominant. The greatest advantage of Zhejiang's institution and mechanism is its private economy.

1. Actions were taken to elevate the private economy to a new level

In Zhejiang's working conference on the private economy in 2004, Xi Jinping stressed that it was necessary to further emancipate the mind, be bold in practice, speed up institutional, scientific and technological and managerial innovation, fully promote the scientific and technological, large-scale, intensive, and international development of the private economy, constantly enhance the overall strength and international competiveness of the private economy, and maintain the leading position of Zhejiang's private economy in China. He pointed out that in order to make the private economy reach a new height, it is essential to push forward five transformations and achieve five improvements: (1) transform from its main dependence on the initial advantages of mechanisms to its main dependence on institutional, scientific and technological and managerial innovations, so as to enhance the overall strength and international competitiveness of the private economy; (2) transform from concentration on the traditional manufacturing industry, commerce and trade to all-round entry into the advanced hi-tech manufacturing industry with high added value, basic industries and the emerging service industry, thus increasing the industrial hierarchy and level of development of the private economy; (3) transform from a principal dependence on domestic resources and domestic markets to full utilization of domestic and foreign resources and markets, with a view to increasing the level of external development of the private economy; (4) gradually transform from the existing massive economy and small-scale operations to cluster and large-scale operations at a higher level in order to make the private economy more intensive and of a larger scale; (5) transform from a relatively extensive operational mode to an operational mode with greater emphasis on credit, quality, ecology, and compliance with laws and regulations, so as to improve the overall quality and sustainable development of the private economy. It is necessary to further reinforce the leadership over the development of the private economy, place the work on lifting the private economy to a new level in the important position of the overall work, optimize the environment, improve management, strengthen party building, and create a new pattern for the development of Zhejiang's private economy.

Under the guidance of this strategy and the corresponding policy measures, Zhejiang's people became more passionate about starting a business, the private economy grew rapidly, and the position and role of the private economy in Zhejiang's economy were further improved.

2. The private enterprises were stimulated to start business and make innovations

With changes in the economic developmental stage and in the developmental environment, the development of Zhejiang's private economy was accompanied by new problems including difficulties in financing, transformation, and upgrading. In 2007, the 12th Party Congress of Zhejiang Province developed the overall strategy of making the people rich by starting a business and of building a strong province through innovation, and the Province vowed to generously support and encourage the development of the private economy, improve and implement the policy measures for promoting that development, encourage private enterprises to carry out innovation, and fully activate various private resources. Actions were taken to actively cultivate various types of market players with an enterprising spirit, support and stimulate all of the people to start a business, venture down a new path suited to Zhejiang's local conditions which ensures that all of the people start a business and that all-round innovation is achieved.

In response to the impact from the financial crisis which broke out in 2008, Zhejiang intensified its support of and guidance for the private economy. In early 2011, based on expanding the theme of "blazing a new trail by starting a business and innovating and making Zhejiang strong through concerted efforts," with a focus on the topic of unswervingly supporting the development of the private economy and steadfastly promoting the transformation and upgrading of private enterprises, the Zhejiang Provincial Party Committee and the Provincial Government convened a province-wide conference on the private economy with ten thousand participants to scientifically develop a new round of blueprints for developing the private economy.

With joint efforts from enterprises and the government, the basic capability of Zhejiang's private enterprises for independent innovation significantly improved, and some conditions and comparative advantages with the improvement of the capability for independent innovation as a breakthrough came into being; a technical innovation system dominated by enterprises and relying on colleges, universities, and scientific research institutions gradually took shape, and the enterprises above the designated size became the leading force in Zhejiang's technical innovation; a number of knowledge and talent-intensive private technology enterprises emerged; Zhejiang's private enterprises utilized domestic and foreign resources and markets, boldly implemented the strategy of "going out of Zhejiang to develop Zhejiang," a new pattern of two-way interaction between "going global" and "bringing in", benign development took shape. In 2003, the registered capital per private enterprise in Zhejiang was 1,150,000 yuan, while that figure reached 3,085,000 yuan in 2013, an increase of nearly two times. A total of 139 private enterprises from Zhejiang were listed among the Top 500 National Private Enterprises released by the All-China Federation of Industry and Commerce in August, 2013, ranking Zhejiang No. 1 nationwide for 15 consecutive years. In 2013, the private economy contributed more than 60% of the tax revenue, more than 70% of the GDP, more than 80% of the foreign trade export and more than 90% of the new jobs in Zhejiang. The private economy became the forerunner and pusher in Zhejiang's market-oriented reform and the main force in Zhejiang's economic transformation and upgrading.

1.2.3 The Innovations and Practice of the "Two-Bird" Philosophy of Transformation and Upgrading

With sustained rapid development for more than 20 years, at the beginning of the 21st century, Zhejiang's economy was subject to more severe challenges and problems, some traditional industries, small and micro enterprises faced the test of life and death, regional transfer of Zhejiang's industries accelerated, while the emerging industries were restricted by scientific and technological talent factors and were hard to sustain. Zhejiang's economic development was at a new crossroads.

1. The innovations in the philosophy of transformation and upgrading

The Zhejiang Provincial Party Committee and the Provincial Government realized that in the new environment, it was necessary for Zhejiang's traditional industries to go global and utilize external resources and markets to sharpen their competitive edge and achieve thorough transformation. In the economic working conference of Zhejiang Province in late 2004, Xi Jinping, then Secretary of the Zhejiang Provincial Party Committee, stressed that in order to solve Zhejiang's bottlenecks to development, it was imperative to proceed from the Scientific Outlook on Development to practically transforming the economic developmental mode. He described this work as "two birds"—"achieving the rebirth of the phoenix amid fire" and "vacating the cage to change birds." "Achieving the rebirth of the phoenix amid fire" means "born of fire" and "born again". "Vacating the cage to change birds" means "getting rid of the stale and bringing in the fresh."

"Achieving the rebirth of the phoenix amid fire" and "vacating the cage to change birds" initiated Zhejiang's structural adjustment and transformation. Transforming the economic developmental mode and promoting economic transformation and upgrading has become the unremitting pursuit of successive Party Committees and governments of Zhejiang Province. After the 12th Party Congress of Zhejiang Province, the Zhejiang Provincial Party Committee and the Provincial Government thoroughly carried out the "Eight-Eight Strategies" and the overall strategy of making the people rich by starting a business and of building a strong province through innovation, thus giving birth to a new pattern of quickening transformation of the developmental mode and pushing forward economic transformation and upgrading. In December, 2009, the economic working conference of Zhejiang Province vowed to further leverage the characteristics and advantages, including the private economy, county economy, and massive economy, solidly push ahead with the construction of great platforms, large industries, large-scale projects, and big enterprises, while that construction was included as a major strategic measure for promoting economic transformation and upgrading into the *12th Five-Year Plan of Zhejiang Province*.

2. The development of the philosophy of transformation and upgrading

The 13th Party Congress of Zhejiang Province set the goal of becoming affluent in material and rich in mind. In the Fifth Plenary Session of the 13th Party Committee of Zhejiang Province, the Zhejiang Provincial Party Committee and the Provincial Government put forward the vision of building a beautiful Zhejiang and creating a good life. "Becoming affluent in material and rich in mind" and "building a beautiful Zhejiang and creating a good life" are consistent with the "Eight-Eight Strategies" of Zhejiang Province and its overall strategy of making the people rich by starting a business and of building a strong province through innovation; they are Zhejiang's goals of economic transformation and upgrading and also the inevitable choices for Zhejiang to stand at the forefront in economic and social development. Under the guidance of this philosophy, Zhejiang persistently accelerated its economic transformation and upgrading. The successive Party Committees and governments of Zhejiang Province carried through one blueprint to consistently pursue development and perseveringly pushed forward Zhejiang's economic transformation and upgrading.

As from June, 2012, Zhejiang further strengthened the mechanism for the promotion of work of "vacating the cage to change birds," and further forced the phase-out of backward production capacity by increasing the costs of factor use relating to backward production capacity. At the opening ceremony of the First Session of the 12th People's Congress of Zhejiang Province in January, 2013, Li Qiang, acting governor of Zhejiang Province, stated that it was necessary for Zhejiang to actively renovate and upgrade its traditional industries, develop and implement a package plan for promoting transformation by "vacating the cage to change birds," guide and support enterprises to speed up technical renovation, spur the application of information technology and firmly phase out some backward production capacities.

On this basis, the new Party Committee and government of Zhejiang Province launched a number of projects, including "Four Changes and Three Famous Things" ("vacating the cage to change birds," replacing the people with machines, optimizing space to save land, expanding the market through e-commerce, and cultivating well-known enterprises, famous products and eminent experts), "Three Renovating and One Demolishing" (renovating old residential areas, old factory areas in urban areas and the villages in cities, and demolishing illegal buildings), and "The Governance for Five Kinds of Water" (treating sewage, controlling flood, discharging the accumulated water, guaranteeing water supply, and saving water). Zhejiang's current economic transformation and upgrading presents the following new characteristics: the projects of cultivating well-known enterprises, famous products and eminent experts serve as the guide; the strategy of "vacating the cage to change birds," replacing the people with machines, optimizing space to save land, and expanding the market through e-commerce constitutes the path; a breakthrough is made by controlling the flood, discharging the accumulated water, guaranteeing water supply and saving water.

1.2.4 The Formation and Practice of the "Two-Mountain" Ecological Economic Philosophy

The ecological environment is the foundation for economic and social development. For a long time, Zhejiang's industrialization was propelled at the expense of the ecological environment. At the beginning of the 21st century, air pollution became increasingly severe and forest resources were destroyed in some economically developed areas, even in particular areas, the safety of the drinking water for residents could not be guaranteed. The Zhejiang Provincial Party Committee and the Provincial Government thoroughly recognized that after Zhejiang's industrialization entered the later stage, it was essential to attach importance to the building of an ecological environment, provide support for sustainable economic development, increase the index of the people's happiness with life, really ensure that economic development focuses on the people's livelihood and is people-centered.

When Xi Jinping served as the Secretary of the Zhejiang Provincial Party Committee, he adopted the dialectical relationship between lucid water and lush mountains and the "gold and silver mountains" to illustrate the construction of Zhejiang as an ecological province. He said that Zhejiang's understanding of the relationship of dialectical unification between two mountains in practice was developed in three stages: During the first stage, the people exchanged lucid water and lush mountains for the "gold and silver mountains" and did not consider or rarely considered the bearing capacity of the environment, recklessly grabbing resources; during the second stage, the people exploited the "gold and silver mountains" but sought to maintain lucid water and lush mountains; at that time, there were contradictions between economic development and lack of resources, environmental deterioration loomed large, the people realized that the environment was fundamental for human survival and development, and only when the lush mountains were kept could development be achieved; during the third stage, the people recognized that lucid water and lush mountains can endlessly bring about the "gold and silver mountains"; lucid water and lush mountains themselves were the "gold and silver mountains", the ecological advantages can be turned into economic advantages, thus forming an integral whole, achieving harmony and unity.

The "two-mountains" philosophy developed by Xi Jinping vividly presents the relationships between ecology and economic development and also summarizes the process in which Zhejiang went profound and became increasingly mature in dealing with the relations between economic development and ecological protection.

In June, 2002, the 11th Party Congress of Zhejiang Province identified the construction of a green Zhejiang as the strategic goal of the whole province at the new historical stage. This congress vowed to actively carry out the sustainable development strategy, and maintain a coordinated development of the population, resources, the environment, the economy, and society mainly by building an ecological province with the construction of a green Zhejiang as the goal. In January, 2003, with the approval of the State Environmental Protection Administration, Zhejiang Province became the fifth pilot province for building an ecological province, following Hainan, Jilin, Heilong, and Fujian nationwide. This marked the beginning of building an ecological province.

1. Ecological construction was combined with economic transformation and upgrading

The building of an ecological civilization was incorporated into the fields of economic, political, cultural, and social construction, the "Eight-Eight Strategies", and the overall strategy of making the people rich by starting a business and of building a strong province through innovation; it was also included in the work on becoming affluent in material and rich in mind, building a beautiful Zhejiang and creating a good life, and the concrete work on promoting economic transformation and upgrading. Efforts were made to properly deal with the relations between ecological construction and construction on other fronts, vigorously develop an ecological economy, constantly optimize the ecological environment, build a richly endowed, scenic, harmonious, healthy, ecological Zhejiang, and achieve sustainable economic and social development.

2. Environmental protection and protection of the resources were intensified

Zhejiang carried out the environmental protection policy of "placing equal emphasis on three tasks" and "developing three projects simultaneously"[10] to control environmental pollution, and took "811"[11] environmental pollution control action; the

[10]"Placing equal emphasis on three tasks" includes placing equal emphasis on strict prevention of new pollution and vigorous control of old pollution; urban pollution abatement and rural pollution abatement; wide adoption of clean production and the construction of environmental protection projects; "developing three projects simultaneously" includes developing simultaneously pollution prevention and control, and ecological protection; industrial pollution prevention and control, prevention and control of domestic pollution, and agricultural non-point source pollution; prevention and control of water pollution and air pollution.

[11]In "811", "8" means 8 major water systems, canals, and plain river networks throughout the province; "11" means 11 cities divided into districts, and it also means 11 provincial key controlled areas under environmental protection, including Jiaojiang Waisha, the Yantou Chemical and Pharmaceutical Base; the Huangyan Chemical and Pharmaceutical Base; the Linhai Shuiyang Chemical and Pharmaceutical Base; the Shangyu Fine Chemical Park; chemical enterprises in the Dongyang and Nanjiang River Basins; the Xinchang-Shengzhou Section of the Xinchang River Basin; chemical enterprises in the Shenjia Industrial Park, Quzhou; printing, dyeing, chemical industries in eastern Xiaoshan; the Pingyang Shuitou Leather Making Base; the electroplating industry in Wenzhou City; the storage battery industry in Changxing.

authorities in various areas of Zhejiang also actively strengthened water and soil erosion control, clear water river channel improvement, ecological restoration of mines, and the construction of ecological public-welfare forests. The authorities in coastal areas regarded the protection and construction of the marine ecological environment as an important task.

3. An ecological compensation mechanism was actively explored, established, and practiced

First, the fiscal support for ecological compensation was increased, the incentive and guiding role of fiscal funds in ecological compensation was leveraged; second, resources were integrated through multiple channels to push forward ecological compensation; third, the market mechanism was introduced, paid use of resources was carried out; fourth, regulations and systems were established to institutionalize ecological compensation.

4. Energy conservation and emission reduction was taken as the important means for adjusting the economic developmental mode

Actions were taken to energetically promote the circular industry, support the development of the resource-conserving, environmentally friendly industries, push ahead with ecological economic construction and initiate the construction of pilot provinces for a circular economy. The "991" projects were arranged and implemented—focusing on 9 key fields, adopting a working means by taking the 9 fields as a batch, and speeded up the implementation of 100 projects involving a circular economy. The guiding opinions on environmental access to the industries of raw chemical medicine, papermaking, printing, and dyeing were unveiled to accelerate the cultivation and development of the circular economy, low-carbon economy, and ecological economy.

1.2.5 The Philosophy and Exploration of Harmonious Development

With significant economic development since reform and opening up, at the beginning of the 21st century, Zhejiang's urban–rural gap and regional gap widened, posing new challenges to Zhejiang's future sustainable economic development and social stability. In the new situation, the Zhejiang Provincial Party Committee and the Provincial Government achieved the harmonious development of the regional economy, urban and rural society and economy by pushing forward the new-type urbanization, developing the marine economy, enabling mountain–sea cooperation, and supporting the development of the underdeveloped areas.

1. Zhejiang took the path of new-tape urbanization

In light of the economic, social, and environmental development and changes, Zhejiang became the first to "take the path of new-tape urbanization," and it stressed intensive, harmonious, and coordinated development during urbanization and incorporated urbanization into scientific development.

First, Zhejiang gave prominence to intensive development and scientific urban developmental planning, carried out strict urban land planning to enhance the efficiency of the use of land resources, and the agglomeration effect of urban economy; Zhejiang improved the layout, pushed ahead with the development of city groups and clusters, reduced the cities and towns which were subject to traffic jams, were empty, were used for sleeping and waterlogged.

Second, Zhejiang placed emphasis on harmonious development, and established a rational urban system to promote harmonious development of small, medium-sized, and large cities and towns. Zhejiang intensified urban environmental protection, and energetically developed green, low-carbon, and smart cities.

Third, Zhejiang laid stress on coordinated development. Zhejiang combined urban development with the construction of the new countryside and the optimization of the layout of the population and productive forces, and ventured down the path of urbanization through coordinated development; Zhejiang extended urban infrastructure to rural areas, made urban public services cover rural areas, expanded urban civilization to rural areas, established and improved a long-term mechanism for driving rural development through urban development and promoting agriculture through industry. Zhejiang encouraged more counties to develop into medium-sized cities with full functions, and gave full scope to the important role of the county economy in coordinated urban and rural development.

2. Zhejiang was turned into a strong province of marine economy and promoted land and sea interaction

As Zhejiang's land area was small and Zhejiang suffered a shortage of resources, the Zhejiang Provincial Party Committee and the Provincial Government called for land and sea interaction, took the development of the marine economy and the construction of a strong province of marine economy as one priority in the implementation of the "Eight-Eight Strategies", made it the new growth point in Zhejiang's economic development and created more room for Zhejiang's social and economic development.

In August, 2003, the Zhejiang Provincial Party Committee and the Provincial Government explicitly set the goal of building a strong province of marine economy. They organized efforts to formulate the *Plan for Building Zhejiang into a Strong Province of Marine Economy*. Major projects were carried out—priority was given to integrating the Port of Ningbo and the Port of Zhoushan—to stimulate the integrative development of the Port of Ningbo and the Port of Zhoushan. Intensified efforts were made in industrial improvement, and according to the requirements of rational layout, structural optimization, dependence on science and technology and sustainable development, emphasis was placed on developing five major marine industries, including the port-based shipping industry, port-based industry, marine fishery, the coastal tourism industry, and the emerging marine industry; the marine ecological construction and improvement of social security for fishermen was promoted.

In 2007, the 12th Party Congress of Zhejiang Province clearly put forward the strategic requirement and task of energetically developing the marine economy and speeding up the construction of a strong province of port and shipping. Zhejiang incorporated accelerated development of the marine economy as a part of the "Eight-Eight Strategies" and an important part of the overall strategy of making the people rich by starting a business and of building a strong province through innovation; Zhejiang actively planned a belt of marine economy development, vigorously developed industries such as marine organism, marine energy and marine tourism, and more rapidly carried out various tasks for building a strong province of port and shipping, thus preliminarily shaping the pattern for the development of a marine economy in which Ningbo and Zhoushan serve as the center and Wenzhou, Taizhou, Hangzhou, and Jiaxing constitute two wings.

In March, 2011, the working conference of the Party Committee focused on implementing the plan approved by the State Council, and made overall arrangements of the work on building Zhejiang's marine economy demonstration areas; the working conference decided to speed up the development of the marine economy and further improved the working thinking and measures for coordinated land and sea development. Meanwhile, with the pilot reform in the Zhoushan New Area, actions were taken to promote great development of Zhejiang's bonded areas, international shipping, and trade.

The construction of the marine economy boosted Zhejiang's economic transformation and upgrading. The development of marine transport and international trade, and land and sea interaction stimulated social and economic development in Zhejiang's other areas, increased the level of the economic development of island areas as well as propelling harmonious regional development in Zhejiang.

3. Zhejiang pushed forward three major projects and gave an impetus to coordinated regional economic development

With sustained rapid development for more than 20 years, at the beginning of the 21st century, Zhejiang entered a new stage of building a well-off society in an all-around way and moving toward modernization. However, the economic foundation was relatively weak in Zhejiang's southwestern mountainous areas, and the self-accumulation and self-development ability of these areas was not high enough due to historical, natural, and social reasons. The development of the underdeveloped areas was the key and difficult point for Zhejiang in building a well-off society in an all-around way and also the potential for Zhejiang's development. Therefore, the Zhejiang Provincial Party Committee and the Provincial Government vigorously carried out, across the province, the Mountain-Sea Cooperation Project, the project for turning the underdeveloped villages and towns into well-off ones and the project with assistance and support for ten-billion for achieving prosperity, so as to promote province-wide coordinated regional economic development.

(1) The Mountain-Sea Cooperation Project. "Mountain-sea cooperation" means economic cooperation between the underdeveloped areas dominated by Zhejiang's southwestern mountainous areas and islands and the developed coastal areas, the economically developed cities and counties.
(2) The project for turning the underdeveloped areas into the well-off ones. In 2003, the Zhejiang Provincial Party Committee and the Provincial Government made a great decision to carry out the project for turning the underdeveloped villages and towns into well-off ones, with the central task consisting in more quickly turning the underdeveloped villages and towns into well-off ones, solving the problem of relative poverty and achieving coordinated regional development.
(3) The project with assistance and support of ten-billion for achieving prosperity. It is the important part of Zhejiang's five major ten-billion projects. This project centers on cultivating the new economic growth points, helping and supporting the disadvantaged groups, improving the conditions of transportation, reinforcing mountain–sea cooperation, guiding the people to descend from mountains to shake off poverty and become prosperous, promoting coordinated regional development.

Under the scientific guidance of the "Eight-Eight Strategies", with a focus on implementing three major projects, Zhejiang's economic and social development preliminarily featured a pattern of interaction and mutual promotion between the developed coastal areas and the underdeveloped inland areas, and a good situation where the developed areas developed in an accelerated way and the underdeveloped areas achieved leaping development.

1.2.6 The Formation and Development of the Opening-Up Philosophy of "Going Out of Zhejiang to Develop Zhejiang"

Zhejiang's rapid economic development since the late 1970s is attributable to the intensification of internal and external opening up. Since the 21st century, Zhejiang's economy has faced the new problems concerning fiercer competition in domestic and foreign markets and increasing resource and factor supply bottlenecks. In the era of accelerated global economic integration, only when internal and external opening up is increased to make Zhejiang's enterprises survive severe tests and thrive can Zhejiang's economy develop in a healthy and sustained way. Zhejiang took the opportunity from China's accession into the WTO to increase internal and external opening up and implement the strategy of "going global", encourage Zhejiang merchants to go out of Zhejiang to develop Zhejiang; while continuing to attract external direct investments, Zhejiang actively encouraged and supported the overseas expansion of Zhejiang's advantageous industries and specialized markets to stimulate Zhejiang merchants to more fully utilize domestic and foreign markets and resources.

1. There was a shift from "bringing in, going global" to "going out of Zhejiang to develop Zhejiang"

After 2003, resource and environmental constraints became the bottlenecks for Zhejiang's economic development. Meanwhile, the structural, organizational, and factor contradictions in Zhejiang's economic development gradually loomed large. Zhejiang needed to participate in domestic and foreign economic and technical cooperation and competition in more fields within a wider scope at a higher level to expand new developmental spaces and maintain sustained, healthy and rapid economic development. "Going out of Zhejiang to develop Zhejiang" became the strategic choice for Zhejiang's economic development in the new historical conditions. When Xi Jinping served as the Secretary of the Zhejiang Provincial Party Committee, he stressed that "going out of Zhejiang to develop Zhejiang" was not only the inevitable requirement for Zhejiang's economic and social development, but also an overall consciousness and political responsibility. "Going out of Zhejiang to develop Zhejiang" extended Zhejiang's industrial chain, propelled gradient transfer of Zhejiang's industries, the rational flow and optimal allocation of resources and factors. In 2011, the 12th Party Congress of Zhejiang Province vowed to expand the developmental spaces with the thinking of "going out of Zhejiang to develop Zhejiang" and maintain a good developmental momentum. The Second Plenary Session of the 12th Party Committee of Zhejiang Province stressed that in order to promote entrepreneurship and innovation across the board, it was necessary to fully utilize domestic and foreign markets and resources. Thus "going out of Zhejiang to develop Zhejiang" became an important part of the overall strategy of making the people rich by starting a business and of building a strong province through innovation and the strategy of expanding Zhejiang's entrepreneurship and spaces for innovation.

2. The openness was increased in an all-round way

In recent years, with great changes in domestic and foreign economic environments, based on the line of thought of "going out of Zhejiang to develop Zhejiang," the Zhejiang Provincial Party Committee and the Provincial Government attached importance to the all-round improvement of the openness to ensure that Zhejiang could fully participate in the system of global economic cooperation and labor division and enhance the international competiveness of Zhejiang's economy.

In the process of pushing forward the strategy of "going out of Zhejiang to develop Zhejiang," Zhejiang insisted on elevating the local economy during participation in interregional and international competition, and amid interaction and integration with the enterprises outside Zhejiang and overseas enterprises as well as in the course of going global.

Zhejiang carried forward the internal and external opening up of Zhejiang's economy on six fronts. First, Zhejiang took the Reform of Yiwu Pilot Comprehensive International Trade as the means for building a new system of open economy, and increasing the openness of Zhejiang's economy in an all-round way; second, Zhejiang developed the opening-up bond for the coordinated expansion of domestic and foreign markets; third, Zhejiang promoted stable and balanced development of import and export trade; fourth, Zhejiang combined "bringing in" with "going global"; fifth, Zhejiang unceasingly innovated the opening-up carriers; sixth, Zhejiang guided Zhejiang merchants to make investments outside Zhejiang and return to Zhejiang.

With unremitting efforts for many years, the level of Zhejiang's open economy was fully increased. Zhejiang's import and export trade grew steadily, its trade structure improved constantly; foreign capital was introduced in a steady way, and the structure and quality of foreign investments in Zhejiang improved significantly; the investments made by Zhejiang merchants outside Zhejiang and overseas showed sustained rapid growth; the markets and resources available outside Zhejiang and overseas were utilized, resulting in the great development of the economy of Zhejiang's people; Zhejiang merchants quickened the pace of returning to Zhejiang for starting a business and carrying out innovation, and they became the new forces for driving Zhejiang's economic transformation and upgrading.

1.3 The Chinese Dream and Zhejiang's Practice in Economic Development

In 2012, General Secretary Xi Jinping put forward the Chinese Dream—realizing great rejuvenation of the Chinese nation; it is the dream of making the country prosperous and powerful. Specifically, it contains the dream and aspiration, cherished by the Chinese nation for thousands of years, of making the people rich in mind and well-off, building a powerful and prosperous country, an enormously innovative country, a strong marine power, a harmonious and beautiful China. As Zhejiang is a developed coastal region at the forefront in China, Zhejiang's level of economic development is about 10 years ahead of the overall national level; Zhejiang's economic development provides an excellent sample for practicing the Chinese dream.

1.3.1 The Dream of Making the People Well-off and Zhejiang's Practice

The affluence of the people is the foundation for building a powerful and prosperous country and the precondition for becoming rich in mind. Becoming well-off is the dream of every Chinese person. In China with a population of nearly 1.4 billion, the dream of making the people well-off is a huge challenge and also a realistic expectation. The way Zhejiang's people have gone from poverty to prosperity since the reform and opening up especially in the past 10 years proves that the dream of making China prosperous is bound to be realized. Zhejiang's per capita GDP rose from USD 2380 to USD 11,878 during the period from 2003 to 2014, representing a fourfold increase in 11 years. Zhejiang's urban per capita disposable income and rural per capita net income increased from 13,180 yuan and 5431 yuan in 2003 to 37,851 yuan and 16,106 yuan in 2013, up 187% and 197%, respectively; Zhejiang was at the forefront among provinces, autonomous regions, and municipalities nationwide in the average living standard of urban and rural residents; the Engel coefficients of urban and rural households decreased from 36.6 and 38.2% in 2003 to 34.4 and 35.6% in 2013,[12] reaching the well-off level; social security, including medical assistance, 9-year compulsory education and subsistence allowance, basically covered both urban and rural areas.

First, Zhejiang's realization of the dream of becoming well-off consisted of encouraging the people to start a business. The Zhejiang Provincial Party Committee and the Provincial Government developed the overall developmental strategy of making the people rich by starting a business and of building a strong province through innovation. The people were willing and bold to start a business, and aspired to becoming bosses; a large number (more than 10 million) of Zhejiang merchants emerged, ranking Zhejiang No.1 nationwide in the per capita number of business owners, laying a solid foundation for Zhejiang's private economy and injecting ceaseless vitality into Zhejiang's economic development.

Second, Zhejiang encouraged the development of the private economy. Zhejiang delegated powers to the lower levels and surrendered profits at the early stage of reform and opening up; afterward, Zhejiang placed emphasis on providing the private economy with an equal market competition mechanism, fully leveraged the mechanism and institutional advantages of private enterprises to spur a leapfrog development of the private economy; as a result, Zhejiang's private economy grew from small to large and from weak to strong, it became the main force in Zhejiang's economic development, and the people employed by private enterprises accounted for more than 75% of all of the employed people, and private enterprises made up the largest source of residents' income.

Third, Zhejiang guided the development of agglomerations of industries. Zhejiang stimulated small and medium-sized private enterprises to aggregate in particular areas, industries or product chains to engage in collaboration and division of labor based on specialization; the city also stimulated them to shape specialized markets and industrial clusters, thus producing an agglomeration effect, making up for diseconomies of scale of small and medium-sized enterprises, enhancing the competitiveness of Zhejiang's products and rapidly moving Zhejiang's products to the areas outside Zhejiang and onto the overseas market. At present, more than 10% of the industrial products from Zhejiang rank No. 1 nationwide in terms of output, and more than 60% of the industrial products from Zhejiang are among the top ten nationwide in output.

Finally, Zhejiang constantly improved the mechanism of distribution. Zhejiang encouraged urban and rural residents to start a business and increase their operating income. Steps were taken to protect the participation of various factors in distribution to increase the property income for residents. The income from labor employment

[12]Data come from the *Zhejiang Statistical Yearbook 2014*.

for residents was guaranteed. On this basis, redistribution-based adjustment was intensified, and the transfer income for low-income residents was increased.

In addition, the developmental environment was continuously improved. The government pressed ahead with the construction of infrastructures, including transportation, energy, and an information network; actions were taken to better serve enterprises, promote the transportation revolution of government institutions, make Zhejiang creditworthy and safe, govern Zhejiang under the rule of law and carry out clean and honest administration in Zhejiang, so as to provide a good environment for economic development.

1.3.2 The Dream of Making the Country Powerful Through Innovation and Zhejiang's Practice

Making the country powerful and prosperous is a dream shared by the Chinese people. The realization of the dream of making the country powerful is based on a powerful economy, while a powerful economy is built on innovation. The sustained development of Zhejiang's economy since the reform and opening up lies in continuous innovation; Zhejiang's practice of innovation offers beneficial experimentation for turning China into an enormously innovative country.

Zhejiang's practice in building an economically strong province mainly covers institutional, organizational, and technical innovations.

First, institutional innovation. Since the beginning of the 21st century, in view of great changes in the environment of economic development, Zhejiang has explored the developmental path for a socialist market economy, and has adopted the "two-hand" innovation philosophy to constantly push forward the innovation of the economic system. The reform of the institutional mechanism was systematically pushed forward through pilot reforms in the Yiwu Comprehensive International Trade Reform, the Wenzhou Comprehensive Financial Reform, the Lishui Rural Financial Reform and the Haining Market-oriented Factor Allocation Reform and pilot provinces for the reform of the cultural system. Government institutional reform was promoted by focusing on expanding the powers of counties and towns. The reform of the administrative approval system was carried out in an all-round way, and a revolution in government efficiency was promoted. The reform of the property rights system involving state-owned enterprises and enterprise reorganization were steadily pushed forward, and actions were taken to guide private enterprises to transform into modern enterprises. The systems and mechanisms suited to the development of the modern market economy were preliminarily established.

Second, organization innovation. In light of the changes in the economic and social environments and the requirements of market economic development, efforts were made to continuously promote the innovation and optimization of industrial organization, and to establish an industrial-organizational system compatible with Zhejiang's economic development. The relationship between the government and enterprises was rationalized, and the government carried out the construction of infrastructures, provided enterprises with good services, and planned and managed the macroeconomy. Enterprises acted in a market-oriented way to build modern industrial clusters and engage in collaboration and division of labor based on specialization, and the vitality of the competition of enterprises was maintained. The intermediary bodies represented by chambers of commerce and industrial associations played an active role of coordinating and serving.

Third, technical innovation. Technical innovation emphasizes the importance of scientific and technical revolution and guides enterprises and the whole society to focus on technical innovation and development. With regard to innovation, the government intensified basic research, basic research for application, especially the input in the research on common technologies for industries, and the government guided technical innovation in the whole society, and ensured that enterprises played the leading role in innovation, in particular, large enterprises leveraged advantages and played the key role in applied (technology) research and test development. Zhejiang established a collaborative innovation mechanism among the government, enterprises, institutions of higher learning, scientific research institutions, investment organizations, and intermediary organs. Zhejiang actively cultivated scientifically and technologically innovative talents, introduced high-end scientific and technological talents and technologies, and increased the introduction of advanced technologies and appropriate technologies through trade in technology.

1.3.3 The Dream of Building a Large Open Country and Zhejiang's Practice

In the era of global economic integration, an internationally competitive economic system cannot be built in a closed country or territory. Only when an open economy is available can resources be allocated around the world to enhance the efficiency and promote development, and can the dream of making the people well-off and the country powerful and prosperous be truly realized. Zhejiang's sustained economic development cannot be achieved without internal and external opening up; only when Zhejiang's people "bring in and go global" and "go out of Zhejiang to develop Zhejiang" can Zhejiang economically break through the constraints from a shortage of resources and can the dream of making the people well-off be realized.

First, the reform of the foreign trade system was constantly intensified in response to the needs of economic development. Zhejiang further relaxed control over the power to engage in foreign trade exportation and encouraged production enterprises to carry out import and export trade. Zhejiang intensified the reform of the property rights system of state-owned foreign trade enterprises. Actions were taken to push forward the reform to achieve the facilitation of foreign trade and the reform of the system of trade management. Efforts were made to build bonded areas and pilot-free trade zones in Zhejiang. The reforms of the system of foreign capital management and the system of outward investments were steadily promoted.

Second, the foreign trade growth mode was transformed. The strategy of diversifying import and export markets was implemented to spread international market risks. The industrial structural upgrading was combined with the upgrading of the structure of trading to optimize the import and export trading structure. Actions were taken to boost the innovation of the types of trading businesses and the transformation and upgrading of the modes of trade. Efforts were made to make import trade large and promote a relatively balanced development of imports and exports. Innovations were made in the mode of international market development to enhance the competitiveness of imports and exports. The development of trade in services was vigorously promoted. Early warning of foreign trade risks and the mechanism for coping with them was established.

Third, the quality of the utilization of foreign capital was improved. Actions were taken to greatly improve the hard and soft environments for investment, integrate the developmental zones and industrial parks, and build large platforms for utilizing foreign capital. The introduction of foreign capital was combined with industrial structural upgrading, and continuous innovations were made in the manner of attracting investments, foreign capital was introduced in a targeted and selective way.

Fourth, the level of "going global" was increased. The reform of the system for the management of outward investments was promoted; innovations were carried out in the mode of Zhejiang merchants' outward investments; the advantages of the private economy were leveraged; Zhejiang merchants were guided to go global, conduct mergers and acquisitions and seek listing overseas, establish R&D centers and marketing organizations, set up stores, build factories and develop markets, engage in the contracting and leasing of farms and mines overseas, fully utilize overseas resources and markets, overcome Zhejiang's resource and environmental constraints to increase investment return.

Fifth, regional economic cooperation was comprehensively promoted. Emphasis was placed on pushing forward the strategy of connecting Shanghai on the north and engaging in close economic cooperation with Shanghai and Jiangsu to create regional economic integration in the Yangtze River Delta. Zhejiang merchants were guided to go west and north, accelerate industrial transfer and regional industrial economic cooperation. Regional economic integration was conducted in various ways. Zhejiang merchants were encouraged to utilize the resources more and expand their markets outside Zhejiang. Steps were taken to actively participate in building economic cooperation regions represented by the Western Taiwan Straits Economic Zone, two Silk Road economic belts, and the Yangtze River economic belt.

Sixth, the enterprises outside Zhejiang were attracted to invest in Zhejiang. Zhejiang merchants were supported with respect to entrepreneurship and innovation. Zhejiang merchants were guided to return to Zhejiang for seeking development and promoting Zhejiang's economic transformation and upgrading.

1.3.4 The Dream of Building a Marine Power and Zhejiang's Practice

The Report of the 18th National Congress of the Communist Party of China makes the building of a marine power a national developmental strategy. This is a highly significant appeal of all Chinese people and also an inevitable process in China's history. China's sea area is more than 3 million km^2, accounting for one-third of the total national territorial area, but the marine economy accounts for only 10% of the GDP. Compared with the USA where the marine economy accounts for 50% of the GDP, it is a long-term, arduous task for building a marine power in China. Zhejiang's sea area reaches 260,000 km^2, which is 2.6 times its land area; Zhejiang's deepwater shoreline is 506 km, accounting for one-third of the national total deepwater shoreline; Zhejiang's islands account for 40% of those in China. Therefore, Zhejiang is a large marine province. In more than a decade, Zhejiang has been committed to building a strong marine province, providing extensive practice for realizing the dream of building China into a marine power.

First, the government attached great importance to the development and utilization of marine resources. In August, 2003, the Zhejiang Provincial Party Committee and the Provincial Government explicitly set the goal of building a strong province of marine economy, and organized efforts to formulate the *Plan for Building Zhejiang into a Strong Province of Marine Economy*. In 2007, the Zhejiang Provincial Party Committee and the Provincial Government identified the strategic requirement and task of vigorously developing the marine economy and more rapidly building a strong province of port and shipping, and actively planned the marine economy developmental belt. In 2011, Zhejiang's demonstration areas for the development of a marine economy and the Zhoushan Archipelago New Area were upgraded to national strategies.

Second, with efforts centering on developing the marine economy, the marine economy was developed into a new growth point of economic development, thus offering new space for Zhejiang's economic transformation and upgrading. According to the requirements of rational layout, structural optimization, dependence on science and technology and sustainable development, prominence was given to key points and plans were carried out. With major projects as the means, efforts were made to energetically develop the emerging marine industries including the port-based shipping industry, the port-based industry, the shipbuilding industry, marine fishery, the coastal tourism industry and marine energy, the marine biological chemical industry, and work was done to build the pattern for the development of a marine economy in which Ningbo and Zhoushan serve as the center and Wenzhou, Taizhou, Hangzhou, and Jiaxing constitute two wings.

Third, a strong province of port and shipping was more rapidly built. The advantages of Zhejiang's natural ports were leveraged; the integration of the Port of Ningbo and the Port of Zhoushan was strengthened to promote the integrative development of the Port of Ningbo and the Port of Zhoushan, and measures were taken to strengthen labor division and cooperation among the Port of Ningbo, the Port of Zhoushan and the Port of Wenzhou, the Port of Taizhou and the Port of Zhapu in shipping. The cooperation between Zhejiang's ports and the surrounding ports, including the Port of Shanghai and the Port of Ningbo, was enhanced. Actions were taken to build closer connections between the Port of Ningbo and the Yiwu market, to develop trade and transportation between the Port of Ningbo, the Port of Wenzhou and the surrounding areas, including Anhui, Jiangxi, and Fujian.

Finally, land and sea interaction was vigorously promoted. On the one hand, actions were taken to enhance economic interaction between coastal areas and the inland area, stimulate the inland areas through the coastal areas, drive the development of other industries through the marine economy, and promote the development of the coastal economy and marine economy through inland economy and non-marine industries, thus shaping a pattern of development of interaction and mutual promotion between land and sea. On the other hand, the "mountain-sea cooperation" was carried out to advance economic cooperation between the developed coastal areas and the underdeveloped mountainous area, islands, stimulate mountainous economic development through coastal areas and promote harmonious regional development.

1.3.5 The Dream of Building a Harmonious China and Zhejiang's Practice

The harmony among regions, between urban and rural areas and among strata guarantees social stability and is an important indicator for measuring the people's happiness; it is also an important part of the Chinese Dream. China has a vast territory and many nationalities; various areas in China are greatly different in natural and transport conditions, economic and humanistic foundations; regional disparity, the urban–rural gap and the income gap among social strata are obvious. With industrialization, under the law of a market economy, regional disparity, the urban–rural gap and the income gap among social strata may still become wider, so harmonious development is particularly important. Great progress has been made in Zhejiang's economy since the reform and opening up; in particular, since the beginning of the 21st century, as Zhejiang's economy has entered the later stage of industrialization, regional disparity, the urban–rural gap and the income gap among social strata have not obviously widened in Zhejiang, and a relatively harmonious developmental pattern has always been maintained among regions, between urban and rural areas and among social strata in Zhejiang. Zhejiang's harmonious developmental practice can serve as an important reference for China's harmonious development.

First, Zhejiang's harmonious development consisted in arousing the people's enthusiasm for starting a business, fostering a humanistic atmosphere in which wealth was respected and the rich were not hated, and encouraging the people to get rich by starting a business, investing and working; it also lay in delegating powers to the lower levels and surrendering profits, mobilizing the initiative of local authorities to develop the economy, stimulating various areas to fully leverage their advantages and promote development in light of local conditions.

Second, Zhejiang became the first to venture down the path of new-tape urbanization, and stressed intensive, harmonious and coordinated development during urbanization; Zhejiang promoted the harmonious development of small, medium-sized, and large cities and towns by saving land resources through the new-type urbanization; Zhejiang combined urban development with the construction of a new countryside, optimization of the population and the layout of productivity to stimulate the transfer of rural residents to urban areas, fully push forward urban–rural integration and narrow the urban–rural gap.

Third, the Mountain-Sea Cooperation Project, the project for turning the underdeveloped villages and towns into well-off ones, the project with assistance and support in the amount of ten billion for achieving prosperity and the project for making low-income rural households become well-off were carried out, and the construction of a beautiful countryside was promoted. The development of mountainous areas and the underdeveloped island areas was stimulated by the coastal economically developed plain areas; the economy of mountain areas and the ecological economy was vigorously developed, the industry supported the agriculture, the strong supported the weak, and the government provided help and support to boost the economic development of the underdeveloped areas and towns, and fiscal transfer payment was intensified to vitalize the underdeveloped areas and low-income groups and achieve harmonious development of the whole province.

Chapter 2
Pursuing Scientific Development and Constantly Promoting Transformation and Upgrading

Feng Xiang

For many years, the successive Party Committees and governments of Zhejiang Province proceeded from the Scientific Outlook on Development to push forward the strategic adjustment of the economic structure and fundamental change in the growth mode, and unremittingly explore Zhejiang's road to economic transformation and upgrading. Sustained exploration of scientific development, transformation and upgrading of Zhejiang's economy since the 21st century is Zhejiang's practice of the Chinese Dream; it provides ample and vivid samples for realizing the Chinese Dream of making the people well-off and the country powerful.

2.1 The Formation and Development of the "Two-Bird" Philosophy

Zhejiang's road to transformation and upgrading started from the "two-bird" philosophy developed by Xi Jinping when he served as Secretary of the Zhejiang Provincial Party Committee. Afterwards, under the guidance of this philosophy, the successive Party Committees and governments of Zhejiang Province carried through one blueprint to consistently pursue development, and perseveringly sought the ways to transform the growth mode.

2.1.1 *The Formation of the Philosophy*

1. Background: the large economic province suffered from growing pains, its development bottlenecks urgently needed to be overcome

F. Xiang (✉)
Zhejiang Academy of Social Sciences, Hangzhou, China

C. Pei and J. Xu (eds.), *Chinese Dream and Practice in Zhejiang – Economy*, Research Series on the Chinese Dream and China's Development Path,
https://doi.org/10.1007/978-981-13-7484-5_2

Zhejiang's economic development since the reform and opening up has been remarkable. Zhejiang's GDP grew annually by an average of 13.1% from 1978 to 2003. In 2004, Zhejiang's GDP was 1.13 trillion yuan; a province with a shortage of resources and covering a land area of only 101,800 km^2 abruptly became the fourth affluent province in China with a GDP above one trillion yuan.

After Zhejiang rapidly spearheaded development for 30 years, Zhejiang first suffered from the ache of constraints and growing pains. On the one hand, the bottlenecks and constraints in factor supply and environmental carrying capacity became increasingly prominent; on the other hand, the extensive growth mode imposed increasingly obvious restrictions on sustainable development.

In November, 2004, the Zhejiang Province Bureau of Statistics released a report entitled *An Analysis of the Price in Zhejiang's GDP Growth*, which for the first time fully stated three major negative effects from Zhejiang's high GDP growth, including lack of cultivated land, energy shortage and environmental deterioration. It became the first to study and analyze the price paid for the growth in the GDP and to release the relevant analysis report; this occurred for the first time nationwide.[1]

First, the cultivated land sharply decreased and land use was inefficient. Zhejiang's cultivated land area was just a little more than 1% of the national amount of cultivated land. Zhejiang's cultivated land decreased annually by an average of 584,500 mu (one mu = 0.0667 ha) from 2001 to 2003.

Second, there was an extreme shortage of energy, while the situation of high consumption remained unchanged. Zhejiang is a province with a severe lack of energy and minerals; more than 95% of the primary energy for the whole province was introduced from the areas outside the province. In Zhejiang, the rate of growth of the consumption of electric power was much higher than the rate of growth of the GDP, electric power supply showed full-scale sustained shortage. Many enterprises had no land to build factories on and no electric power to start work. In 2004, the actual maximum gap in Zhejiang's electrical load for unified dispatching exceeded 7 million kW, Zhejiang's cumulative loss from power rationing accounted for 50% of that in State Grid Corporation of China and 92% of that in the East China Power Grid.

Third, the environmental pollution caused by economic development worsened. In 2003, every 100 million yuan of GDP led to 288,000t wastewater, every 100 million yuan industrial added value resulted in 238 million standard m^3 industrial waste gas and 4,500t industrial solid wastes in Zhejiang. These indicators increased by 84.8%, 3 times and 1.3 times compared with 1990, respectively.

In addition, the low cost and low price advantages formed during many years were weakening in Zhejiang where small private enterprises grew and flourished. Compared with the central and western regions, the prices of factors including labor, land and energy, in Zhejiang were noticeably high. Take labor price as an example: in 2003, Zhejiang's annual average staff wage was 21,000 yuan, while that figure

---

[1]The Party History Research Office of Zhejiang Provincial Party Committee compiled *Carrying out Solid Work and Taking the Lead—Since the 11th Party Congress of Zhejiang Province*, Zhejiang People's Publishing House, 2007, p. 50.

was 12,300 yuan, 10,290 yuan and 10,570 yuan in Sichuan, Shanxi and Hubei, lower than half of Zhejiang's figure.

Meanwhile, Zhejiang's products were also subject to heavy pressure on the international market. Since 2002, Zhejiang faced 54 anti-dumping, countervailing and safeguard measure investigations initiated by 12 countries including the USA and India; these investigations covered lighters, bearings, glasses, textiles, tea, furniture and footwear and involved almost all of Zhejiang's bulk export commodities. In fact, these contradictions mirrored Zhejiang's long-standing problems, including extensive economic development and growth mode and its low industrial level.

2. Formation of the Philosophy: "Achieving the Rebirth of the Phoenix Amid Fire" and "Vacating the Cage to Change Birds"

At the beginning of the 21st century, the leaders of the Zhejiang Provincial Party Committee and the Provincial Government gained insight into the importance and urgency of Zhejiang's economic transformation and upgrading. In order to overcome the bottlenecks in Zhejiang's development, it was necessary to proceed from the Scientific Outlook on Development to practically transform the manner of economic development. When Xi Jinping served as Secretary of the Zhejiang Provincial Party Committee, he compared this work to "two birds"—"achieving the rebirth of the phoenix amid fire" and "vacating the cage to change birds".

"Achieving the rebirth of the phoenix amid fire" means that enormous courage is required to break away from extensive growth, vigorously enhance the capability for independent innovation, build a scientifically and technologically strong province and a province with great brands, promote industrialization through information development, set up advanced manufacturing bases, develop the modern service industry, turn manufacturing into creation, change the OEM into brand creation, achieve thorough transformation of industries and enterprises.

"Vacating the cage to change birds" means that it is imperative to actively push ahead with the optimization and upgrading of the industrial structure, energetically guide the development of efficient ecological agriculture, advanced manufacturing and modern service industries. Meanwhile, it is necessary to carry forward the enterprising spirit of Zhejiang's people, go out of Zhejiang to develop Zhejiang, and zealously engage in regional cooperation and exchange nationwide according to the requirements of coordinated regional development, thus making available developmental space for Zhejiang's industrial supererogation; it is essential to combine "going global" with "bringing in" to introduce high-quality foreign capital and domestic capital, promote the adjustment of the industrial structure, make up for the deficiency in the industrial chain, cater to the international market, cultivate and introduce "new birds" and "good birds" which eat less, lay more eggs and fly high.[2]

[2]Xi Jinping, *Zhijiang Xinyu*, Zhejiang People's Publishing House, 2007, p. 185.

2.1.2 The Development of the Philosophy: Carrying Through One Blueprint to Consistently Pursue Development

The 10th Party Committee of Zhejiang Province determined that the main work consisted in promoting economic transformation from quantitative expansion to qualitative improvement, which initiated the way of exploring Zhejiang's transformation of its economic developmental mode. Comrade Xi Jinping, then Secretary of the 11th Party Committee of Zhejiang Province, put forward the "Eight-Eight Strategies", and vowed to push forward the transformation of the developmental mode with the courage of "achieving the rebirth of the phoenix amid fire" and by "vacating the cage to change birds", thus kicking off Zhejiang's efforts in adjusting the structure and promoting transformation, and elevating Zhejiang's transformation of the economic developmental mode to a new level.

2.1.2.1 The Implementation and Promotion of the Philosophy of Economic Transformation and Upgrading by the Zhejiang Provincial Party Committee and the Provincial Government

The 12th Party Committee of Zhejiang Province deeply carried out the "Eight-Eight Strategies" and the overall strategy of making the people rich by starting a business and of building a strong province through innovation, thus giving rise to a new pattern of accelerating the transformation of the developmental mode and promoting economic transformation and upgrading. The 13th Party Congress of Zhejiang Province set the new goal of becoming affluent in material and rich in mind and decided to carry through one blueprint to consistently pursue development.

As from June, 2012, Zhejiang further strengthened the mechanism of work promotion of "vacating the cage to change birds", and further forced the phase-out of the backward production capacity by increasing the costs of factor use relating to backward production capacity. At the opening ceremony of the First Session of the 12th People's Congress of Zhejiang Province in January, 2013, when delivering the government work report on behalf of the People's Government of Zhejiang Province, Li Qiang, acting governor of Zhejiang Province, stated that it was necessary for Zhejiang to actively renovate and upgrade the traditional industries, develop and implement a package plan for promoting transformation by "vacating the cage to change birds", guide and support enterprises to speed up their technical renovation, spur the application of information technology and firmly phase out some backward production capacities.

2.1.2.2 Several Major Systematic Projects for Zhejiang's Current Economic Transformation and Upgrading

On the previous basis, the new Party committee and government of Zhejiang Province launched a number of projects, including "Four Changes and Three Famous Things", "Three Renovating and One Demolishing", and "The Governance for Five Kinds of Water".

1. Taking the strategy of "Four Changes" as the route

The project "Four Changes and Three Famous Things", namely more rapidly "vacating the cage to change birds", replacing the people with machines, optimizing space to save land, expanding the market through e-commerce, and vigorously cultivating well-known enterprises, famous products and eminent experts, solves a series of current structural problems in Zhejiang's economy.

"Vacating the cage to change birds" means that it is necessary to intently develop the industries with high added value, low energy consumption and low emissions including the strategic emerging industries, new and hi-tech industries, the high-end equipment manufacturing industry and the modern service industry, and actively phase out the industries with low added value, high energy consumption and a high degree of pollution, achieve the strategic adjustment of the economic structure; its essence is industrial innovation.

Replacing the people with machines means that it is essential to encourage and support enterprises to quicken technical renovation, adopt the processes and equipment with more advanced technologies and a higher degree of automation to replace the existing relatively backward processes and equipment, and use advanced equipment to replace low-end labor, so as to enhance the labor productivity, the quality of the products and the market competitiveness of enterprises; its essence is innovation of technology, process and management with equipment renewal as the carrier.

Optimizing space to save land focuses on saving and intensively utilizing the land, continuously increasing the yield of factors including unit land, energy and environmental capacity; its essence is innovation in the manner of factor utilization.

Expanding the market through e-commerce means that actions are taken to vigorously develop e-commerce, actively use the Internet to develop new markets, new spaces and new fields, and adopt the Internet of Things, cloud computing and big data to boost crossover operations, crossover competition and crossover development; its essence is change and innovation in the business model.

For the effect of implementation, "vacating the cage to change birds" generated new industries: in 2013, more than 18,000 low-end backward enterprises (workshops, processing points) were phased out and shut down, the added value from new and hi-tech industries, the equipment manufacturing industry increased by 10.3% and 9.4% in Zhejiang. "Replacing the people with machines" produced new efficiency: in 2013, technical renovation investment involving replacing the people with machines grew by 25.8%, the number of people necessary for delivering 10,000-yuan industrial added value decreased by 9.2% compared with the previous period, more than 600,000 people were replaced in industrial and economic fields. "Optimizing space to save land" engendered a new pattern: as of late December, 2013, Zhejiang's 3998 inefficiently utilized construction land lots were redeveloped, covering an area of 99,500 mu; 39,099,000 m^2 underground space was developed and utilized. "Expanding the market through e-commerce" brought about new vitality: in 2013, Zhejiang delivered online retail sales amounting to 382,125 million yuan, up 88.48% from the previous period, 16.9% sales were carried out through e-commerce, and Zhejiang's residents spent 226,198 million yuan online, up 73.26% from the previous period.

2. Being spearheaded by the project for cultivating well-known enterprises, famous products and eminent experts

Cultivating well-known enterprises, famous products and eminent experts means that it is necessary to more rapidly cultivate a number of well-known enterprises, famous brands and celebrated entrepreneurs, build industry leaders, shape a structure of industrial organization in which large enterprises play the dominant role and small, medium-sized and large enterprises collaborate and supplement one another; its essence is industrial organizational innovation. It is essential to cultivate and build enterprises to be listed among the top 500 global companies, turn them into the enterprises with "geographical indication" in Zhejiang's economic development and the "locomotive" of Zhejiang's transformation and upgrading.

3. Making breakthroughs by the project "The Governance for Five Kinds of Water"

"The Governance for Five Kinds of Water" means tTreating sewage, controlling flooding, discharging the accumulated water, guaranteeing water supply and saving water, which is a major policy recently introduced by the People's Government of Zhejiang Province and also the key policy for a new round of transformation and upgrading in Zhejiang. Zhejiang is really a region of rivers and lakes, but the extensive industrial developmental mode has posed severe challenges to the sustainable development of Zhejiang's water areas. Uncontrolled urban domestic sewage is becoming the source of more and more black rivers, stinking rivers and trash-ridden rivers. In order to guarantee the role of Zhejiang's water resource system in supporting social development, become the first to achieve sustainable development of water resources nationwide and build the model of water control and treatment, the Zhejiang Provincial Party Committee and the Provincial Government vowed to make breakthroughs by the project "The Governance for Five Kinds of Water" in order to force Zhejiang's industrial transformation and upgrading.

The CPC Central Committee and the State Council paid high attention to Zhejiang's water control and treatment, the successive Party Committees and governments of Zhejiang Province also attached great importance to water control and treatment. When comrade Xi Jinping worked in Zhejiang, he made important instructions and arrangements numerous times, and repeatedly stressed that it was necessary to adopt the philosophy and method of scientific development to study water utilization, water control and treatment, water saving, seriously work on the project of "Four-Water" for safe drinking water, scientific water diversion, effective water saving and sewage treatment. In recent years, with a number of measures for the reform of water control and treatment including three rounds of "811" action, drinking water projects for numerous farmers, the ten-billion project for the guarantee of water resources, long-distance seawalls, the dike and reinforcement project, phased achievements were made in Zhejiang's water control and treatment.

As the successive Party Committees and governments of Zhejiang Province have always carried out the "Eight-Eight Strategies" in an all-round way and actively pressed ahead with "vacating the cage to change birds", much experience in transformation and upgrading was gained, the overall strength and competiveness of Zhejiang's economy was greatly enhanced, and the living environment for Zhejiang's people improved significantly.

2.2 From Traditional Agriculture to Efficient Modern Ecological Agriculture

Since the beginning of the 21st century, Zhejiang has fully entered the new developmental stage of promoting agriculture through industry and stimulating rural development by urban areas, thus it has been increasingly urgent to accelerate the transformation of traditional agriculture and develop modern agriculture.

On the one hand, with rapid industrialization, urbanization and marketization, the young and strong rural labor force has massively migrated to the secondary and tertiary industries, agricultural operations have tended to feature side lines, by-business and aging; on the other hand, with the improvement of the people's living standard and fierce competition in domestic and international agricultural product markets, the following problems have become increasingly acute: the levels of quality and safety of agricultural products are not high; the organizational degree of agriculture is low; market players are less competitive. Meanwhile, the agricultural land resources have decreased year by year; there is a shortage of water resources; infrastructure is weak; capital input is not sufficient; the consumption of production energy and costs are on the increase; these problems have also hindered Zhejiang's agricultural development. In order to solve these problems, it is necessary to speed up the transformation of the agricultural growth mode, innovate the agricultural developmental mode, and explore a path that leads not only to leveraging Zhejiang's comparative advantages but also to overcoming the difficulties in the traditional agricultural development so as to achieve sound and fast agricultural development.

Subject to resource constraints characterized by less land for more people, Zhejiang has always focused on the market and on innovation, guided agriculture by means of the market, carried out innovations to lead agriculture, and promoted a great transformation and upgrading of traditional agriculture towards modern agriculture. Zhejiang has carried out active experimentations in building an industrial system of efficient ecological agriculture and a modern mechanism for agricultural development of promoting agriculture through industry and stimulating rural development by urban areas, so as to guarantee food security and bring about efficient ecological agriculture, taking a unique and fruitful path of modern agricultural development and gathering extensive successful experience.

2.2.1 The Formation of the Philosophy of the Development of Efficient Ecological Agriculture

Based on fully analyzing Zhejiang's resource endowment, its level of economic and social development and the new situation of its agricultural development, Xi Jinping, then Secretary of the Zhejiang Provincial Party Committee, farsightedly made the strategic decision to develop an efficient type of ecological agriculture, took the efficient type of ecological agriculture as the target pattern for Zhejiang's modern agriculture, and regarded the development of that efficient ecological agriculture as the concrete practical form of Zhejiang's development of its modern agriculture.

An efficient type of ecological agriculture is driven by green consumption needs and centers on enhancing market competitiveness and the capacity of sustainable development; it is characterized by high input, high output, high performance and sustainable development. The efficient type of ecological agriculture has the general characteristics of modern agriculture and also reflects the special nature of agricultural development in the ecologically developed areas with more people and less land.

In order to develop an efficient type of ecological agriculture, it is essential to properly deal with the relations between high efficiency and ecology; high efficiency and food; high efficiency and agricultural multifunctionality. Under the guidance of such a philosophy, Zhejiang classified the agricultural industries and stressed that grain and oil was a strategic industry and must be unswervingly developed, while ten major industries, including vegetables, tea, fruit, animal husbandry and silkworm breeding and mulberry growing, can be considered as the leading industries; it also stated that play should be given to the sustainable comparative advantages; meanwhile, Zhejiang also developed the emerging industries, took the path of ecological development, and exploited the multifunction value of leisure and sightseeing agriculture, ornamental fishery, forest tourism and other agricultural aspects.

In 2006, based on industrial segmentation, Zhejiang released the efficient ecological agricultural development plan, which for the first time specified the division and construction of four major industrial belts and key industrial developmental fields which were market-oriented and characterized by resource agglomeration, and stated the guiding principles for ten major industries from an ecological perspective.

The formation of the concept "efficient ecology" reflects the forward-looking market philosophy and innovation awareness of Zhejiang's people; it has also kept Zhejiang's agriculture away from a range of quality and safety problems and has created a path towards industrialization for agriculture.

2.2.2 The Innovative Development and Cultivation of Agricultural Players

Modern agriculture calls for strong agricultural organizations and urgently needs to be led by talents. During three leaps in the development of Zhejiang's agriculture during the period of a decade, Zhejiang intensified the cultivation of agricultural players. Along with each leap, the organizational degree of Zhejiang's agriculture increased to some extent, new agricultural players emerged, the capability for innovation and the overall quality of new agricultural players significantly improved.

1. The project for the cultivation of leading agricultural enterprises

As from 2004, Zhejiang rated leading provincial agricultural enterprises, subsequently carried out the "Project of 100 Leading Enterprises" to support a number of those leading agricultural enterprises with a high capability for stimulating the development of rural households and high market competitiveness. This triggered a wave of investments in agriculture made by industrial and commercial capital, which not only injected capital for Zhejiang's modern agricultural development, but also brought some advanced managerial experience and forward-looking market awareness to the agricultural field.

2. The project for the cultivation of farmers' cooperatives

In parallel with the project for the cultivation of leading agricultural enterprises, Zhejiang's project for the cultivation of cooperatives was carried out. Compared with other provinces, Zhejiang was more obvious in the decentralized operations of numerous households. In order to ensure that agricultural production is performed in an organized way, only leading enterprises are obviously not enough, it is essential to establish such organizations as associations and farmers' specialized cooperatives to organize rural households, and enable a division of labor based on specialization and cooperative operations under the "leading enterprise + cooperative + rural household" mode.

In 2004, Zhejiang became the first in China to introduce the *Regulations on Farmers' Specialized Cooperatives*. In the same year, the first federation of farmers' specialized cooperatives—the Wenling Federation of Farmers' Specialized Cooperatives—was established. In late June, 2011, Zhejiang was home to more than 22,000 cooperatives with 900,000 members and involving more than 1.30 million mu of cultivated land. Zhejiang has also developed relatively stable modes for connecting the agricultural players: the industries directly entering the market, including grain, vegetable, melon and fruit, are mostly dealt with in such a way that the cooperatives play the leading role, and rural households are directly connected; some industries involving heavy investment, high technological content and complicated market conditions, such as the processing of agricultural products, are addressed under the mode that enterprises play the leading role and rural households are connected through cooperatives.

At present, Zhejiang's farmers' specialized cooperatives have entered a new stage of development, and have shifted focus from quantity to quality, while relevant government departments have regulated and improved specialized cooperatives—helping them become large and strong.

3. Relevant supporting work for the project aimed at cultivating cooperatives

In order to make cooperatives large and strong, Zhejiang worked on establishing land circulation service organizations, developing and growing the village collective economy and addressing the shortage of agricultural talents.

First, a fairly complete land circulation service system was built at the county, town and village levels. Farmers can entrust a village collective cooperative to circulate their land to others; if someone had the desire to obtain land from others through circulation, it was not necessary for him or her to deal with each farmer, his or her desire can be satisfied merely by signing a contract with village collective.

Second, full play was given to the role of the village collective. With the development of the village collective economy, various benefits for farmers, including old-age care, were guaranteed and increased year by year, the agglomeration of rural collective land and the land contracted by farmers obviously quickened.

Third, the shortage of high-caliber agricultural talents was addressed. Zhejiang introduced a number of policies for encouraging and supporting university graduates to engage in modern agriculture, such as increasing remuneration, providing allowance and addressing the issue concerning personnel arrangement.

2.2.3 The Construction of the Grain Production Function Zone and the Modern Agricultural Park—the Establishment of a Factor-Intensive Platform for Agricultural Production

Zhejiang had always been at the forefront nationwide in industrialization and urbanization. However, the modernization of Zhejiang's agriculture obviously lagged behind vigorous industrialization and urbanization, which was mainly attributable to difficulties in overcoming factor constraints. In view of this situation, in recent years, Zhejiang adopted various means for expanding its spaces; although some measures were effective to a certain extent, the situation of increasingly marginalizing agriculture was not reversed. There were severe challenges for improving the capacity for agricultural production and agricultural performance.

In 2010, Zhejiang released the *Opinions Concerning Strengthening the Construction and Protection of a Grain Production Function Zone* and the *Opinions Concerning the Construction of a Modern Agricultural Park*. The construction of a grain production function zone and a modern agricultural park was initiated in Zhejiang. Such construction is designed to creatively build a unified platform for introducing industrial notions and adopting the mode of the construction of an industrial park to innovate systems and mechanisms. Policies and services are offered to integrate agricultural production factors, including manpower, materials and financial resources, into one platform.

1. The construction of a grain production function zone

With respect to the issues concerning where construction will be carried out, who will be responsible for the construction and how to perform the construction, Zhejiang clearly stated that the grain production function zone should be built on standard farmland suitable for planting rice and having a flat terrain, even surface and contiguous areas above 100 mu (mountainous areas 50 mu). Moreover, the farmland cannot be used for other projects within a period of ten years. The grain production function zone should be built in such a way that the government plays the leading role and various players are guided to participate in its construction. The key point in the grain production function zone consists in guaranteeing the quality of the construction of the infrastructure, so the towns and villages are required to carry out design, project budgeting, bid invitation, supervision, management and protection in a unified way.

In order to guarantee the quality, Zhejiang also developed construction standards and acceptance measures, and numbered the identified function zones, as well as establishing an electronic map and database files which can clearly show the personnel in charge of management and protection, agricultural technicians and the personnel responsible for managing and protecting the roads, ditches, pump stations and protection forests. Meanwhile, based on guaranteeing the quality, Zhejiang followed up the three-in-one services to ensure that grain was really planted and produced within the grain production function zones.

The government-led construction of grain production function zones embodies Zhejiang's highly market-oriented determination about guaranteeing grain production safety. From 2008, 1199 grain production function zones covering an area of 1,424,000 mu have been built in Zhejiang.

2. The construction of a modern agricultural park

Modern agricultural parks present higher requirements compared with traditional agricultural demonstration zones and demonstration bases. According to the relevant plan, provincial comprehensive modern agricultural zones can contain about three leading industries, and in principle, the contiguous area should exceed 20,000 mu, a demonstration effect should be produced to stimulate the development of the surrounding areas above 50,000 mu. The leading industry demonstration zones should give prominence to a particular industry and have a contiguous area above 3000 mu, with a demonstration effect produced to drive the development of the surrounding areas above 10,000 mu; the featured agricultural parks should focus on a featured agricultural product and have a contiguous area above 1000 mu, and they can produce a demonstration effect to stimulate the development of the surrounding areas. It is also necessary to ensure that products are of a high quality and safe, and the rate of coverage of the improved variety in provincial modern agricultural parks reaches 100% and 100% of the agricultural products pass nuisance-free agricultural product certification.

With regard to the application of modern science and technology in modernization, modern agricultural parks are required to place emphasis on integration, transformation and demonstration application of advanced agricultural technologies, and provincial modern agricultural parks are required to achieve a science and technology contribution rate above 70%.

2.2.4 The Establishment of a Public Service System for Agricultural Marketization

Marketization is the motive power for Zhejiang's agricultural development. However, because of constraints from objective conditions, most of Zhejiang's agricultural enterprises were small and weak, the driving role of cooperatives was not ideal. With the adoption of the household contract responsibility system, the original service system, which merely focused on production and disregarded sales, gradually disintegrated, but the needs of rural households for services still increased.

In 2008, a province-wide arrangement was made in Zhejiang to build a three-in-one public service system in the vast rural areas, covering popularization of agricultural technologies, animal and plant disease prevention and control, agricultural product quality supervision, in which the government provides public services to gradually guide small farmers to venture down the path towards modern agricultural methods. The characteristic of this measure is that the government assumes a part of the responsibilities, and the government's guiding role is combined with the market's fundamental role. For example, regional public brands are basically operated by industrial associations, while the government supports the management center for agricultural product marketing under whole-budget management; its main task lies in providing a service of policy information and guaranteeing the prompt exchange of market information.

Xianju's agricultural public service system is a typical case in this regard. Xianju is a mountainous county with less access to transportation and information, but its ecological environment is very good. In response to this situation, Xianju leveraged advantages and avoided shortcomings, attached great importance to the development of an efficient ecological agriculture, thus rapidly fostering characteristic leading industries including grain, vegetable, livestock and waxberry. Xianju also developed a four-tier interaction structure at the county, town, village and household levels; a system of chief experts, agricultural technology instructors, responsible agricultural technicians and local talents; a personnel training plan; special supporting fiscal funds at the county and town levels, and reintegrated the fragmented and structurally loose grass-roots agricultural technical force in a three-in-one way. The three-in-one public service system promoted Xianju's agricultural transformation and upgrading and turned Xianju into a typical case in Zhejiang's modern agricultural development.

2.2.5 The Coordinated Exploitation of Domestic and International Markets

After modern agriculture has developed to a certain degree, the spillover of production factors is imperative, while outward agricultural development is the key to enhancing the international competitiveness of agriculture. With the construction of grain production function zones and modern agricultural parks, besides guaranteeing the production capacity of Zhejiang's agriculture and agricultural performance, Zhejiang also further leveraged its advantages in capital, management and talent, and fully utilized the non-local abundant land resources and low-cost labor to rapidly develop Zhejiang's agriculture into the agriculture of Zhejiang's people—exploiting domestic and international markets in a coordinated way, and combining "bringing in" with "going global" to allocate agricultural resources nationwide and worldwide.

In March, 2011, with the support of the Economic & Technical Cooperation Office and the Department of Agriculture of Zhejiang Province, the Zhejiang Association for the Promotion of Agricultural Investment and Regional Cooperation was established. Soon the Association signed a strategic cooperation agreement with the Kunming Municipal People's Government. According to statistical data, as of June, 2011, 500,000 Zhejiang merchants engaged in agriculture, forestry, animal husbandry and fishery and contracted about 3 million mu of land in more than 40 countries and territories worldwide. In China, people from Zhejiang contracted 50 million mu of land in other provinces to carry out agricultural development, with the area surpassing that of Zhejiang's cultivated land, being equivalent to the creation of another agriculture in Zhejiang Province.

Shaoxing is the representative of Zhejiang's outward agricultural development. Since the reform and opening up, Shaoxing's agriculture has developed rapidly; however, with urbanization and industrialization, new contradictions and difficulties occurred in Shaoxing's agricultural development: on the one hand, the space for development became increasingly small; on the other hand, with accumulation for a long time, it was an urgent need for agricultural enterprises to consider spillover of production factors including capital, talent and management. Under the active guidance of the government, Shaoxing took the path of outward agricultural development. Some people from Shaoxing raised grain in Northeastern China, while some farmed fish in Northwestern China and some sought development overseas. According to statistical data in late 2010, 194 agricultural enterprises, large planting and farming households from Shaoxing set up 8.48 million mu bases in more than 20 provinces, autonomous regions and municipalities outside Shaoxing, which were double the size of Shaoxing's cultivated land area.

2.3 From "Made in Zhejiang" to "Created in Zhejiang" and Intelligent Manufacturing in Zhejiang

Industry is the leading force in Zhejiang's economic and social development. In more than 30 years since the reform and opening up, Zhejiang has taken a relatively successful distinctive industrialization path to rapidly achieve an important leap from a small industrial province to a large industrial province, and to a great extent realize historical transformation from an agricultural society to an industrial society, significantly improving Zhejiang's overall strength and the people's living standard.

Since the beginning of the 21st century, in the new situation of strengthened macro control and cyclical economic adjustment, subject to new constraints from production factors and the ecological environment and new pressure from fiercer international competition and global economic fluctuation, Zhejiang's industry has entered an important period of strategic opportunity and is undergoing accelerated transformation and upgrading, making Zhejiang leap from a large manufacturing province to a large province of creation, even a strong province of intelligent manufacturing.

2.3.1 Building Advanced Manufacturing Bases, Venturing Down the New Path of Industrialization

Building advanced manufacturing bases is one of the major measures in the "Eight-Eight Strategies" developed by the Zhejiang Provincial Party Committee and the Provincial Government; this measure was put forward mainly on the basis of understanding the characteristics and problems of Zhejiang's manufacturing industry at that time.

2.3.1.1 The Characteristics and Problems of Zhejiang's Manufacturing Industry

Zhejiang's manufacturing industry presented distinctive local characteristics during its development: First, a manufacturing structure dominated by featured advantageous industries took shape, and there were a number of industries and products with certain features and advantages nationwide. Second, a large cluster of regional characteristic economies, characterized by industrial agglomeration development, were built. In the 1980s, Mr. Fei Xiaotong, a famous Chinese sociologist, called them massive economies. According to a survey conducted by the Policy Research Office of the Zhejiang Provincial Party Committee in 2001, Zhejiang was home to 519 massive economies with a total industrial output value above 100 million yuan, which delivered total industrial output value amounting to 600 billion yuan and involved 175 industries and 237,000 production units.

Zhejiang's manufacturing industry developed very rapidly; its aggregate was very large, but the overall quality was not high and greatly lagged behind industrially developed countries. This was mainly embodied in the following four aspects: First, industrial supererogation was not enough, the dual structure in the manufacturing industry was relatively salient. Second, the technical level of its industries was low; the capability for technical innovation was not high; technological development input was insufficient; the technological content of products and the degree of modernization of the equipment were not high; an effective mechanism for the transformation of scientific and technological achievements towards realistic productive forces had not yet really taken shape. Third, the degree of industrial organization was not high; the enterprises which should have become large were not large and strong enough; the labor division and collaboration system of small, medium-sized and large enterprises on the foundation was imperfect. Fourth, sustainable industrial development was subject to great challenges, the pressure on the ecological environment was heavy and the problems concerning sustainable development became increasingly prominent.

2.3.1.2 Decision Regarding the Building of Advanced Manufacturing Bases and Its Implementation

Based on a profound understanding of the current situation of Zhejiang's manufacturing industry, given the general situation of economic globalization and international manufacturing development, the Zhejiang Provincial Party Committee and the Provincial Government developed the major strategy of building advanced manufacturing bases and taking to the path of new industrialization.

1. The making and implementation of the decision to build advanced manufacturing bases

The report delivered at the 11th Party Congress of Zhejiang Province in June, 2002 gives very high priority to the building of advanced manufacturing bases and specifies the main goals and developmental priorities. In 2003, the Zhejiang Provincial Party Committee and the Provincial Government put forward the major strategy of leveraging "eight advantages" and pushing forward "eight measures"; one of the measures consisted in further drawing on the advantages of massive characteristic industries in Zhejiang, speed up the building of advanced manufacturing bases, take the path of new industrialization.

In June, 2003, the Zhejiang Provincial Party Committee and the Provincial Government convened a provincial industry conference to make overall arrangements for building advanced manufacturing bases. In August, the People's Government of Zhejiang Province released the *Plan of Zhejiang Province for the Building of Advanced Manufacturing Bases*. The Plan specifies the overall goal: by 2020, Zhejiang's manufacturing industry will be fully integrated into the global modern manufacturing system, and the international advanced manufacturing bases led by new and high technology and characterized by coordinated development of high-value-added processing and manufacturing industry and modern equipment manufacturing industry will have basically taken shape.

According to the Plan, Zhejiang will build advanced manufacturing bases by focusing on technical support, further opening up, increased input, agglomeration development and brand strategy to carry out eight major projects, including the project for enterprise informationalization, the technical innovation project, the investment promotion project, the outward stimulation project, the industrial park integration and improvement project, the project for the cultivation of large enterprises, the brand development project and the sustainable development project.

In 2005, Zhejiang started to put into practice some concrete measures for building advanced manufacturing bases.

In various counties, cities and districts, industrial structural adjustment was made by means of upgrading massive economies and turning them into the important industrial support for the future advanced manufacturing bases and for the county economy. Thanks to these economically strong counties (cities, districts) and towns based on characteristic industries, Zhejiang ranked No. 1 nationwide in terms of the proportion in the national top 100 counties and national top 1000 towns.

2. Achievements made with the decision to build advanced manufacturing bases

From 2003 to 2007, guided by the government and led by enterprises, with interaction and concerted efforts in the whole society, staged achievements were made from quantitative change to qualitative change in Zhejiang's building of advanced manufacturing bases.

During the period of the 10th Five-Year Plan, the manufacturing industry became the dominant one among Zhejiang's industries and almost accounted for more than 90% of the industrial aggregate. The cumulative industrial added value and total profit and taxes from the enterprises above the designated size in Zhejiang reached 1.64 trillion yuan and 0.699 trillion yuan, 2.82 times and 3.1 times that during the period of the 9th Five-Year Plan, an annual increase of 25.8% and 22.3%, respectively.

For the industrial structure, the total amount of investments in technical transformation during the period of the 10th Five-Year Plan exceeded 740 billion yuan, up 2.1 times compared with that during the period of the 9th Five-Year Plan. The ratio of added value from the heavy industries above the designated size to that from the light industries above the designated size increased from 49.1:50.9 in 2000 to 56.4:43.6 in 2005. That ratio reversely changed for the first time; this was a historical change in the manufacturing pattern traditionally dominated by light industries.

For enterprise vitality, the proportions of the number and sales revenue of the private enterprises above the designated size in Zhejiang in the total number and sales revenue of enterprises in Zhejiang increased from 45% and 47% in 2000 to 80% and 71.5% in 2005, respectively. During the period of the 10th Five-Year Plan, the number of the enterprises above the designated size showed two-fold increase.

For the development of industrial clusters, the total industrial output value of massive economies dominated by small and medium-sized enterprises in Zhejiang accounted for more than 60% of the whole industry; there were 95 massive economies with the output value above 5 billion yuan in 2005, accounting for more than 1/4 of the total number; the scale of the single massive economy increased by about 115% compared with 2003.

For the factor composition, the net value of fixed assets for the industrial enterprises above the designated size in Zhejiang annually grew by an average of 13.3% during the period of the 10th Five-Year Plan period, being 1.1 percentage points higher than the national level; the investment intensity per unit of land increased markedly, the consumption of raw materials was on the decrease, the labor productivity continuously improved, the levels of automation and digitization of equipment constantly increased.

2.3.2 *Relying on Independent Innovation as the Driving Force to Help Leap from "Made in Zhejiang" to "Created in Zhejiang"*

After the developmental strategy of relying on independent innovation as the driving force was established, Zhejiang's manufacturing entered a new stage of industrial transformation—the stage of "Created in Zhejiang".

2.3.2.1 The Stage of Industrial Transformation of Relying on Independent Innovation as the Driving Force

The Fifth Plenary Session of the 16th CPC Central Committee gave priority to the enhancement of the capability for independent innovation as a national strategy in economic and social development. In light of Zhejiang's actual conditions, the Zhejiang Provincial Party Committee and the Provincial Government set the goal of turning Zhejiang into an innovative province within 15 years, with the core task focusing on rapidly leaping from "Made in Zhejiang" to "Created in Zhejiang".

In this regard, the Zhejiang Provincial Party Committee and the Provincial Government developed the major strategy of accelerating industrial innovation and pushing forward industrial transformation and upgrading. On November 12, 2007, the Zhejiang Provincial Party Committee and the Provincial Government convened the provincial video and telephone conference on industrial innovation. Under the overall strategy of making the people rich by starting a business and of building a strong province through innovation, Zhao Hongzhu, the Secretary of the Zhejiang Provincial Party Committee, made overall arrangements for the general requirements, goals, tasks and working measures for industrial innovation in this conference. This conference called for proceeding with the Scientific Outlook on Development to fully push ahead with industrial innovation, make Zhejiang leap from a large province of manufacturing to a strong province of creation, speed up the transformation of the economic developmental mode, constantly improve the overall industrial economic strength, international competitiveness and capacity for sustainable development, turn Zhejiang into a global advanced manufacturing base and take the new path of industrialization with Chinese and Zhejiang's characteristics.

2.3.2.2 Enhancing the Capability for Independent Innovation, More Rapidly Leaping from "Made in Zhejiang" to "Created in Zhejiang"

1. Unceasingly improving the core competitiveness of enterprises by independent technological development and innovation and proprietary intellectual property rights

Some large private enterprises in Zhejiang Province attached great importance to the protection of intellectual property rights. A total of 31,000 patents were granted in Zhejiang Province in 2006, up 62.5% compared with the same period of the previous year, being 37.3 percentage points higher than the national average. In 2005, Zhejiang ranked No. 2 and No. 4 nationwide in the number of granted patents and the number of granted patents per one million people. Eighteen enterprises from Zhejiang were listed among the "National Top 50 Private Enterprises of Independent Innovation in 2006" released by the Chinese Academy of Social Sciences, accounting for 36.0%, ranking Zhejiang No. 1 nationwide. A large number of enterprises set up high-level research and development organizations and postdoctoral workstations, forged alliances with universities and research institutions, introduced academicians and engaged in international cooperation, thus bringing about industry-university-research integration and shaping a distinctive kind of independent enterprise innovation, research and development systems.

2. Strengthening brand building to enhance the core competitiveness of enterprises

Industrial brand building is a vigorous means for addressing excessive market competition in some manufacturing sectors and increasing industrial concentration in Zhejiang. Zhejiang relied on the features and advantages of industrial clusters and massive economies to make leading enterprises larger and stronger, build regional brands and well-known domestic brands, further expand the enterprises and markets of the existing famous-brand products; Zhejiang supported the enterprises and products where conditions permitted it to become well-known international brands, encouraged enterprises to upgrade and transform from OEM and ODM to OBM, and turned more enterprises and products into national well-known trademarks and famous-brand products. Youngor Group is a successful model in this regard.

3. Vigorously developing the supporting service sectors

The service sectors, especially modern commerce, trade and logistics relating to production and manufacturing, and the third-party organizations which provide services relative to production processes can greatly optimize various segments of manufacturing, including research and development, purchasing, production, marketing and management; it can also reduce transaction costs, improve the overall efficiency, sharpen the competitive edge of the manufacturing industry and speed up the development of the manufacturing industry. On the one hand, Zhejiang strove to accelerate the development of the modern logistics, commerce and trade service, information service and modern financial industries; on the other hand, Zhejiang energetically developed the productive service industry which offered services before, during and after the production process to the traditional advantageous industries, it extended the product value chain, encouraged the traditional production enterprises to develop towards upstream materials, research and development, innovation and downstream marketing and promotion, after-sale service and logistics, so as to create the enduring advantages of enterprise competition.

4. Building an effective service-oriented government

The People's Government of Zhejiang Province has always actively guided enterprises to improve their capability for independent innovation, optimize their service mode and service contents, boost the quality of their services, proactively guided and stimulated enterprises to enhance their capability for independent innovation in technology, institutions, management and brands.

2.3.3 The Strategy of Building an Industrially Strong Province: From a Large Province of Manufacturing to a Strong Province of Intelligent Manufacturing

With global industrial restructuring and a new round of industrial revolution after the global financial crisis, Zhejiang's manufacturing industry has faced unprecedented challenges and opportunities.

2.3.3.1 The Opportunities and Challenges Facing Zhejiang's Manufacturing Industry in a New Round of Industrial Revolution

A new round of industrial revolution after the global financial crisis is a digital revolution and also a value chain revolution. The breakthroughs, integration and interaction in the Internet, the Internet of Things, robot technology, artificial intelligence, 3D printing and new materials will promote the rise of new industries, new business types and new modes, a world of post-mass production is coming; this revolution will exert an impact on how to make products and where products will be made.

At present, the intelligent industrial equipment has become the foundation for the transformation and upgrading of the global manufacturing industry; the developed countries have taken the upgrading of the manufacturing industry as the primary task in a new round of industrial revolution. The U.S. reindustrialization, German Industry 4.0 and connected factory strategy, the manufacturing transformation in Japan and South Korea do not simply represent a return to the traditional manufacturing industry, but they are accompanied by the improvement of production efficiency, innovation in production modes and the development of emerging industries. It is urgently necessary for Zhejiang, which has entered the post-industrialization era, to speed up its transformation from the traditional industries to the modern industries, expedite the transformation of the developmental mode, and vigorously develop high-end intelligent manufacturing, modern manufacturing, integrated and systematic manufacturing, service-oriented manufacturing, joint manufacturing and cooperative manufacturing. They have become the intrinsic requirements and inevitable choices for the accelerated building of Zhejiang into an industrially strong province during the period of the 12th Five-Year Plan.

2.3.3.2 The Formulation and Implementation of the 12th Five-Year Plan of Zhejiang Province for Building an Industrially Strong Province

1. The formulation and goals of the *12th Five-Year Plan of Zhejiang Province for Building an Industrially Strong Province*

On April 28, 2012, the People's Government of Zhejiang Province officially released the *12th Five-Year Plan of Zhejiang Province for Building an Industrially Strong Province*, which specifies the overall goal of developing Zhejiang from a large industrial province to an industrially strong province, a large province of manufacturing and a strong province of intelligent manufacturing. It is the programmatic document for guiding the industrial transformation and upgrading of Zhejiang and the accelerated building of Zhejiang into an industrially strong province in the next five years.

The Plan states that it is necessary to energetically implement the *Industrial Transformation and Upgrading 310 Promotion Plan*, cultivate and develop the strategic emerging industries, renovate and improve the traditional advantageous industries, speed up the development of the productive service industry to carry out 10 major tasks including cultivating trans-provincial and transnational enterprise groups, enhancing the capability for the independent innovation of enterprises and building industrially strong cities, counties, districts and towns, so as to push forward Zhejiang's overall industrial transformation and upgrading. Actions are taken to turn Zhejiang into the national forerunner of industrial transformation and upgrading, the advanced manufacturing and modern productive service base with a certain influence in the world.

2. Route to Implementing the *12th Five-Year Plan of Zhejiang Province for Building an Industrially Strong Province*

Trans-provincial and transnational enterprise groups are cultivated. Scope is given to the leading role of large enterprises in promoting the building of an industrially strong province. Measures are taken to guide the leading and backbone enterprises of industries to build brand-supported, listed, hi-tech, industrial alliance-led, headquarters enterprises, give prominence to developing enterprises that are headquarters in integrating research, development, design, operational management, integrated manufacturing and marketing services.

The innovation-driven developmental strategy is vigorously carried out. Efforts are made to support enterprises in strengthening the construction of research and development organizations, encourage enterprises to undertake major national and regional scientific and technological projects, enhance the capability for independent innovation of enterprises. With a focus on cultivating the strategic emerging industries and transforming and upgrading the traditional industries in Zhejiang, the *Double-Ten Plan* is implemented to make breakthroughs in major key technologies which restrict Zhejiang's industrial development.

The construction of pilot smart cities is promoted. Steps are taken to actively explore the effective smart city construction service and business model, innovate systems and mechanisms, achieve interaction between high and lower levels, deeply promote the construction of pilot smart cities, stimulate economic transformation and development, make innovations in the mode of social management in Zhejiang Province.

The construction of industrially strong cities, counties, districts and towns is boosted. Actions are taken to comprehensively build the cities divided into districts, large industrial counties (cities, districts), large industrial towns, key industrial parks or agglomeration zones into industrially strong cities, strong counties (cities, districts), strong towns and strong districts, speed up the development of modern factories, urban industrial zones and new urban zones of the new-type urbanization, new-type industrial satellite towns and new-type industrially strong towns.

The cultivation of the strategic emerging industries is accelerated. The Thousand-Hundred-Ten Cultivation Project for the strategic emerging industries is thoroughly carried out to promote the accelerated development of Zhejiang's strategic emerging industries.

2.3.3.3 Zhejiang's Practice in Transformation from "Made in Zhejiang" to Intelligent Manufacturing in Zhejiang

During transformation from "Made in Zhejiang" to intelligent manufacturing in Zhejiang, "replacing the people with machines" and "expanding the market through e-commerce" become the main modes of Zhejiang's manufacturing transformation and upgrading.

Yongkang's hardware industry is a typical representative in Zhejiang's manufacturing industry. With its international convention and exhibition center as the industrial agglomeration platform, China (Yongkang) Sci-Tech Hardware City greatly introduces famous e-commerce platform enterprises, e-commerce service enterprises and large-scale entrepreneurs, and taps new potential by "expanding the market through e-commerce". It has introduced more than 20 e-commerce enterprises, including www.99114.com, IBM, China National Credit Information Service, Inc, Cofortune and www.jhjcw.net.

Wenzhou also relies on light industrial agglomeration and the resource advantages of global Wenzhou merchants to actively develop cross-border e-commerce and achieve the integrative development of the cyber economy and the real economy.

In recent years, Zhejiang's manufacturing industry, dominated by labor-intensive sectors, has suffered an obvious labor shortage. In order to solve this problem, many Zhejiang enterprises have carried out transformation by replacing the people with machines. The speed of replacing the people with machines at enterprises has been increased in an all-round way, thus bringing huge development opportunities for the development of the robot equipment manufacturing industry. The renovation and upgrading of the traditional industries, the cultivation and development of the emerging industries cannot be achieved without the "mother of industry"—the equipment manufacturing industry.

Ningbo has always attached great importance to developing the equipment manufacturing industry; it has become the important equipment manufacturing base in Zhejiang Province; it has reached the advanced domestic level in such fields as medium and high-grade numerical control machine tools, high-end injection molding machines, photovoltaic power generation equipment, computerized flat knitters and complete equipment of high-voltage power transmission and transformation.

2.4 From the Traditional Service Industry to the Modern Service Industry

In parallel with promoting industrial and agricultural economic transformation and upgrading, Zhejiang took the service industry as the important way to carrying forward industrial structural adjustment and transforming the economic developmental mode.

2.4.1 Gradually Cultivating and Developing the Service Industry into the Leading Driving Industry for Promoting Economic Development

1. The determination of the service industry as the leading driving industry

After many years of great efforts, a certain amount of progress was made in the development of Zhejiang's service industry. The ratio of the primary, secondary and tertiary industries in Zhejiang was adjusted from 11:52.7:36.3 in 2000 to 6.6:53.4:40 in 2005. However, in general, the development of the service industry still lagged behind Zhejiang's industrialization and urbanization. In a meeting held in 2005, Xi

Jinping, then Secretary of the Zhejiang Provincial Party Committee, pointed out, "accelerating the development of the service industry is the objective requirement for conforming to the economic development law and promoting growth transformation; it is essential to observe the economic law to gradually cultivate and develop the service industry into the leading driving industry for promoting economic development; the developed service industry boosts the improvement of the manufacturing industry, and the first-class manufacturing industry calls for support from the first-rate service industry."[3]

2. The work arrangement for the accelerated development of the service industry

In August, 2005, Zhejiang convened the provincial conference on the service industry for the first time, which vowed to speed up the development of the service industry and turn it into the new engine for economic development and new support for social transformation. Afterwards, the Zhejiang Provincial Party Committee and the Provincial Government convened the provincial conference on developing the service industry and stressed that in order to quicken the development of Zhejiang's service industry, it was imperative to combine it with the building of an advanced manufacturing base, rational regional distribution, the expansion of consumption needs, employment and opening up; it was necessary to focus on five major advantageous service sectors with a certain foundation and at a certain scale, including the sector of commerce, trade and logistics, the financial and insurance sector, the tourism sector, the cultural sector and the real estate sector; it was essential to more rapidly cultivate five major emerging service sectors with developmental potential and consistent with developmental trends, including the information service sector, the science and education service sector, the intermediary service sector, the community service sector and the public service sector.

Afterwards, the Zhejiang Provincial Party Committee and the Provincial Government issued *Several Opinions Concerning the Accelerated Development of the Service Industry*, which specifies the overall goals for developing Zhejiang's service industry as follows: by 2010, make the added value from Zhejiang's service industry be the double of what it was in 2004 and account for about 45% of Zhejiang's GDP; increase the contribution from the service industry to economic growth and the employment in the whole society, transform the industrial structure and employment structure from "the secondary, tertiary, and primary industries" to "the tertiary, secondary, and primary industries", overcome the institutional and talent constraints and the bottlenecks to opening-up on the development of the service industry.

In order to carry out the Opinions, the government decided to establish the work coordination meeting system of the service industry for organizing and coordinating the development of the service industry throughout the province, making overall planning, providing policy guidance and studying major issues.

Under the correct guidance of the Zhejiang Provincial Party Committee and the Provincial Government, Zhejiang's service industry entered a new stage of accelerated development. In the first half of 2006, a large number of investment projects in

[3]Xi Jinping, *Zhijiang Xinyu*, Zhejiang People's Publishing House, 2007, p. 120.

the service industry were carried out in Zhejiang Province. Among the fixed asset investment projects above the designated size in Zhejiang Province, the investments in the service industry amounted to 138.2 billion yuan, up 12.7% compared with the same period of the previous year—the investments in the transport sector were 30.7 billion yuan, up 24.6%, accounting for 22.2% of the investments in the service industry; that in water conservation, the environment and public facility management reached 23.06 billion yuan, accounting for 16.7%, up 31.8%; that in real estate amounted to 66.24 billion yuan, accounting for 47.9%, up 8.4%; that in the wholesale and retail sector, the leasing and commercial service sector increased by 71.7% and 21.2%, respectively; that in the health, social security and social welfare sector and the cultural, sports, radio and television sector increased by 61.1% and 24.1%, respectively.

3. Foreign capital in the service industry

Meanwhile, with coordination and interaction among provincial departments, Zhejiang established an open and transparent, industrially unified market access system with standardized management to relax control over market access to the service field and break the industrial monopoly, with a view to permitting various kinds of capital to enter the service sectors and fields to which access was not prohibited by laws, encouraging foreign capital and non-public sectors of the economy to participate in the development of the service industry in more fields in various flexible ways.

Under the guidance of these policies, foreign capital utilized by the service industry substantially grew, its proportion significantly increased. In 2006, foreign direct investments actually utilized by Zhejiang's service industry were USD 1.96 billion, accounting for 22.1% of the total amount of actually utilized foreign direct investments, up 33.6%. Hong Kong was one of the most important trading partners of Zhejiang, the largest foreign capital source and fourth largest export market for Zhejiang.

With increasing input in the service industry, Zhejiang's service industry quickly developed and a number of large service enterprises rapidly rose. Meanwhile, Zhejiang's market was developed and transaction scale was large; 27 out of the top 100 national commodity transaction markets came from Zhejiang, ranking Zhejiang No. 1 nationwide in this regard. A group of large department stores, chain retail stores, supermarkets, lodging, catering and modern logistics enterprises also grew rapidly. In 2006, the added value from Zhejiang's service industry was 628.8 billion yuan, up 14.8%, being 1.5 percentage points higher than the rate of growth of the GDP. Its proportion in the GDP reached 40.2%, up 0.2 percentage points compared with the previous year.

Overall, the structure of Zhejiang's service industry was gradually optimized during development. On the one hand, the industrial concentration increased, characteristics and advantages were obvious. The commercial circulation sector, dominated by the characteristics of specialized markets, was developed; the transport sector with advantages from deepwater ports developed swiftly; new development was achieved in the tourism sector mainly enhanced by the brand that there are idyllic regions south of the Yangtze River, and Zhejiang is full of scenic waters and mountains. On the other hand, the emerging service sectors developed rapidly—fast progress was made in the modern logistics sector; the convention and exhibition sector showed a pattern of interactive development of integrated and specialized conventions and exhibitions; Zhejiang became one of the provinces having the fastest-growing financial sector with the best asset quality nationwide.

2.4.2 The Modern Service Industry: New Engine for Zhejiang's Economic Development

The transformation from the traditional service industry to the modern service industry is the goal of Zhejiang's economic transformation and also the new driving force for economic development. According to statistical data, the growth of Zhejiang's service industry was faster than the growth of the GDP in the same period for many consecutive years. For Zhejiang at the crucial stage of transformation and upgrading, the service industry, which is greatly developing, is undertaking a special and important mission—becoming a new engine for Zhejiang's economic development. As indicated by the data concerning the aggregate of Zhejiang's service industry, the added value from Zhejiang's service industry was 1.7 trillion yuan in 2013, up 8.7% compared with 2012, being 0.5 percentage points higher than growth rate of the GDP and 0.3 percentage points higher than the growth rate of the secondary industry. The growth of the added value from the service industry was faster than the growth of the GDP for nine consecutive years. During the period of the 11th Five-Year Plan, the added value from Zhejiang's service industry grew annually by an average of 13.3%, being 1.4 and 1.7 percentage points higher than the growth rates of GDP and the secondary industry in the same period.

The rapid development of the emerging and high-end service sectors became a bright spot. The roles of productive service sectors, including logistics and finance, in supporting industrial transformation and upgrading were continually strengthened. According to statistical data, in 2012, the added value from Zhejiang's financial, transport and warehousing and postal sectors accounted for nearly 30% of that from its service industry. The emerging and high-end service sectors, including service outsourcing and e-commerce, enjoyed a considerable market share in China, and even on the global market. As the business and consumption model of e-commerce became increasingly mature, Zhejiang delivered 382.1 billion yuan online retail sales in 2013, up about 88.5%, accounting for 25.2% of Zhejiang's total retail sales of consumer goods.

In addition, the life service sectors, including commerce, trade and tourism, also transformed from the traditional service sectors to the modern service sectors through innovations in the technical pattern, management mode and business model.

The investments in the service sectors also played an obvious role in stimulating effective investments in Zhejiang Province. In 2013, the investments in the service sectors above the designated size in Zhejiang Province reached 1.3 trillion yuan, up 19.2%, accounting for 64% of total investments, contributing 65.2% to the total amount of new investments. The dominant position of the service industry among three industries in terms of investment further stood out, and the investments in the service industry played an important role in expanding Zhejiang's effective investments. An industrial structure dominated by the modern service industry is taking shape.

The experience in this period is mainly summarized as follows.

1. Identifying the clear direction and providing policy support

Since the 12th Party Congress of Zhejiang Province initiated the service industry as a new engine for economic development, the government has introduced a raft of policies. The *Decision Concerning Deeply Learning and Practicing the Scientific Outlook on Development, Accelerating Transformation of the Economic Development Mode and Promoting Economic Transformation and Upgrading,* deliberated and adopted in the Fourth Plenary Session of the 12th Party Committee of Zhejiang Province in September, 2008, specifies the goal of ensuring that the proportion of the added value from Zhejiang's service industry in the GDP will reach 47% by 2012.

Afterwards, also during the financial crisis, Zhejiang became the first in China to release the *Plan of Zhejiang Province for the Development of the Service Industry (2008–2012)* and the *Implementation Opinions Concerning Further Accelerating the Development of the Service Industry*. The Plan was the first industrial development plan released by Zhejiang since the financial crisis exerted an impact on the real economy. The Opinions presented 16 concrete measures in three major parts and constituted the measure providing the most support to the development of the service industry among the measures introduced by provinces, autonomous regions and municipalities nationwide at that time. Meanwhile, Zhejiang developed a working mechanism for the development of the service industry, which is composed of the executive meeting of the provincial government, a joint meeting of provincial departments responsible for the service industry, the person in charge assigned by the provincial government, functional departments and industry associations.

In 2011, the People's Government of Zhejiang Province released *Several Policy Opinions Concerning Further Accelerating the Development of the Service Industry*, which specify the policies for further supporting the development of that industry. In order to support the development of the service industry, 50 million yuan, 50 million yuan and 100 million yuan were allocated from provincial finance in 2009, 2010 and 2011, respectively, as the funds for guiding the development of the service industry.

With great attention from the Zhejiang Provincial Party Committee and the Provincial Government, local authorities unveiled about 100 supporting policy measures, so a relatively complete policy system for developing the service industry basically took shape. The corresponding leading body and working mechanism were also established; the systems for promoting the key sectors of the service industry were built in some cities.

In order to optimize resource allocation, based on the master plan, Zhejiang developed and implemented a number of special plans for the key sectors of the service industry. As from 2009, Zhejiang annually formulated and carried out major project plans for Zhejiang's service industry, Zhejiang chose a number of large service projects which were innovative and feasible and were able to produce a driving effect so as to guide and stimulate the accelerated development of Zhejiang's service industry. There were 159, 184 and 200 major service projects with a total investment of 228.3 billion yuan, 202.9 billion yuan and 207.4 billion yuan that were arranged in 2009, 2010 and 2011 respectively. In 2011, Zhejiang developed and released the 12th Five-Year Plan for 11 key sectors, including commerce and trade, finance, logistics, information, science and technology, tourism, culture, real estate, community, service outsourcing and e-commerce, to further promote the expedited development of key sectors of the service industry.

2. Making service enterprises large and strong

In order to build a strong service industry, a number of large enterprises are required. In March, 2010, Zhejiang Provincial Development and Reform Commission released the *Measures of Zhejiang Province for Recognition and Determination of Key Enterprises of the Service Industry and Support Policies* to determine 108 provincial-level key enterprises in the service industry, and the Commission also introduced relevant policies for further supporting the development of key enterprises. The following means are mainly adopted to speed up the cultivation of key enterprises in the service industry: separately cultivating a group of enterprises, introducing and transplanting a group of enterprises, integrating and improving a group of enterprises.

Separately cultivating a group of enterprises means that industrial enterprises engage in separate development of the service industry. Separation is made to develop a number of scientific and technological service enterprises, modern logistics enterprises, commercial and trade service enterprises, construction and installation enterprises and specialized supporting service enterprises.

Introducing and transplanting a group of enterprises means making the service industry open wider to the outside world. In March, 2009, the People's Government of Zhejiang Province released the *Opinions on Supporting and Encouraging the Accelerated Development of the International Service Outsourcing Industry*, which specify 20 measures for quickening the development of Zhejiang's international service outsourcing industry and establish special funds for service outsourcing and relevant supporting policies.

Integrating and improving a group of enterprises means enhancing enterprises' competitive edge through the implementation of the brand strategy and standardization. Such measures as fiscal incentives, tax preferences, credit support and talent cultivation are taken to support service enterprises in building self-owned brands, encouraging well-known service brand enterprises to become large and strong through merger, acquisition and restructuring. The standardization of the service industry is strengthened while carrying out the brand strategy.

With the implementation of various policies, large enterprises have constantly emerged in Zhejiang's service industry. With the annual scale of operations surpassing 100 billion yuan since 2008, Zhejiang Materials Industry Group enjoys the leading position nationwide in the overall scale, economic performance and comprehensive strength. Hangzhou Tower, a leading enterprise in the retail industry, saw a sales volume exceeding 5.3 billion yuan in 2010. Alibaba (China) Network Technology Co., Ltd. under Alibaba Group had the main operating revenue of more than 4 billion yuan in 2010.

3. Achieving agglomeration development, building the highland of the service industry

Along with efforts to cultivate and develop enterprises, Zhejiang has also striven to build the highland of the service industry to make the modern service industry break away from scattered development and move toward development into agglomeration. In July, 2010, the General Office of the People's Government of Zhejiang Province transmitted the *Opinions on Building the Modern Service Industry Agglomeration Demonstration Zones in Zhejiang Province* released by Zhejiang Provincial Development and Reform Commission, which state that Zhejiang Province will focus on building nine types of modern service industry agglomeration demonstration zones including logistics parks, bases for headquarters, science and technology parks and creative cultural parks and specify the developmental goal of building about 100 modern service industry agglomeration demonstration zones in Zhejiang Province by 2012.

The modern service industry agglomeration zones, officially launched in 2010, serve as the important carriers for developing the service industry in Zhejiang Province. In recent years, throughout the province, actions have been taken to actively guide the development of agglomerations of the service industry, solidly push forward the planning and construction of service industry agglomeration demonstration zones, and 100 provincial-level modern service industry agglomeration demonstration zones have been recognized and determined, the agglomeration and radiation effect has been preliminarily produced. According to the statistical data on 75 provincial-level modern service industry agglomeration demonstration zones in Zhejiang Province, at the end of November, 2013, these demonstration zones were home to 86,000 units and 473,000 people, up 6.4% and 13.9%, respectively, compared with the same period of the previous year.[4]

The agglomeration effect of the service industry is also embodied in promoting the agglomeration development of the primary and secondary industries. The Zhejiang Transfer Logistics Base has cultivated 10 national Grade A logistics enterprises; such agglomeration zones as the Hangzhou Hi-tech Zone China Internet Economic Industrial Park and the East E-commerce Park have actively promoted the transformation and upgrading of the manufacturing industry by introducing a number of leading industrial enterprises, including Alibaba, NetEase, China Crystal Online and gangji.com.

Platform building is crucial for the development of agglomerations in the service industry. One hundred provincial-level modern service industry agglomeration demonstration zones and more than 200 service industry agglomeration zones under planning and construction in various areas are becoming the important engines for

[4]The Development of Zhejiang's Service Industry 2013 released by Zhejiang Provincial Bureau of Statistics.

leading the development of the service industry in Zhejiang Province. At the same time, in order to cater to the needs for transforming and upgrading the massive economy toward modern industrial clusters, various areas have also actively investigated the building of regional productive public service platforms in key fields such as finance, information, science and technology, logistics, commerce, marketing, conventions and exhibitions.

The Zhejiang Provincial Party Committee and the Provincial Government have also encouraged the regional central cities and economically strong counties where conditions permit to speed up the development of the service industry. Many cities, including Hangzhou, Ningbo, Wenzhou, Huzhou and Jinhua, have developed and released the plans for modern service industry agglomeration zones. Hangzhou City has energetically moved toward becoming the Yangtze River Delta Modern Service Industry Center and the National Cultural Creative Industry Center; Ningbo City has planned seven logistics parks including the main one and six subsidiary ones, it has intensified efforts to develop the port logistics industry and the international shipping service industry, and has actively promoted the building of an international shipping service center and the fourth-party logistics platform; Wenzhou City has more rapidly developed modern commerce and trade, and has become home to a number of enterprises under innovative business models and operation models; Jinhua City and Yiwu City have made all-out efforts to build modern logistics hubs, and have seen preliminary formation of a modern logistics network under comprehensive operations covering urban distribution logistics, transfer logistic, aviation logistics and a public logistics platform; Taizhou City has made breakthroughs through the project for the creation of a service agglomeration zone for the modern manufacturing industry to orderly push ahead with the shipbuilding industry service center and the auto parts industry service center in agglomeration zones.

2.5 From Massive Economy to Modern Industrial Clusters

Massive economy, dominated by the manufacturing industry, has the characteristics of industrial clusters and is a regional economic form with Zhejiang's characteristics. After many years of development, starting from traditional specialty industries with one product at one village and one industry in one area, from small to large, from weak to strong, massive economic mosaics with distinctive features and under various modes have been prevalent throughout Zhejiang Province; the massive economy has become the important industrial organization form for supporting Zhejiang's regional economic development. As the massive economy serves as the important support for building bases for the advanced manufacturing industry, incorporated into the "Eight-Eight Strategies", the path of transforming the massive economy into modern industrial clusters reflects, to some extent, the industrial transformation path with Zhejiang's characteristics.

2.5.1 *Massive Economy: An Important Support for the Bases of the Advanced Manufacturing Industry*

Actions should be taken to further leverage the advantages of Zhejiang's massive specialty industries, speed up the building of the bases for the advanced manufacturing industry and start down the new industrialization road; this is the important developmental strategy among the "Eight-Eight Strategies" made by the Zhejiang Provincial Party Committee and the Provincial Government. Massive economy is the important foundation for Zhejiang's manufacturing industry; developing the massive economy is a new industrialization road with Zhejiang's characteristics.

Since the second half of 2003, like other areas of the country, Zhejiang has entered a period of rapid expansion amidst a new round of economic growth. At the new growth stage, in Zhejiang Province, the massive economy has developed strongly, the economic aggregate has increased greatly, and the industrial structure has changed significantly, thus vigorously boosting the building of the bases for the advanced manufacturing industry. The "Eight-Eight Strategies" have preliminarily produced good effects. The statistical data during the period 2003–2005 clearly show the trajectory of developmental changes in the massive economy.

First, the industrial scale has increased rapidly. In 2005, the industrial output value from the massive economy was 1,840.5 billion yuan, accounting for 60.9% of the total industrial output value of 3,021.24 billion yuan. The industrial output value from the massive economy grew annually by an average of 34.23% compared with 1,021.56 billion yuan in 2003; the proportion of the massive economy in the total industrial output value increased by 8.1 percentage points. In other words, about 60% of the industrial economic aggregate in Zhejiang Province was reflected in the massive economy; this was second to none nationwide. Moreover, the improvement of the massive economy was combined with the construction of industrial parks, delivering fruitful results. During the period 2003–2005, a total of 296.26 billion yuan was invested in industrial parks in Zhejiang Province, accounting for 50.4% of the total investments in the manufacturing industry at the same period. Th large-scale construction of industrial parks, especially the construction of specialty industrial parks, has decidedly boosted the massive economy and has stimulated the development of agglomerations and technical transformation of enterprises; as a result, a number of new industrial parks have taken shape and the situation of low output, small scale and scattered distribution has been changed to a great extent.

Second, obvious changes have taken place in the industrial structure. The massive economy has a large industrial coverage and is available in the majority of manufacturing sectors. The massive economy exists in 31 large statistical categories of manufacturing sectors except for petroleum processing, coking and nuclear fuel processing, tobacco products, and arms and ammunition manufacturing.

The massive economy, with featured advantageous industries as the pillars, gives birth to the growth poles for regional economic development and produces a prosperity effect on the local economy. A relatively developed massive economy brings about a relatively developed county economy. The massive economy epitomizes the new industrialization road with Zhejiang's characteristics. Its most distinctive feature is that specialized markets and specialty manufacturing support each other and develop in a coordinated way. Specialized markets largely address market information, raw materials supply and product marketing channels necessary for the development of specialty manufacturing and small and medium-sized enterprises, especially their initial development. Now, specialized markets have extended from Zhejiang Province to other provinces, from the tangible fields to the intangible ones, they have built connections with nearly three million Zhejiang merchants outside Zhejiang Province and enterprises' sales terminals to form product sales networks at home and abroad, thus greatly expanding the spaces for the development of the massive economy and promoting industrial integration and upgrading.

The Zhejiang Provincial Party Committee and the Provincial Government vowed to, during the period of the 11th Five-Year Plan, further develop the bases for the advanced manufacturing industry according to the overall requirement of building those bases and starting down the new industrialization road, and to speed up the overall transformation towards the internationally competitive industrial clusters. Under the guidance of this goal, the People's Government of Zhejiang Province has called for focusing on cultivating a host of large enterprises and conglomerates, a number of massive economic areas and a group of small growth enterprises. Most importantly, efforts are being made to cultivate 100 massive economic areas and turn them into featured advantageous industrial clusters with a sales scale above 5 billion yuan, a high capability for innovation and competitiveness, a high industrial level and regional brands, and to shape a number of national manufacturing centers and important industrial bases.

2.5.2 *More Rapidly Transforming and Upgrading the Massive Economy to Modern Industrial Clusters*

Although the massive economy has contributed tremendously to making Zhejiang's people rich and Zhejiang Province strong, it has inherent defects—the level is low, the structure is scattered, innovation is weak and brands are small; in general, it is still available in the initial form of an industrial cluster, it is not a modern industrial cluster. In recent years, the advantages of Zhejiang's private economy—swift, ingenious and flexible—have been gradually weakened, the disadvantages—low, small and scattered—have been greatly enlarged.

The Zhejiang Provincial Party Committee and the Provincial Government realized the weaknesses of Zhejiang's economy early: In order to improve Zhejiang's economy, it is essential to change the low-end position of the engine of Zhejiang's economy—the massive economy—in the global industrial value chain, and to unlock industries and products from the low end. The fundamental way to achieving such change lies in transforming Zhejiang's economic developmental mode and accelerating the efforts to transform and upgrade the massive economy towards modern industrial clusters.

Since 2008, with the impact from the global financial crisis, Zhejiang's massive economy was one of the economic groups that was hit the hardest: Export markets in many areas shrank, the production capacity of the same kind was severely excessive so that production sharply declined; some private enterprises provided guarantees for each other in an excessive way, financial crises occurred like dominos at enterprises. Against such a background, in the second half of 2008, the Zhejiang Provincial Party Committee and the Provincial Government explicitly put forward, at the beginning of their arranging for addressing the global financial crisis, the strategy and line of thought of resolving the current problems and removing the root causes at the same time, maintaining stability and promoting adjustment; they called for taking the financial crisis as a historic opportunity for transformation and upgrading, drawing on strengths to overcome the structural and quality-related contradictions in Zhejiang's economy; and they made the major strategic decisions about more rapidly transforming and upgrading the massive economy towards modern industrial clusters.

1. The construction of industrial cluster demonstration zones

In the summer of 2009, the People's Government of Zhejiang Province issued the *Guiding Opinions on Accelerating the Transformation and Upgrading of the Massive Economy towards Modern Industrial Clusters* ("the Guiding Opinions"), which specify the path to follow to achieve transformation and upgrading by focusing on five major projects, including the cultivation of leading enterprises, space and platform optimization, stimulation through major projects, promotion based on innovation platforms, policy factor support, and determining 42 industrial cluster demonstration zones from 312 massive economic areas at a scale above one billion yuan to carry out pilot work ("industrial cluster demonstration zones"). Afterwards, the leading provincial group for industrial transformation and upgrading was established to push forward the transformation and upgrading of the massive economy in Zhejiang Province in an integrated way; 42 industrial cluster demonstration zones saw the establishment of coordination mechanisms in the charge of the main leaders from local governments and with a clear division of labor among departments and with responsibilities put in place.

The decisions and requirements of the Zhejiang Provincial Party Committee and the Provincial Government have been quickly carried out throughout the province; the departments and organizations at various levels have taken the construction of industrial cluster demonstration zones as an important means for economic transformation and upgrading, as an important carrier for developing the emerging industries, as the planning for exploring the new modes involving intensive, agglomeration and cluster development of Zhejiang's industry; they have intensified work on planning guidance, policy support, demonstration promotion, atmosphere creation, intellectual support and joint stimulation. This mainly covers the following areas.

(1) Formulating implementation plans, identifying transformation tasks. Relevant departments have taken the formulation of implementation plans as an important

means for pushing forward the pilot construction of demonstration zones, they have distributed the plan formulation guidelines to specify the main points of formulation, regulate the study of feasibility and approval procedures, so as to ensure that implementation plans are more strategic, macro, open and operable.

In order to foster a good atmosphere and promote the transformation of the massive economy from points to areas, local authorities of Zhejiang Province held 9 seminars on transformation and upgrading, covering textile, equipment manufacturing and new materials, in which 19 academicians of the Chinese Academy of Sciences and the Chinese Academy of Engineering, well-known national experts and leading industrial figures were invited to deeply analyze the current situation, background, trends of Zhejiang's major industries and countermeasures. With insights, experts brought new perspectives and lines of thought to grass-roots cadres and the personnel in charge of enterprises. Moreover, the chief expert system has been established in 42 demonstration zones, with 303 academicians, professors and experts available to provide high-end consulting, technological breakthroughs, scientific and technological services and policy publicity concerning the economic transformation and upgrading of the massive economy.

(2) Exploring the specific path of transformation and upgrading at industrial cluster demonstration zones while carrying out practical work. Since the launch of the pilot work on industrial cluster demonstration zones in Zhejiang Province, the people throughout the province have continuously explored different paths of transformation and upgrading at 42 industrial cluster demonstration zones, and have gathered much successful experience. In sum, at present, the paths of transformation and upgrading at industrial cluster demonstration zones mainly include interactive improvement of industries and markets; developmental promotion by leading enterprises; government planning and guidance; improvement through value chain integration.

In September, 2010, the People's Government of Zhejiang Province issued *Several Opinions on Further Accelerating the Construction of Demonstration Zones for Transforming and Upgrading the Massive Economy towards Modern Industrial Clusters*. In October, the second batch of 21 provincial-level demonstration zones were launched on a pilot basis, with a focus on guiding and cultivating the massive economy in new technologies, new energy, new materials, a circular economy, high-end manufacturing, business model innovation to renovate and improve the traditional massive economy. With these efforts, 42 provincial-level industrial cluster demonstration zones took shape in Zhejiang Province. In November, 2011, the People's Government of Zhejiang Province issued *Several Opinions on Promoting the Construction of Featured Industrial Design Bases and Accelerating Transformation and Upgrading of the Massive Economy*, which provide strong impetus in planning guidance, intellectual support, scientific and technological support, project promotion, product innovation, brand cultivation and policy support. At the same time, various cities chose, in light of reality, the regional massive economy with excellent basic conditions, large developmental space and great potential for transformation and upgrading as the key support target.

Because of the several years of pilot efforts, Zhejiang Province has made great achievements in building industrial cluster demonstration zones. The most obvious change was steady improvement in scale and performance. The number of industrial cluster demonstration zones with an annual sales revenue of more than 100 billion yuan increased from 3 in 2008 to 5 in 2010; in addition, there were 4 demonstration zones with an annual sales revenue between 50 and 100 billion yuan.

Moreover, 42 industrial cluster demonstration zones have increasingly improved in their capability for innovation and their brand influence has become further evident; the leading role of leading enterprises has been constantly reinforced, the public service support system has gradually improved.

2. Construction of industrial cluster zones

In September, 2009, the *Master Plan of Zhejiang Province for the Development of Industrial Cluster Zones* was released. According to the Plan, Zhejiang will build 14 provincial-level industrial cluster zones and their key planning area will reach 1000 m^2. As of March, 2011, all the developmental plans for the 14 industrial cluster zones were approved by the People's Government of Zhejiang Province.

With the construction of 14 industrial cluster zones, their advantages in resource agglomeration have preliminarily taken effect. For example, the Hangzhou Dajiangdong New Area integrates the Linjiang Industrial Park, the Jiangdong Industrial Park, the Airport Economic Zone and the Qianjin Industrial Park, with an area covering 500 km^2. After integration, its developmental advantages have multiplied; such large enterprises and conglomerates as Gonow Automobile, Sany Heavy Industry, Dongfeng Yulong, China South Railway Group, ABB invested several billion yuan in it. In 2014, the Dajiangdong Industrial Agglomeration Area saw 8.74 billion yuan added value from the secondary and tertiary industries[5] and completion of 17.86 billion yuan fixed asset investments. The large platform in the Shaoxing Binhai New Area has become the main site for transforming and upgrading the traditional advantageous industries and for developing high-tech industries including clean energy, new materials and intelligent equipment. The Huzhou Nantaihu Industrial Cluster Zone has enjoyed a certain industrial foundation and comparative advantages in biological medicine, new energy, advanced equipment, energy conservation and environmental protection.

Accelerated construction of large platforms including 14 provincial-level industrial cluster zones has provided a great stage for industrial transformation and upgrading: the enterprises managed by the Central Government, such as PetroChina and Sinopec, have cooperated with private enterprises through these platforms, and Fortune Global 500 companies have entered these platforms; the strategic emerging industries, the modern service industry and modern ecological agriculture have become the main industrial forms in industrial cluster zones. According to relevant statistical data, in 2014, in 14 provincial-level industrial cluster zones, fixed asset investments amounted to 271.8 billion yuan; a number of projects for the advanced manufacturing industry, the modern service industry and strategic emerging indus-

[5]Zhejiang Provincial Bureau of Statistics, *Zhejiang Statistical Abstract 2015*, the same below.

tries were introduced and signed; the added value from the secondary and tertiary industries stood at 175.96 billion yuan, the output value from new industrial products reached 198.89 billion yuan, while that from strategic emerging industries hit 206.89 billion yuan.

At present, the plan for the 15th provincial-level industrial cluster zone—the Wenzhou Zhenan Coastal Advanced Equipment Industrial Cluster Zone—has been completed. The *Development Plan for the Wenzhou Zhenan Coastal Advanced Equipment Industrial Cluster Zone* was deliberated and approved during the executive meeting held by the Wenzhou Municipal Government on June 5, 2014. According to the Plan, the overall layout of the Industrial Cluster Zone features one center, two belts and four areas.

The transformation and upgrading of Zhejiang's massive economy toward modern industrial clusters will promote the cluster and high-end development of industries, and inject a strong impetus for industrial and economic transformation and upgrading; it will help explore the path and provide samples for transforming from "Made in Zhejiang" to "Created in Zhejiang", thus delivering new performance and brilliant achievements for Zhejiang Province to thoroughly carry out the overall strategy of mass entrepreneurship and innovation and promote scientific development.

2.6 Summary and Outlook

Economic transformation and upgrading is a process in which structural transformation interacts with institutional transition to stimulate the economy in a country or territory to gradually develop from a low stage to an advanced one.[6] Zhejiang's economy underwent two great transformations from the launch of the reform and opening up to the early 21st century. The first transformation was that Zhejiang's economy preliminarily achieved transformation from the traditional economic system under the planned system into the industrial economic system under the market system during the period 1978–1991. The second transformation was that from 1992 to the early 21st century, with a focus on pushing forward market-oriented reform, speeding up opening up and optimizing the urban and rural structure; Zhejiang's economy basically transformed from an endogenous economy with both ends of the production process on the world market and the private sector being dominant to a preliminarily open economy with two types of resources and two markets.

A new round of transformation and upgrading—the third transformation—started after the Third Plenary Session of the 16th Central Committee of the Communist Party of China put forward the Scientific Outlook on Development in 2003. During this period, the long-standing quality-related and structural contradictions in Zhejiang's economy became prominent, as evidenced by the following: First, the pattern in which economic growth mainly depended upon material resource consumption

[6]Li Zhihai, Thinking on Promoting Economic Transformation and Upgrading in Zhejiang Province, *China Economic & Trade Herald*, 2009(12).

was not fundamentally changed. Second, the pattern in which enterprise competition was mainly based on low costs and low prices was not fundamentally changed. Third, the pattern in which the industrial level was low, distribution was scattered and competitiveness was weak was not fundamentally changed. The extensive developmental mode characterized by high input, high consumption, heavy pollution and low output became unsustainable; if no economic transformation was made, the problem of survival would emerge; if no industrial upgrading was conducted, being eliminated would be inevitable amidst fierce market competition.

Speeding up economic transformation and upgrading is a major decision and arrangement made by the Zhejiang Provincial Party Committee and the Provincial Government for thoroughly carrying out the Scientific Outlook on Development and comprehensively implementing the overall strategy of making the people rich by starting a business and of building a strong province through innovation; it is the strategic choice for Zhejiang to achieve a new round of development and continue remaining at the forefront, and this is a long-term and pressing task.

More than a decade of experience in transformation and upgrading of Zhejiang's economy shows that the following is most important: The choice of path was definitely correct. Thus, as long as the paths and directions for Zhejiang's future transformation and upgrading are clear Zhejiang's economy will certainly be able to "achieve the rebirth of the phoenix amid fire" and "vacate the cage to change birds".

Path One: develop the modern service industry. Transformation and upgrading is necessary because the economic structure is irrational. Such irrationality is mainly reflected in the great overcapacity in the manufacturing sectors. Transformation and upgrading aims at phasing out the manufacturing sectors with overcapacity, backwardness, pollution and high consumption, decreasing the proportion of those industries and increasing that of the modern service industry in the economy. The integration between industrialization and IT application and that between the manufacturing industry and the service industry represent two major trends in the development of industrialization in developed countries. For Zhejiang Province at an important juncture in the middle and later periods of industrialization, developing the modern service industry should be taken as an extremely important path for transforming and upgrading its economic structure, whether in carrying out the new-type urbanization or adjusting much of its excessive backward production capacity.

Path Two: drive development forward through scientific and technological innovation. First, development driven by scientific and technological innovation plays a decisive role in enterprise transformation and upgrading. Enterprise transformation and upgrading is a process of development driven by enterprise innovation. Second, development driven by scientific and technological innovation is closely related to transformation of the economic developmental mode. Only when emphasis is placed on the core strategy—development driven by scientific and technological innovation—will it be possible for transformation of the economic developmental mode to yield great benefits.

Path Three: protect the ecological environment. Once protecting the ecological environment is taken as the precondition for economic development, the economic developmental mode can be greatly promoted in a quicker way. In the future, it is necessary to, under the scientific philosophy of "two mountains", intensify the protection of the ecological environment to boost the harmonious and interactive development of the economy and the ecology.

Path Four: develop the information economy. Developing the information economy is a strategic choice for Zhejiang's economic transformation and upgrading.[7] The information economy is one of the major industries in support of Zhejiang's future development. In the future, it is necessary for Zhejiang to actively develop the information economy and develop the information industry into an important pillar industry in Zhejiang Province, transform Zhejiang Province from a large province of manufacturing to a large province of information economy, and build the national pioneering area for developing the information economy to promote Zhejiang's economic transformation and upgrading.

[7]Li Qiang, The Information Economy Is the Strategic Choice for Zhejiang's Transformation and Upgrading, *Zhejiang Daily*, June 25, 2014.

Chapter 3
Upholding Innovative Development and Building an Innovative Province

Ying Guo

Since 2003, the successive Party Committees and governments of Zhejiang Province have always placed innovative development in an important strategic position, they have made relevant arrangements in a profound way and have carried out sustained practical work; the overall scientific and technological strength and competitiveness of the whole province have been elevated to a new level, with an important supporting role played in promoting economic and social development. In 2006, the provincial conference on independent innovation explicitly put forward the goal of innovative development: By 2020, turn Zhejiang Province into an innovative province with a sustained capability for innovation; the 12th Party Congress of Zhejiang Province identified independent innovation as the core strategy for achieving sound and fast development of the whole province; the 13th Party Congress of Zhejiang Province and the Second Plenary Session of the 13th Party Committee of Zhejiang Province vowed to comprehensively carry out the strategy of innovation-driven development.

3.1 The Formation of the Philosophy of Building an Innovative Province

3.1.1 The Background of Putting Forward Innovative Development

1. Innovative development is an inevitable way to achieve Zhejiang's economic and social developmental goal

Since 2003, Zhejiang has been in a period of accelerated structural transformation, quickened institutional transition and more rapid social transformation. This is a

Y. Guo (✉)
Zhejiang Academy of Social Sciences, Hangzhou, China

C. Pei and J. Xu (eds.), *Chinese Dream and Practice in Zhejiang – Economy*, Research Series on the Chinese Dream and China's Development Path,
https://doi.org/10.1007/978-981-13-7484-5_3

period of opportunities for speeding up development and also a period during which various problems and contradictions become prominent. Zhejiang Province's capability for innovation is not high; this remains a bottleneck and weakness in its overall economic and social development. In order to ensure that Zhejiang can seize the period of strategic opportunities in the first 20 years of the 21st century to maintain sustained, rapid, sound and coordinated economic development and build a harmonious and stable society, the most fundamental and most crucial solution consists in firmly upholding and implementing the Scientific Outlook on Development and adopting the Scientific Outlook on Development to lead economic and social development. In order to achieve the goal of development, it is essential to rely on innovation; as long as innovation is put in place, we can hold the strategic basic point of scientific and technological development, the central link of structural adjustment and transformation of the mode of growth, and seize the key to leveraging the period of strategic opportunities to achieve long-term rapid and sound economic development.

2. Innovative development is essential to optimizing the industrial structure and transforming the mode of growth

It is necessary to break away from the low-level operational mode with high energy consumption, optimize the industrial structure and press ahead with the transformation of the mode of growth and institutional innovation; this is the inevitable choice for sustainable economic development in Zhejiang Province. During the period of the 11th Five-Year Plan, the adjustment of Zhejiang's industrial structural should focus on addressing the issues concerning industrial upgrading and sustainable development rather than filling the gap. In this regard, the overall requirement is as follows: optimizing agriculture, strengthening industry and revitalizing the tertiary industry, while the difficulty is that the space for introducing new industries, new products and new technologies is not large and the capability for innovation is insufficient.

Collaboration based on the division of labor among enterprises is widespread in Zhejiang Province. First, there is extensive collaboration among small enterprises. Zhejiang Province comes out in front among provinces, autonomous regions and municipalities across the country in the proportion of small and medium-sized enterprises and their output value. These enterprises started from making a certain product or spare part, they have spontaneously formed a close system of collaboration based on a division of labor in production. Second, small capital is brought together on a large scale. As originally one product was made at one village (or town), with imitation and diffusion, finally industrial clusters took shape to form regional specialty industries with small capital and great agglomeration. In Zhejiang Province, the cultivation of advantageous industries and the development of specialized markets are combined with urban construction to create a regional specialty economy and foster the growth poles for regional economic development. However, small and medium-sized enterprises, constituting the absolute majority of Zhejiang's enterprises, make products mainly through imitation. A total of 80% of small and medium-sized enterprises throughout the province do not conduct new product development, those with a product renewal cycle above two years account for about 55%. Most of the small and medium-sized enterprises imitate products from large domestic and foreign enterprises; the business of processing materials supplied by clients makes up a relatively high proportion. Therefore, the adjustment and upgrading of industrial structural should be relied upon to fully transform thousands of massive economic areas from simple enterprise clusters to the clusters with performance delivered on a large scale.

According to a survey conducted by the Zhejiang Federation of Industry and Commerce in 2005, more than half of the surveyed private enterprises "admitted" that there were no scientific research funds; this shows that the enterprises' capability for innovation did not adapt to the requirement of transforming the mode of economic growth. Less than half of the new products made by enterprises are self-developed.[1] Many enterprises are willing to spend money to purchase first-class equipment but unwilling to allocate financial resources to cultivate first-class talents. "First-class equipment, second-class quality and third-class prices" really reflect the reality of many private enterprises in Zhejiang Province. This production mode certainly leads to this consequence: the developmental road for enterprises becomes narrower, performance is increasingly low. Private enterprises must change their mode of development under which emphasis is placed on development, less attention is paid to transformation and great importance is attached to quantity. The governments at various levels should also continue intensifying policy support to enhance the enterprises' capability for independent innovation and more rapidly help transform the mode of economic growth of private enterprises.

3. Innovative development is imperative for building a resource-conserving and environmentally friendly society

Zhejiang Province has a large population with relatively little land and a shortage of per capita basic resources. The extensive mode of economic growth aggravates the contradiction from a lack of resources and causes increasingly severe environmental pollution.

Since 2003, Zhejiang's economy has faced the "growing pains" from a shortage of resources and factors, mainly evidenced by constraints from production factors and the environment, including land, electricity, water, raw materials and funds. The prices of raw materials and energy have risen; power supply for enterprises is insufficient, power shortage is severe; environmental disruption and acts of God have caused a severe water shortage in some areas. These constraints and pressures will increase within a certain scope; the restrictions from production factors on economic development will not be mitigated in a short period of time.

The extensive economic growth has led to increasing resource constraints and environmental pressure. In the later part of the period of the 10th Five-Year Plan, Zhejiang's energy supply featured full and persistent shortage instead of the previous local and staged shortage and Zhejiang became the province with the greatest power shortage nationwide. The environmental situation was also very severe. In ten major water systems throughout the province, 31.3% of the sections being monitored showed Grade V and inferior Grade V water quality; canals, plain river networks

[1]Zhejiang Provincial Development and Reform Commission: A Reader on the 11th Five-Year Plan of Zhejiang Province, January, 2006, p. 49.

and urban inland rivers were severely polluted; lakes suffered different degrees of eutrophication. There was no Grade I sea water in offshore areas, 70.7% of the sea water showed Grade IV and inferior Grade IV quality; Zhejiang Province ranked No. 2 among coastal provinces, autonomous regions and municipalities in the degree of pollution.

Innovation is the fundamental solution for overcoming the resource and environmental constraints. Strengthening scientific and technological progress and innovation is the fundamental way to transforming the mode of growth and resolving the resource and environmental constraints in order to promote economic and social development.

4. Innovative development is the necessity for enhancing the international competiveness and the capacity to resist risks of the whole province

The capability for independent innovation is the core of national competiveness. The practice of the world's scientific and technological development proves that only when there is a high degree of capability for independent innovation, can one country seize the opportunities in fierce international competition to gain the upper hand. In particular, in the key fields having a vital bearing on the national economy and national security, the real core technologies and key technologies must be based on independent innovation. It is necessary to enhance the awareness about improving the capability for independent innovation, master a number of core technologies, enjoy a raft of proprietary intellectual property rights and build a group of internationally competitive enterprises, in several important fields, so as to greatly improve national competitiveness.

Since the reform and opening up, Zhejiang Province has ceaselessly increased the level of industrial technology and production capacity by massively introducing advanced foreign technologies, thus boosting rapid development of the featured advantageous industries and the massive economy. However, the degree of dependence upon foreign technologies is high, and technology introduction is obviously characterized by more emphasis on hardware, introduction and imitation, less emphasis on software, assimilation and innovation. A lack of technologies and products with proprietary intellectual property rights has become the main factor restricting the transformation of the mode of growth, so enhancing the capability for independent innovation is a pressing task.

3.1.2 The Birth of the Philosophy of Innovative Development

Strengthening scientific and technological progress and independent innovation is the fundamental way to transforming the growth mode and overcoming the resource and environmental constraints on promoting rapid and sound economic and social development.

1. The birth of the line of thought on building an innovative province

In the provincial conference on independent innovation in 2006, Xi Jinping, then Secretary of he Zhejiang Provincial Party Committee, stressed that Zhejiang had entered an important period of transforming from investment-driven development to innovation-driven development, and it was particularly important to more rapidly enhance the capability for independent innovation and work hard to build an innovative province and a scientifically and technologically strong province in response to the new requirement of carrying out the Scientific Outlook on Development and building a harmonious society, the new goal of building a moderately prosperous society in all respects and continuing coming out in front nationwide, the new task of building a resource-conserving and environmentally friendly society.

In order to transform from "Made in Zhejiang" to "Created in Zhejiang" and build an innovative province and a scientifically and technologically strong province, it is crucial that actions should be taken to constantly improve the capability for independent innovation of the whole province, especially enterprises, achieve the dynamic transformation of comparative advantages, namely, transform the original low-cost advantages and expansion model into new comparative advantages and competitive advantages focusing on increasing technical content and added value. Vigorous support can be provided for building an innovative province and a scientifically and technologically strong province only when: new breakthroughs are made in several important aspects of science and technology, and a number of core technologies involving the equipment manufacturing and information industries are mastered to make several key industries and product technologies come out in front nationwide; actions are taken to ensure that the overall strength of agricultural science and technology is at the forefront nationwide; great progress is made in energy development, energy saving technologies and clean energy technologies; a technical developmental mode for the circular economy is basically established; the level and technology of preventing and treating high-incidence serious diseases are significantly increased; a number of well-known domestic scientists, technical experts and research teams are brought together, a crop of innovation achievements with great influence are made in some advantageous fields; a system for domestic first-class open regional innovation is built.

During the provincial conference on independent innovation in 2006, participants vowed to finish the building of an innovative province and a scientifically and technologically strong province within 15 years. By 2020, the total R&D input will account for more than 2.5% of the GDP; scientific and technological progress will make contributions of more than 65%, making Zhejiang Province become an innovative province in which science and technology play a decisive role in economic and social development, new and hi-tech industries become the pillar industries, the traditional industries are fully transformed and upgraded, the innovation and entrepreneurial environment is excellent, and sustainable innovation is achieved; and it will make Zhejiang Province become a scientifically and technologically advanced province which comes out in front nationwide in overall scientific and technological strength, capability for regional innovation and in the public scientific quality.

2. The guiding principles for building an innovative province

In the provincial conference on independent innovation in 2006, Xi Jinping, then Secretary of the Zhejiang Provincial Party Committee, stressed that Zhejiang Province would speed up efforts to build an innovative province, and the following areas must be properly addressed in work guidance.

(1) Cultivating and carrying forward the Zhejiang spirit which advances with the times, further arouse the innovative and creative vitality of the whole society. Zhejiang's people enjoy the fine cultural tradition and quality of starting businesses with diligence and forging ahead in an innovative way. It is necessary to further enrich and develop the Zhejiang spirit, keep pace with the times to cultivate and carry forward the spirit of seeking truth and being pragmatic, honest and harmonious, and striving to be strong in an open manner, develop the innovation culture with Zhejiang characteristics to lay the most extensive and most solid social and humanistic foundation for independent innovation. Great efforts should be made to build and uphold an innovative value system; respect the pioneering spirit of the people; create a fair, competitive and cooperative innovation and entrepreneurial environment; foster a policy and cultural atmosphere in which the people dare to be the first, take risks and make experimentations; raise the people's enthusiasm about innovation.

(2) Doing something in some areas but refraining from acting in other areas, make key breakthroughs and achieve leapfrog development. The strategic priorities for Zhejiang's scientific and technological development during the period of the 11th Five-Year Plan: First, give priority to developing the technologies for energy, mountainous and marine resource development, water resource conservation and environmental protection; concentrate efforts on overcoming the major bottlenecks restricting economic and social development. Second, speed up the development of electronic information, biological medicine, new materials, advanced equipment manufacturing and other hi-tech industries, take the acquisition of proprietary intellectual property rights involving core technologies as the breakthrough in improving Zhejiang's industrial competiveness. Third, accelerate the application of information technology, biotechnology and new material technology in traditional industries, fully increase the technical level of traditional industries. Fourth, quicken popularization and application of biotechnology and information technology in agriculture, energetically develop efficient ecological agriculture. Fifth, more rapidly make scientific and technological progress in population health, public security and other social development fields to provide scientific and technological support for building a harmonious society. It is essential to focus on these strategic priorities and the needs of economic and social development to better carry out eight major scientific and technological innovation[2] projects, identify the priority areas where

[2]New and hi-tech industry, traditional manufacturing industry, equipment manufacturing industry, modern agriculture, environmental resource, marine development, health and safety, IT application in the service industry.

there is a good technical foundation and breakthroughs are expected to be made in the near future, and screen out several strategic products or key generic technologies as major special tasks for making breakthroughs through concentrated efforts, so as to achieve leapfrog development.

(3) Focusing on strengthening the dominant position of enterprises, speed up the building of a regional innovation system. In order to turn Zhejiang into an innovative province, the key lies in letting enterprises make decisions and investments in technical innovation and to share interests and risks, and establishing an enterprise-dominated and market-oriented open regional innovation system with cooperation among industries, universities and research cooperation. It is necessary to rely on large enterprises and conglomerates, encourage and support enterprises to actively seek intellectual support from scientific research institutions and the institutions of higher learning; engage in cooperation among industries, universities and research cooperations, set up enterprise engineering centers and technical centers with high capability for R&D. While reinforcing the research on strategic high technologies and basic scientific research, universities and scientific research institutions should attach importance to achievement transformation and proactively offer solid scientific and technological support for enterprises to conduct technical innovation. Steps should be taken to vigorously support the technical innovation activities of small and medium-sized enterprises, focus on building various enterprise incubators, and cultivate a number of small and medium-sized hi-tech enterprises with capability for innovation and growth potential. It is necessary to more quickly develop various kinds of scientific and technological service intermediary bodies for serving enterprises, promote knowledge flow and technology transfer among enterprises and between enterprises and the institutions of higher learning, scientific research institutions. Actions should be taken to study and make the policies for encouraging enterprises' independent innovation, reduce enterprises' innovation costs and improve enterprises' innovation impetus.

(4) Combining independent innovation with brand strategy to build a strong province of brand. The brand strategy is implemented to stimulate independent innovation which then supports the brand strategy; the basic brand-related work is carried out with respect to trademark, quality, standard and management; a brand cultivation and development system is carried out according to a relevant plan and priorities; emphasis is placed on improving enterprises' capability for building brands, with efforts to build a number of internationally well-known competitive brands with proprietary intellectual property rights. An intellectual property and standardization strategy is actively implemented to make technologies patented, patents standardized and standards internationalized.

(5) Upholding reform, innovation and open integration to further enhance the impetus and vitality for independent innovation. The innovation factors are assembled and allocated in an open-minded and market-oriented way to promote scientific and technological progress and innovation; this is a great characteristic and advantage of Zhejiang's work on science and technology. It is necessary to continue innovating systems and mechanisms, establish and improve the technical

innovation mechanism and modern intellectual property system. Actions should be taken to deepen the reform of the scientific research system, encourage the development of private scientific research institutions, and make a number of key scientific research institutions large and strong. Quicker actions should be taken to build key disciplines at the institutions of higher learning; measures should be adopted to support Zhejiang University and the China Academy of Arts to develop towards world-class universities, turn the provincial institutions of higher learning where conditions permit into research universities or teaching and research universities; great efforts should be made to develop vocational and technical education; full scope should be given to the basic role of the market in allocating the scientific and technological resources; the disconnection between science, technology and the economy should be further addressed. Zhejiang Province should make good use of innovative resources by allocating them nationwide, even worldwide. Actions should be taken to actively integrate the existing technologies, push forward integrated innovation, encourage enterprises to really assimilate and further innovate advanced foreign technologies while introducing them.

(6) Putting the people first to build an innovative talent force with a rational structure, good quality and high strength. The leading cadres at various levels should raise the awareness that human resource is the first resource, be eager to seek talents, highly treasure and fully utilize those talents, with a strong sense of responsibility and urgency for cultivating and utilizing them. The strategy of building a strong province through talents should be comprehensively carried out; accelerated efforts should be made to push forward the Million and Ten-Million Scientific and Technological Innovation Talent Project and the Leading Innovative Talent Program so as to build a large innovative talent force with a rational structure and high quality. At the same time, efforts should be made to improve the talent incentive mechanism, better carry out and improve the policy for including technical factors into distribution, increase the scientific and technological rewards to fully arouse the enthusiasm and creativity of innovative talents, scientific and technological personnel.

3.2 The Practical Construction of an Innovative Province

3.2.1 Carrying Out the Strategy of Making the Province Strong Through Innovation

1. Independent innovation has become the core strategy for economic transformation and development

Since the reform and opening up, Zhejiang Province has achieved a historic leap from an economically small province to an economically large province. In order to ensure that Zhejiang Province continues staying ahead, the 12th Party Congress of Zhejiang Province put forward the overall strategy of making the people rich by starting a business and of building a strong province through innovation, and called for taking independent innovation as the core strategy for promoting Zhejiang's rapid and sound development and the primary task for economic construction. It is necessary to deepen the reform of the scientific and technological system, improve the policy system for supporting independent innovation and achievement transformation, guide various kinds of innovation players to increase R&D input, mobilize the initiative of various social forces to participate in and push forward independent innovation. It is essential to more rapidly build a regional system for innovation; actively introduce innovation carriers built in cooperation with large institutions and famous universities; foster a number of domestic first-class scientific research institutions and public innovation platforms; improve an enterprise-dominated and market-oriented technical innovation system with cooperation among industries, universities and research cooperation; establish a knowledge innovation system with scientific and technological personnel as the main force and a combination of scientific research and higher education. It is necessary to uphold original innovation, integrated innovation, close integration of introduction, assimilation and further innovation; carry out a number of major scientific and technological innovation projects and major technical renovation projects, and make fresh progress in the research and development of key technologies and generic technologies. Efforts should be made to earnestly carry out the standardization strategy and intellectual property strategy, cultivate a number of self-owned brands with high international influence and competitiveness, and more quickly transform Zhejiang Province from a large province of brand to a strong province of brand. Continued efforts should be made to boost national economic construction and IT application in the society. The construction of an innovative talent force should be strengthened, and importance should be attached to cultivating and introducing leading hi-tech talents. It is necessary to extensively and persistently carry out popular innovation activities and scientific knowledge popularization activities to improve the people's awareness of innovation and scientific quality. It is imperative to foster an innovation culture, protect the enthusiasm for innovation, tolerate the setbacks in innovation and nurture a social atmosphere conducive to innovation.

The *Report on the Work of the Government*, adopted in the First Session of the People's Congress of Zhejiang Province in January, 2008, put the "action plan for improving the capability for independent innovation" in the first place among six major action plans for building a moderately prosperous society in all respects, and made specific arrangements. In September, 2008, the Fourth Plenary Session of the 12th Party Committee of Zhejiang Province identified "making major breakthroughs in the capability for independent innovation" as the primary goal for making great progress in transforming the economic developmental mode, achieving economic transformation and upgrading in Zhejiang Province. The Fifth Plenary Session of the 12th Party Committee of Zhejiang Province, held in May, 2009, took the improvement of the capability for independent innovation as the main impetus for promoting economic transformation and upgrading. In that year, Zhejiang Province became the first pilot province for national technical innovation projects to fully carry out eight projects covering a number of areas,[3] thus the effort to turn Zhejiang Province into an innovative province entered a new stage.

2. Fully implementing the strategy of innovation-driven development

The *Decision on Fully Carrying out the Strategy of Innovation-driven Development, Accelerating the Building of an Innovative Province*, made in the Second Plenary Session of the 13th Party Committee of Zhejiang Province in December, 2012, states that by 2020, a relatively perfect regional innovation system will be established, innovation resources will be effectively gathered, the capability for innovation will be significantly improved and the innovation performance will be greatly enhanced, making Zhejiang Province one of the innovative provinces, and basically forming the pattern of innovation-driven development. The following problems in the work on science and technology need to be overcome: scientific and technological input mismatches with output; the integration among industries, universities and research is not close; the evaluation of scientific and technological achievements is not scientific; there is inadaptation in the systems and mechanisms of scientific and technological innovation; in order to do this, in the next five years, the following main goals for innovation-driven development should be achieved: double the size in eight areas, achieve increases on two fronts, to be specific: by 2017, double the amount of province-wide R&D fund expenditure, the number of R&D personnel, the number of the patents granted for invention, the output value of new products from the industries above the designated size, the output value of new and hi-tech industries, the amount of transactions concluded in the technology market, the number of new and hi-tech enterprises and the number of small and medium-sized technology enterprises; increase the rate of contribution from scientific and technological progress and the total labor productivity. The R&D fund expenditure will exceed 140 billion yuan, accounting for about 2.7% of the GDP; the full-time equivalent of R&D personnel will exceed 600,000 man-years; the number of the patents granted for invention will reach 23,000; the output value of new products from the industries above the designated size will reach 2700 billion yuan; the output value of new and hi-tech industries will reach 2850 billion yuan; the amount of transactions concluded in the technology market will exceed 16 billion yuan; the number of new and hi-tech enterprises will be close to 10,000; the number of small and medium-sized technology enterprises will exceed 20,000; the rate of contribution from scientific and technological progress will reach 60%; the total labor productivity will reach 140,000 yuan/person.

[3]Improving the work on a number of innovative enterprises; building a number of public platforms for scientific and technological innovation; developing a number of industrial technical innovation strategies; introducing a number of innovation systems built in cooperation with large institutions and well-known universities; improving a number of new and hi-tech developmental zones (parks) and specialty industrial bases; carrying out a number of enterprise-led major special scientific and technological projects; widely applying a number of important scientific and technological achievements and generic technologies; cultivating a number of enterprise innovative talents.

3.2.2 *Greatly Enhancing the Capability for Independent Innovation*

1. The enterprises' capability for technical innovation was steadily improved

(1) Constantly increasing enterprises' R&D input. In 2012, the R&D fund expenditure of the industrial enterprises above the designated size throughout the province reached 68,436 million yuan, ranking Zhejiang Province No. 4 nationwide in this regard, its scale increased by 10.3 times over 2003; the intensity of the R&D fund input reached 1.18%, ranking Zhejiang Province No. 5 nationwide in this regard, up 0.75 percentage points over 2003.[4]

(2) Continuously strengthening the construction of enterprise R&D bodies. As of late 2013, the number of provincial-level new and hi-tech enterprise R&D centers reached 1870, up 7.1 times over 2003; the number of national-level engineering technical research centers reached 14, up 9 over 2003; there were 67 provincial-level engineering technical research centers. In 2009, the construction of provincial-level enterprise research institutions was initiated, and their cumulative number has reached 155. Zhejiang Province ranks No. 2 nationwide in both number and proportion of the industrial enterprises above the designated size with R&D bodies.

(3) Speeding up efforts to cultivate the echelon of innovative enterprises. In 2007, the work on building innovative enterprises was launched. As of late 2013, 416 provincial-level pilot (demonstration) innovative enterprises were cultivated and 44 national-level pilot innovative enterprises were approved. As of late 2013, Zhejiang Province was home to 5160 new and hi-tech enterprises and more than 10,000 small and medium-sized technology enterprises.

(4) Taking continued actions to push forward the construction of industrial technical innovation strategic alliances. Given that there were a large number of enterprises and the capability for scientific and technological innovation was low, Zhejiang Province integrated various resources and forces to build strategic alliances for industrial technical innovation. In July, 2010, Zhejiang Province made the *Measures of Zhejiang Province for the Construction and Management of Strategic Alliances for Industrial Technical Innovation*, which state that about 50 of those strategic alliances will be built by 2015. As of late 2013, 31 strategic alliances were built, there were 471 members, including 390 enterprises. In response to the issues of common concern for alliances, 126 scientific and technological projects were jointly organized and carried out, with the R&D fund input being 1.26 billion yuan. Four provincial-level strategic alliances for industrial technical innovation, including those involved in the food cold chain and industrial design, were designated as national pilot alliances by the Ministry of Science and Technology.

(5) Incessantly intensifying the research and development of new products within enterprises. In 2013, the output value of new products from the industrial enter-

[4] *Zhejiang Statistical Yearbook* over the years, the same below.

prises above the designated size hit 1.58 trillion yuan in Zhejiang Province, up 10.5 times over 2003; the proportion of the output value from new products reached 24.88%, up 14.26 percentage points over 2003.

2. Large institutions and well-known universities gathered together more quickly

In 2003, Xi Jinping, then Secretary of the Zhejiang Provincial Party Committee, made the strategic decision to introduce innovation carriers built in cooperation with large institutions and well-known universities, with commitments to encouraging local authorities to focus on introducing team-type talents and core technologies and to cooperate with large domestic and foreign institutions and well-known universities to build various kinds of innovation carriers, so as to enhance Zhejiang's capability for independent innovation and boost economic transformation and upgrading. In order to carry out this strategic decision, Comrade Xi Jinping directly participated in planning and pushed forward relevant work, he led delegations to visit Tsinghua University many times, raised and discussed the issues concerning the joint construction of innovation carriers through cooperation between the province and universities. In December, 2003, the Yangtze Delta Region Institute of Tsinghua University, Zhejiang was officially built in Jiaxing, Zhejiang Province. Afterwards, Zhejiang Province stepped up its efforts to introduce innovation carriers built in cooperation with large institutions and well-known universities, including the Ningbo Institute of Material Technology & Engineering, the Chinese Academy of Sciences, the Zhejiang-California International NanoSystems Institute; the Jiaxing Center for Applied Technology Research & Transformation, the Chinese Academy of Sciences; the Advanced Manufacturing Institute of Hong Kong University of Science and Technology, Zhejiang; the Hangzhou Branch of the ChangChun Institute of Applied Chemistry, the Chinese Academy of Sciences; the Taizhou Center for Applied Technology Research, Development & Industrialization, the Chinese Academy of Sciences; Shaanxi University of Science and Technology. As of late 2013, 970 jointly-built scientific and technological innovation carriers were introduced. The Ningbo Institute of Material Technology & Engineering, the Chinese Academy of Sciences and the Yangtze Delta Region Institute of Tsinghua University, Zhejiang have made major breakthroughs in several fields, with the achievements involving high-strength carbon fiber and butyl rubber successfully industrialized in Zhejiang Province.[5]

3. The scientific and technological talent force kept growing

Since 2003, Zhejiang Province has acted more quickly to cultivate and gather various kinds of innovative talents, with the introduction of a number of policy measures including the *Opinions on Accelerating the Building of Innovation Teams*, the *Measures of Zhejiang Province for the Building of Key Scientific and Technological Innovation Teams (Trial)* and the *Implementation Measures of Zhejiang Province for the Introduction and Cultivation of the Leading Innovation Teams*. In order to move faster to gather excellent domestic and foreign scientific and technological innova-

[5]Data come from the *Zhejiang Statistical Yearbook 2013*.

tion resources, Zhejiang Province thoroughly carried out the strategy of making the province strong through talents.

Zhejiang Province continued to carry out the national and provincial Recruitment Program of Global Experts, the New Century 151 Talent Project, the Million and Ten-Million Scientific and Technological Innovation Talent Project, the New Talent Program and the Qianjiang Talent Program. As of late 2013, Zhejiang Province introduced 678 people under the Recruitment Program of Global Experts, including 236 people included in the national Recruitment Program of Global Experts, ranking Zhejiang Province No. 4 nationwide in this regard; 130 provincial-level teams for scientific and technological innovation and 100 provincial-level teams for key enterprise technical innovation were approved and built in Zhejiang Province. During the period of the 12th Five-Year Plan, about 30,000 new scientific and technological talents were cultivated, 201 high-skilled scientific and technological talent teams were financially aided, and 1435 skilled talents were cultivated.[6]

The number of people engaged in scientific and technological activities throughout the province and in the whole society increased from 188,400 in 2003 to 610,300 in 2012, up 2.24 times; Zhejiang Province increased its ranking of the scale of personnel from the 6th place to the 4th place nationwide. The full-time equivalent of R&D personnel rose from 46,600 man-years in 2003 to 278,100 man-years in 2012, up 4.97 times, making Zhejiang Province improve its nationwide ranking from the 10th place in 2003 to the 3rd place in 2012. According to the *National Statistical Monitoring Report on Scientific and Technological Progress 2012*, Zhejiang Province sharply increased its nationwide ranking of human resources from 15th place in 2003 to 1st place in 2012.[7]

4. The environment for policies regarding innovation was significantly improved

(1) Continued to intensify the reform of system for scientific and technological management. The system for scientific and technological planning was adjusted to shape a four-in-one work layout covering the environment, talents, platforms and projects. The philosophy that technical innovation is mainly conducted by enterprises was upheld to guide innovation factors to enterprises. A system of consultation between or among provincial, municipal and local departments was established.
(2) Improving the policy system for laws and regulations. A number of policies for promoting independent innovation were introduced; a system of regular meetings for implementing the independent innovation policy was built; the publicity and training relating to the innovation policy were intensified. In 2004, the Seventh Session of the Standing Committee of the 10th People's Congress of Zhejiang Province adopted the *Regulations of Zhejiang Province on Promoting the Transformation of Scientific and Technological Achievements*. In 2005, the *Regulations of Zhejiang Province on Patent Protection* was revised and adopted, the *Measures of Zhejiang Province for the Protection of Technical Secrets* was

[6]Data come from the *Zhejiang Statistical Yearbook 2013*.

[7]Data come from the *Zhejiang Statistical Yearbook 2013*.

released. In 2006, the Zhejiang Provincial Party Committee and the Provincial Government held the provincial conference on independent innovation, releasing *Several Opinions on Accelerating the Improvement of the Capability for Independent Innovation and the Building of an Innovative Province and a Scientifically and Technologically Strong Province* and the *Building of Scientifically and Technologically Powerful Zhejiang Province and the 11th Five-Year Plan for Scientific and Technological Development*, giving unprecedented priority to independent innovation. In 2008, the Science and Technology Department of Zhejiang Province worked with relevant departments to release the *Action Plan for Improving the Capability for Independent Innovation (2008–2012)*, making great strategic arrangements for improving the Zhejiang Province's capability for independent innovation in the next five years and putting that improvement effort in the first place among six major action plans for building a moderately prosperous society in all respects. The 13th Session of the Standing Committee of the 11th People's Congress of Zhejiang Province adopted the *Regulations of Zhejiang Province on the Promotion of New and High Technologies* in 2009, regularizing and promoting the research and development of new and high technologies, achievement of transformation and industrialization throughout the province; the People's Government of Zhejiang Province issued the *Incentive Measures of Zhejiang Province for the Transformation of Scientific and Technological Achievements*, further speeding up the transfer and transformation of innovation achievements. In 2010, the Science and Technology Department of Zhejiang Province worked with relevant departments to release *Several Opinions on Further Strengthening the Construction of Innovative Enterprises* and the *Measures of Zhejiang Province for the Construction and Management of Strategic Alliances for Industrial Technical Innovation*, more rapidly pushing forward innovative enterprises. Since 2011, Zhejiang Province has revised the *Regulations of Zhejiang Province on Scientific and Technological Progress*, and released a number of policies and regulations including the *Guiding Opinions on the Building of Innovative Cities (Counties, Districts)*, the *Circular Concerning the Work on Upholding and Improving the Evaluation of the County-level Party and Government Leaders under the Scientific and Technological Progress Goal Responsibility System*, *Several Opinions on Further Supporting Enterprises' Technical Innovation and Accelerating the Transformation and Industrialization of Scientific and Technological Achievements* and the *Decision of the Party Committee of Zhejiang Province on Comprehensively Implementing the Strategy of Innovation-driven Development and Accelerating the Building of an Innovative Province*.

3.3 Science and Technology Supports Economic Transformation and Upgrading

3.3.1 Enhancing the Capability for Public Scientific and Technological Service

1. A marked effect was produced in building platforms for innovation service

(1) Policy background

In 2003, China unveiled the *National Plan for the Construction of Scientific and Technological Foundation Platforms 2004–2010*, calling for focusing on establishing a sharing mechanism and integrating resources to push forward the construction of scientific and technological foundation platforms in an all-round way. Platform construction stresses innovations in institutions and mechanisms, gives prominence to resource sharing, and breaks up the current scattered distribution of resources, relative closure and monopoly with active exploration of a new management system and operating mechanism to continuously improve the efficiency of scientific and technological resource utilization in China. With the introduction of the *National Plan for the Construction of Scientific and Technological Foundation Platforms 2004–2010* and the *11th Five-Year National Implementation Opinions on the Construction of Scientific and Technological Foundation Platforms*, local authorities proceeded from respective characteristics and advantages to combine platform construction with industrial technical innovation and economic development and to build different kinds of platforms for supporting and serving enterprises' technical innovations. The *Report on the Work of the Government*, delivered in 2008, identified the construction of a number of enterprise-oriented innovation support platforms as the government work priority. The *Opinions of the State Council on Giving Play to the Supporting Role of Science and Technology to Promote Rapid and Sound Economic Development*, released in 2009, call for building and improving technical innovation service platforms. In the national technical innovation project jointly launched and carried out by six ministries, including the Ministry of Science and Technology and the Ministry of Finance, in July, 2009, the construction of technical innovation service platforms was taken as one of the three major implementation carriers and thus the work priority. Given the actual situation, Zhejiang Province worked out the *Plan of Zhejiang Province for the Construction of Public Scientific and Technological Foundation Platforms*. Based on the main spirit, the Plan adds the connotation and service requirements for platform construction as well as the construction of industrial scientific and technological innovation platforms and regional scientific and technological innovation platforms.

(2) Developmental process

In response to the requirements of the *National Plan for the Construction of Scientific and Technological Foundation Platforms*, Zhejiang Province endeavored to push forward the construction and development of local public scientific and technological service platforms. As from the second half of 2004, based on the basic line of thought regarding platform construction—integration, sharing, service, innovation, improvement and enhancement, the pilot work on platform construction was carried out. The platforms built on a pilot basis are the Zhejiang Scientific and Technological Service Platform for New Medicine Development and the Zhejiang Public Technical Service Platform for Integrated Circuit Design. Zhejiang Scientific and Technological Service Platform for New Medicine Development was jointly built by Zhejiang University of Technology, Zhejiang Chinese Medical University, the Zhejiang Academy of Medical Sciences, Zhejiang University and the Zhejiang Institute for Food and Drug Control; it integrates the advantageous scientific research forces engaged in the clinical study of new medicines and covering pharmacy, pharmacodynamics and toxicology within Zhejiang Province to conduct a pharmacy, pharmacodynamics and safety evaluation study concerning new medicines and provide full service for the development of new medicines.

In April, 2006, Zhejiang Province launched the construction of three public scientific and technological foundation platforms including the Scientific and Technological Literature Resource Co-construction and Sharing Platform, the Large Instrument and Equipment Collaboration and Sharing Platform and the Public Service Platform for Experimental Animals. In order to effectively integrate scientific and technological resources and build a resource sharing mechanism, as from 2006, the Science and Technology Department of Zhejiang Province approved a number of provincial-level innovation platforms. These platforms involve a wide range of industries including textiles, software, environmental protection equipment, hardware, mechanical manufacturing, garments, the sea, rice, tea, bamboo, wood processing, fishery, animal husbandry, automobile and auto parts, and border security.

The People's Government of Zhejiang Province also released the *Building of Scientifically and Technologically Powerful Zhejiang Province and the 11th Five-Year Plan for Scientific and Technological Development* and the *Action Plan for Improving the Capability for Independent Innovation*, which take the accelerated construction of innovation platforms as the foundation project for enhancing the capability for independent innovation and specify the following goal: By 2012, 8 scientific and technological foundation platforms, about 50 industrial innovation platforms and regional innovation platforms will have been built. The Science and Technology Department of Zhejiang Province worked with a number of departments and commissions, including the Finance Department, the Development and Reform Commission, the Education Department and Economics and Trade Commissions of Zhejiang Province to develop the *Plan of Zhejiang Province for the Construction of Public Scientific and Technological Foundation Platforms*, specifying the guiding line of thought, basic principles, main tasks, work priorities and safeguard measures for platform construction. Zhejiang Province also released a number of relevant documents including the *Trial Measures of Zhejiang Province for the Construction and Management of Provincial-level Industrial and Regional Innovation Platforms* and *Several Opinions on Pushing Forward Collaboration and Sharing of Large Scientific Instruments and Equipment in Zhejiang Province*, providing the institutional and policy guarantee for regularizing platform operation and management and promoting platform development.

As of late 2013, Zhejiang Province completed 60 public scientific and technological foundation platforms, industrial innovation platforms and regional innovation platforms across units, departments and regions under three major categories of scientific and technological service platforms, including 7 public scientific and technological foundation platforms covering collaboration on and sharing of large scientific instruments and equipment and public service for experimental animals, and 26 industrial scientific and technological innovation platforms covering new medicine development and integrated circuit design, as well as 27 regional scientific and technological innovation platforms, including XinChang Bearing and Special Equipment and the Jiaxing Sweater Industry.[8]

2. Focusing on the construction of "two cities" to orderly promote the construction of major scientific and technological innovation centers

In the construction of major scientific and technological innovation bases, the Qingshan Lake Sci-Tech City and the Future Sci-Tech City are two major cores in the whole province and are of typical significance.

(1) The Qingshan Lake Sci-Tech City

In 2009, the Zhejiang Provincial Party Committee and the Provincial Government made a great decision concerning the construction of Qingshan Lake Sci-Tech City and released *Several Opinions on Further Supporting the Construction and Development of Qingshan Lake Sci-Tech City*, which state that 100 million yuan will be allocated from provincial finances each year to support its construction. As of late 2013, the conceptual planning of Qingshan Lake Sci-Tech City and the urban design of its core areas were completed; the formulation of three guide rules for low carbon, environmental protection and intelligentization was fully completed; infrastructure and supporting works were pushed forward in an all-round way; 28 large institutions and well-known universities, including the Science and Technology Institute of University of Hong Kong, Zhejiang, the Zhejiang Research Institute of the ChangChun Institute of Applied Chemistry and the Chinese Academy of Sciences were introduced, with a total investment of 5.15 billion yuan; 6 projects for cooperation among industries, universities and research, including the Insigma National Engineering Center for Train Intelligentization, were signed and launched in Qingshan Lake Sci-Tech City; 7 scientific research projects, including the Shanghu Science and Technology Industrial Park, with a total investment of 2.1 billion yuan were launched in Qingshan Lake Sci-Tech City; 35 industrial projects with a total investment of 12.5 billion yuan were introduced to the Hengfan Industrialization Zone.

[8]Data from the website of the Zhejiang Science and Technology Department, http://www.zjkjt.gov.cn.

(2) Future Sci-Tech City

Hangzhou Future Sci-Tech City is one of the four national future science and technology cities highly contacted by the Organizational Department of the Central Committee of the Communist Party of China and the State-owned Assets Supervision and Administration Commission under the State Council; it is the talent-focused special zone built by Zhejiang Province for attracting overseas high-level talents to start businesses and conduct innovations; it is also the core block in the Hangzhou Chengxi Scientific & Technological Innovation Industrial Agglomeration Zone intensively built by Zhejiang Province during the period of the 12th Five-Year Plan (one of the 14 provincial-level industrial agglomeration zones). Since inception in 2011, the Future Sci-Tech City has focused on carrying out the "private enterprise + capital + talent" developmental mode in light of the local characteristic according to which the private economy is developed and the private capital is ample in Zhejiang Province; it is unique among the four national future science and technology cities; a number of overseas talents started businesses and a crop of scientific research achievements emerged in the Future Sci-Tech City. As of late 2013, 717 overseas high-level talents were introduced, and there were 101 talented people under the Recruitment Program of Global Experts. A total of 752 projects were introduced. Seven high-level R&D bases under research institutions and 8 enterprises managed by the Central Government settled here; 370,000 m^2 initial R&D incubation platforms were put into use.[9]

3. The transformation and upgrading of new and hi-tech parks was constantly accelerated

With a focus on "high" and "new", the transformation and upgrading of new and hi-tech industrial parks is taken as the priority in the cultivation and development of new technologies and industries. During the period of the 11th Five-Year Plan, Ningbo and Shaoxing were successfully upgraded to become national new and hi-tech parks; during the period of the 12th Five-Year Plan, Wenzhou and Quzhou were successfully upgraded to national new and hi-tech parks; there were 5 national-level new and hi-tech parks in Zhejiang Province. The Hangzhou Hi-tech Zone was approved as the provincial-level independent innovation demonstration zone for network information technology and strives to become the national-level independent innovation demonstration zone. Eighteen provincial-level new and hi-tech industrial parks with distinctive industrial features were newly built, including Jiaxing Photovoltaic, Quzhou Fluorosilicone New Materials, Hangzhou Qingshan Lake High-end Equipment, Zhoushan Shipping Equipment and Yongkang Modern Agricultural Equipment; there were 29 provincial-level new and hi-tech parks. In 2012, the *Guiding Opinions on Accelerating the Transformation and Upgrading of New and Hi-tech Industrial Parks* was released; in 2013, the *Measures of Zhejiang Province for Evaluation of New and Hi-tech Parks (Trial)* was established, improving the system for monthly ranking, quarterly analysis and annual evaluation, and the elimination of the

[9]He Quan, Thinking of Countermeasures for the Development of the Hangzhou Future Sci-Tech City, *Northern Economy and Trade*, 2014(1).

lowest place, in order to create a good atmosphere of comparison, learning, catching up with and surpassing the competitors. The output value of new and hi-tech industries throughout the province increased from 0.57 trillion yuan in 2006 to 2.08 trillion yuan in 2013, up 2.65 times; the proportion of the added value of new and hi-tech industries in the industrial added value rose from 18.9% in 2006 to 32.26% in 2013, up 13.36 percentage points.[10]

4. The development of scientific and technological enterprise incubators was generously supported

In September, 2005, the People's Government of Zhejiang Province issued *Several Opinions on Accelerating the Construction and Development of Scientific and Technological Enterprise Incubators*, specifying the basic line of thought regarding speeding up the construction and development of scientific and technological enterprise incubators as follows: adopting the Deng Xiaoping Theory and the Important Thought of Three Represents as a guide, fully carrying out the Scientific Outlook on Development, taking the construction and development of scientific and technological enterprise incubators as the important means for pushing ahead with scientific and technological innovation, cultivating proprietary intellectual property rights and transforming the economic growth mode, fully arousing enterprises' enthusiasm for participating in construction; conducting system and mechanism innovation to intensify policy support, enabling scientific and technological enterprise incubators to achieve a new leap in the service field, service function and service quality. The goal of the construction and development of scientific and technological enterprise incubators is as follows: by 2010, in Zhejiang Province, more than 100 scientific and technological enterprise incubators will be officially put into operation; there will be more than 3000 incubated enterprises; the total building area of incubators will exceed 1.20 million m^2, thus gathering scientific and technological talents involved in innovation and entrepreneurship, quickening the transformation of new and hi-tech achievements and cultivating a number of hi-tech enterprises at an internationally advanced technical level for Zhejiang Province.

In order to support the development of scientific and technological enterprise incubators, the People's Government of Zhejiang Province vowed to increase support for public service conditions and infrastructure for scientific and technological enterprise incubators, enhance service function and service quality. A certain amount of funds should be allocated from provincial fiscal funds for science and technology each year to support the construction of public service platforms for national and provincial key scientific and technological enterprise incubators in coordination with the construction of public scientific and technological innovation platforms. The units and people making outstanding contributions to the construction and development of scientific and technological enterprise incubators should be commended and rewarded. Venture capital should be encouraged to make equity investments in the incubated enterprises. Actions should be taken to increase the financial support

[10]Data from the website of the Zhejiang Science and Technology Department, http://www.zjkjt.gov.cn.

for the enterprises incubated in scientific and technological enterprise incubators. Various kinds of financial institutions should improve credit service, increase credit varieties, rationally determine loan terms, and actively perform better credit services for the incubated enterprises. Various kinds of guarantee institutions and venture capital institutions should proactively provide credit guarantees for the incubated enterprises. Efforts should be made to strengthen intellectual property management and protection for scientific and technological enterprise incubators and the incubated enterprises. The intellectual property management departments at various levels should actively organize efforts to carry out publicity and training activities relating to intellectual property laws and regulations to guide incubators and the incubated enterprises to enhance the awareness about intellectual property protection; an intellectual property management system should be established and improved. The building of a talent force at scientific and technological enterprise incubators should be reinforced. The talents introduced by scientific and technological enterprise incubators can enjoy the preferential policies adopted by the governments at various levels for introducing talents. The personnel exchange centers at various levels should actively provide incubators and the incubated enterprises with the services concerning talent recruitment, recommendations and personnel agency, and encourage college graduates to work at incubators and the incubated enterprises. Actions should be taken to support scientific and technological enterprise incubators and the incubated enterprises to engage in domestic and foreign cooperation and exchange. The incubators should draw upon the successful domestic and foreign experience in incubator construction to provide the incubated enterprises with good services; the incubators should engage in exchange and cooperation with domestic and foreign enterprise incubation institutions to establish an incubator information network for resource sharing. Efforts should be made to improve the work on the recognition and determination of provincial-level scientific and technological enterprise incubators and key provincial-level scientific and technological enterprise incubators. Actions should be taken to make public and improve the conditions for the recognition and determination of provincial-level scientific and technological enterprise incubators and key provincial-level key scientific and technological enterprise incubators, the procedure for applying for recognition and determination as well as the conditions relating to the incubated enterprises and the "graduated" enterprises. A performance evaluation system for scientific and technological enterprise incubators should be established to carry out a dynamic kind of management.

3.3.2 Earnestly Pushing Forward the Construction of Innovative Enterprises

An innovative enterprise refers to the enterprise which enjoys core technologies with proprietary intellectual property rights, a well-known brand, excellent innovation management techniques and culture, the advanced position in the same industry in terms of the overall technical level, and one that has advantages and a capacity for sustainable development in market competition. In January, 2011, such departments as the Science and Technology Department of Zhejiang Province issued *Several Opinions on Further Strengthening the Construction of Innovative Enterprises*, specifying the guiding opinions on the construction of innovative enterprises.

1. Guiding thoughts

With the Scientific Outlook on Development as a guideline, emphasis should be placed on the province-wide economic transformation and upgrading and the enhancement of the enterprises' capability for independent innovation; work should focus on guiding innovation factors to enterprises; steps should be taken to conduct trials at a number of enterprises, produce a demonstration effect through a number of enterprises and drive the development of a number of enterprises to further gather innovation resources, activate innovation factors and transform innovation achievements, foster a good entrepreneurial and innovation environment, more quickly establish and improve an enterprise-dominated and market-oriented technical innovation system with close cooperation among industries, universities, research and application, give full scope to the leading role of innovative enterprises in independent innovation, transformation and upgrading, guide efforts to the enterprises' capability for independent innovation and core competitiveness.

2. Work goals

By 2015, more than 5000 innovative enterprises above the county level will have been built, including more than 500 provincial-level innovative enterprises and more than 50 national-level innovative enterprises; the innovative enterprises above the provincial level will cover the leading and backbone enterprises in industries throughout the province; the pilot innovative enterprises above the provincial level will cover the traditional pillar industries and strategic emerging industries; the innovative enterprises at the municipal and county levels will cover the demonstration zones for transforming and upgrading the massive economy toward modern industrial clusters; the innovative enterprises will be developed into the pacesetters for cultivating strategic emerging industries, the forerunners for transforming and upgrading the traditional pillar industries, the main force for integrating and utilizing industry-university-research-application resources for innovation, the leaders for leading industrial technical innovation and progress, so as to form the innovative enterprise groups with national-level innovative enterprises and pilot innovative enterprises as the flagships, with provincial-level pilot innovative and demonstration enterprises as the backbone and county-level innovative enterprises as the foundation.

3. Guiding principles

(1) Ensuring that enterprises play the dominant role with guidance provided by the government. Full play should be given to the basic role of the market mechanism in allocating scientific and technological resources; the dominant role of enterprises in technical innovation should be further strengthened; efforts should be made to stimulate enterprises to become the main body in R&D input, technical

innovation activities and transformation and application of innovation achievements, and improve the enterprises' capability for continuous innovation. Full scope should be given to the government's incentivizing function in public scientific and technological resources and foster an institutional environment for innovation and entrepreneurship.

(2) Combining points with areas, providing classified guidance. Different kinds of enterprises should be chosen to carry out pilot work, the targeted support measures and the corresponding evaluation measures should be explored in light of respective characteristics.

(3) Keeping coordination among higher and lower levels and pushing forward relevant work in a coordinated way. The work should be further intensified; the scale of pilot efforts should be expanded; the content of pilot efforts should be expanded; innovation should be made in the pilot mode; the construction of municipal and county-level innovative enterprises should be performed in an all-round way; upper to lower coordination, joint promotion, hierarchical cultivation and level-to-level upgrading should be carried out to build the innovative enterprise echelons at the national, provincial, municipal and county levels.

4. Main tasks

(1) Establishing the enterprise systems conducive to independent innovation. Actions should be taken to establish and improve the modern enterprise systems; the legal person governance structure should be improved; systems beneficial for technology and human resource investments need to be set up; an internal mechanism favorable for innovations in philosophy, product, process, organization, brand, management and business model should be established and improved.

(2) Establishing and improving the enterprise technical innovation system. Steps should be taken to set up and improve enterprise R&D centers, technical centers, design centers, creative centers and other R&D bodies; the enterprises which are industrial leaders and considered the backbone of industries should be relied upon to build enterprise research institutes, key laboratories, engineering laboratories, engineering technical (research) centers, pilot scale test bases, academician workstations; the scale of postdoctoral research workstation carriers should be increased; it is necessary to encourage and support the enterprises where conditions permit to set up R&D bodies in central cities, even in foreign countries, or master core technologies and proprietary intellectual property rights by various means, including merger ad acquisition; enterprises should be supported to establish long-term stable cooperative relationships or alliances among industries, universities and research with domestic and foreign institutions of higher learning and scientific research institutions to enhance the capability of enterprises for allocating innovation resources, researching and developing key generic technologies and their capability for introducing, assimilating and further innovating technologies.

(3) Building a mechanism for introducing, cultivating and motivating enterprise innovation talents. Actions should be taken to improve the incentive mechanism for enterprise innovation, actively explore equity and option incentives,

accumulative funds for scientific and technological talent contributions, a wage system for R&D personnel based on their capability and level and the mechanism for internal flexile movement of scientific and technological personnel; the leading innovative talents and R&D backbone should be introduced and cultivated to promote the building of key enterprise technical innovation teams, form the R&D and management teams suited to the independent innovation of enterprises; exploration should be made to establish such systems as chief technician and build a high-caliber and high-skilled employee force.

(4) Establishing a mechanism for the stable growth of independent innovation input. Steps should be taken to stimulate enterprises to become the main body in innovation decision-making, input, execution, benefit and risk-sharing. It is essential to establish and improve the enterprise financial system and statistical accounting system conducive to independent innovation. It is necessary to make good use of the policies for encouraging enterprises to increase their scientific and technological input and really increase R&D fund input. Measures should be taken to support enterprises to raise funds for innovation by various means, such as attracting venture capital, obtaining stock right pledge loans, issuing collective bonds and raising funds within domestic and foreign capital markets.

(5) Forging strategic alliances for industrial technical innovation. With a focus on the cultivation and development of the strategic emerging industries and the transformation and upgrading of key pillar industries in Zhejiang Province, actions should be taken to work with institutions of higher learning and scientific research institutions to establish strategic alliances for market-oriented industrial technical innovation in which the leading backbone enterprises in industries play the dominant role and interests and risks are shared, with a view to enable the connection and integration between the upstream and downstream of the innovation chain and the industrial chain.

(6) Establishing a mechanism for the transformation of major scientific and technological achievements. It is necessary to carry out projects for the transformation and popularization of major scientific and technological achievements involving energy saving technology, emission reduction technology, photovoltaic technology, IT applications in the manufacturing industry, new materials and major supporting technologies for projects; boost the transformation and popularization of scientific and technological achievements from institutions of higher learning and scientific research institutions.

(7) Building the intellectual property system for motivating and protecting innovations. The intellectual property strategy should be thoroughly carried out; activities for the creation of inventions should be encouraged and supported; actions should be taken to strengthen the construction of intellectual property management bodies and management systems, cultivate intellectual property management personnel, improve the capability for creating, applying, protecting and managing intellectual property; the standardization strategy should be carried out in a profound way; enterprises should be encouraged and supported to lead or participate in the making (revision) of international, national and industrial technical standards, and a technical standard system should be estab-

lished and improved; the brand strategy should be thoroughly implemented to strengthen the building of self-owned brands of enterprises and products, enhance the international competitiveness of enterprises and products; a system for the building of brands should be established and improved.

(8) Fostering an enterprise culture beneficial for independent innovation. It is should further carry forward the entrepreneurs' spirit for innovation of daring to be first, of taking risks and striving unceasingly and with a scientific spirit, advocate scientific methods, popularize scientific knowledge, enhance the awareness of enterprise employees regarding scientific quality and innovation, organize and guide employees to participate in the activities of building learning organizations and nurturing knowledge-based employees, carry out all-employee innovation, popularize and apply innovative methods; the spirit of seeking truth and being pragmatic should be advocated further, innovation should be encouraged, failure tolerated, the enthusiasm for independent innovation protected and the enterprise culture built that is conducive to independent innovation.

5. Safeguard measures

(1) Increasing fiscal fund support for innovative enterprises; steps should be taken to gradually increase fiscal funds relating to science and technology for national-level and provincial-level innovative enterprises, special funds need to be continually arranged for enhancing enterprises' capability for independent innovation. At the same time, the evaluation system and dynamic monitoring system for innovative enterprises should be established and improved. Intensified efforts should be made to make coordinated arrangements of provincial science and technology programs, industrial, science and technology and talent programs involving talent cultivation, energy conservation and emission reduction, brand cultivation and standard construction and special funds; relevant departments should provide vigorous support to innovative enterprises according to the directions of respective fund use and the corresponding management methods.

(2) Further supporting innovative enterprises to carry out independent innovation policy. Emphasis should be placed on supporting innovative enterprises in implementing preferential policies relating to value added tax transformation and reform, increased reduction of enterprise R&D expenses, collection of corporate income tax from new and hi-tech enterprises at a rate of 15%. The recognized and determined new software production enterprises enjoy the following preferential policy concerning corporate income tax: corporate income tax is exempted within two years as from the profit-making year and halved within three years as from the profit-making year. The integrated circuit design enterprises are considered software enterprises and thus enjoy the above corporate income tax policy. Measures are taken to support the recognized and determined technical service enterprises to enjoy relevant preferential tax policy according to the regulations. Regarding the expenditure of funds for employee education incurred by innovative enterprises, the portion not exceeding 2.5% of the total wages and salaries is permitted to be deducted, while the portion in

excess of 2.5% of the total wages and salaries is permitted to be carried over to and deducted in the subsequent tax years.

(3) Increasing government procurement support for innovative enterprises. More government procurement support should be provided for the enterprises involved in independent innovation and the products based on independent innovation. It is necessary to study and make specific implementation measures for the first purchase and ordering, in government procurement, of the products based on independent innovation, and carry out the system for the first purchase, ordering or compulsory purchase, in government procurement, of the products based on independent innovation.

(4) Providing more support to R&D bodies of innovative enterprises. Priority should be given to recommending the national-level and provincial-level innovative enterprises to independently or work with the institutions of higher learning and scientific research institutions to apply for establishing national enterprise engineering (technical) research centers, national engineering laboratories, national key laboratories and national enterprise technical centers. Actions should be taken to support the national-level and provincial-level innovative enterprises to work with domestic and foreign institutions of higher learning, scientific research institutions, large enterprises and conglomerates to build various kinds of innovation carriers. Steps should be taken to support the provincial-level innovative enterprises in working with the institutions of higher learning and scientific research institutions to establish provincial-level industrial innovation platforms. Innovative enterprises should be encouraged to set up provincial-level scientific and technological enterprise incubators. Innovative enterprises should be supported in expanding to both ends of the industrial chain, acquiring or controlling domestic and foreign R&D design, famous brands and marketing channels and other high-end links in the value chain to quickly master core technologies and proprietary intellectual property rights.

(5) Increasing support for the scientific and technological projects of innovative enterprises. Priority should be given to supporting the national-level and provincial-level innovative enterprises to, with these enterprises playing the dominant role, work with the institutions of higher learning and scientific research institutions to carry out major special scientific and technological projects and undertake major national special projects, science and technology support programs, 863 Program, 973 Program, national innovation funds and international scientific and technological cooperation programs. The national-level and provincial-level innovative enterprises should be supported to carry out major scientific and technological projects for the achievement of transformation and popularization involving energy-saving and emission-reduction technologies; a manner for cooperation among industries, universities and research institutions should be adopted to build a number of pilot scale transformation bases involving demonstration projects regarding major scientific and technological achievement transformation.

(6) Further supporting the building of talent forces at innovative enterprises. In coordination with the implementation of the national Recruitment Program of Global Experts and the Overseas High-level Talent Introduction Program of Zhejiang Province, priority should be given to introducing a crop of overseas high-level talents who directly engage with innovative enterprises and master core key technologies. Overseas high-level talent stations should be built at large institutions and well-known universities. In the Provincial Special-class Expert, 151 Talent Project and the Million and Ten-Million Scientific and Technological Innovation Talent Project, preferential policies should focus on innovative enterprises, and the proportion of innovative enterprise talents included should be increased. With a focus on innovative enterprises, efforts should be organized to carry out a program for the improvement of the quality of enterprise operation management personnel, 5111 Talent Cultivation Project for Fine Management of Enterprises, action plans for improving the innovative and entrepreneurial capability of entrepreneurial talents, and high-skilled talent training projects. Priority should be given to recommending innovative enterprises to participate in the decision-making consulting and evaluation of national and provincial scientific and technological projects. Measures should be adopted to support the high-level talents of public institutions who engage in technology research and development and achievement transformation to work at national-level and provincial-level innovative enterprises. Where the personnel of public institutions whose age is less than 5 years (inclusive) away from the statutory retirement age and who have worked for 20 years or 30 years voluntarily seek employment at innovative enterprises, their public institutions should be permitted to complete the retirement formalities in advance.
(7) Further supporting innovative enterprises to engage in cooperation among industries, universities and research institutions. Efforts should be made to support the national-level and provincial-level innovative enterprises to focus on the cultivation of the strategic emerging industries and the transformation and upgrading of key pillar industries. Strategic alliances for industrial technical innovation should be encouraged to participate in the pilot work on national strategic alliances for industrial technical innovation, support them in undertaking national science and technology programs and projects. The institutions of higher learning, scientific research institutions and testing bodies should be guided to open their large instruments and equipment, scientific data and scientific literature to innovative enterprises, provide them with services concerning testing and standards and other services. Enterprises should be supported in working with the institutions of higher learning and scientific research institutions to cultivate talents; enterprises' scientific and technical personnel should be supported in participating in scientific research at the institutions of higher learning and scientific research institutions in the capacity of visiting scholars. Measures should be taken to fully carry out the following tax policy: business tax is exempted for the income from technology transfer, technology development and the technical consulting and technical services relating to it. Innovative enterprises should be supported in participating in the 432

Project jointly carried out by Zhejiang Province and the Chinese Academy of Sciences, with efforts to enable high-end scientific and technological achievements to be transformed at innovative enterprises; high-level talents should be supported in taking temporary posts at innovative enterprises. Innovative enterprises should be supported in enhancing cooperation with various sectors, such as science and technology, for national defense; efforts should be made to promote the joint development of military-to-civilian and dual-use technologies, achievement transformation and industrialization, where conditions permit, priority should be given to providing support. With projects as means, innovative enterprises serve as the main body to vigorously introduce advanced technologies and high-end talents to build a number of international scientific and technological cooperation bases, joint research centers, where conditions permit, priority should be given to offering support. Actions should be taken to support innovative enterprises in cooperating with the institutions of higher learning and scientific research institutions to carry out the transformation and industrialization of major scientific and technological achievements. Venture capital enterprises are encouraged to make equity investments in the major scientific and technological achievement transformation and industrialization projects jointly carried out by provincial-level innovative enterprises and the institutions of higher learning, scientific research institutions, and transfer the equities generated by investments to the scientific and technological personnel, operation management teams and original shareholders of the invested enterprises.

(8) Further supporting innovative enterprises' work on intellectual property. It is necessary to guide and help innovative enterprises to improve their internal intellectual property system, better manage, protect and apply the intellectual properties of core technologies. It is important to strengthen intellectual property law enforcement, protect the intellectual properties of innovative enterprises according to laws, give full play to the self-disciplinary role of the industrial associations incorporating innovative enterprises in intellectual property protection, and constantly improve the intellectual property protection system of innovative enterprises.

(9) More energetically supporting innovative enterprises in innovating the standards. The national-level and provincial-level innovative enterprises should be encouraged to lead or participate in the making (revision) of international, national and industrial standards and given support in doing so, and substantively in adopting advanced international and national standards. Innovative enterprises should be encouraged to transform independent innovation achievements into standards of regional alliance. The national-level and provincial-level innovative enterprises should be encouraged to strengthen the development of the standards for the productive service industry; the standards development projects where conditions permit should be included in the local standards development plan and should be first recommended in making international or national standards. The national-level and provincial-level innovative enterprises should be encouraged to become secretariat units at national

and provincial specialized standardization committees, and then supported in doing so; the building of an enterprise technical standard innovation system should be continuously improved.

(10) Increasing financial support for independent innovation at innovative enterprises. Financial institutions should be encouraged to increase credit support for innovative enterprises, further expand the financing based on the pledge of equity, patent rights and trademark rights, and be supported then in their efforts. Insurance institutions should be encouraged to develop product liability insurance, product quality insurance, environmental pollution liability insurance, export credit insurance, executive and key R&D personnel team health insurance and accident insurance for innovative enterprises. Priority should be given to including the innovative enterprises, whose shareholding reform has been completed, in the rank of Zhejiang Province's potentially listed enterprises for cultivation and recommending them to the unlisted company share transfer platform of Zhejiang Province to go public for raising funds on domestic and foreign capital markets. Priority should be given to supporting innovative enterprises in issuing enterprise bonds. The innovative enterprises where conditions permit should first be supported in issuing short-term financing bonds and medium-term notes; active experimentations should be made to permit small and medium-sized innovative enterprises to issue SMEs' collective notes.

3.3.3 Boosting the Transformation of Scientific and Technological Achievements

1. The big market of science and technology was built more rapidly

In 2002, Zhejiang Province became the first in China to establish China's Zhejiang Online Technology Market. At present, there is a service system consisting of 1 provincial management center, 11 municipal markets, 94 county (municipal, district) submarkets and 29 specialized markets, with 94,000 online members. As of late 2013, it released 64,000 enterprise technical difficulties, 154,000 scientific and technological achievements, with a total amount of transactions at 27.1 billion yuan. In 2012, *Several Opinions on Further Cultivating and Regulating the Zhejiang Online Technology Market* was developed and released; preparations were made to build Zhejiang Online Technology Market Co., Ltd. and a provincial technology exchange, a great impetus was given to building the five-in-one big market of science and technology, covering display, trading, sharing, service and exchange; Wuyi Technology Market Co., Ltd. was established to push forward market-oriented operations and well-regulated management. Explorations were made to improve the system for competitive auctions of scientific and technological achievements; the contract transaction amount in technology markets in Zhejiang Province reached 8131 million yuan in 2012, up 53.3% over 2003.[11]

2. Intensified efforts were made to cultivate science and technology intermediary bodies

A number of policy measures including the *Five-Year Special Action Plan for Nurturing Technology Markets and Promoting Technical Achievement Transactions (2013–2017)* and the *Interim Measures of Zhejiang Province for Evaluation of Technical Intermediary Service Institutions and Technology Brokers* were introduced, thus a number of scientific and technological service sectors, intermediary bodies and technology brokers were earnestly cultivated and developed. The added value of the scientific and technological service sectors in Zhejiang Province was 34.5 billion yuan in 2012, up 88.52% over 2008.

3. The combination between science, technology and finance was constantly extended

According to the requirement of separately focusing on banking credit, venture capital investments, intellectual property pledges, science and technology guarantees, science and technology insurance and fiscal support, actions were taken to improve the scientific and technological investment and financing system for the transformation of scientific and technological achievements, and press ahead with national pilot work on scientific and technological finance in Hangzhou, Wenzhou, Huzhou and Ningbo. As of late 2012, Zhejiang Province was home to 213 venture capital enterprises, with total venture capital amounting to more than 40.8 billion yuan, Zhejiang Province ranked No. 3 among provinces, autonomous regions and municipalities nationwide in the number of venture capital institutions and the total amount of capital under management. The *Circular Concerning Pilot Work on Financing Based on Patent Right Pledges* was issued; the balance of credit involving financing based on patent right pledges was about 900 million yuan. In Zhejiang Uni-Power Financial Services of Sci-Tech Co., Ltd. with a registered capital of 300 million yuan jointly established at the provincial, municipal and county levels, there is a fiscal input of 120 million yuan from various levels.

4. The projects for the transformation of scientific and technological achievements were carried out more quickly

During the period of the 12th Five-Year Plan, with a focus on key fields, including treating sewage, controlling floods, discharging the accumulated water, guaranteeing a water supply and saving water, preventing and controlling haze, addressing food and drug safety, public security, energy conservation and emission reduction, and improving the quality and performance of agricultural products, great efforts were made to carry out 10 major scientific and technological achievement transformation projects, more rapidly replace the people with machines, expand the market through e-commerce and "vacate the cage to change birds", enable science and technology

[11]Data come from the *Zhejiang Statistical Yearbook 2013.*

to better benefit the people. Efforts were made to vigorously push forward agricultural and rural scientific and technological innovation, and carry out major special scientific and technological projects for selecting and cultivating 12 new agricultural varieties, including paddy rice, dry crops, vegetables, fruits and aquatic products. The level of science and technology having a bearing on the people's livelihood was increased in an expedited way; relevant departments are being organized to carry out two environmental protection achievement transformation projects including ten-million-ton industrial wastewater and pollutant emission reduction technology and one–million-ton sewage sludge treatment technology, and eight major projects for transforming the achievements of appropriate technologies for grass-roots health, including the Double-10 and the Double-100 minimally invasive technology and national innovative medical equipment products and technologies. With the implementation of scientific and technological achievement transformation projects, a number of scientific and technological achievements were transformed and significant economic and social benefits were delivered. For example, the yield of indica/japonica hybrid rice "Yong You 12" per mu (one mu = 0.0667 ha) in small areas reached 936.9 kg, the highest level across the country.

3.3.4 *Carrying Out Major Special Scientific and Technological Projects*

Based on the national plan for major special projects, according to the *National Medium and Long-term Plan for Scientific and Technological Development (2006–2020)*, Zhejiang Province proceeded from national objectives and addressed strategic key technologies and major projects by integrating various resources to identify a number of major strategic products, key generic technologies or major projects as major special scientific and technological projects of Zhejiang Province, gave full scope to the advantages of the socialist system in concentrating forces on doing great work and the role of the market mechanism to promote the transformation of scientific and technological achievements.

1. Implementation goals

The major special scientific and technological projects of Zhejiang Province are the priorities in the provincial scientific and technological plan; they involve key fields of Zhejiang Province's economic and social development; they represent the major measures for implementing the strategy of making the people rich by starting a business and of building a strong province through innovation.

(1) Great innovation achievements will be made in the industrial fields. A number of highly influential innovation achievements will be made in the pillar industries of Zhejiang Province including the textile, medical chemistry, electromechanical, material and communications industries, bringing Zhejiang Province to the forefront nationwide in the overall technical level of the manufacturing industry

and the information industry, and providing an important support for yielding the following results: by 2010, the output value of new and hi-tech industries in Zhejiang Province will be redoubled and reach 1000 billion yuan, the added value of new and hi-tech industries will account for about 25% of the industrial added value.

(2) The agricultural scientific and technological strength will be higher than that of the rest of the country. Regarding the coverage rates of the main improved animal and plant varieties, planting and breeding technologies will be higher than 95%; the rate of loss caused by crop diseases and pests and livestock mortality will decrease to lower than 15%; the rate of processing of agricultural products will exceed 40%; more than 60% of agricultural scientific and technological achievements will be transformed; scientific and technological progress will contribute more than 60%.

(3) Great progress will be made in science and technology underpinning the harmonious development of the society. Breakthroughs will be made in energy conservation, clean energy and environmental protection technologies; remarkable achievements will be made in the demonstration and popularization of the circular economy. National requirements will be satisfied in terms of key indicators including the overall energy consumption per 10,000 yuan GDP, the overall utilization rate of industrial solid wastes and total emissions of the main pollutants. The morbidity and mortality of infectious diseases and serious diseases will markedly decrease; the technical support system for disaster prevention and reduction will be basically completed; the level of marine science and technology will lead the country.

(4) A number of leading high-level figures in scientific and technological innovation and innovation teams with rational structure and high quality will emerge. The number of applications for patents of inventions and the number of the patents of inventions granted will lead the country.

2. Characteristics of special plans

(1) Being representative and advanced. Twenty-six major special scientific and technological plans include 14 in the industrial field, 5 in the agricultural field and 7 in the social development field; they cover the key fields of Zhejiang Province's economic and social development. These special plans focus on domestic and foreign scientific and technological development frontiers and aim at making significant achievements in breakthroughs in key generic technologies, the development of major products and the implementation of major projects, making Zhejiang Province reach the advanced domestic level in the capability for R&D in relevant industries.

(2) Giving prominence to active design, strengthening the integration of technology and concentrating advantageous scientific and technological resources on making breakthroughs in a number of major technological fields. Under the principle of achieving limited goals and making breakthroughs in key fields, in light of the technical developmental trend of relevant industries and the existing

basic conditions of Zhejiang Province's enterprises and scientific research institutions, active design is conducted, accurate positioning, a clear direction and feasible goals are guaranteed in project selection and goal setting, with great efforts to make breakthroughs in major key technologies restricting Zhejiang Province's economic and social development.

(3) Reflecting guidance and operability. Being different from general project guides, special implementation plans cover the main technical directions for making breakthroughs, the desired technical and economic goals, and they show a relatively high level of guidance; meanwhile, they are highly operable and specify clear requirements for scientific and technological resource integration, project arrangement and work progress; moreover, they divide tasks and goals according to major and key projects.

(4) Attaching importance to original innovations, giving prominence to integrated innovation, introduction, assimilation and further innovation, strengthening the transformation and industrialization of achievements. Where resources and conditions permit, great efforts are made to boost original innovations, and master core technologies for industrial development. The advantages in technology integration and industrial connections are utilized to strengthen integrated innovation and develop a combination of individual technologies into new integrated technology so as to seize developmental opportunities. Advanced and proven domestic and foreign technologies are actively introduced and fully utilized, with efforts made to reinforce introduction, assimilation and further innovation.

(5) Enabling the cooperation industries, universities and research with enterprises playing the dominant role to make breakthroughs through collaboration across various institutions and multi-disciplinary efforts. The activities for the development of technology of the leading industrial enterprises are incorporated into major special scientific and technological plans; enterprises are encouraged to actively participate in carrying out major special scientific and technological plans and play the leading role in cooperation among industries, universities and research. The institutions of higher learning and scientific research institutions actively participate in enterprises' R&D and mainly undertake public welfare projects and the projects at the R&D stage.

(6) Making rolling arrangements and dynamic adjustments. Special implementation plans will be adjusted and improved amidst the implementation in light of situation development and the progress made in the implementation of the projects under the principle of making rolling arrangements and dynamic adjustments. Where there are major technologies or industrial development during the period of the 11th Five-Year Plan, the corresponding plans can be greatly adjusted or new special major plans for relevant fields are added.

3. Main achievements

With the implementation of major special plans, Zhejiang Province made breakthroughs in a number of core key technologies and scored many innovation achievements at advanced domestic and foreign levels in such fields as rice breeding, minimally invasive medicine, liver transplant, the development of new medicines and wind power generation, vigorously supporting economic transformation and upgrading. According to statistical data on 2031 major and key projects, project investments totaled 19.06 billion yuan. As of late 2012, the total output value, sales revenue, total profits, total tax payments and saved and earned foreign exchange reached 165,168 million yuan, 231,424 million yuan, 24,777 million yuan, 8448 million yuan and 6.59 billion yuan, respectively. The scientific and technological input from every 100 million yuan realized 870 million yuan output value and 174 million yuan total profits and taxes. Applications were filed for 6658 patents, including 3449 patents for inventions; 4234 patents were granted, including 1258 granted patents for inventions; there were 587 software copyrights; 171 new animal and plant varieties were examined and approved; there were 13 new medicine certificates; Zhejiang Province led or participated in the making of 197 national standards and 203 industrial standards; 37 national awards for science and technology and 251 provincial awards were won.

3.3.5 Accelerating the Development of New and Hi-Tech Industries and Strategic Emerging Industries

1. Boosting the development of new and hi-tech industries

The new and hi-tech industries are the strategic forerunner industries in the national economy and the decisive factors for measuring the core competiveness and developmental potential of a region. Based on making tremendous achievements during the periods of the 10th and 11th Five-Year Plans, the Zhejiang Provincial Party Committee and the Provincial Government put forward the 12th five-year plan for the development of the new and hi-tech industries.

The overall requirement is as follows: Taking the Deng Xiaoping Theory and the Important Thought of Three Represents as guidelines, thoroughly carrying out the Scientific Outlook on Development, comprehensively implementing the "Eight-Eight Strategies" and the overall strategy of making the people rich by starting a business and of building a strong province through innovation, stressing transformation and development led by the new technology industries, focusing on eight major industrial fields, taking the action plan for improving the capability for independent innovation and national pilot technical innovation project as carriers to speed up the industrialization of independent innovation achievements, more rapidly push forward spatial development agglomerations, constantly enhance the capability for independent innovation, the capability for the achievement of transformations, the leading driving capability and the international competiveness of the new technology industries, make the new technology industries become the important forces for helping transform the economic developmental mode and building a moderately prosperous society in all respects for everyone in Zhejiang Province.

The basic principles are as follows: (1) Keeping the dominant role of enterprises with the driving effect produced by the government. We should maintain the leading role of enterprises in technology research and development and industrialization, and the guiding and supporting roles of the government in building up the capacity for innovation, industrialization and base construction, to shape a pattern of benign development of the high technology industries. (2) Combining research and development innovation with industrialization. We should strengthen the original innovation of high technologies, integrated innovation, assimilation and further innovation of the introduced technologies to master a number of core technologies in several important fields and own a number of proprietary intellectual property rights. At the same time, we should further enhance the cooperation among industries, universities and research institutions and the capability for the industrialization of scientific and technological achievements, to achieve a close combination of technology research and development with market development and accelerate the industrialization of independent research and development achievements. (3) Combining making breakthroughs in key fields with achieving overall improvement. We should give play to the core role of bases and the leading enterprises, concentrate forces on making breakthroughs in the key fields with a great influence on industrial upgrading, capability for high technical radiation and high capability for driving sustained development, and extend from points to areas to push forward the overall improvement of the high technology industries in multiple fields and at various levels and enhance the leading driving capability and the international competitiveness of the high technology industries. (4) Combining agglomeration development with characteristic economy. We should give full scope to the advantages of Zhejiang's regional specialty industries to boost penetration of the high technology industries into the traditional specialty industries, effectively increase the rate of resource utilization, extend the industrial chain to gradually develop a number of highly competitive hi-tech industrial groups with high capability for innovation which are combined with the specialty economy. (5) Combining high technologies with the traditional industries. Along with efforts to cultivate and develop the key fields in eight major high technology industries, more attention should be paid to adopting high technologies to transform and upgrade the traditional industries, fully utilizing IT applications, new materials and high technology service industries to promote the transformation and upgrading of the manufacturing industry in Zhejiang Province and finally achieve the adjustment of the industrial structure.

The development goals are as follows: (1) Increasing the industrial scale to a new level. During the period of the 12th Five-Year Plan, the total output value of the high technology industries will reach 900 billion yuan, the added value of the high technology industries will exceed 180 billion yuan, 320 billion yuan of exported hi-tech products will be delivered, the capability for transforming the traditional industries will be further improved, they will become the important forces in Zhejiang Province's industrial transformation and upgrading. (2) Making great breakthroughs in the capability for independent innovation. By 2015, Zhejiang Province's total R&D funds will account for more than 2.5% of the GDP, the full-time equivalent of all R&D personnel will reach 400,000 man-years—that of the enterprises' R&D personnel will reach 320,000 man-years, the number of the patents granted for inventions will hit 10,000, continuing to stay ahead nationwide. (3) The agglomeration of hi-tech industrial bases will become more prominent. By 2015, there will be 7 national-level hi-tech industrial bases and 10 provincial-level hi-tech industrial bases; the proportion of the output value of the hi-tech industrial bases in that of the high technology industries throughout the province will be effectively increased; the hi-tech enterprises will feature large-scale, group-oriented and transnational development. (4) The leading position of the new and hi-tech enterprises will become more prominent. By 2015, there will be more than 5000 new and hi-tech enterprises, more than 2000 new and hi-tech enterprises with the main operating revenue above 100 million yuan, including more than 200 with the main operating revenue above 1 billion yuan, in Zhejiang Province.

2. Speeding up the cultivation of the strategic emerging industries

The strategic emerging industries are the knowledge and technology-intensive industries which are based on major technical breakthroughs and great developmental needs, and which can play a big leading driving role in the overall and long-term economic and social development and are characterized by less material and energy consumption, great growth potential and a good comprehensive performance. In 2008, the People's Government of Zhejiang Province released the *Action Plan for Improving the Capability for Independent Innovation*. In 2010, after China identified seven major strategic emerging industries, Zhejiang Province proceeded from reality to put forward nine major strategic emerging industries including biology, the Internet of Things, new energy, new materials, high-end equipment manufacturing, energy conservation and environmental protection, the emerging marine industry, new energy automobile and nuclear power-related industry. In 2011, Zhejiang Province issued the *Implementation Opinions on Accelerating the Cultivation and Development of the Strategic Emerging Industries*, specifying five major basic principles, including: the government promotes relevant work, enterprises play the dominant role, development is driven by innovation, talent support is sought; rational layout takes shape, agglomeration development is achieved, open cooperation is fostered, joint creation is pursued through collaboration, breakthroughs are made in key areas and a demonstration effect is produced to drive development.

The developmental goals for the strategic emerging industries are as follows: the added value of the strategic emerging industries will grow annually by an average of more than 15% during the period of the 12th Five-Year Plan, with its growth rate higher than the level during the period of the 11th Five-Year Plan, that of the same year's GDP and the nation's average growth rate. By 2015, it will reach about 500 billion yuan, its proportion in the GDP will reach about 12%; there will be a number of large enterprises with core competitiveness and a number of small and medium-sized enterprises with great innovative vitality; several industries will lead the country in scale and innovation capability; a number of domestic first-class strategic emerging industry bases with distinctive features will preliminarily take shape, they will become the new growth poles for Zhejiang Province's economy, and their role in stimulating economic transformation and upgrading will be significantly enhanced.

According to the planning layout of the strategic emerging industries, first, actions should be taken to carefully carry out the developmental plan for the strategic emerging industries, and intensify the cultivation and support to boost industrial development according to the developmental plans for nine emerging industries including biology, new energy, the Internet of Things, high-end equipment manufacturing, energy conservation and environmental protection, new materials, new energy automobiles, the emerging marine industry and the nuclear power-related industry. Second, efforts should be made to more rapidly build the strategic emerging industry bases, plan and build the provincial-level industrial agglomeration zones and the new and hi-tech industrial development zones (parks) above the provincial level by taking them as the main areas for cultivating and developing the strategic emerging industries. Finally, the priorities in the development of the strategic emerging industries in various areas are specified, and the requirements for industrial development in key fields are put forward for 11 cities: Hangzhou City focuses on cultivating such industries as biology, the Internet of Things, energy conservation and environmental protection, and high-end equipment manufacturing; Ningbo City focuses on cultivating and developing such industries as new energy and new emerging industries; Wenzhou City focuses on cultivating and developing such industries as new energy, new material and high-end equipment manufacturing; Huzhou City focuses on cultivating and developing such industries as high-end equipment manufacturing; new energy and biological medicine; Jiaxing City focuses on cultivating and developing such industries as the Internet of Things, new energy and nuclear power-related industry; Shaoxing City focuses on cultivating and developing such industries as high-end equipment manufacturing; new material and biological medicine; Jinhua City focuses on cultivating and developing such industries as new energy automobile, new energy and biology; Quzhou City focuses on cultivating and developing such industries as new energy, new materials and high-end equipment manufacturing; Zhoushan City focuses on cultivating and developing such industries as new energy, high-end equipment manufacturing and the emerging marine industry; Taizhou City focuses on cultivating and developing such industries as biology, high-end equipment manufacturing and the emerging marine industry; Lishui City focuses on cultivating and developing such industries as high-end equipment manufacturing, biological medicine and new materials.

3.4 Summary and Outlook

Since the 21st century, Zhejiang Province has moved faster to build an innovative province; the environment for the policy of innovation has significantly improved; large institutions and well-known universities have gathered more rapidly; the scientific and technological talent forces have constantly expanded; innovation service platforms have mushroomed; enterprises' capability for technical innovation has steadily improved; the information economy has risen rapidly; high technology industries and the strategic emerging industries have grown rapidly, their status in Zhejiang's economy has improved constantly; innovation has become the main driving force for boosting Zhejiang's economic transformation and upgrading and sound development. The effort to build Zhejiang into an innovative province has also offered beneficial reference for China in carrying out the strategy of making the country strong through innovation.

The main successful experience of Zhejiang Province in innovative development is as follows: First, the systems and mechanisms suitable for innovation were established. Zhejiang Province has better combined the "invisible hand" with the "visible hand" in carrying out the strategy of innovation-driven development; in the field of scientific and technological innovation, Zhejiang Province first explored the formation of a pattern in which the decisive role of the market in resource allocation and the government's role mutually complement, coordinate, promote and form a unity. Second, emphasis has been placed on enhancing the public capability for scientific and technological service by building innovation service platforms; with a focus on building Qingshan Lake Sci-Tech City and Future Sci-Tech City, actions have been taken to push forward the construction of major scientific and technological innovation centers in an orderly fashion. Efforts have been made to propel the transformation and upgrading of new and hi-tech parks, earnestly support the development of scientific and technological enterprise incubators and promote the construction of innovative enterprises. Third, importance has been attached to the market-oriented transformation of scientific and technological achievements. The transformation of scientific and technological achievements has been driven forward by building a big market of science and technology, further cultivating science and technology intermediary bodies, intensifying the integration among science, technology and finance and carrying out projects in the transformation of scientific and technological achievements. Finally, scientific and technological innovative development has been promoted by carrying out major special scientific and technological projects.

The key to addressing future challenges lies in more rapidly fostering a general environment conducive to innovation and creation. It is necessary to further carry forward the innovation culture with the characteristics of the times and Zhejiang's characteristics, launch more publicity relating to major scientific and technological achievements, typical innovative figures and enterprises, more earnestly commend and reward innovators and creators; it is essential to foster a strong atmosphere in which creation is respected, people are bold in making innovations and failure is tolerated. Intellectual property protection is a basic system for respecting creative labor and stimulating innovation. It is essential to uphold the policy of stimulating creation, ensuring effective application, law-based protection and scientific management, move faster to establish and improve the intellectual property protection mechanism, improve the honesty and credibility system, purify the market environment to turn Zhejiang Province into a strong province of intellectual property. It is imperative to closely combine science and technology with finance; encourage the development of angel investment, venture capital investment and venture investment; guide venture capital investment and social capital to further support small and medium-sized technology enterprises, speed up the formation of a diversified, multi-level and multi-channel system for scientific and technological innovation and financing; the government should focus on improving the innovation environment and carrying out its innovation strategy better, further study and improve the way in which government funds support innovation, accelerate efforts to build an open, active and efficient regional innovation system and foster a looser environment for enterprises' innovative development.

Chapter 4
Scientifically Using "Two Hands" and Intensifying the Reform of the Economic System

Guo Ying

During the period of the 10th Five-Year Plan, Comrade Xi Jinping, then Secretary of the Zhejiang Provincial Party Committee, quoted the theory of "two hands" from the *Wealth of Nations* written by Adam Smith in the process of intensifying reform to further enrich innovation and put forward the new philosophy of "two hands": the visible hand—the government—and the invisible hand—the market—should mutually coordinate, perform and play different functions and roles in light of different stages and requirements of economic development. The government should be keenly aware of the orientation of its function in the development of the market economy, and promptly transform government functions according to the requirements of the market economy: where the market can work, the government should not intervene; where the market has functional defects, the government should endeavor to make up for those defects. Only in this way can sound, efficient and sustainable development be better promoted.

G. Ying (✉)
Zhejiang Academy of Social Sciences, Hangzhou, China

C. Pei and J. Xu (eds.), *Chinese Dream and Practice in Zhejiang – Economy*, Research Series on the Chinese Dream and China's Development Path, https://doi.org/10.1007/978-981-13-7484-5_4

4.1 The Development and Expansion of the Philosophy of "Two Hands"

4.1.1 The Background of Intensifying the Reform of the Economic System

1. Great changes have taken place in the macro environment

The great changes in the macro environment are mainly as follows: (1) The developmental stage has changed. Based on finishing the first two steps in the strategic goal of modernization, China has entered the new stage of building a moderately prosperous society in all respects and speeding up efforts to push forward socialist modernization. (2) The relation of market supply and demand has changed. The productive forces have reached a new level, the people have generally become well-off, and there are higher requirements in consumption needs. (3) The road to development has changed. Industrialization remains the historic task for pushing ahead with modernization; in order to achieve the integration between IT application and industrialization, it is imperative to take the new road to industrialization. (4) The institutional environment for development has changed. The pattern in which the public ownership remains the mainstay and the economy with different types of ownership develops side by side has basically taken shape; the socialist market economic system has been preliminarily established. (5) The foreign economic relations have changed. China's accession to the WTO marks the entry of China's opening up into a new stage, and economic development has more rapidly integrated into the process of globalization.

2. The new situation presents new requirements for intensifying the reform of the economic system

The overall situation is the one based on the preliminary establishment of the market economic system, it is necessary to make local breakthroughs in removing the traditional institutional barriers and holistically make progress in establishing a well-enhanced socialist market economic system. To be specific: (1) With the basic completion of the reform of the enterprise system, it is essential to move from the micro level to macro fields including the government administration system and the social security system. (2) With the intensification of the reform of the economic system, it is necessary to advance from the economic field to social and political fields including science and technology, culture and health. (3) With increasing opening up, it is necessary to March from the internal autonomous reform to the establishment of a management system complying with the WTO rules and international practices. (4) With tremendous achievements made in industrialization and urbanization, it is essential to holistically move from city-centered development to coordinated urban and rural economic and social development.

3. New thinking regarding the reform of the economic system

Given the new situation and new requirements, it is essential to address that new situation and the new challenges, seize new opportunities to make new breakthroughs in the reform of the economic system, and to develop an understanding and a line of thought on the following aspects.

(1) Actively coping with new challenges amidst economic globalization and China's accession to the WTO, combining the intensified reform with opening up, promoting reform and development through opening up. China's accession to the WTO means that we will engage in international economic and technical cooperation and competition in a wider scope in more areas and at higher levels; this brings opportunities for us to more rapidly develop an open economy; at the same time, this also presents new challenges to the reform of the system. In order to take advantage of the new opportunities from increasing opening up and respond to the new challenges from economic globalization, it is essential to combine the intensification of the reform with the opening up, turn pressure into impetus, convert challenges into opportunities, and promote development through opening up.
(2) Combining reform with well-regulated development according to the new requirements for further improving the socialist market economic system, so as to further create new institutional advantages. Zhejiang's first-mover institutional advantages mainly come from first-ever breakthroughs in the traditional planning system. With continuous improvement in the nation's socialist market economic system, in order to ensure that Zhejiang Province continues to maintain and develop the first-mover institutional advantages, Zhejiang Province must change from a first-ever breakthrough to first-ever well-regulated development—becoming the first to pursue well-regulated development according to the contract system governing the socialist market economy and the economic management system complying with WTO rules. After reform develops to the new stage of further moving toward a well-enhanced market economic system and keeping in line with WTO rules and international practice, it is necessary to continue to carry forward the innovative spirit of daring to make breakthroughs, take risks and blaze new trails, resolutely reform all practices and rules which hinder development, firmly remove the institutional defects which affect development. At the same time, it is essential to correctly deal with the relations between reform and well-regulated development, avoid the passive situation in which well-regulated development is valued only after reform, and rectification is not made until development is achieved. Various means, including laws and regulations, should be adopted to opportunely, regulate the successful prac-

tices and experience well, further create new institutional advantages amidst well-regulated development.

(3) Focusing on the new task of more rapidly building a moderately prosperous society in all respects and basically achieving modernization in advance, carrying out reform to make breakthroughs and maintain social stability at the same time, correctly deal with the relations among reform, development and stability. According to the guiding principles adopted in the 16th CPC National Congress, the Second Plenary Session of the 11th Party Committee of Zhejiang Province set the goal of more rapidly building a moderately prosperous society in all respects and basically achieving modernization in advance; in order to achieve this goal, it is essential to further emancipate and develop the productive forces, improve the basic economic system in which the public ownership remains the mainstay and the economy with different types of ownership develops side by side; further reform the urban-rural dual structure, promote urban and rural coordinated social development and urbanization; further intensify the reform of the administrative management system, really transform government functions. Given new goals and tasks, the task of intensifying reform becomes more arduous, it involves more areas and higher levels, and reform has entered a new crucial stage. It is essential to closely follow the hotspots and difficult issues in the society to passionately overcome the difficulties affecting the immediate interests of the people, making every effort to improve employment and reemployment, constantly improve the social security system so that the people feel the care from the Party and the government and enjoy the tangible benefits of reform, thus creating a stale social environment for development.

4.1.2 The Birth and Practice of the Philosophy of "Two Hands" in the Reform of the Economic System

1. The birth of the philosophy of "two hands"

After the Third Plenary Session of the 16th CPC Central Committee decided to improve the socialist market economic system, the relations between government and the market entered a new developmental stage. As a national big uniform market basically took shape, and after China joined the WTO, the competition among countries and among the areas in China became increasingly fiercer, Zhejiang's relative advantages in leading the market-oriented and privatization reforms faded away, Zhejiang's institutional advantages over other provinces, autonomous regions and municipalities also gradually disappeared. Against such a background, Zhejiang Province intensified government reform and took a number of effective measures in transformation of government functions, agency reform, reform of the examination and approval system, efficiency building and reform of the government performance evaluation system; the government shifted its focus to fostering a good environment for market operations and increasing the supply of public goods and services.

During the rapid development of Zhejiang Province's market economy, local governments of Zhejiang Province have promptly assumed the responsibility of supervising the market economy. The market mechanism has a dual nature: competition reduces costs and improves efficiency, but excessive pursuit of interests by market players results in disorderly competition. As Zhejiang Province has led the country in a market economy, Zhejiang Province has early enjoyed high efficiency, and it has also early encountered problems from market competition. Given the conflicts caused by the poor quality of products and environmental pollution, the government's oversight over the market economy has become more urgent.

When delivering the special report on studying and implementing the guiding principles adopted in the Fifth Plenary Session of the 16th CPC Central Committee during the Zhejiang Forum held in October, 2005, Xi Jinping, then Secretary of the Zhejiang Provincial Party Committee, pointed out, "Zhejiang's economy" is an economy of the people, the people have a burning desire to start businesses and a strong awareness about a commodity economy. An economy of the people does not mean that the Party Committee and the government have nothing to do; as the Party Committee and the government respect the pioneering spirit of the people and steadily push forward the market-oriented reform, Zhejiang Province has led the country in the degree of marketization. Under the planned economic system, only the government as one hand worked, so at the early stage of reform, emphasis should be placed on the other hand—the market, with play given to the fundamental role of the market in resource allocation. With the intensification of the reform, it is necessary to transform the functions of the government as one hand, shift government functions to economic regulation, market regulation, social management and public services, build a service-oriented, limited government under the rule of law, better leverage, regulate and coordinate the relations between the "two hands". When reform is gradually promoted to a certain degree, the "two hands" should have the following relations: with respect to economic and social regulation, the market as one hand regulates the economy more, while the government as the other hand strengthens the functions of exercising social management and performing public services; with regard to economic operations, the market as one hand regulates the economic activities in micro fields, while the government as the other hand makes game rules and exercises macro control; in terms of equity and efficiency, the market as one hand activates efficiency, while the government as the other hand pays more attention to equity; for urban and rural development, urban development relies more on the market as one hand, while rural development is promoted with more functions undertaken by the government as the other hand. This entails a certain process, but we must continuously expand reform in this direction.[1] The government should dedicate more energy to improve services, better carry out the work which should be done by the government and hand over the work which should not be done by the government to the market.

2. Major practical measures in the reform of the economic system

[1] *Zhejiang Daily*, March 17, 2006.

The major measures in the reform of the economic system guided by the philosophy of "two hands" include the following.

(1) Major decisions in reform and opening up. During the period of the 11th Five-Year Plan, the Zhejiang Provincial Party Committee and the Provincial Government opportunely made a number of major reform decisions. In 2008, the Zhejiang Provincial Party Committee and the Provincial Government held a conference on commemorating the 30th anniversary of reform and opening up, fully summarizing the tremendous achievements made in Zhejiang's first-ever endeavor to promote market-oriented reform, and stressing that it was essential to steadfastly push forward reform and opening up at a new historical starting point. In 2009, the Fifth Plenary Session of the 12th Party Committee of Zhejiang Province made the *Decision on Intensifying Reform and Opening up and Promoting Scientific Development*, arranging 31 reform tasks in 8 areas. In late 2009, a decision was made with respect to the pilot work on comprehensive reform in the transformation of the developmental mode, pilot reform in 11 areas was carried out in the cities divided into districts and Yiwu City. These major reform decisions further built a reform consensus and helped develop firm confidence, creating a new pattern in which the whole society pays attention to and values reform.
(2) Major adjustments in the focus of reform. During the period of the 11th Five-Year Plan, subject to the impact from the global financial crisis, cyclical and structural contradictions in economic operations, reform shifted from more emphasis on promoting rapid development to a clearer focus on sound development, from economic fields to social fields with more emphasis on guaranteeing and improving the people's livelihood. Within the theme of scientific development, with a focus on institutional reform in promoting the transformation of the economic developmental mode and economic structural adjustment, the institutional reform in guaranteeing and improving the people's livelihood and promoting all-round development of the people was taken as the fundamental solution, accelerated efforts were made to establish the systems and mechanisms conducive to scientific development, thus providing a strong impetus and an institutional guarantee for boosting integrated, coordinated and sustainable economic and social development.
(3) Great breakthroughs in pilot reforms. A number of reforms were designated as national pilot reforms, with first-ever trials and first-ever breakthroughs conducted in key fields and key links. The Yiwu Pilot Comprehensive International Trade Reform was approved by the State Council; it is a pilot comprehensive reform approved by the State Council after 9 comprehensive reform pilot areas were established by the Central Government; it is the first national-level pilot comprehensive reform in Zhejiang Province; it is also the first pilot comprehensive reform at the level of county-level city approved by the State Council nationwide. Solid progress was made in a number of national pilot areas including pilot province for the development of the marine economy, pilot province for the circular economy, pilot province for national technical innovation projects,

pilot province for transportation logistics, pilot province for the reform of the cultural system; the comprehensive reform pilot area for transforming the economic developmental mode was elevated to be the contact point of development for the National Development and Reform Commission.

(4) Major innovations in the reform mode. Zhejiang Province became the first in China to establish a working mechanism for promoting reform in a coordinated way; the provincial and municipal governments set up the leading groups for reform led by main government leaders; a number of systems were established, including medium and long-term reform plans and annual implementation opinions; a preliminary study and a feasibility study of major reform matters; a major reform project library and expert library; evaluation of reform goal responsibility; reform situation debriefing; reform information exchange, thus creating a new reform pattern in which the Party Committee and government make the overall arrangements, reform departments lead relevant work, with the participation of functional departments and concerted efforts for making breakthroughs.

(5) Comprehensive intensification of reform. In recent years, Zhejiang Province has further intensified economical and intensive land use innovations, financial factor innovations and differentiated allocation of such resources and factors as water and electric power; in Haining, pilot reform was carried out in the market-oriented allocation of factors to constantly improve the efficiency in the utilization of resources and factors; the output rate per mu in construction land throughout the province in 2012 increased by 58.7% over 2007. The direction of the overall reform for the market-oriented allocation of factors is as follows: all factors which can be allocated by the market should be handed over to the market, resources and factors should be allocated through market competition in a rational, high-quality, lawful and efficient way. In 2013, the Zhejiang Provincial Party Committee and the Provincial Government put forward the following main tasks: first, intensifying the reform of the land factor allocation. The philosophy of "defining a hero by the output per mu" should be adopted to establish and improve the system of linking revitalization of stock land, land output performance with new construction land, push forward the reform involving the system of flexible management of industrial land, and establish the mechanism for making the inefficiently used land exit in a market-oriented way. Second, intensifying the reform involving the allocation of such factors as water, electricity and gas. Actions should be taken to improve the mechanism for differentiated and ladder-like prices of electricity, gas and water used by enterprises and residents, carry out a pilot reform involving total quantity control of river basin water and water rights trading system, make investigations in carrying out the trading of regional energy utilization rights. Third, intensifying the reform of environmental resource allocation. Innovations should be made in the mechanism of ecological protection and paid use of resources; explorations should be made in the reform involving total quantity control of carbon emissions and the trading system; steps should be taken to innovate on the mode of evaluating regional and river basin environmental management; pilot construction of ecological function zones in Kaihua and other areas should be launched; efforts should be made

to further improve the systems and mechanisms for building a beautiful Zhejiang. Fourth, intensifying the reform of financial factor allocation. Intensified efforts should be made to overcome difficulties and the high costs in enterprise financing; substantive breakthroughs should be made in the establishment of private banks, online finance and other areas; actions should be taken to build connections between small capital from private sources and large projects, large industries, between large capital from banks and small enterprises, between the capital market and the real economy. Fifth, further reforming the scientific and technological system, promoting market-oriented allocation and efficient flow of technologies and talent factors.

4.2 Transformation of Government Functions

4.2.1 Building Up Government Efficiency

In February, 2004, the Zhejiang Provincial Party Committee and the Provincial Government issued the *Decision on Building up the Efficiency of Agencies*, kicking off the building up of government efficiency.

1. Important significance of building up the efficiency of agencies

The building up of the efficiency of agencies is the inevitable requirement for studying and implementing the Important Thought of Three Represents and improving the ability to lead and govern; it is an important measure for improving the socialist market economic system and more rapidly pushing forward the transformation of government functions; it is an effective guarantee for earnestly carrying forward the spirit of seeking truth and being pragmatic and carrying out the "Eight-Eight Strategies". The building up of the efficiency of agencies is conducive to promoting reform, development and stability; putting in practice the essential requirement of serving the public good and exercising power in the interests of the people; transforming agency functions, regularizing agency behaviors, improving the work style of agencies and administrative efficiency; exercising rigorous governance over the Party and the government, stepping up efforts to improve Party conduct and government integrity and fight corruption; expanding intra-party democracy, strengthening democratic supervision and pushing forward the all-round construction of agencies.

2. Overall requirement and basic principles

(1) The overall requirement for building up the efficiency of agencies is as follows: taking the Deng Xiaoping Theory and the Important Thought of Three Represents as a guide, carefully carrying out the guiding principles adopted in the Third Plenary Session of the Central Commission for Discipline Inspection, following the overall arrangement of solid work made in the Fifth Plenary Session

of the 11th Party Committee of Zhejiang Province to focus on keeping government functionaries honest and industrious, improving the efficiency, optimizing the environment, governing for the people and promoting development; stress ideological education and strengthen the establishment of rules and regulations, be strict with evaluation, reward and punishment to integrate the resources of agency management, optimize the factors of agency management, regulate agencies' management behaviors, improve the operational mode of agencies in order to overcome the outstanding problems in agency efficiency, ensure that agencies at various levels and agency cadres make new breakthroughs in the execution of their duty, reform and innovation, and further improve the quality of services and the efficiency of their work; enhance the people's satisfaction with the work of the agencies, establish the well-regulated, operationally coordinated, fair and transparent, honest and efficient management system and operation mechanism.

(2) The basic principles for building up the efficiency of agencies are as follows: focusing on central tasks, serving the overall interests, concentrating on thoroughly carrying out the "Eight-Eight Strategies", using the results of the implementation and the people's satisfaction to test the effect of building up efficiency; making breakthroughs in key areas, holistically pushing forward relevant work, addressing key issues, identifying the main directions, stimulating the building up of the efficiency of agencies by breakthroughs at points; carrying out fair, open and strict evaluation, establishing an evaluation system, improving the incentive mechanism, actively fostering a strong atmosphere of valuing and strengthening the building up of the efficiency of agencies; persisting in and inheriting innovations, keeping pace with the times, learning and drawing upon the successful experience and practices, boldly innovating the line of thought and measures regarding work to constantly improve the building up of the efficiency of agencies.

3. Work priorities

(1) Enhancing service awareness. According to the requirement of arming brains, guiding the practice and promoting the work, actions should be taken to deeply study and carry out the Deng Xiaoping Theory, the Important Thought of Three Represents and the important speech delivered by President Hu Jintao during the Third Plenary Session of the Central Commission for Discipline Inspection. It is necessary to earnestly carry out education concerning the outlook on purpose and political achievements, guide agency cadres, especially the leading cadres, to integrate the correct outlook on political achievements with the correct outlook on power, firmly uphold the philosophy of putting the people's interests first, continuously enhance the consciousness regarding seeking truth and being pragmatic, raise the quality and level of serving the people.

(2) Regularizing the behavior of agencies. It is essential to take law as the criterion, base actions on rules, uphold administration under the rule of law and act according to rules and regulations and regularize behavior. Steps should be taken to fully clear away the policies, rules, regulations and normative documents that are contrary to the existing laws, international practices and the cur-

rent economic and social developmental requirements; those which should be abolished are resolutely abolished; those which should be revised are promptly revised and improved, so as to remove the policy obstacles to the economic and social development.

(3) Improving the administrative efficiency. It is necessary to develop the notion of limited government, do certain things and refrain from doing other things, simplify the procedure for handling affairs to improve the efficiency of work. It is essential to continuously intensify the reform of the administrative examination and approval system, focus on addressing the excessive, overly concentrated and undue matters subject to examination and approval. Actions should be taken to make government affairs public, strengthen e-government construction, further release the procedures of work, the criteria and results regarding the matters of concern to the people and the society, including project examination and approval, certificate handling and examination, money and material examination and approval, law enforcement and punishment; make commitments regarding the quality of the work, service attitude, the time limit and the effect of work and constantly improve transparency.

(4) Improving institutional construction. According to the requirement of carrying out innovation and reform, transforming functions and exercising strict management, it is necessary to act in a well-regulated, standardized and scientific way to fully carry out the post responsibility system, the system of commitment to service, the system of finishing work within the specified time, the first-inquiring responsibility system, the work responsibility system of two similar posts; gradually establish and improve the accountability system for dereliction of duty, the negation filing system and the system of one-time notification at windows and departments; adopt systems to govern personnel and affairs.

(5) Improving the work style of agencies. It is necessary to overcome the difficulties in handling affairs, which still exist in some areas and departments, properly deal with the relationship with the people, enhance the consciousness of public servants and the initiative of serving the people.

(6) Improving the quality of forces. Actions should be taken to carefully carry out the guiding principles adopted in the national and provincial working conferences on talents, actively foster a working environment favorable for outstanding talents to stand out, and really establish a mechanism under which the competent personnel are promoted while the mediocre ones are demoted.

(7) Strengthening the supervision mechanism. A supervisory body for the building up of the efficiency of agencies should be established; a supervisory force should be built; duties and responsibilities should be specified; responsibilities should be put in place; coordination should be strengthened to ensure that the supervisory function for the building up of the efficiency of agencies is really performed. It is necessary to continue to thoroughly carry out the activities involving democratic appraisal of the work style of agencies, promptly sum up experience, constantly improve the appraisal mechanism and measures, guarantee supervision, examination and rectification better. Scope should be further given to the supervisory role of the people's congress, the people's political

consultative conference, news media and the masses; measures should be taken to build a power operation mechanism with a rational structure, a scientific arrangement, a rigorous procedure and effective constraint.

(8) Being strict with evaluation, reward and punishment. Actual conditions should be considered to study and establish a scientific, quantitative and highly operable performance evaluation system, and the implementation measures for efficiency warning, admonition education and responsibility investigation in order to carry out strict evaluation. Performance evaluation should be combined with the evaluation of the goals of work, Party and government should conduct an evaluation of responsibility, leading cadres' year-end reporting on work and an annual evaluation of public servants; evaluation results serve as an important basis for evaluating the performance of agency cadres, rewarding, punishing, selecting and appointing agency cadres.

4.2.2 *Reforms of Government Institutions and the Administrative Approval System*

1. Reform of government institutions

Since 2003, Zhejiang Province has earnestly pushed forward the reform of government institutions, with the largest institution reform conducted in 2009. According to the requirement of building an administrative management system with responsibilities commensurate with the powers, rational division of labor, scientific decision-making, smooth execution and vigorous supervision, government functions were further transformed, institution setting was regularized, the organizational structure was optimized and the operational mechanism and management mode were improved. After the reform, the People's Government of Zhejiang Province had 42 working departments and 6 department management bodies. Zhejiang Province has always strictly controlled its institutions and the authorized size of those institutions. As of late 2013, the administrative authorized size of the Party, government and mass organization throughout the province was 151,997 people—that of the government system was 114,355 people, accounting for 75.4% of the total authorized size; Zhejiang Province ranked No. 4 among provinces, autonomous regions and municipalities nationwide in terms of relative scale, so the governments in Zhejiang Province can be regarded as small governments.[2]

Zhejiang Province has actively delegated administrative powers to the lower levels in the process of marketization, creating a good environment for the development of regional economy, especially the county economy. In the reforms on expanding the powers of strong counties and towns, the following measures have been mainly

[2]The Institution Reform Plan of the People's Government of Zhejiang Province in 2009.

introduced since 2003[3]: (1) In 2003, the economic management authority which had been delegated to 17 counties and 3 districts including Yuhang, Xiaoshan and Yinzhou was given to all counties (cities, districts) of Zhejiang Province; (2) In 2006, pilot reform on expanding Yiwu's economic management authority was carried out; except for important resource allocation, planning management and management of major social affairs, 763 items of management authority at the provincial-level departments were twice delegated to the departments at the lower levels; (3) In 2007, the central town cultivation project was carried out, 141 central towns were given ten items of economic and social management authority, covering land, finance, project examination and approval, and administrative law enforcement; (4) In 2008, the reform on expanding the powers of strong counties was comprehensively promoted to fully delegate powers to 61 counties and cities throughout the province, with 618 items of economic management authority delegated to the lower levels, involving 38 provincial-level departments and 21 prefecture-level departments; (5) The reform on expanding the powers of strong towns was carried out in an all-round way, the policy documents on accelerating the development and reform of central towns were developed and released; the economic and social management authority of 200 provincial-level central towns was expanded; 27 provincial-level central towns were chosen to carry out the pilot cultivation of small towns and were given the economic and social management authority equivalent to that of county-level governments; (6) In 2013, the Zhoushan Archipelago New Area was given the provincial-level economic and social management authority.

In order to ensure the smooth delegation of powers to the lower levels, in June, 2009, the People's Government of Zhejiang Province made the first regulation on expanding the powers of strong counties in China—*Several Regulations of Zhejiang Province on Strengthening the Administrative Management Functions of the County-level People's Government*, issued in the form of a government decree, delegating partial management authority of the governments of higher levels to the county-level government and making the reform of power expansion more law-based and regulation-based.[4] Expanding the powers of strong counties means that almost all county-level governments in Zhejiang Province can enjoy more economic management authority to the extent permitted by laws, so that the county economy becomes the main means for transforming Zhejiang's economic developmental mode, injecting impetus for Zhejiang to effectively allocate resources and improve the developmental environment, stimulating vitality and further promoting the rapid development of the county economy.

While expanding the powers of strong counties, Zhejiang Province made explorations to expand the powers of strong towns. With rapid economic development and deepening urbanization, the contradiction that responsibilities were not commen-

[3]Yu Jianxing, Zhang Liping, Adjustment and Adaptation of the Roles of Local Governments in the Process of Marketization and Management Innovations, *Theoretical Investigation*, 2013(4).

[4]Party History Research Office of Zhejiang Provincial Party Committee, *Making the People Rich by Starting Business and of Building a Strong Province through Innovation—Since the 12th Party Congress of Zhejiang Province*, Zhejiang People's Publishing House, 2012.

surate with powers became increasingly acute in Zhejiang's towns. Given the new situation, the Zhejiang Provincial Party Committee and the Provincial Government conducted system and mechanism innovations to make breakthroughs in overcoming the development bottlenecks at central towns, and introduced relevant policy measures in registered permanent residence management, land system, administrative management and in the law enforcement system, thus adding reform impetus and vitality for the construction and development of central towns.

2. Reform of the administrative examination and approval system

After the *Administrative Licensing Law* was promulgated in 2003, according to the requirement of building a service-oriented government under the rule of law, Zhejiang Province extended the reform of the examination and approval system to the following areas: administration under the rule of law; making government affairs public; examination and approval network construction; the construction of a system of electronic supervision; clearing and regularization of administrative licensing items and non-administrative licensing items; integration and reform of the licensing function within administrative organs and the standardization of administrative service center. Main tasks focused on reducing the items subject to examination and approval, examination and approval steps, preconditions and levels; promoting th innovation in the examination and approval mode; regularizing the content and process of examination and approval; improving the long-term mechanism of administrative examination and approval. As of late 2013, 470 provincial-level items subject to examination and approval were delegated to the lower levels, accounting for 50% of the total number of provincial-level items subject to examination and approval.

Intensifying the reform represents self-improvement of the government's governance system and governance mode; this is the precondition for the market to play a decisive role. After the Third Plenary Session of the 18th CPC Central Committee, the Zhejiang Provincial Party Committee and the Provincial Government launched a new round of reform, three lists[5] and one network,[6] and made dramatic reductions in three areas.[7] This round of reform traces back to the source of government powers. The "unresting hand"—the government—was really withdrawn, while the "invisible hand"—the market—was unleashed, and the "hand of autonomy"—the

[5]The negative list of enterprise project investments was promoted, in which where the market mechanism can exercise effective regulation, examination and approval is cancelled, and where management by the grass-roots departments is more convenient and effective, the examination and approval powers are delegated to the lower levels; the list of government powers was set down, in which government powers were fully overhauled; the management list of special funds of government departments was made, the provincial-level government departments generally no longer directly distributed and allocated funds to enterprises and they also no longer directly collected administrative charges from enterprises.

[6]A province-wide online government hall was built, thus providing one-stop online services and exercising whole-process efficiency supervision.

[7]Greatly reducing the government's direct allocation of resources, the government's management of and intervention in micro affairs, the government's intervention in resources and factor prices.

society—was reinforced, so that the market and the people became bold in making innovations and experimentations for jointly promoting reform and development.

As of late 2013, the number of provincial-level items subject to administrative licensing was reduced by 41% from 718 to 424, while that of provincial-level items not subject to administrative licensing was reduced by 78% from 560 to 125. The number of authorities for non-administrative licensing examination and approval was reduced by 47.4% from 57 to 30; 27 departments no longer conducted non-administrative licensing examination and approval. Moreover, with regard to great improvement in the efficiency of examination and approval, the network of the provincial government was relied on to build a joint examination and approval network platform covering joint examination and approval, efficiency supervision and information service; the examination and approval networks of 14 provincial departments and more than 500 municipal and county-level departments were launched.[8]

4.2.3 Active Market-Oriented Reform of Resource and Factor Allocation

1. Market-oriented reform of land resource allocation

Land resource is one of the greatest bottlenecks restricting Zhejiang's sustainable development. In order to overcome bottlenecks, on the one hand, Zhejiang Province continued to expand economical and intensive land use. In 2008, the People's Government of Zhejiang Province released the *Action Plan for Resource Saving and Environmental Protection*, and decided to holistically push forward economical and intensive land use in six main areas including urban construction, industrial construction, housing construction, infrastructure construction, rural construction, land development and consolidation, with a view to increasing the land utilization rate. The consumption of new construction land newly increased per unit of GDP, fixed asset investment decreased by 20 and 15% in 2012 over 2007, while the land use intensity increased by 15%. In 2008, Zhejiang Province became the first in China to put forward and carry out the system of linking the division of the annual land use plan with the intensive land use level, it carried out the "zero land increase" technical renovation, and adopted the following policy: where an enterprise rebuilds old factory buildings into multi-storey factory buildings and uses open spaces within a factory to build factory buildings above 3 storeys, land transfer fees and the locally-retained portion of the surcharge on urban infrastructure construction will be reduced or exempted. In May, 2009, the People's Government of Zhejiang Province issued the *Circular Concerning Implementation of the One-Million Land Creation Safeguard Project*, and vowed to newly increase the area of cultivated land by guaranteeing the total quantity of newly increased cultivated land from the development of mild slope of low mountains and hills, increasing the scale of land from tideland reclamation,

[8]http://www.raresd.com.

pushing forward the reclamation of rural construction land and tapping the potential of land consolidation. In October, 2009, the People's Government of Zhejiang Province issued the *Circular Concerning the Work on the Linking of the Increase or Decrease in Urban and Rural Construction Land*, and decided to establish account books of the indicators involving the linking of the increase or decrease in urban and rural construction land with city, county (city, district) as unit so as to enable unified management and use.

On the other hand, a uniform urban-rural construction land market was established. First, actions were taken to improve the industrial land bidding, auction and listing system, actively carry out a pilot reform of the system of differentiating industrial land transfer fees by the number of years, and specify the provisions for the lowest control standard for industrial land. Second, various types of homestead nature change modes were actively and steadily put into practice. Third, steps were taken to establish an effective mechanism for openly transferring the rural collectively operated construction land according to laws, and speed up the reform of the system of coastal tideland reclamation and comprehensive utilization of the mild slope of low mountains and hills.

2. Pilot market-oriented reform of other factor allocation

Since the 12th Party Congress of Zhejiang Province, Zhejiang Province has reformed the prices of water, electricity and refined oil products. Actions have been taken to establish and improve the ladder-like water price and water rights trading system, push forward the system of ladder-like prices of urban domestic water and the system of increasing the prices of water used by enterprises in excess of plan or quota, and press ahead with the transfer of the rights for water resource use. The system of unifying industrial and commercial electricity prices has been reformed more quickly. The policy for on-grid prices of the electricity generated by renewable energy sources, photovoltaic system and biomass has been developed; pilot work has been carried out with respect to direct purchase of electricity by big consumers. The mechanism for the formation of electricity prices has been further improved; Zhejiang Province has become the first to conduct a reform involving the system of ladder-like prices of domestic electricity, with full adoption of the policy of peak and valley electricity prices among urban and rural residents. The People's Government of Zhejiang Province developed and issued the *Implementation Opinions on Carrying out the Refined Oil Product Reform*, and cancelled road maintenance fees, channel maintenance fees, road transportation management fees, road passenger and freight transportation surcharges, waterway transportation management fees and water passenger and freight transportation surcharges, the mechanism for the formation of refined oil product prices has gradually taken shape.

The system of paid use and trading of emission rights has been fully reformed on a pilot basis. Based on first carrying out pilot reform on the trading of emission rights in Jiaxing, Hangzhou, Shaoxing and Taizhou, Zhejiang Province fully established the urban sewage treatment charging system as from 2007, and fully implemented the urban and rural domestic refuse disposal charging system as from 2009. The provincial emission rights trading center was established; Zhejiang Province developed and released the *Guiding Opinions Concerning the Pilot Work on Paid Use and Trading of Emission Rights* and the *Administrative Measures for Paid Use and Trading of Main Pollutant Emission Rights*.

4.3 Multidimensional Pilot Reforms

4.3.1 The Wenzhou Comprehensive Financial Reform Experimental Area

The State Council approved Wenzhou's comprehensive financial reform in April, 2012. According to the *Master Plan for Comprehensive Financial Reform Experimental Area in Wenzhou City, Zhejiang Province* approved by the State Council, the experimental area is designed to undertake 12 main tasks including regularizing and developing private financing and accelerating the development of new-type financial organizations; it focuses on overcoming the difficulties in two fields,[9] regularizing private finance and putting it in the sunshine, establishing a financial system suited to the economic system, pushing ahead with the construction of four major systems including the financial organization system, the capital market system, the financial service system and the local regulatory system, making reform experimentations, thus it is of important experimental significance for national financial reform and economic development.

1. Overview of the Wenzhou Comprehensive Financial Reform Experimental Area

The developmental goal and strategic orientation of the Wenzhou Comprehensive Financial Reform Experimental Area are as follows: making system and mechanism innovations to build a diversified financial system commensurate with economic and social development, so as to significantly increase the level of financial service, markedly enhance the capability for guarding against and defusing financial risks, apparently optimize the financial environment, offer experience for national financial reform. The main tasks are as follows: regularizing and developing private financing; speeding up the development of new-type financial organizations; developing specialized asset management bodies; studying and carrying out the pilot work on individual overseas direct investments, investigating to establish the well-regulated and convenient direct investment channels; intensifying the reform of local financial institutions; innovating and developing the financial products and services for small and micro enterprises, agriculture, farmers and rural areas; exploring the establishment of a multi-tier financial service system; cultivating and developing local capital markets; actively developing various types of bond products; broadening the insurance service fields, innovating and developing the insurance products for specialized

[9]It is difficult for small and medium-sized enterprises to seek more loans; it is difficult for private capital to make more investments.

markets and industrial clusters, encouraging and supporting commercial insurance to participate in building the social security system; reinforcing the construction of the social credit system; improving the local financial management system, preventing regulatory vacuums, guarding against systemic and regional risks; setting up a comprehensive financial reform risk prevention mechanism. The experimental area was built to guide, regularize and promote the benign development of private finance, make finance serve the real economy better and boost sound, rapid and healthy economic and social development.

Since the implementation of the pilot work, Wenzhou's comprehensive financial reform has featured first-ever implementation of pilot programs and has delivered positive results. Wenzhou became the first to work on the following areas: preparing and releasing the Wenzhou Index; issuing the first local financial regulation—the *Administrative Regulations of Wenzhou City on Private Financing*; establishing a private lending service center; launching the local off-site financial regulation system; setting up private capital management companies with local characteristics; carrying on private placement business; initiating the "Happiness Share"; issuing a private placement bond involving small loan companies; setting up the first prefecture-level branch of the Credit Reference Center of the People's Bank of China; issuing the first prefecture-level private placement bond involving government-subsidized housing. Ten major pilot reform projects have been or will be duplicated and popularized nationwide—five projects, including a private capital management company, a private lending service center, the Wenzhou Index, the construction of a local regulatory system, the construction of a credit system, have been duplicated on a pilot basis nationwide; the following aspects are of referential significance for national endeavor: implementation of the *Administrative Regulations of Wenzhou City on Private Financing*; the further intensification and improvement of five pilot reform projects: efforts to regularize private lending and putting it in the sunshine; pilot work on private placement involving private capital management companies, private placement bonds involving small loan companies and on the issuance of the "Happiness Share"; pilot work on the rural fund mutual benefit association and the rural mutual insurance association; pilot work on the community banking system and rural inclusive finance; pilot work on the mechanism for guarding against financial risks and disposition of non-performing assets.

2. Pushing forward major projects, presenting four main bright spots

The Wenzhou Comprehensive Financial Reform Experimental Area guides the well-regulated development of private financing and enhances the capability of finance for serving the real economy; this is crucial for Wenzhou's healthy development and is also of important significance for provincial and national financial reform and economic development.

(1) It is a leader in regularizing private financing and putting it in the sunshine. On November 22, 2013, the Standing Committee of the People's Congress of Zhejiang Province deliberated and adopted the *Administrative Regulations of Wenzhou City on Private Financing*, for the first time making the compulsory

filing system for large-amount private lending and taking the form of legislation to put the huge semi-light semi-dark private financing on the table.[10]

(2) It is a leader in stimulating formal finance to serve the real economy. Commercial banks innovatively launched more than 80 financial products to serve small and micro enterprises, involving more than 70 billion yuan; in 2013, 56,000 small and micro enterprises were newly supported and newly increased small and micro loans amounting to 28.8 billion yuan, up 8.3 billion yuan or 40.5% over the previous year. Actions were taken to develop export credit insurance, domestic trade credit insurance and small loan guarantee insurance and to utilize insurance instruments to deepen financial services for small and micro enterprises. Securities institutions actively served the reform of enterprise shareholding and private placement to enhance the developmental potential.[11]
(3) It is a leader in innovatively expanding the application of capital market instruments. As of late 2013, the private placement bond involving small loan companies was carried out on a pilot basis in an innovative way, with 400 million yuan filed and 50 million yuan issued; 3 private capital management companies carried out collective funds based on private placement to raise and register 330 million yuan; 3 enterprises registered 50 million yuan from private placement bonds; 4 companies were newly-added to the list, raising funds amounting to 3393 million yuan, accounting for 19.7% of the total funds raised by listed companies.[12]
(4) It is a leader in improving the construction of the local financial regulatory system. Such institutions as the local financial management bureau, the financial arbitration court, the financial crime investigation division and the financial court orderly carried out their work. On-site inspection was conducted of the players on the local financial market; the non-site regulatory system was launched to stimulate local financial organizations to perform operations according to regulations and guard against local financial risks.

3. Serving the real economy, consolidating four major foundations

(1) Pushing forward the construction of the modern enterprise systems. In order to improve enterprises' financing capability and potential for development, a regional capital market was cultivated to promote economic transformation and upgrading; the reform of enterprise shareholding was launched; the preferential and support policies were formulated to drive enterprises to establish the modern enterprise systems suited to modern finance.[13]
(2) Boosting the construction of a financial ecological environment. Measures were adopted to help the enterprises subject to risks, identify and classify the enterprises subject to risks. Intensified efforts were made to control the new non-

[10]Zhang Zhenyu, Ke Yuanyuan, Wenzhou's Solution for Local Comprehensive Financial Reform, *China Finance*, 2014(11).

[11]Data come from the *Zhejiang Statistical Yearbook 2013*.

[12]Data come from the *Zhejiang Statistical Yearbook 2013*.

[13]Data come from the *Zhejiang Statistical Yearbook 2014*.

performing loans of banks and defuse the old ones. With time exchanged for space, the risks at the enterprise guarantee chain were dissolved. Continued actions were taken to crack down on and deal with illegal fund-raising. The activities of service personnel at enterprises and financial service personnel were actively carried out.

(3) Promoting the construction of financial infrastructures. The integrated statistical information platform for the financial industry and the Wenzhou Financial Monitoring and Reporting Platform were built; intensified efforts were taken to analyze the operations of the financial industry and monitor financial risks. A branch of the Credit Reference Center of the People's Bank of China, the first prefecture-level one in China, was built and it shares information with the enterprise-related public credit information platform of the Wenzhou Municipal Government. The first credit-rating agency was established to rate the borrowing enterprises, grade small and micro enterprises and evaluate the trustworthy ones in rural areas[14]; great efforts were made to restore a good social credit environment in which private mutual trust is built, enterprises are trustworthy and banks honor commitments.

(4) Pressing ahead with the construction of the enterprise financing platforms. Five integrated service centers for small and micro enterprise financing were built to provide more than 1400 enterprises with financing service above 2.8 billion yuan. The construction of two libraries and one network was reinforced[15]; platform development was initiated in Cangnan at the early stage; it is expected to be officially launched at the 2nd anniversary of financial reform.

4.3.2 *The Lishui Rural Pilot Financial Reform*

Lishui is the first pilot city for rural financial reform approved by the People's Bank of China in China. The People's Bank of China and the People's Government of Zhejiang Province adopted, on a pilot basis, the mode of joint construction by the central bank and a province. On March 30, 2012, the People's Bank of China and the People's Government of Zhejiang Province jointly issued the *Circular Concerning Rural Pilot Financial Reform in Lishui City, Zhejiang Province*, calling for first-ever implementation of pilot programs and provision of experience demonstration in the following eight areas: innovating the system of rural financial organization; enriching the system of rural financial products; bolstering the policy system for making financial services accessible to agriculture; improving the system for the rural financial market; enhancing the rural financial credit system; building a system for a financial service platform; improving the system of rural payment services; optimizing the rural financial ecological system.

[14]Trustworthy towns, trustworthy villages and trustworthy households.

[15]Two libraries mean enterprise demand library and financial product library; one network means the integrated service network for micro, small and medium-sized enterprises.

1. Priorities and measures of the pilot reform

The priorities and measures of pilot reform cover the following several aspects.

(1) Innovating the rural financial organization system. First, actions are taken to expand the reform of rural credit cooperatives, push forward the shareholding reform of rural cooperative financial institutions, increase capital strength, enhancing the capability for serving agriculture, farmers and rural areas. Second, financial institutions are encouraged to extend their outlets and business to counties and towns; the financial service system of central towns is improved. Finally, social capital and private capital are guided to enter the financial field; the areas where conditions permit are encouraged to take counties (cities, districts) as units to establish various kinds of small and medium-sized financial institutions and organizations, including community banks, financial leasing companies, pawnshops; explorations are made to build the rural insurance organization system including a rural insurance marketing service department and insurance service stations for agriculture, farmers and rural areas.
(2) Enriching the systems of rural financial products. In the rural pilot financial reform, innovations are made in credit mode and the scope of loan pledges and mortgage collaterals is expanded; domestic and foreign well-proven small loan techniques are actively introduced and popularized to build a three-in-one rural credit product system covering small credit loans, mortgage-secured loans and guarantee institution guarantee loans.
(3) Bolstering the policy system for making financial services accessible to agriculture. Government policy support is the greatest impetus in rural financial reform. Lishui increases government support for rural financial policies, and improves various mechanisms involving fiscal discounts for agriculture-related loans, risk compensation, evaluation and incentives, thus promoting the rapid development of rural inclusive finance.
(4) Improving the system of a rural financial market. With respect to the improvement of a multi-level financial market system, Lishui comprehensively leverages various financial resources including credit, securities, insurance, trust and guarantee, and increases the proportion of direct financing. During the rural financial reform, actions are taken to actively cultivate large-scale agricultural operation entities including high-quality agricultural enterprises and large households engaged in the industrialized operation of agriculture, and recommend them to seek listing and financing at the SME board and on the growth enterprise market.
(5) Improving the rural social credit system. Zhejiang expands the construction of the rural credit system, steadily carries out the credit rating of community residents as well as small and medium-sized enterprises; it builds a three-in-one credit information database covering rural households, residents and enterprises; it comprehensively promotes the construction of an integrated urban and rural social credit system. First, steps are taken to fully collect the credit information concerning the main agriculture-related players including rural households, rural enterprises and rural economic organizations. Second, the gov-

ernment, banks and main agriculture-related players work together to conduct asset appraisal, credit rating and credit line evaluation, thus pushing forward credit loans, mortgage loans and joint guarantee loans in an interactive way; the resulting operational mechanism of the rural credit information collection and evaluation system has been established; a good social practice of honesty and trustworthiness has been fostered.

(6) Building a platform system of financial services. Given that rural financial service intermediaries are absent t counties, great efforts are made to build integrated rural financial service platforms with complete supporting facilities, effective support and excellent services. At the same time, actions are taken to push forward the construction of a diversified system of rural financing guarantees.

(7) Improving the rural payment service system. Based on the existing work, the modern communication and network information technologies are relied upon to further improve the outlets of banking institutions, encourage payment institutions to provide payment service in rural areas, offer low-cost basic financial services including deposits, withdrawals and transfers in rural areas. More efforts are being made to popularize and apply non-cash payment instruments, including cheques, bills of exchange, promissory notes and bank cards, in rural areas. Innovations and applications are being encouraged with respect to emerging electronic payment operations including mobile phone payments, fixed phone payments and Internet payments.

(8) Optimizing the rural system of financial ecology. Zhejiang Province attaches importance to legal protection of the rights and interests of private investors, and the maintenance of a fair, impartial and open market investment environment. Actions are taken to crack down on financial criminal activities, including evasion of financial debt repayment, insurance and claims fraud, bank card crime, according to laws; severely deal with illegal fund-raising, illegal private banking, illegal withdrawal of cash from credit cards, illegal insurance policies and illegal foreign exchanges. At the same time, education on financial knowledge is being carried out at primary and middle schools throughout the city; the Rural Financial Reform Development & Research Center has been established in local institutions of higher learning to intensify education and the popularization of financial knowledge, building a good financial ecological system at the source.

2. Main achievements in the pilot reform[16]

(1) The pilot promotion mechanism was constantly improved. The organizational mechanism was improved; with the mode of joint construction by the central bank and a province as an opportunity, plans were actively developed, organization and implementation were strengthened, six coordinated promotion groups, including financial innovation, were established to solidly and smoothly carry out the pilot work; the survey and research mechanism was improved, a strategic cooperation agreement was signed with Zhejiang University of Finance and

[16]http://www.lsstats.gov.cn.

Economics to jointly establish the Lishui Institute of Rural Financial Reform, with a view to strengthening research on the theories concerning rural financial reform and development. The work implementation mechanism was improved; the *Plan of Lishui City for the Rural Pilot Financial Reform*, the *Three-Year Action Plan of Lishui City for the Rural Pilot Financial Reform* and 14 implementation measures for the rural pilot financial reform were developed. The work evaluation mechanism was improved to exercise special supervision and inspection of the rural pilot financial reform at municipal units and counties (cities, districts), and the work on the rural pilot financial reform was incorporated into the evaluation of the governments at various levels and relevant departments throughout the city.

(2) The impetus for reform and development continuously improved. Scope was given to the advantages of the mode of joint construction by the central bank and a province; pilot policies were further studied; feasible implementation plans were practically formulated, and full play was given to the leading role of financial institutions in reform; more financial resources were guided to the agricultural, farming and rural areas. In 2013, the balance of agriculture-related loans was 60,998 million yuan throughout the city, an increase of 5377 million yuan, accounting for 54.41% of all newly increased loans, the balance increased by 21.00%, 2.46 percentage points higher than the growth rate of all loan balances.

(3) The level of financial support for agriculture persistently increased. Continued efforts were made to push forward the project of credit support for agriculture, and promote the high quality and steady growth of forestry rights mortgage loans. In 2013, 94,600 forestry rights mortgage loans amounting to 7349 million yuan were extended throughout the city, with a balance of 3029 million yuan, ranking it No. 1 in Zhejiang Province. Continued actions were taken to push forward the project of extending benefits from credit to agriculture, to promote credit rating of farmers' specialized cooperatives and the borrowing enterprises and to steadily advance the construction of the three-in-one social credit system covering rural households, community residents, small and medium-sized enterprises. As of late 2013, credit rating covered 100% of administrative villages and 92% of rural households throughout the city. The project of making payment convenient for agriculture continued to be promoted. In 2013, 614,300 small-amount cash withdrawals with an amount of 141 million yuan were completed at 2114 service points for withdrawing money for agriculture throughout the city, 14,700 agency-based transfer transactions with an amount of 8,150,000 yuan were concluded.

(4) Financial product innovation continuously intensified. Further innovations were made in agriculture-related credit products. In 2013, 490 million yuan stone carving mortgage loans, 1460 tea garden mortgage loans, with a balance of 90.33 million yuan, were extended. The financial institutions engaged in agriculture were guided to utilize the rural household credit information system to fully promote the business of centralized credit extension and holistic wholesale of small agricultural loans in 9 counties (cities, districts) throughout the

city, thus further increasing the level of financial support for agriculture. Efforts were made to more rapidly build the city-wide demonstration zone for making insurance serve the people's livelihood; it became the first to conduct pilot innovation in students' safety insurance nationwide; its policy-based insurance, including forest, rice, oilseed rape and public liability insurance for natural disasters, became the first to fully cover the whole province and the whole nation. The work on small loan guarantee insurance was carried out across the board, with 736 million yuan in loans extended as of late 2013. The mode of bank-government-insurance company cooperation was adopted to first carry out a pilot loan project for helping low-income rural households in Jingning; in 2013, 1746 loans with an amount of 46.35 million yuan were extended to low-income rural households.

(5) The construction of the system for the organization of rural financial services was constantly promoted. A rural financial organization system was established and improved. Joint-stock commercial banks and village banks were guided to establish 10 branches in counties and rural areas. The first village-level foreign currency exchange point in China was set up; in 2013, it completed 44,400 agency-based exchange transactions with an amount of 203 million yuan. The service system for the settlement of rural payments was improved; actions were taken to fully initiate the construction of more than 2000 rural financial service stations covering small-amount cash withdrawal, agency-based transfer, RMB anti-counterfeiting, exchange of small denomination and damaged currencies, collection of basic credit information on rural households, wealth management consulting, financial knowledge publicity, assistance for securing securities, insurance transactions and rural household loans. The construction of the farmer guarantee system was actively promoted; efforts were taken to fully push forward the construction of the four-tier guarantee system which is funded by city-wide government finance, built by industrial associations and features the village-level establishment of a guarantee fund and commercial operations. Active pilot work was carried out with respect to the village-level organizations of mutual financial assistance; 220 village-level organizations for mutual financial assistance were established by introducing government funds; 13,000 rural households joined these organizations; 4896 small loans with an amount of 51 million yuan were extended.

4.3.3 The Yiwu Pilot Comprehensive International Trade Reform

On March 4, 2011, the State Council approved the pilot comprehensive international trade reform in Yiwu City. Since the pilot reform was launched, according to the overall pilot plan approved by the State Council, Yiwu City has focused on speeding up the transformation of its economic development mode, increasing the level of openness, transforming the manner of developing foreign trade, building an open economic system; intensifying the reform in and enabling first-ever implementation of pilot programs in promoting the transformation of government functions and fostering new advantages in regional development, thus making great progress and breakthroughs.

1. Breakthroughs have been made in innovating the international trade system; the new-type trade mode and trade system have been basically established

According to the *Three-Year Overall Implementation Plan for the Yiwu Pilot Comprehensive International Trade Reform*, by 2015, a new-type trade system framework conducive to scientific development will basically have taken shape; great breakthroughs will have been made in the reforms of the international trade management and promotion system, etc., making that system keep in line with international practices. With more than two years of efforts, Yiwu's new-type trade mode and trade system have been basically established, and international trade facilitation and standardization have been achieved.

(1) Innovating the international trade mode, establishing the market purchase trade mode and improving the management system of the new-type trade mode. In April, 2013, eight ministries and commissions, including the Ministry of Commerce and the National Development and Reform Commission, agreed to the pilot adoption of the market purchase trade mode in Yiwu City and called for experimenting and innovating in order to establish the corresponding management system. Foreign-funded partnership enterprises have been permitted to make filing registrations of foreign trade operations and open current-account foreign exchange accounts. The added-value tax exemption policy has been implemented for the goods exported under the market purchase trade mode. The customs office has additionally adopted the market purchase trade supervision mode. Under the principle of ensuring that risks are controllable, sources can be traced and the people involved can be held accountable, the customs office and the department for quality inspection have taken customs clearance facilitation measures for the goods exported under the market purchase trade mode, and RMB settlement has been permitted under that mode. The people involved are encouraged and guided to faithfully make declarations; the maximum limit for the value of each batch of goods declared at customs under the market purchase trade mode has been temporarily increased from the original USD 50,000 for tourism shopping to USD 150,000.
(2) Innovating the international trade management mode, establishing the supporting supervision system and comprehensive management mechanism, striking a balance between facilitation of the new-type trade mode and its well-regulated implementation. Actions have been taken to gradually establish the supporting supervision system suited to the market purchase trade characterized by the following: participants are diverse, less-than-contained-load transportation is prevalent, and both domestic trade and foreign trade are involved. Efforts are being made to study and improve the supporting supervisory measures involving

customs, inspection and quarantine, foreign exchange and industry and commerce, with a focus on making greater breakthroughs in the large-scale implementation of customs clearance procedures across customs districts; determination of a code of customs supervision and simplified declarations; the first-ever reform of the statutory inspection system; the simplification of tax administration procedures; trade settlement and financing. Steps have been taken to change the previous management mode under which there was segmentation between departments and local authorities; according to the requirement of ensuring that the source can be traced, risks are controllable and the people involved are held accountable, experimentations have been made to establish a government-led integrated management mechanism jointly managed by departments and with information sharing; guide facilitation for observing laws and acting in a well-regulated way; promote basic establishment of a long-term mechanism for the sustained and healthy development of market purchase trade.

2. The institutional reform has been pushed forward in a systemic, coordinated and holistic way; the combined effect of the supporting reforms has preliminarily become evident

(1) Reforming the administrative management system, expanding administrative authority, breaking through the constraints on reform as imposed by institutional contradictions. The reform of the administrative examination and approval system has been deepened; actions have been taken to establish an examination and approval service mechanism characterized by relaxed control over entry, strict management and high efficiency. The administrative licensing functions have been merged; the municipal administrative service center has incorporated 93.8% of administrative adjudication items from 18 departments; the items subject to examination and approval have been constantly cleared, with 262 items subject to administrative examination and approval having been cancelled, merged or stopped in 2013. Online examination and approval has been explored, 185 items subject to examination and approval can be handled online, making it lead the province in administrative efficiency. It has become the first in the province to initiate the provincial-level pilot work in the following three areas: the reform of the industrial and commercial registration system; holistic before-licensing examination and approval in the Yiwu Commercial and Trade Service Industrial Agglomeration Zone; the reform involving rapid examination and approval of those engaged in foreign trade.

(2) Pushing forward special financial reforms in response to the needs of international trade reform to overcome the difficulties in financial service under the new-type trade mode. In August, 2013, nine ministries and commissions, including the People's Bank of China, jointly approved the *Special Financial Plan for the Yiwu Pilot Comprehensive International Trade Reform*, calling for focusing on developing trade finance and thus making great progress and staged achievements in building a system for financial organization; innovating trade finance products; developing cross-border RMB business and broadening enterprise financing channels. With respect to institutional innovation, it presents a

foreign exchange management system with the following characteristics: the flow of goods exported under the market purchase trade mode matches the total fund flow, dynamic monitoring is exercised and post-mortem verification is conducted. With regard to innovation in trade finance products, the "E Tou" supply chain financing product, the first one in China, was launched, adjusted and upgraded to the "Guo Mao Tong" supply chain financing product; GM Supply Chain Service Co., Ltd., the first integrated trade service enterprise in the province and the only enterprise, in China, capable of applying for credit extension for individual foreign buyers, was established. For pilot cross-border RMB settlement, on December 28, 2012, the People's Bank of China approved Yiwu as the only pilot city, in China, for cross-border RMB settlement. For offshore business, preparations have been made to establish the Yiwu Offshore Business Operations Sub-center of SPD Bank, the first offshore sub-center in China. For innovation in the financing of small and medium-sized enterprises, the first private placement bond of private enterprise in China was issued by Zhejiang Wadou Co., Ltd. For innovation in Internet finance, innovations were made to launch a number of e-commerce products including "Dian Shang Tong", "Dian Shang Dai" and "Wang Dai Tong".[17]

(3) Pressing ahead with special reform of the land management system, properly dealing with the relations between security development and the red line of protection to increase the level of intensive land use. In November, 2012, the Ministry of Land and Resources approved the *Special Plan for the Reform of the Land Management System in the Yiwu Pilot Comprehensive International Trade Reform*, with a focus on carrying out the evaluation of the master plan for land use; exploring a cross-regional cooperation mechanism, preliminarily reaching multi-field strategic cooperation intention with Ganzhou City, Jiangxi Province; pushing forward economical and intensive land use, establishing the industrial land guidance mechanism of "defining a hero by the output per mu", experimenting in carrying out, on a pilot basis, the redevelopment of inefficiently-used urban land, the development and utilization of the spaces under agricultural land; exploring the reform involving the examination and approval of the change in land use; more quickly building a new pattern of land and resources administration; conducting a special study of the utilization of land and resources.

3. Innovations have been made in the forms of both market and business; the market structure has been optimized; great breakthroughs have been made in promoting market transformation and upgrading

(1) Building a modern market system, unceasingly enhancing the market's capability for agglomeration and radiation. Great efforts have been made to move forward with market transformation and upgrading, and with the improvement of the strategic position and the agglomeration and radiation role of the physical market in the international and domestic trade chains. The goods structure has been incessantly expanded and the international production material market

[17]http://www.raresd.com.

has been moderately developed. Continuous extension has been made in the field of trade; import trade has been cultivated and developed; imported goods halls have been established; African and ASEAN product exhibition and sales centers have been completed; an Eastern European product exhibition and sales center is under construction. The market trade structure has been constantly optimized; the market network has been continuously expanded; the strategic plan for developing the market by "going global" has been formulated; efforts have been made to actively expand the domestic trade market and push forward the construction of overseas foreign economic and trade cooperation zones. The market functions have been constantly enhanced; the service platforms covering market settlement, credit, training and law have been built; the system of the Yiwu–China Small Commodity Index has been improved. Continuous innovations have been made in the form of market service business; the exhibition and convention economy has kept growing; various kinds of exhibitions have become more specialized, market-oriented, internationalized and enjoy a higher level of brand influence.

(2) Making innovations in the manner of market trade, basically shaping the modern trade pattern of integrated online and offline development. With a focus on cultivating e-commerce by taking it as the strategic and forerunner industry, the integration between online trade and offline trade has accelerated. The e-commerce transactions throughout the city amounted to 85.6 billion yuan in 2013, up 64%. The e-commerce operation entities were growing. There were 120,000 Taobao seller accounts in the whole city, accounting for 1.3% of the nation's total accounts. The e-commerce enterprise incubation and introduction project has been carried out, with a number of famous e-commerce enterprises, including Alibaba, Global Sources, DHgate.com and Amazon, setting up offices or purchasing centers in Yiwu. Business incubation parks have been established; 8 billion yuan have been invested in building the international e-commerce city; explorations have been made to develop a virtual e-commerce park and cross-border e-commerce park.[18]

(3) Building a modern logistics network system, fully opening the international logistics channel for integration into the Asia Pacific area. With the goal of moving toward the international logistics center, the strategic and fundamental position of modern logistics has been reinforced. The international land port construction mode has been explored. In May, 2013, Yiwu was designated as an international land port by the United Nations Economic and Social Commission for Asia and the Pacific, Yiwu became the only inland city in the eastern region in this regard. Efforts have been made to more rapidly integrate into the national transportation logistics hub; 8 transportation logistics projects in Yiwu City have been included in the overall national plan for road transportation hubs. In September, 2013, Yiwu was identified as the national Grade II logistics park city in the *National Plan for the Development of Logistics Parks*. The land port platforms and collection and distribution functions have been

[18]http://www.raresd.com.

continuously improved; the inland port station has been put into full operation. Multimodal transportation has been evolving; there is further seamless connection with coastal ports, inland border ports and important airports. The functions of the inland port have been improved, the inland port has engaged in comprehensive strategic cooperation with the Port of Ningbo. Efforts are being made to open the airport. The agglomeration development of modern logistics has been pursued; the international land port logistics park has been planned and built, with a centralized arrangement of functional blocks, including express logistics, railway logistics, airport logistics and a comprehensive bonded zone.

4. Market transformation and upgrading has been promoted in coordination with industrial transformation and upgrading; driving forces have been derived from "two wheels"—commercial and trade circulation, advanced manufacturing

Reform has been carried out by further combining the market system, commercial and trade circulation enterprises, financial enterprises and others with industrial enterprises, and forming a mechanism under which the market and the manufacturing industry promote and interact with each other. Scope has been given the leading role of circulation in the economy; actions have been taken to integrate and upgrade the provincial-level commercial and trade service industrial agglomeration zone, the national-level economic and technological development zone and the provincial-level Yiwu industrial park. Intensified efforts have been made to develop the headquarters economy and the advanced manufacturing industry; an agglomeration of industrial developmental features; the industrial structure has become advanced; competitive and high-end development has picked up pace in industries. At the same time, public service platforms have been built—a number of public innovation platforms, including the China (Yiwu) Industrial Design Center, the Yiwu Creative Park and the Business Incubation Center of Zhejiang University, have taken shape; 32 provincial-level or national-level enterprise and industrial R&D centers (technical centers) have been completed. Since the reform, the transformation of traditional industries and the development of the advanced manufacturing industry have accelerated; such industries as stockings and ornaments have become the first to carry out innovations. The industrial structural adjustments have continued to improve, with a continuous decline in the proportions of the primary and secondary industries and a steady increase in the proportion of the tertiary industry; the ratio of the primary, secondary and tertiary industries was adjusted from 2.8:43.2:54.0 in late 2010 to 2.5:40.5:57 in late 2013.[19]

5. The mechanism for promoting the pilot work has been improved, some pilot work has seen the formation of a pattern with a clear division of labor, appropriate implementation of responsibilities and interaction between the upper and lower levels

(1) Establishing an organizational leadership mechanism at the provincial and municipal levels. In order to strengthen organizational leadership over the pilot

[19]http://www.jhstats.gov.cn.

work, the People's Government of Zhejiang Province set up a leading group for the pilot work and added member units. The leading group has an office located at the Zhejiang Provincial Development and Reform Commission. A supervisory group for pilot work promotion was specially established. Yiwu City set up a working group for the pilot work which has an office and 11 staff members and is responsible for strengthening organizational guarantee for the pilot work.

(2) Establishing a mechanism for the promotion of pilot work for interaction between the upper and lower levels. The province-ministry cooperation has been further enhanced; the leaders of the Zhejiang Provincial Party Committee and the Provincial Government specially consulted with and sought alignment in the pilot reform with relevant ministries and commissions many times. More than 30 ministries and commissions, including the National Development and Reform Commission, the Ministry of Commerce, General Administration of Customs, General Administration of Quality Supervision and State Administration of Taxation, went deep into Yiwu in order to guide the pilot work; the General Administration of Customs and General Administration of Quality Supervision signed a memorandum of cooperation with the People's Government of Zhejiang Province for jointly promoting Yiwu's pilot work. A system of inter-ministerial joint meetings was established; 11 key matters for which support should be coordinated were identified. Provincial-municipal interaction has been continuously intensified; the People's Congress of Zhejiang Province specially made a relevant decision on guaranteeing and promoting Yiwu's pilot work; 15 provincial departments, including the Department of Commerce of Zhejiang Province and the Zhejiang Administration for Industry and Commerce, released relevant documents for supporting Yiwu's pilot work; the Organization Department of the Zhejiang Provincial Party Committee assigned the first 50 cadres to Yiwu for taking temporary posts.

(3) Building a pilot task decomposition mechanism with clear responsibilities. In January, 2012, the General Office of the State Council released the work division plan for key pilot work, dividing 41 key tasks among 30 ministries and commissions; this occurred for the first time with respect to a national experimental area for comprehensive reform. According to the above plan, the People's Government of Zhejiang Province specially unveiled a three-year implementation plan and the key work arrangements for the years covered, dividing relevant work among relevant provincial departments and Jinhua City. Yiwu City also determined the responsible leaders and departments for various tasks, exercised management by project and incorporated them into the scope of evaluation under the annual goal responsibility system.

4.3.4 The Pilot Comprehensive Reform of Market-Oriented Factor Allocation in Haining City

In September, 2013, the People's Government of Zhejiang Province approved the *Master Plan for the Pilot Comprehensive Reform of Market-oriented Factor Allocation in Haining City*; in November, 2013, the pilot comprehensive reform of market-oriented factor allocation in Haining City was launched in an all-round way, with a view to gradually removing the institutional obstacles to factor allocation by proceeding from reforming the allocation of such factors as land, energy, finance and scientific and technological talents.

1. Content of pilot work

The priorities of pilot work are as follows: giving scope to the roles of the market and the government, resulting in a mechanism of linking factor allocation with enterprise quality and performance, thus enabling the market to play the decisive role in resource and factor allocation, ensuring that enterprises transform themselves from factor-driven development to innovation-driven development, and the government shifts its management focus to actively delivering benefits and strengthening services, so that various factors are allocated in a rational, efficient and high-quality way, and economic structural adjustments and industrial transformation and upgrading are promoted. Haining's goals are as follows: the investment intensity per mu of newly increased industrial land in the whole city will increase by 45% in 2017 over 2012, the tax per mu from the industrial enterprises above the designated size will rise by 45%, the energy consumption per unit of GDP will decrease by 15%, the water consumption per 10,000-yuan industrial added value will decline by 30%.

2. Main measures and achievements

(1) Making the rules governing market operation, giving play to the role of the "visible hand"—the government. First, steps are taken to establish an open and impartial mechanism for the comprehensive evaluation of the yield per mu. For the industrial enterprises above the designated size, the following six indicators have been developed: tax per mu; sales per mu; industrial added value per mu; industrial added value per unit of energy consumption; industrial added value per unit of COD emission; overall labor productivity. For the industrial enterprises below the designated size, the following three indicators have been developed: tax per mu; sales per mu; industrial added value per unit of energy consumption; a comprehensive score is given to the industrial enterprises with land above 3 mu in the whole city, and then classification and ranking are conducted by four main industries including textile, leather, mechanical electronic manufacturing and others; enterprises from various industries are classified into A (development and upgrading type), B (rectification and upgrading type) and C (backwardness and phaseout type). At the same time, a dynamic ranking system is established; comprehensive evaluation and ranking are conducted and the result is released each year. Second, actions are taken to establish a mechanism

for classified implementation of policies for managing factor prices. In order to better reflect the scarcity of resources and the costs for ecological environmental damage, enterprises from Categories A, B and C are imposed with differentiated policies for electricity prices, water prices, urban land use tax, emission rights trading prices and energy trading prices, and other differentiated management measures. Third, an exit incentive mechanism for backward production capacity is established. A relevant incentive policy is developed to encourage shutdown, shift and phaseout of inefficient and backward production capacity; policy incentive support is provided for the substantive actions in dealing with backward production capacity, including vacation of land, voluntary trading of land, merger and acquisition, phaseout and shutdown, improvement and renovation; efforts are made to guide the good use of the resources at hand and optimized allocation of resources. As of late 2013, in the whole city, the tax per mu from the industrial enterprises above the designated size increased by 11.78%, the sales per mu grew by 9.6%, 57 inefficiently used land lots covering an area of 1418 mu were vacated.[20]

(2) Building market trading platforms, actively giving play to the role of the "invisible hand"—the market. First, a factor trading market has been established. Zhejiang Jiangnan Factor Trading Co., Ltd. was established; it is mainly responsible for undertaking the primary and secondary market trading of land, emission rights, energy and other scarce resources; it is striving to become an integrated factor trading platform which keeps a foothold on the local level and stimulates the development of the surrounding areas. Second, human resource agglomeration zones have been introduced. Shanghai BRIDGE Talent Service Co., Ltd. has been successfully introduced to cooperate in building the provincial Huzhe Human Resources Service Industry Park which is mainly engaged in industrial agglomeration, service expansion, business incubation and market cultivation, and provides industrialized, information-based, well-regulated and international human resource services to boost economic development. Third, a technology factor market has been set up. Xiamen Zhongkai Information Co., Ltd. has been introduced as the operator for jointly building an online technology trading platform covering information display, achievement evaluation, online matchmaking, technology trading, and broker cultivation. Innovations have been made to enable deep cooperation between institutions (universities) and localities to jointly build a mechanism for industry-university-research cooperation; actions are being taken to more quickly build such innovation platforms as the Technology Transfer Center of the International Campus of Zhejiang University, the Caohejing Science and Technology Oasis and the Zhongke Chuangzhi Industry Park.

(3) Expanding the supporting systems to support reform, improving the factor reform guarantee mechanism. First, efforts have been made to make the government more rapidly delegate powers to the market, push ahead with efficient administrative examination and approval. The following pilot reform has

[20]http://www.jxstats.gov.cn.

been comprehensively promoted: The enterprise investment projects outside the catalogue of examination and approval are no longer subject to examination and approval. The negative list of access to industrial enterprise investment projects has been developed so that the industrial projects outside the negative list have been fully put under the commitment filing system, and the practice through which the construction is not allowed unless approval is obtained has been changed to the practice by which construction is first performed and then inspection is conducted. Steps have been taken to fully clear and reduce the items subject to examination and approval; examination and approval before construction has been changed to operational and post-operational overseeing. Measures have been adopted to expand the mechanism for completing the procedures relating to investment projects through six stages in the whole process. The reform of the commercial registration system has been carried out; the practice of applying for and obtaining a business license before relevant permits are obtained has been adopted in 35 industries. Second, innovations have been made in the guarantee of the local financial factor to vitalize private capital. Differentiated credit policies have been adopted and differentiated insurance services have been provided for enterprises in Categories A, B and C. In 2013, a market-oriented private financing management center, which is managed like a company and in which the government participates, was put into operation, and the Zhejiang Equity Exchange set up a sub-center in Haining. Third, a mechanism for gathering innovative, scientific and technological talents has been established; a good investment environment has been created. Innovative enterprises have united as one to apply for establishing provincial-level enterprise research institutes. Actions have been taken to speed up the construction of innovation platforms including the Caohejing Science and Technology Oasis, the Zhongke Chuangzhi Industry Park, the Haining Park in the Science Park of Shanghai University of Engineering Science; moves have been taken to build a mechanism for joint construction, by various capital providers, of major science and technology platforms including the Leather Research Institute and the Zhongfang Warp Knitting Technology Research Institute.

4.4 The Utilization of Institutional and Mechanism Advantages

4.4.1 Invigorating the State-Owned Economy

Since the State-owned Assets Supervision and Administration Commission of Zhejiang Province was established in 2004, Zhejiang Province has pushed forward the reform of state-owned enterprises according to the principle of ensuring that those which should become strong are made strong, those which should be retained are retained and those which should be phased out are phased out; this reform has delivered remarkable results. In 2004, the Zhejiang Provincial Party Committee and the Provincial Government put forward the above principle and explicitly focused the reform of state-owned enterprises on diversifying property rights.[21]

1. Thoughts and ideas of invigorating the state-owned economy

When serving as the Secretary of the Zhejiang Provincial Party Committee, Comrade Xi Jinping put forward the following thoughts and ideas about invigorating the state-owned economy: first, fully finishing the reform of state-owned and urban collective enterprises which focuses on reforming the property rights system and transforming employees' labor relations; improving the mechanism of distribution incentives within enterprises; strengthening enterprise management; further improving the corporate governance structure; establishing the modern enterprise systems. Second, building and improving a state-owned assets administration system under which powers are commensurate with obligations and responsibilities at the provincial and municipal levels, and assets administration is combined with the administration of personnel and affairs. Third, quickening strategic adjustment in the layout of the state-owned economy, making the state-owned economy better and stronger. Combining the reform of state-owned enterprises with actions designed to promote enterprise integration and increase the vitality of enterprises; providing classified guidance for the existing state-owned enterprises, developing and growing a number of state-owned enterprises, optimizing and organizing a group of state-owned enterprises, shutting down and phasing out some state-owned enterprises. More rapidly cultivating a number of large internationally competitive enterprises and conglomerates in the key fields and advantageous industries. Fourth, boldly exploring various ways of realizing a state-owned economy. Providing foreign and private capital with more access, vigorously developing the mixed ownership economy.[22]

According to the guiding principles adopted in the 16th CPC National Congress and the Third Plenary Session of the 16th Central Committee of the Communist Party of China, in light of Zhejiang's reality, in 2004, the Zhejiang Provincial Party Committee and the Provincial Government put forward the main goals for reforming the provincial state-owned enterprises: With about three years of great efforts, the provincial state-owned enterprises will basically complete a new round of reform focusing on investor diversification, and improvement will be made in the mechanism, under which the state-owned capital advances in some areas while retreating in other areas, rationally flows; continued efforts will be made to adjust and optimize the layout and structure of the state-owned economy; measures will be adopted to stimulate the state-owned assets to gather in key areas and advantageous enterprises. Moves will be taken to more rapidly establish modern enterprise systems, boost innovations in enterprise systems and mechanisms, and make new progress in improving the

[21] With the Reform under the Specified Principle, Zhejiang's State-owned Enterprises Increased State-owned Assets by More Than One Trillion Yuan within a Decade, Xinhuanet, 2014-07-14, http://financeifeng.com/a/20140714/12716653_0.shtml.

[22] Xi Jinping, Remaining Steadfast on Two Fronts, Creating New Advantages for Zhejiang in Developing the Economy with Different Types of Ownership, *Economic Times*, March 15, 2003.

corporate governance structure and transforming the enterprise operational mechanism; steps will be taken to basically establish a state-owned assets supervision and administration system under which powers are commensurate with obligations and responsibilities, and assets administration is combined with the administration of personnel and affairs. With the above requirements and goals, the following guidance of the work must be upheld.

(1) Giving prominence to development, allowing full play to the leading role of the state-owned economy. Asset reorganization and structural adjustment are carried out to further optimize the layout and structure of the state-owned assets, cultivate a number of large internationally competitive enterprises and conglomerates, improve the overall quality of the provincial state-owned enterprises, preserve and increase the value of the state-owned assets, better reflect and give scope to the leading role of the state-owned economy. This is the starting point and goal of reforming the provincial state-owned enterprises and also represents the important signs for measuring the success in the reform of the provincial state-owned enterprises. Individual enterprises should, according to the requirements of the modern enterprise systems, actively carry out well-regulated issuance under the joint-stock system to diversify the property rights, transform the enterprise operational mechanism to invigorate enterprises, enhance their overall strength and market competitiveness. The provincial state-owned enterprises and state-owned assets, as a whole, should push forward strategic adjustment in the layout and structure of the state-owned assets, concentrate the state-owned assets in key areas and advantageous enterprises, further improve the overall competitiveness, influence and driving effect of the provincial state-owned enterprises.
(2) Taking actions in an active and sound way, continuously exploring new ways of reforming the provincial state-owned enterprises. Since reform and opening up, rapid progress has been made in the reform of the state-owned enterprises in Zhejiang Province, making the province lead the country in this regard and creating much successful experience. However, the reform of Zhejiang's provincial state-owned enterprises is currently at a crucial stage—after many years of unremitting reforms and explorations, the problems for which it is easy to find solutions have been basically solved, while all the remaining problems are the key unavoidable difficult problems. In order to solve these problems, it is essential to seek the truth and be pragmatic, bold to explore, focus on key areas in reform, overcome the institutional bottlenecks, make breakthroughs in the diversification of property rights owners, corporate governance structure and the state-owned assets administration system, earnestly develop the mixed ownership economy and proactively explore various effective ways for realizing public ownership.
(3) Upholding classified guidance, adopting various effective means of reforming. The conditions of the provincial state-owned enterprises are greatly different; the enterprise groups under provincially authorized operation vary in industrial characteristics, enterprise scale, asset quality and operating performance.

Therefore, the reform must be based on the following principle: starting with the conditions of the enterprise, following the classified guidance, adopting different ways of reform to different types of enterprises, refraining from indiscriminately imposing a uniform approach and a single mode, proceeding from the reality to actively explore and practice. Any means adopted should be beneficial to transforming the operational mechanism, building the modern enterprise systems, optimizing the layout and structure of the state-owned economy, preserving and increasing the value of the state-owned assets and promoting Zhejiang's development.

(4) Putting the people first, safeguarding the rights and interests of workers. This is the fundamental principle for pushing forward the reform of the provincial state-owned enterprises and also fully embodies the philosophy of governing for the people. It is necessary to firmly uphold the line of thought that puts the people first, fully respects the democratic rights of workers, ensures that a reform plan is deliberated by the congress of workers and staff, and that a worker resettlement plan is adopted by the congress of workers and staff, as well as one that makes reform achievements shared by workers. The legitimate interests of workers are put first; full considerations are given to the bearing capacity of workers; actions should be taken to address the issues concerning the basic life and social security of the workers and retirees from the reformed enterprises, transformation of workers' identity and employment of workers.

(5) Keeping a well-regulated operation to strictly prevent the loss of state-owned assets. China has issued the *Opinions on Regularizing the Reform of the State-owned Enterprises* and the *Interim Administrative Measures for the Transfer of State-owned Property Rights of Enterprises.* Both documents specify the explicit provisions for main links in the reform of the state-owned enterprises and the transfer of state-owned property rights. In specific operations, in order to press ahead with reform, some necessary supporting policies should be made and implemented, but it is imperative to effectively prevent the loss of the state-owned assets. The following three key areas must be valued: First, be well-regulated in the whole process; second, be open in an all-round way; third, be subject to supervision by the whole society.

2. Main measures and achievements[23]

(1) Intensifying enterprise reform, constantly rationalizing the systems and mechanisms for enterprise development. First, actions have been taken to stimulate the provincial enterprises to engage in strategic cooperation with the enterprises managed by the Central Government, private enterprises and overseas enterprises, energetically push forward shareholding reform and listing; as of 2013, there were 9 listed holding companies. Second, the provincial enterprises have been reorganized and integrated; 3 provincial foreign trade groups have been reorganized to establish the International Business Group; the Energy Group

[23]Data come from the *Zhejiang Statistical Yearbook 2013.*

has reorganized into the Water Resources & Hydropower Group. Third, the levels of enterprise management have been gradually reduced, with the number of management levels at provincial enterprises decreased to be less than 4; the corporate governance structure has been improved; actions have been taken to actively promote the construction of the board of directors and the board of supervisors; the worker director and supervisor system has been built; 4 boards of supervisors externally dispatched to provincial enterprises have been set up; all enterprises except joint ventures have been basically covered by externally dispatched boards of supervisors.

(2) Adjusting and optimizing the industrial structure, shaping the pattern of the development of accelerated transformation. First, development is pursued by focusing on the main businesses. The main businesses of provincial enterprises have been fully determined, with a focus on cultivating six main advantageous industries, including energy, transportation, commerce and trade, iron and steel, chemicals, construction. The Double-100-Billion Project has been vigorously implemented. Three groups engaged in produce, transport and energy have a scale of operations or assets above 100 billion yuan; 8 groups have seen both assets and revenue exceeding 10 billion yuan; 7 provincial enterprises have been listed among the top 500 enterprises of China. Third, the emerging industrial fields have been constantly expanded; new growth points, including the marine economy and finance, have been cultivated. The opinions on integration of industry and finance have been issued; financial service has been actively cultivated.

(3) Innovating the developmental mode, continually improving the quality and efficiency of enterprise operations. First, active innovations have been made in the control system. Efforts have been made to reinforce the group control system, stimulate enterprises to exercise total budget management, centralized management of funds and total cost management, reduce the financial, production and management costs of enterprises. Second, efforts have been concentrated in innovating the development platforms. Enterprises have been guided to enhance strategic cooperation with the enterprises managed by the Central Government, local governments and provincial enterprises; arrangements have been made to successfully hold the signing ceremony for the memorandum of strategic cooperation between the State-owned Assets Supervision and Administration Commission under the State Council and the People's Government of Zhejiang Province, and the meeting on discussing cooperation affairs between Zhejiang and the enterprises managed by the Central Government. Third, actions have been taken to promote innovation in the business model. Active measures have been taken to encourage commercial and trade service enterprises involving produce, international trade and commerce to innovate new forms of operation. Fourth, technical innovations have been solidly promoted.

(4) Improving the supervisory service mode, making continuous improvement in the supervisory system of service development. First, the supervisory service mode has been further improved. Innovations have been made in the supervisory system, policy and mode for prompting enterprises to reform and develop; the

efficiency of supervising and serving enterprises has been improved. Second, the institutional system of supervision has been further improved. More than 100 systems and normative documents concerning the supervision of state-owned assets have been issued, with a focus on establishing and improving the national supervisory system represented by 4 main reporting systems and 9 operational flows. Third, the supervisory system has been further improved. The reform of the county-level state-owned assets supervisory system is conducted in a strong atmosphere and presents unique features.

(5) Performing three major responsibilities, constantly improving the enterprises' social image. First, contributions have been made to national and local finance. In the past five years, the total state-owned assets of provincial enterprises increased by 52.35 billion yuan, the accumulated profits have totaled 83.93 billion yuan, the total tax amount has reached 75.55 billion yuan. Second, market supply and production orders have been guaranteed. The Energy Group has sought coal and gas resources to guarantee power supply for the whole province; the Salt Industrial Group has properly addressed the salt panic to maintain the market supply and price stability of the products vital to the people's livelihood. Third, actions have been taken to actively support the construction of major projects and the projects relating to the people's livelihood. The enterprises engaged in transportation, energy, railways and Xiaoshan Airport have greatly pushed forward the construction of infrastructures and have played the leading role in improving the energy safeguard network and integrated transportation network.

4.4.2 Achieving a New Leap in the Private Economy

The private economy is an important part of the socialist market economy. With a more prominent position and role in Zhejiang Province, the private economy has become Zhejiang Province's advantage and source of vitality.

1. The basic course of achieving the new leap in the private economy

The year 2003 was an important period for the economic development of Zhejiang Province. In 2003, Zhejiang Province suffered the SARS epidemic, persistent high temperature and drought, a shortage of electric power and energy, but its economy grew by 14.7% over the previous year, so brilliant performance was delivered: the economy has grown annually by an average 13.1% since the reform and opening up. The highly vibrant non-governmental forces are the magic weapons for Zhejiang's sustained and rapid development. In 2003, the added value from the non-public sectors of the economy in Zhejiang Province accounted for 59.5% of the GDP. In 2004, Zhejiang Province held a large high-level working conference on the private economy, in which the *Several Opinions on Promoting a New Leap in the Private Economy* was issued. Based on the above opinions, local Party Committees and governments at various levels in Zhejiang Province introduced more concrete, pragmatic and operable policy measures, and did away with various unfair policies to make sure that the individual private economy can fully enjoy national treatment and thrive in a loose environment. In the working conference on the private economy held in 2004, Xi Jinping, then Secretary of the Zhejiang Provincial Party Committee, vowed to further emancipate the mind, be bold in practice, speed up innovation in systems, science and technology, management, fully increase the scientific, technological, intensive and international levels and the scale of the private economy, incessantly enhance the overall strength and international competitiveness of the private economy, maintain the leading position of Zhejiang's development of the private economy in the country. He stressed, "in order to achieve a new leap in the private economy, it is necessary to press ahead with five transformations and make five improvements (as shown in the part "Introduction" in this book). It is essential to strengthen leadership over the development of the private economy, give high priority to achieving a new leap in the private economy in the whole work, optimize the environment, improve management and intensify Party building, and break new ground in Zhejiang's development of the private economy.

On February 25, 2005, the State Council officially issued *Several Opinions on Encouraging, Supporting and Guiding the Development of the Non-public Sectors of the Economy Including the Individual Private Sector*; this shows that the Central Government started to more vigorously support the development of the private economy. The People's Government of Zhejiang Province refined the above opinions and issued the *Implementation Opinions on Encouraging, Supporting and Guiding the Development of the Non-public Sectors of the Economy Including the Individual Private Sector*; this fully reflects the stance that the private capital can get access to all the industries and areas to which access is not explicitly prohibited by laws and regulations. In 2006, the Zhejiang Provincial Party Committee and the Provincial Government held the provincial conference on independent innovation and issued *Several Opinions on Accelerating the Improvement of the Independent Innovation Capability and Building an Innovative Province and a Scientifically and Technologically Strong Province*, which specially stipulates that the actual income tax payable in the current year is deducted by 150% of the technology development expense actually incurred by enterprises in the current year so as to stimulate enterprises to increase capital input in research and development.

Against the general background of accelerated economic globalization, Zhejiang's private economy still maintained rapid development; however, since 2008, with the impact of the global financial crisis, the structural and quality-related contradictions have become increasingly acute in Zhejiang's private economy. At this stage, the development of Zhejiang's private enterprises mainly presented the following characteristics: First, the areas in which private enterprises operated have continued to increase; as the Central Government introduced relevant policy to provide private enterprises with equal access to the market, private enterprises have gradually entered some traditional monopolized industries such as telecommunication and oil, while previously, private enterprises were mainly present in the highly competitive industries. Second, private enterprises have paid more attention to enterprise social responsibilities, while in the past, private enterprises merely focused on seeking profits. During enterprise development, Zhejiang's private enterprises have gradually realized the social responsibilities of private enterprises at the following three levels: obligation, responsibility and morality. Third, they have stressed harmony; they have attached greater importance to social resources, ecological environment and workers' rights and interests and have been committed to building harmonious enterprises and a harmonious society. Fourth, their basic capability for making independent innovation has significantly improved; some conditions and comparative advantages for making breakthroughs by enhancing the independent innovation capability have started to take shape: a technical innovation system with enterprises as the main body and relying on the institutions of higher learning and research institutions has gradually taken shape; the enterprises above the designated size have become the leading forces in Zhejiang's technical innovation; a number of knowledge and talent-intensive private technology enterprises have emerged. Fifth, Zhejiang's private enterprises have utilized the resources from both domestic and foreign markets, boldly carried out the developmental strategy of "going out of Zhejiang to develop Zhejiang" and "going global" to make overseas investments, thus shaping a new pattern of two-way interaction between "going global" and "bringing in" and benign development.

In early 2011, the Zhejiang Provincial Party Committee and the Provincial Government held the provincial 10,000-people conference on the private economy. With a focus on the topic of unswervingly supporting the development of the private economy and firmly pushing forward the transformation and upgrading of private enterprises, the conference scientifically charted a blueprint for a new round of development of the private economy. The Zhejiang Provincial Party Committee and the Provincial Government vowed to increase policy support, remove the institutional obstacles to the development of the private economy to give play to the guiding and supporting role of fiscal and tax policies, build an integrated local financial support system and introduce other measures to promote new development of Zhejiang's private economy.

In 2013, the Fourth Plenary Session of the 13th Provincial Party Committee adopted the *Decision of the Zhejiang Provincial Party Committee on Carefully Studying and Implementing the Guiding Principles Adopted in the Third Plenary Session of the 18th Central Committee of the Communist Party of China and Comprehensively Intensifying the Reform to Create New Advantages in Systems and Mechanisms*; as stressed in the Session, private capital is ample, the private economy is developed, there are many small and medium-sized enterprises, the group of Zhejiang merchants is huge; all these are the outstanding advantages of Zhejiang Province; it is essential to, to the greatest extent, activate the private forces by intensifying the reform to promote the private economy to achieve a new leap. It is necessary to act unswervingly on two fronts, and actively develop the mixed ownership economy amidst the reform of state-owned enterprises to arouse the developmental vitality and creativity of the private economy, ensure that the economic sectors under various types of ownership can utilize production factors on an equal footing according to laws, openly, fairly and impartially participate in market competition and equally enjoy legal protection.

2. Achievements in the development of the private economy[24]

The achievements made in the development of Zhejiang's private economy can be summarized as follows.

(1) The group was huge. In 2003, the registered capital per private enterprise in Zhejiang Province was 1.15 million yuan; in 2013, that figure reached 3,085,000 million yuan, up nearly two times. There were more than 11 million Zhejiang merchants, including 1.5 million, 6 million and 3.5 million Zhejiang merchants who started businesses overseas, in China's other provinces and Zhejiang Province, respectively. The total wealth created by 7.5 million Zhejiang merchants making investments and doing business overseas, in China's other provinces and Zhejiang Province was similar to Zhejiang's annual GDP, equivalent to the creation of another Zhejiang in foreign countries and China's other provinces. More than 6 million Zhejiang merchants doing business and running enterprises in various parts of the country established more than 260,000 enterprises, more than 2000 specialized markets and 373 development parks, with the planned investment parks covering an area of 906,000 mu. The total investments made by Zhejiang merchants nationwide exceeded 3 trillion yuan, there were more than 3000 projects above 100 million yuan and more than 500 projects above one billion; the accumulated tax paid to local authorities exceeded 150 billion yuan, and they employed more than 14 million people.
(2) The growth rate was high. As of late 2013, there were 3,779,000 main market players in Zhejiang Province, up 9.25%. There were 1,108,000 enterprises of record, up 19.34%; 1,078,000 domestic enterprises, up 19.88%, with a total registered capital of 5 trillion yuan, up 18%; 2,609,000 individual businesses, up 5.37%, with a fund amount of 166 billion yuan, up 16.42%; 2492 enterprise groups, up 7.55%.
(3) The enterprise scale was large. A total of 139 Zhejiang enterprises were included in the list of the "500 Top National Private Enterprises" released by the All-China Federation of Industry and Commerce in August, 2013, ranking Zhejiang No. 1 nationwide for 15 consecutive years. In 2013, there were 823 private enterprises with an operating revenue above 500 million yuan in Zhejiang Province, including 5 enterprises above 50 billion yuan, 94 above 10 billion yuan, 202 above 5 billion yuan and 557 above 1 billion yuan; the scale of private enterprises was far ahead nationwide.
(4) The economic contributions were enormous. In 2013, the private economy contributed more than 60% of the taxes, 70% of the GDP, more than 80% of foreign trade exports and more than 90% of the new jobs in Zhejiang Province. There were 258 private enterprises with a total tax payment above 100 million yuan, including 163 enterprises above 200 million yuan, 63 above 500 million yuan, 25 above 1 billion yuan, 7 above 1.5 billion yuan and 3 above 3 billion yuan. In particular, the Geely Group and the Wahaha Group annually paid taxes reaching 8587 million yuan and 5876 million yuan, respectively, showing tremen-

[24] *Zhejiang Statistical Yearbook* over the years.

dous contributions. In Zhejiang Province, there were 82 private enterprises with 10,000 employees, including 41 enterprises with more than 20,000 employees, 22 with more than 30,000 employees, 13 with more than 40,000 employees and 7 with more than 50,000 employees, making important contributions to solving the problem of employment.

4.5 Summary and Outlook

There are contradictions between the government and the market. In many areas, an active market is often accompanied by the weakening role of the government, while the government plays its role often at the price of the contraction of market functions. However, in Zhejiang Province, an active market does not contradict the government, they have complemented each other's advantages.

Zhejiang Province has better dealt with the relations between the government and the market to vigorously promote a market-oriented reform of the economy, so Zhejiang Province has gained the institutional and mechanism advantages for developing first. In the future, Zhejiang Province will intensify the reform of its economic system to push forward the transformation of the economic developmental mode, so as to achieve the economic and social development goals set in the 18th CPC National Congress; this calls for respecting the law of the market, better giving scope to the government's role and further properly handling the relations between the government and the market. At present, the breadth of reforms is unprecedented, so reforms must coordinate with each other, more attention should be paid to carrying out reforms in a systematic, coordinated, associated and interactive way, and the supporting efforts, local and full coordination should be made among reforms at the upper and lower levels, so that the reform policies can deliver the best results. As there are unprecedented difficulties in reform, planning and rolling implementation require supporting efforts. It is necessary to overcome some reform difficulties, and make a raft of effective achievements for popularization; actions should be taken to further expand reform hotspots and thus make substantive progress; continued efforts should be made to push forward a number of pilot reforms and actively respond to the economic and social developmental needs. It is necessary to promote a number of pilot reforms in due time, and initiate in advance the study of various reform plans; with respect to the reforms which urgently need to be carried out but whose conditions are not mature, further study should be conducted and a relevant reform plan should be developed as soon as possible. As the delegation of powers to the lower levels is unprecedented, the supporting efforts are necessary for accelerating the delegation of powers to the lower levels and strengthening supervision.

It is essential to continue to intensify the reform involving the market-oriented allocation of factors, and ensure that resources and factors are allocated in a rational, high-quality, legal and efficient way through market competition. Under the principle of being market-led and policy-guided, efforts are being made to build a 1 + X factor allocation platform—one factor trading center, with a property rights exchange market under market-oriented operations, a human resources market and a technology market—to enhance the efficiency of factor allocation in an integrated way, refine and improve the system for comprehensive evaluation of the yield per mu; intensify the implementation of differentiated prices to further strengthen the role of selecting the superior and eliminating the inferior.

Explorations should be made to establish a system for evaluating the effectiveness of pilot reforms. The third party should be introduced to objectively evaluate the pilot reforms. It is necessary to build a system for summarizing and popularizing the experience from pilot reforms to generate a number of characteristic reform modes which can be duplicated and popularized, so as to stimulate extensive reforms. Actions should be taken to encourage other areas to learn and draw upon the reform measures adopted in pilot areas, encourage pilot reform areas to undertake and superimpose reform matters on each other. It is necessary to establish a joint meeting system for pilot reforms in order to solve major problems in pilot reforms in a coordinated way; moreover, a reform information sharing mechanism should be built to enhance communication concerning pilot work.

It is necessary to further clarify the boundary between the government and the market. In the socialist market economy, the government and the market perform different functions and work in different fields. The market enjoys unique advantages in information transmission and benefit motivation, thus the foundation for economic resource allocation in the micro fields is the market. The government is responsible for providing different main market players with a fair and orderly market environment. The relations between the government and the market should be constantly adjusted and improved; such relations are not eternally unchanged and vary with time, location and conditions. The government and the market should coordinate with each other to form an optimal combination; in the socialist market economy, it is necessary to give full play to the role of the market mechanism in effectively allocating resources and improving economic performance, and fully consider social equity to prevent an excessive wealth gap, while the latter cannot be achieved by the market itself and calls for macro regulation and overall arrangement by the government. Only when the relations between the government and the market are properly handled to make them work together can a high rate of economic development and efficiency, social equity and equality be maintained and can the ultimate goal of achieving common socialist prosperity be realized.

Chapter 5
Pursuing Open Development and Establishing a New System of an Open Economy

Jianfeng Xu

Zhejiang is an economically developed province in the southeastern coastal area. The opening of Zhejiang's economy includes not only opening to the outside world (international opening), but also opening to the domestic market (inter-regional opening). As Zhejiang's economy enjoys a relatively high degree of marketization, Zhejiang's economy is closer to an open economy. Since the reform and opening up, great progress has been made in Zhejiang's foreign trade and introduction of foreign direct investment. In particular, since the beginning of the 21st century, the Zhejiang Provincial Party Committee and the Provincial Government have proceeded from Zhejiang's actual conditions and have followed the developmental trend of the world economy to "go out of Zhejiang to develop Zhejiang" so as to continuously increase the level of Zhejiang's open economy. The development of Zhejiang's open economy is the best practice of the Chinese dream of a large open country.

5.1 The Formation and Development of the Philosophy of "Going Out of Zhejiang to Develop Zhejiang"

In the mid-1990s, with the development of the private economy and the rise of industrial clusters, the international competitiveness of Zhejiang's products was constantly enhanced, Zhejiang's export trade greatly developed. In particular, after China's accession to the WTO in 1999, Zhejiang's export trade grew rapidly in successive years, Zhejiang ranked No. 1 nationwide in export surplus; foreign investments in Zhejiang Province maintained a momentum of rapid growth. An open economy has become the strong support and driving force for Zhejiang's overall economic and social development. However, Zhejiang's open economy has been subject to many threats and challenges: the prices of such factors as land resources, labor and capital

J. Xu (✉)
Zhejiang Academy of Social Sciences, Hangzhou, China

C. Pei and J. Xu (eds.), *Chinese Dream and Practice in Zhejiang – Economy*,
Research Series on the Chinese Dream and China's Development Path,
https://doi.org/10.1007/978-981-13-7484-5_5

continue to rise; Zhejiang's export products are mainly labor-intensive textiles and other light industrial products, which are subject to enormous competition pressure from the products made in China, developing countries and territories; Zhejiang's export products prevail through low prices and large quantities, the economic benefits are low; Zhejiang's external investments mainly come from Hong Kong, Taiwan and overseas Chinese, the scale is relatively small, the industrial technical level is not high, enterprises have less connection with local private capital. How to push forward the continued growth of Zhejiang's import and export trade, inter-regional trade and the absorbed foreign capital, inter-regional and international economic cooperation, and stimulate Zhejiang's economic transformation and development has become a new major issue.

5.1.1 From "Bringing in, Going Global" to "Going Out of Zhejiang to Develop Zhejiang"

Given the new opportunities and new problems in Zhejiang's open economy, the Zhejiang Provincial Party Committee and the Provincial Government have profoundly realized that only when the opening to the domestic market and the outside world is increased and the openness is improved in an all-round way can Zhejiang's enterprises withstand tests, gain more vitality and become more competitive on the international market, and can Zhejiang's economy maintain a healthy and sustained development. In September, 2001, the People's Government of Zhejiang Province decided to more rapidly implement the strategy of "going global". It vowed to actively encourage and support Zhejiang's advantageous industries and specialized markets to develop overseas while continuing to earnestly attract foreign direct investments, so as to make Zhejiang Province more fully utilize both domestic and foreign markets and resources. This is the objective need of enterprise development and also an important strategy developed by the Zhejiang Provincial Party Committee and the Provincial Government in light of the situation.

In December, 2002, the Zhejiang Provincial Department of Finance and the Zhejiang Provincial Department of Foreign Trade and Economic Cooperation jointly issued the *Circular Concerning Several Opinions on the Administration of the Use of Special Funds for Implementing the Strategy of "Going Global"*, establishing the special fund for "going global" with a view to providing financial subsidies and incentives to Zhejiang's enterprises establishing overseas the specialized commodity markets, production enterprises and R&D centers. The Zhejiang Provincial Department of Foreign Trade and Economic Cooperation and the Zhejiang Provincial Administration of Foreign Exchange jointly issued the *Administrative Measures of Zhejiang Province for Examination and Approval of the Establishment of Overseas Enterprises and Institutions (Trial)*; at the same time, the examination and approval power over some items was delegated to the foreign trade and economic departments of cities (the counties whose powers had been expanded) so as to mobilize the initiative of local authorities to stimulate enterprises to "go global".

With the implementation of the strategy of "going global", Zhejiang's enterprises have achieved leapfrog development in keeping in line with the international market. Zhejiang's enterprises have gradually obtained the brands, technologies and markets of foreign enterprises by establishing overseas production bases, R&D centers, carrying out overseas mergers and acquisitions and overseas listings and in other new ways, thus rapidly expanding their market share and entering new markets. For such markets as Zhejiang's China Commodity City, Zhejiang has also set up submarkets in Latin America, Europe and Africa, stimulating massive exportation of small commodities. Zhejiang's enterprises have gradually improved their capability for resisting risks and participating in international competition in the process of "going global". "Going global" has also driven the exportation of Zhejiang's commodities and has promoted foreign investment in Zhejiang, so it has played an active role in Zhejiang's foreign trade cooperation.

In early summer, 2003, a power shortage occurred throughout Zhejiang Province; in Wenzhou, Taizhou and other areas, as electric power was cut, factories had to frequently halt production, and many small enterprises had to buy diesel engines to generate electricity. This shows that the rigid constraint of resources on economic development was particularly salient in Zhejiang where metallic ore falls short, there is less kerosene energy, a large population and little land; resource and environmental constraints had become the bottlenecks for Zhejiang's economic development. At the same time, structural, organizations and factor contradictions loomed large in Zhejiang's economic development. In order to follow the requirements of the Scientific Outlook on Development, realize the call of the Zhejiang Provincial Party Committee and the Provincial Government for "doing solid work, staying ahead", participate in domestic and foreign economic and technical cooperation and competition within a wider scope in more areas at higher levels and seek new developmental spaces to maintain sustained, healthy and rapid economic development, "going out of Zhejiang to develop Zhejiang" has become the strategic choice for Zhejiang's economic development under the new historical conditions. Xi Jinping, then Secretary of the Zhejiang Provincial Party Committee, stressed that "going out of Zhejiang to develop Zhejiang" was the inevitable requirement for Zhejiang's economic and social development and also an overall awareness and political responsibility. "Going out of Zhejiang to develop Zhejiang" contributed to the nation's coordinated regional development, extended Zhejiang's industrial chain, promoted the gradient transfer of Zhejiang's industries, the rational flow and optimal allocation of resources and factors. In the 12th Party Congress of Zhejiang Province in 2011, he pointed out that we should adopt the line of thought of "going out of Zhejiang to develop Zhejiang" to expand developmental spaces and maintain the good development momentum. In the Second Plenary Session of the 12th Party Committee of Zhejiang Province, he emphasized, "in order to comprehensively push forward innovation and entrepreneurship, it is essential to fully utilize both domestic and foreign markets and resources." Therefore, "going out of Zhejiang to develop Zhejiang" has become an important part of the overall strategy of making the people rich by starting a business and of building a strong province through innovation, and it is also the strategic move for expanding new spaces for innovation and entrepreneurship throughout the province.

"Going out of Zhejiang to develop Zhejiang" is an improvement in the strategy of "bringing in and going global" under the new situation.

1. "Going out of Zhejiang to develop Zhejiang" aims at keeping a foothold in Zhejiang to develop Zhejiang

Since the reform and opening up, Zhejiang's economic development has been mainly driven by the local private economy and has been a kind of endogenous development. However, in an open economic system, endogenous development is not closed development, it should be combined with opening up and external expansion. Keeping a foothold in Zhejiang does not mean confining the development to Zhejiang Province; instead, it is necessary to actively integrate into the national and global economic systems, better utilize domestic and global markets, the resources outside the province and overseas resources to promote the rational flow and optimal allocation of resources and factors. This can help Zhejiang overcome the bottleneck constraints on the supply of advanced factors, including resources, the environment and technologies to enhance Zhejiang's industrial competitiveness, move forward with Zhejiang's economic transformation and upgrading, so that Zhejiang's economy can keep a foothold in Zhejiang to develop Zhejiang.

Therefore, with an effort to push ahead with the strategy of "going out of Zhejiang to develop Zhejiang", Zhejiang put forward the following requirements: (1) Participate in inter-regional and international competition to improve the local economy. (2) Interact and integrate with the enterprises outside the province and overseas enterprises to improve the local economy. (3) "Go global" to improve the local economy. Only when a cage is vacated can a bird be changed; only when development is achieved can contributions be made.

2. "Going out of Zhejiang to develop Zhejiang" covers both inter-regional opening and international opening

First, "going out of Zhejiang to develop Zhejiang" is designed to encourage Zhejiang merchants to go beyond Zhejiang and invest in the rest of the country, better utilize the nation's resources and factors to reduce production costs, enhance industrial competitiveness and the investment efficiency; it encourages Zhejiang to further engage in inter-regional trade, introduce more low-price intermediate goods from other provinces, process, manufacture and market them, and then deliver the finished products to various markets across the country, carry out extensive two-way inter-provincial trade, further optimize the structure of the commodities from Zhejiang, stimulate the adjustment and upgrading of Zhejiang's industrial structure.

Second, "going out of Zhejiang to develop Zhejiang" encourages Zhejiang merchants to go abroad, leverage their own advantages to develop markets, run factors, farms and mines, establish sales organizations and R&D centers in foreign countries; it encourages labor exportation and economic and technical cooperation with foreign countries. This aims at better utilizing global resources and advanced factors to cover the shortage of factors and resources in Zhejiang; integrating into the global industrial chain to further take full advantage of the overseas market; increasing the exportation of Zhejiang's products; upgrading Zhejiang's export commodities and improving their quality; more rapidly adjusting the structure of Zhejiang's export commodities. At the same time, this helps improve and further attract overseas enterprises to invest and develop in Zhejiang Province.

3. "Going out of Zhejiang to develop Zhejiang" aims at building a new system of open economy

Zhejiang's economic development in 30 years since the reform and opening up has been mainly based on the endogenous development of the local private economy, while import and export trade and introduction of foreign capital are the ways of promoting economic development. With growing inter-regional trade and overseas trade, inter-provincial investment and introduction of foreign capital, Zhejiang's economy has constantly integrated into the national economy and the global economy, so the original system of Zhejiang's economy must be greatly adjusted. "Going out of Zhejiang to develop Zhejiang" also aims at building an open economic system in Zhejiang Province.

In order to build an open economic system, it is essential to follow the principle of comparative advantages to allocate market elements, factors and resources worldwide, proactively utilize the resources, factors and markets outside the province and foreign countries; adopt the principle of comparative advantages to bring in, go global, go out of Zhejiang to develop Zhejiang, establish an open production system nationwide and worldwide so that Zhejiang's enterprises can participate in the global industrial chain.

5.1.2 Comprehensively Increasing the Level of Zhejiang's Open Economy

In the second half of 2008, the American subprime mortgage crisis became a financial crisis, exerting an impact on the global economy. The market demand tended to decline in the developed countries. At the same time, with the appreciation of the RMB against the main currencies, including the U.S. dollar, the prices of Zhejiang's commodities denominated in foreign currencies were on the increase; this also imposed restrictions on the price competitiveness of Zhejiang's export commodities. As from late 2008, Zhejiang's import and export trade and foreign direct investment were greatly affected, the import and export growth rate decreased from about 20% to a single digit; negative growth occurred in January. As Zhejiang's export trade accounted for more than 50% of the GDP, the decrease in the growth of export trade affected the steady growth of Zhejiang's economy.

Moreover, Zhejiang's per capita GDP exceeded USD 6000 in 2008. According to relevant research,[1] Zhejiang's economy entered the stage of developed industrialization—a period of transition from industrialization to a developed economy. According to the empirical research based on the economics theory and the development experience from Japan, South Korea and Taiwan, at this stage, the prices of factors and resources such as labor, land and energy will rise rapidly, the environmental protection pressure will increase, the currency will continuously appreciate, the gap among enterprises, among regions and among classes will widen, the economic growth rate will decline noticeably. All these aspects will restrict the growth of foreign trade, outward investment and labor exports. Zhejiang's economic development since 2008 has basically proved this characteristic.

In the new environment, increasing the breadth and depth of opening up, the level of the open economy has become the inherent requirement of Zhejiang's economic development at the new stage. In order to promote the rapid and sound development of Zhejiang's economy, it is essential to give play to the role of opening up, as a driving force in economic and social development; achieve an all-round increase in the level of open economy; fully take advantage of both domestic and foreign markets amidst economic globalization; really give scope to the fundamental role of the market in resource allocation to enable optimal allocation of resources, foster the new advantages of Zhejiang Province in participating in international cooperation and competition under the condition of economic globalization.

Therefore, the Zhejiang Provincial Party Committee and the Provincial Government vowed to continue putting into practice the strategy of "going out of Zhejiang to develop Zhejiang", fully increase the level of Zhejiang's open economy. It is necessary to increase the areas for opening up; optimize the structure of opening up; include regional opening up into the framework of global labor division and competition; take promoting independent innovation, industrial upgrading and regional coordinated development as important goals of participating in international labor division; fully leverage both domestic and foreign markets and resources to enhance the international competitiveness of Zhejiang's economy during integration into the international industrial division.

1. Building a new system of an open economy, increasing the level of opening up in an all-round way

Since 2009, Zhejiang Province has given full play to the role of four main national strategic measures to further increase the areas for opening up, innovate the opening up mode, optimize the opening up structure and improve the quality of opening up, so as to build a new system of open economy, fully increase the level of opening up. Emphasis has been placed on actively creating a strategic platform for fully utilizing both domestic and foreign resources.

2. Forging an opening up bond for coordinated development of both domestic and foreign markets

[1]Xu Jianfeng, Zhejiang's Economic Development at the Stage of Developed Industrialization, *Zhejiang Academic Journal*, 2010(1).

Economic opening up includes international opening up and inter-regional opening up. Zhejiang's economy is an economy with large-volume imports and exports—Zhejiang imports a great deal of resources and semi-finished products from foreign provinces, and massively exports finished products to foreign countries after processing and manufacturing them; this becomes the Triangular Mode of Zhejiang's economy. With the intensification of opening up, Zhejiang has strengthened the opening up bond for coordinated development of both domestic and foreign countries.

3. Promoting stable and balanced development of import and export trade

As the development of the trade in goods faced bottlenecks, the pressure on foreign trade exportation was mounting. Zhejiang has fully realized that it is necessary to speed up its structural adjustment to achieve sound and rapid development of foreign trade. First, actions were taken to accelerate the transformation of the foreign trade developmental mode, increase the exportation of the products with high added value and high technical content. Efforts were made to strengthen the coordination of trade and industrial policies, push forward the building of self-owned export brands and the construction of export bases and export quality safety demonstration zones, so as to form the export-related competitive advantages in technology, brand, quality and service. Steps were taken to earnestly develop new-type trade modes including cross-border e-commerce, market purchasing and foreign trade supply chain management. Second, it is necessary to more rapidly increase the scale of the exportation of trade in services, expand the outsourcing of services, especially the electronic information service industry, move faster to develop the trade in culture and promote the trade in technology, and gradually increase the proportion of the trade in services in its total amount of exports. Third, it is essential to improve the import trade support policy, further introduce advanced technologies and key equipment to promote the development of import trade.

4. Combining "bringing in" with "going global" better

"Bringing in" is one of the three ways of expanding effective investments, while "going global" is conducive to breaking through the bottlenecks in the resource and environmental capacity, vacating the cage to change birds; utilizing the high-quality factors including the market, capital, resources, talents, information and technologies obtained overseas to expand the economic developmental spaces for Zhejiang Province and grow and upgrade the local economy. First, actions were taken to boost the steady growth of foreign capital. The control over the conditions for access for foreign capital were relaxed; explorations were made to adopt a pre-establishment national treatment and the negative list management mode for foreign capital; an international, market-oriented foreign investment environment under the rule of law was built. Second, all favorable opportunities were taken to speed up efforts to "go global". Measures were taken to reform the overseas investment management mode, improve the outward investment service, and constantly increase the facilitation of overseas investments. An international marketing network was built so that Zhejiang's goods could be sold better to foreign countries through the self-owned marketing network. Actions were taken to develop contracted projects in foreign countries and to make projects more able to stimulate the export of complete equipment and technologies. It is necessary to cultivate local multinational corporations and enhance enterprises' capability for global resource allocation and international operations. Various players were actively guided and encouraged, in an innovative way, to go global in making greenfield investments, conducting cross-border mergers and acquisitions and engaging in technical cooperation. The construction of overseas economic and trade cooperation zones was accelerated, and partial production capacity was shifted in an orderly fashion to foreign countries. Explorations were made to establish the administrative measures and service system for individual overseas direct investment.

5. Making continuous innovations to the carriers of opening up

In a new round of opening up, it is necessary to further enhance the role of the opening up platforms of developmental zones to build a number of domestic first-class developmental zones. First, actions should be taken to expand the integration and upgrading of developmental zones, improve the mechanism for the evaluation of developmental zones; it is necessary to adopt various means, including classified guidance, comprehensive evaluation, rewarding the superior and punishing the inferior, special funds and statistical monitoring, to effectively stimulate developmental zones to forge ahead, build brands and improve performance; moreover, the upgrading of the provincial-level developmental zones needs to be supported where conditions permit; the construction of the strategic emerging industry demonstration bases and featured brand parks should be pushed forward to achieve innovative development. Second, efforts should be made to promote the construction of special customs supervision zones including comprehensive bonded zones, making them play a bigger role in Zhejiang's opening up. Third, steps should be taken to speed up the construction of the Zhejiang-Taiwan Economic and Trade Cooperation Zone and continuously innovate the cross-Strait economic and trade cooperation mode. Fourth, it is necessary to actively respond to the nation's call for and participate in building a high-standard global network of free trade zones, adapt to the new pattern of opening up inland and along the border; it is also necessary to integrate into the external economic corridor covering the eastern, central, western, northern and southern regions; it is necessary to proactively participate in pushing forward strategic arrangements including the construction of the Silk Road Economic Belt and the Marine Silk Road and thus seize the opportunity in China's new round of opening up.

6. Guiding Zhejiang merchants to invest in other provinces and return to Zhejiang Province

Given the characteristics of the new developmental stage, Zhejiang merchants should be guided to transfer the traditional manufacturing industry with declining comparative advantages to the central and western regions, so as to promote the economic development of the central and western regions while seeking new developmental spaces for Zhejiang's traditional industries and improving the investment efficiency.

Zhejiang's enterprises should be encouraged to set up R&D centers and marketing centers in Shanghai, Beijing and other areas, introduce more technologies and talents to Zhejiang and drive forward the exportation of Zhejiang's products. As Zhejiang merchants make outward investments, "vacating the cage to change birds" will be achieved to boost the improvement of the structure of Zhejiang's local production factor, and the transformation and upgrading of its industrial structure.

At the same time, intensified efforts should be made to enable Zhejiang merchants to return home. A number of well-targeted projects should be arranged and launched at the World Zhejiang Entrepreneurs Convention, investment fairs and product trade shows; play should be given to the roles of the federation of industry and commerce, Zhejiang's chambers of commerce outside the province and professional associations to guide Zhejiang merchants to return home in order to invest and make contributions.

Under the guidance of the developmental strategy and policy measures developed by the Zhejiang Provincial Party Committee and the Provincial Government, new progress has been made in Zhejiang's open economy. During the period 2001–2012, Zhejiang's exports grew annually by an average of 23.0%, ranking Zhejiang No. 3 nationwide, accounting for 1.22% of global exports; the trade in services developed rapidly, its proportion in foreign trade increased steadily; in particular, the trade in technology grew rapidly; foreign direct investments maintained stable growth; investment projects were continually optimized in terms of quality and industrial composition; Zhejiang merchants' investments in other provinces and foreign countries soared.

5.2 Adjustment and Optimization of the Structures of Foreign Trade and Foreign Capital

5.2.1 Transforming the Manner of Trade Development

1. Intensifying the reform of the foreign trade and economic system

(1) Further relaxing control over the power to engage in foreign trade exportation. As of late 2005, 25,000 enterprises (or individual households) in Zhejiang Province became entitled to engage in importation and exportation. A large number of private enterprises entered the foreign trade field, so more products with excellent quality at low prices from Zhejiang were exported to overseas markets, the volume of Zhejiang's general trade exports surged, and Zhejiang became a large province of general trade exportation and the province with the largest foreign trade surplus in China.

(2) Intensifying the reform of the property rights system involving state-owned foreign trade enterprises. Zhejiang's abundant capital and the advantages of the Yangtze River Delta in foreign capital agglomeration have been fully utilized, and various means, including private capital's equity participation, mergers and

acquisitions, employee stock ownership and engagement with foreign capital, have been adopted to diversify investors.

(3) Pushing forward the reform of foreign trade facilitation. Actions have been taken to continuously open up airports and seaports wider to the outside world, innovate the supervisory mechanism, simplify the arrangements relating to export rebates, inspection and quarantine, intensify the construction of the customs clearance and electronic customs declaration and clearance information system to improve the efficiency of customs clearance. Measures have been taken to promptly handle the export rebate procedures in full, expand the scale of the foreign trade development fund and export credit insurance, carry out pilot RMB settlement of cross-border trade.

(4) Promoting the construction of Zhejiang's bonded zones and free trade zones. On February 24, 2008, the State Council officially approved the establishment of the Ningbo Meishan Bonded Port Area. The Bonded Port Area represents the development and upgrading based on 15 bonded zones in China. Ningbo City of Zhejiang Province has proceeded from a high starting point to plan the development of a bonded port area, solidly pushed forward the construction of infrastructures and established an advanced bonded port area management mechanism with a view to turning the Ningbo Meishan Bonded Port Area into a new platform for Zhejiang's opening up. On March 14, 2011, the Zhoushan Archipelago New Area was officially approved. On September 29, 2012, the State Council approved the establishment of the Zhoushan Comprehensive Bonded Zone. In March, 2015, the establishment of the Hangzhou Cross-border E-commerce Comprehensive Pilot Area was officially approved by the State Council. The plan for and application filing relating to the Wenzhou Comprehensive Bonded Zone are underway.

2. Optimizing the structure of import and export trade

First, efforts have been made to diversify export markets. Actions have been taken to consolidate the developed economic markets, including the EU, North America and Japan, actively develop such emerging markets as those of Southeast Asia, the Middle East and Latin America, and maintain the advantages in general trade. Intensified efforts have been made to develop the markets in Taiwan and South Korea, improve the market structure of trade.

Second, the transformation and upgrading of the trade mode have been promoted. In response to the needs of economic development and the changes in overseas market demand, Zhejiang has constantly strengthened the advantages in general trade and the integration among agriculture, industry and trade, stimulated more production enterprises and commodities from Zhejiang to "go global", utilize overseas markets to drive production development forward. General trade has accounted for more than 80% of Zhejiang's total exports for a long time, providing strong support for the development of Zhejiang's manufacturing industry.

Third, the industrial structural upgrading has been combined with the upgrading of the trade structure. The export marketing mode characterized by large quantities and low prices has been changed and the differentiation strategy has been implemented, with more emphasis on winning the market through good quality. The strategy of revitalizing trade through science and technology and making trade strong through brands has been thoroughly carried out, actions have been taken to transform export products towards excellent quality performance and upgrade export commodities. Steps have been taken to more rapidly establish "Created in Zhejiang", "Intelligent Manufacturing in Zhejiang", "Channel in Zhejiang" and "Price in Zhejiang" so as to improve the economic performance of trade.

Fourth, measures have been adopted to make import trade large, promote a relatively balanced development of imports and exports. Enterprises have been encouraged to import important energy which is scarce in Zhejiang, including oil, and such resources and raw materials as iron ore and nonferrous metals, advanced technologies, key equipment, medium and high-quality consumer goods, to reduce the production costs of Zhejiang's enterprises, and to enhance the export competitiveness of Zhejiang's products; efforts have been made to cultivate specialized import markets, especially online import trade, open up the markets to the outside world.

3. Establishing a mechanism for addressing foreign trade risks

(1) The Bureau of Fair Import & Export Trade has been established to guide the enterprises involved in cases to respond to litigations. Since China's accession to the WTO, the anti-dumping cases and other trade barriers that Zhejiang's enterprises have faced have apparently increased. In 2003, Zhejiang's enterprises were subject to 24 anti-dumping and safeguard measure investigations initiated by 7 countries and territories, including the USA, Turkey, the EU, India, Egypt, South Africa and Mexico, 2 intellectual property barrier cases from the USA and 1 Category III textile safeguard measure case from the USA, putting Zhejiang in the first place nationwide in this regard. In 2004, Zhejiang's enterprises encountered 33 anti-dumping, countervailing and safeguard measure investigations initiated by 14 countries and territories, including the USA, the EU, Canada, India and Turkey.

Given increasing international trade barriers, the Zhejiang Provincial Department of Foreign Trade and Economic Cooperation actively organized efforts to make a response. In April, 2002, the Zhejiang Provincial Department of Foreign Trade and Economic Cooperation specially set up the Bureau of Fair Import and Export Trade for further guiding the enterprises involved in cases to respond to litigations; it provided work guidance to Zhejiang's import enterprises engaged in bearing, lighters, glasses, pharmaceutical and chemical, animal derived products, tea and vegetables subject to technical barriers and green barriers. The work on fair trade produced a certain effect. The Zhejiang Provincial Department of Foreign Trade and Economic Cooperation also established and improved Zhejiang's foreign trade early-warning mechanism and the special fund for encouraging enterprises to actively respond to investigations regarding anti-dumping, countervailing and safeguard measures.

(2) Actions have been taken to intensify international trade and economic situation early-warning and macro guidance, to improve the mechanism for addressing trade frictions, to actively respond to international trade barriers and effectively

guard against trade risks. The foreign trade operation monitoring points have been established throughout Zhejiang Province to monthly monitor the orders at the hands of key export enterprises, export prices, enterprise operation conditions and entrepreneurs' judgment about export trends, closely follow the impact of RMB foreign exchange reform and the adjustment of the export rebate policy on foreign trade enterprises, release the comprehensive climate index of foreign trade exportations; the exportation of the enterprises on which contact focused accounted for more than 45% of Zhejiang Province's exports. As from 2007, Zhejiang also made bold explorations in the innovation of the fair trade system, and became the first to set up early-warning points at the industrial associations of the massive economy; as of late 2011, 100 early-warning points had been established, key industries had been basically covered. One hundred lawyers have been available at the early-warning points for conducting "law-based physical examination" of foreign trade enterprises, thus making key enterprises involved in the transformation and upgrading more able to address the trade friction early-warning and carry out early-warning measures. A number of Zhejiang's enterprises involved in foreign trade investigation cases[2] have been organized to engage in project cooperation with overseas cooperation zones to push forward the transfer of Zhejiang's traditional industries and make structural adjustments.

4. Innovating the international market developmental mode to improve export competitiveness

Actions have been taken to actively organize and hold various types of targeted international exhibitions and strengthen classified guidance for exhibitions. In parallel with efforts to hold important domestic international exhibitions, including the China International Consumer Goods Fair and the China Yiwu International Commodities Fair, steps have been taken to build major overseas self-run exhibition platforms, including the Zhejiang Export Trade Osaka Fair, the Dubai Trade Fair, the fairs in the USA and in India.

Enterprises have been guided to speed up the construction of overseas marketing networks; a diversified integrated marketing system has been established and improved. Enterprises have been encouraged to set up overseas marketing headquarters, exclusive stores and trade representative offices in the developed countries and emerging markets, with a view to stimulating major commodity markets to establish submarkets and production distribution centers overseas, build self-owned marketing networks, so that Zhejiang's enterprises can gradually transform from pure suppliers to distributors and brand owners.

More support has been provided for branded export commodities. A mechanism for export brand cultivation, development and protection has been established and improved; enterprises have been encouraged to increase the proportion of their export products with a high technical content, high added value and high returns. Enterprises have been encouraged to increase their input into product research and development to

[2] Anti-dumping, countervailing, safeguard measures and special safeguard measures.

enhance their capability for independent innovation; special funds are allocated from finance each year to support technical transformation and independent innovation at enterprises. Intensified efforts should be made to build national and provincial export bases.

Such trade modes as online display, online negotiation, offline goods delivery and offline check on samples have been promoted. Actions are being taken to boost B2B, B2C, C2C, O2O online trade transactions. Measures have been taken to push forward online declaration and trials at the free trade zone in Hangzhou, reinforce the construction of the opening carriers such as bonded zones, bonded port areas, export processing zones, logistics parks and bonded logistics centers, and elevate the construction of foreign trade transaction platforms.

With concerted efforts on the part of the Zhejiang Provincial Party Committee and the Provincial Government as well as enterprises, Zhejiang's import and export trade maintained rapid growth. Zhejiang's export trade volume hit USD 30 billion, USD 50 billion and USD 100 billion in 2003, 2004 and 2006, respectively. Zhejiang's export trade volume hit USD 200 billion and USD 355.05 billion in 2011 and 2014, respectively,[3] the structure of export commodities also improved steadily. At the same time, given the needs of economic development, Zhejiang has earnestly organized the importation of the urgently needed energy, raw materials and key equipment, the import trade has kept a relatively rapid balanced growth, the structure of import commodities improved significantly, making Zhejiang's import and export structure balanced and providing factor guarantee for Zhejiang where resources are scarce.

5.2.2 *Improving the Quality of Foreign Capital Utilization*

1. Combining foreign capital with the industrial structural upgrading

In April, 2004, the Zhejiang Provincial Party Committee and the Provincial Government issued *Several Opinions on Further Expanding Opening Up*, and vowed to focus investment attraction on the manufacturing industry and the new and hi-tech fields, and concentrate on infrastructure, agriculture and the service industry to make breakthroughs in attracting investments. They called for moving forward with investment attraction by attracting the large investors, introducing the strong investors and choosing the excellent investors, placing equal emphasis on quantity and quality, attracting both capital and intellectuals, combining "bringing in" with "going global".

In an effort to attract investment, Zhejiang has guided and encouraged foreign investors to invest in the new and hi-tech industries, high-end manufacturing, modern service industry, new energy, energy conservation and environmental protection industries, and Zhejiang has strictly restricted particular underperforming enter-

---

[3]The Zhejiang Provincial Bureau of Statistics, Zhejiang Statistical Abstract 2015, the same below.

prises[4] and the projects characterized by the expansion of low-level and excessive production capacity. Multinational corporations have been encouraged to establish regional headquarters, R&D centers, purchasing centers, financial management centers, settlement centers, cost and profit accounting centers and other functional organizations in Zhejiang.

2. Building large platforms for utilizing foreign capital

In order to encourage the construction of development zones, Zhejiang has intensified the construction of infrastructures in development parks, thus laying a good foundation for attracting foreign investment and promoting a new round of development. With a focus on producing a scale agglomeration effect in three main industrial belts around Hangzhou Bay, along the coastal areas in Wenzhou and Taizhou, and the Jinhua-Quzhou-Lishui Highway, Zhejiang has integrated and upgraded various types of development zones (parks). Intensified efforts have been made to remove the institutional obstacles to the healthy development of development zones, strengthen the integration and upgrading of various types of development zones, focus on upgrading the functions of the development zones above the provincial level, including economic and technological development zones and national high-tech zones, to make them become the key platforms for introducing excellent foreign capital.

3. Innovating the investment attraction mode to improve the soft environment for investment

(1) Improving and innovating the investment attraction mode. Importance has been attached to attracting foreign investment through private enterprises, foreign-funded enterprises, trade and overseas Chinese, and attracting investments from Taiwan through the eastern areas. With enterprises playing the leading role in attracting investment, scope has been given to the advantage of the private economy—that advantage is that it is developed—with a view to more quickly attracting foreign investment and turning mere private capital into Sino-foreign joint ventures. Play has been given to the advantages Zhejiang has as a large province of foreign trade, and new ways for attracting foreign investment through trade have been explored to turn the trading partners into joint venture partners. The advantages of the foreign trade agglomeration zones have been utilized to earnestly implement the strategy of attracting foreign investment through foreign-funded enterprises and turn sporadic investments into cluster investments.

(2) Introducing the top 500 global companies through targeted investment attraction and customized design. A series of economic and trade activities have been held in Hong Kong, Macao, Singapore, Japan, South Korea and France to promote a number of major projects of investment attraction in a well-targeted way, with emphasis placed on attracting large enterprises, including the top 500 global companies, and hi-tech industrial projects to Zhejiang Province. Given

[4]High energy-consuming enterprises, heavily polluting enterprises and highly resource-focused product enterprises.

the investment demand of such enterprises as the top 500 global companies, particular projects have been specially designed to improve the efficiency and quality of investment attraction. As a result, more and more top 500 global companies have invested in Zhejiang, new and hi-tech and large projects launched in Zhejiang through investment attraction have been on the increase.

(3) Improving the soft environment for investment. Zhejiang has actively increased the areas of opening up and have steadily pressed ahead with opening up in such service areas as banking, insurance, tourism, education and health according to the national layout. Zhejiang has constantly intensified the reform of its foreign investment mechanism, simplified its foreign investment examination and approval procedures to improve the working efficiency of the government, the service efficiency of the government and social intermediaries as well as the soft environment for investment. Zhejiang has carefully put into practice the policy opinions of the State Council on land, tax and credit involving the utilization of foreign capital; Zhejiang has solved the practical difficulties for foreign investors in life, medical service and children's education, so as to attract investment and retain investors in earnest.

With the concerted efforts of the government, enterprises and the whole society, Zhejiang has maintained sustained and rapid growth in investment attraction and has greatly improved the quality of the foreign capital that has been introduced. In 2014, the contractual foreign investments in Zhejiang reached USD 24.4 billion, the actual foreign investments were USD 15.8 billion, both reaching a record high. At the same time, the quality of the introduced foreign capital had significantly improved, while the new and hi-tech industries, the equipment manufacturing industry, the modern intermediary service industry and ecological agriculture have become the hotspots for foreign investment. The scale of the projects launched through investment attraction has continuously increased; the large projects above USD 10 million have accounted for more than 90% of the investment projects from the areas outside Zhejiang; nearly 100 of the top 500 global companies have presence in Zhejiang, the proportion of their investments in the direct investments from the areas outside Zhejiang has continuously and steadily increased.

5.2.3 Increasing the Level of "Going Global"

1. Propelling the reform of the system for the management of outward investments

In September, 2001, the People's Government of Zhejiang Province issued the *Opinions on Accelerating the Implementation of the Strategy of "Going Global"*. According to the Opinions, Zhejiang would, based on the market mechanism, actively encourage and support the advantageous industries and specialized markets in the province to expand overseas, energetically guide Zhejiang's private enterprises to make outward investments, utilize overseas resources and markets more. In December, 2002, the Zhejiang Provincial Department of Finance and the Zhejiang Provincial

Department of Foreign Trade and Economic Cooperation jointly issued the *Circular Concerning Several Opinions on Administration of the Use of a Special Fund for Implementing the Strategy of "Going Global"*, establishing the special fund for "going global" with a view to providing financial subsidies and incentives to Zhejiang's enterprises that establish specialized commodity markets, production enterprises and R&D centers overseas. In 2003, the Ministry of Commerce designated Zhejiang as the pilot province for the reform of the overseas investment examination and approval system, thus presenting a new opportunity for Zhejiang to carry out the strategy of "going global". After the financial crisis broke out in the USA in 2008, given the new situation and the developmental needs of the market economy and an open economy, Zhejiang specially revised the *Measures of Zhejiang Province for the Administration of the Use of the Special Fund for Implementing the Strategy of "Going Global"*, providing financial support and incentives for overseas investment projects, overseas engineering contracting projects, foreign aid projects, overseas labor service cooperation projects, outward public service projects and the investment projects launched by outward investment enterprises returning to the province, so that Zhejiang's enterprises could "go global" in a more robust way. In 2009, global outward direct investments declined by 39%, but Zhejiang's outward investments grew, Zhejiang approved 427 overseas investment projects with a total investment of USD 920 million, being 10 times that in 2003. In 2014, the Chinese investment amount in Zhejiang's overseas investments reached USD 5820 million.

2. Innovating the mode under which Zhejiang merchants make outward investments

At the initial stage of overseas investment, Zhejiang merchants generally adopted such traditional modes as the establishment of trade representative offices and specialized markets, enterprises started businesses overseas mostly in the manufacturing of automobile parts, clothing, leather shoes and building project contracting. With growing strength, they gradually developed so as to establish overseas production bases and R&D centers, conduct overseas mergers and acquisitions, overseas listing and they also adopted other new means to obtain the brands, technologies and markets of foreign enterprises, to rapidly expand their market share and enter new markets.

In recent years, overseas merger and acquisition has become a new trend presented by Zhejiang's enterprises in "going global" for outward investment. In 2009, Zhejiang had 20 overseas merger and acquisition projects with a total investment of USD 250 million; both the number of projects and investment amount in 2009 were equivalent to the sum total of previous years. In 2010, Zhejiang had 33 projects involved in overseas investment through merger and acquisition and 12 R&D projects. In 2011, Zhejiang carried out 39 overseas merger and acquisition projects with the merger and acquisition amount of USD 1190 million. With overseas merger and acquisition, Zhejiang's enterprises have obtained technologies, brands, marketing networks and resource channels to enhance their competitiveness.

3. Giving play to the advantages of the private economy, attaching importance to the construction of main players

In the process of implementing the strategy of "going global", Zhejiang has paid great attention to the construction of main players, and has focused on expanding the enterprise force in the endeavor to "go global". As a province with a developed private economy, Zhejiang has, while enabling state-owned enterprises and collective enterprises to "go global", encouraged the private enterprises, where conditions permit, to apply for obtaining the power to engage in foreign trade and to cooperate with international counterparts in contracted labor service; Zhejiang stimulated its private enterprises to go abroad, take the path of normalized development, thus private enterprises have become Zhejiang's main force for "going global".

In the symposium on foreign trade of Zhejiang Province in December, 2011, comrade Xia Baolong, then Acting Governor of Zhejiang Province, stated, "during the period of the 12th Five-Year Plan, Zhejiang Province will focus on supporting 100 overseas investment cooperation demonstration projects, cultivating more than 100 multinational corporations with a certain international competitiveness, and building 10 platforms for overseas agglomeration development of Zhejiang's traditional advantageous industries, 10 demonstration platforms for the development of Zhejiang's overseas enterprises in the province; the scale of both outward direct investments and foreign economic cooperation will be doubled."

With the implementation of the strategy of "going global", Zhejiang's enterprises have achieved leapfrog development in keeping in line with the international market. After more than a decade of painstaking efforts, Zhejiang's implementation of the strategy of "going global" has produced remarkable effects, Zhejiang has enjoyed the leading position nationwide in this regard and presents the following main characteristics: First, private enterprises have become the main force in the campaign of "going global"; second, investments have taken various forms, including the establishment of trade windows, overseas processing bases, R&D centers, resource development, overseas listing; third, a new pattern of two-way interaction between "going global" and "bringing in" has taken shape, so that Zhejiang's enterprises can integrate into the major cycle of the international economy at a higher level, they can develop, grow and play an active role in mitigating the province-wide factor bottlenecks and upgrading industries, and Zhejiang's opening up will reach a new level.

5.3 Keeping in Alignment with Shanghai, Enhancing Regional Economic Cooperation

5.3.1 Connecting Shanghai on the North, Integrating into the Yangtze River Delta

1. Integrating into the Yangtze River Delta in a government-led way

In late 2002, based on surveying the economic development in Zhejiang and the Yangtze River Delta soon after serving as the Secretary of the Zhejiang Provincial

Party Committee, Xi Jinping put forward the strategy of connecting Shanghai on the north. In early 2003, the Zhejiang Provincial Party Committee and the Provincial Government decided to actively keep in alignment with Shanghai and energetically engage in cooperation and exchange with the Yangtze River Delta, and identified this decision as one of the decisions in the "Eight-Eight Strategies". Xi Jinping, then Secretary of the Zhejiang Provincial Party Committee, and Lu Zushan, then Governor of Zhejiang Province, led a delegation of officials from the Zhejiang Provincial Party Committee and the Provincial Government to visit Shanghai and Jiangsu, and jointly explore the way of "government-led, market-driven interactive development" with the Yangtze River Delta; they separately signed the *Agreement on Further Promoting Shanghai-Zhejiang Economic Cooperation and Development* and the *Agreement on Economic and Technical Cooperation and Exchange between Zhejiang Province and Jiangsu Province*. In May, 2003, the Zhejiang Provincial Party Committee and the Provincial Government issued *Several Opinions on Actively Keeping in Alignment with Shanghai and Energetically Engaging in Cooperation and Exchange with the Yangtze River Delta*, stating that according to the overall requirement of modestly learning, actively keeping in alignment and sincerely cooperating to achieve a win-win outcome, Zhejiang would proactively engage in cooperation and exchange with the Yangtze River Delta in carrying out the construction of infrastructures, including transportation; cooperation also included building the advanced manufacturing bases, developing the ecological, high-quality and efficient agriculture, further utilizing foreign capital, developing tourism resources and markets, and on the scientific and technological, educational, cultural and talent fronts, Zhejiang promoted economic integration in the Yangtze River Delta and further increased the level of Zhejiang's inter-regional opening and international opening. In November, 2011, the leaders of Zhejiang Province, Jiangsu Province and Shanghai met in Shanghai. During this meeting, these leaders reached a high degree of consensus on the integration of the Yangtze River Delta and decided to expand the space of the Yangtze River Delta from the original 15 cities plus one municipality to two provinces plus one municipality. In December, during the meeting of the industrial and commercial administration circles of Jiangsu Province, Zhejiang Province and Shanghai, which was held in Shanghai to discuss the interactive development and cooperation of the Yangtze River Delta, it was announced that actions would be taken to first remove administrative fences, establish a joint meeting system and introduce the unified market access policy implemented in the Yangtze River Delta Region. During that month, Jiangsu Province, Zhejiang Province and Shanghai signed the *Cooperation Agreement on the Service Industry in the Yangtze River Delta*.

In order to make the Yangtze River Delta Region take the lead in development and achieve sound development, in September, 2008, the State Council issued the *Guiding Opinions on Further Promoting Reform, Opening Up and Economic and Social Development in the Yangtze River Delta*, elevating the integration of the Yangtze River Delta to a national strategy. In December, the main leaders from the Yangtze River Delta Region held a meeting in Zhejiang Province to discuss and adopt the *Opinions on Implementing the Guiding Opinions of the State Council and Jointly Pushing Forward Several Important Matters in the Yangtze River Delta Region*, and to discuss the framework for the regional cooperation mechanism and the priorities of a new round of cooperation. In May, 2010, the State Council approved the *Regional Plan for the Yangtze River Delta Region*. Under the guidance of the national strategy, Jiangsu Province, Zhejiang Province and Shanghai have further improved the regional cooperation mechanism of three-level operations, unified centralization and decentralization, pragmatic action and high efficiency. At the provincial level, a cooperation mechanism with the following characteristics was adopted among Jiangsu Province, Zhejiang Province and Shanghai: high-level leaders engage in communication and consultation; tasks are determined through meetings; the liaison group is responsible for overall coordination; special groups push forward the relevant work. The exchange visits among provincial governments have been institutionalized. At the municipal and county levels, a platform for horizontal communication and cooperation among cities has been built; in the past, the major coordination meeting was held once every two years, but now it is held once a year. There are cooperation coordination mechanisms involving more than 40 industries and sectors among cities, with positive progress having been made in planning, science and technology, information, property rights, talents, tourism, customs, ports and collaboration. On this basis, emphasis has been placed on building four major cooperation platforms covering transportation, science and technology, energy and environmental protection.

2. Fully integrating into the Yangtze River Delta

In the process of promoting the integration of the Yangtze River Delta, Zhejiang has actively integrated into the Yangtze River Delta and made active efforts; it has materialized the relevant strategies and goals of the Zhejiang Provincial Party Committee and the Provincial Government to introduce a number of measures for boosting economic cooperation in the Yangtze River Delta. First, promoting the integration of the Yangtze River Delta has been included in the 11th Five-Year Plan; the goals, priorities and tasks of keeping in alignment and engaging in cooperation have been further identified. There is coordination with the nation in piloting the formulation of the plan for the Yangtze River Delta. Second, emphasis has been placed on putting into practice the cooperation and exchange system at four levels: the first level is an annual meeting of the main leaders from Jiangsu Province, Zhejiang Province and Shanghai in the Yangtze River Delta; the second level is the economic cooperation and development symposium among Jiangsu Province, Zhejiang Province and Shanghai; the third is the establishment of special groups for key cooperation among Jiangsu Province, Zhejiang Province and Shanghai and the meeting of economic coordination among cities in the Yangtze River Delta; the fourth level is the enterprise-led cooperation and exchange system. Third, the activities for keeping in alignment have been widely carried out.

First, more investments have been made in the construction of infrastructures. Actions have been taken to more rapidly build the highway connecting Shanghai, Jiangsu Province, Zhejiang Province and Anhui Province, which was fully completed and open to traffic in 2008. The inland channel at the Huzhou Section of the Huzhou-Jiaxing-Shanghai Waterway has been open to traffic, with the channel capacity increasing from the original 100t to 1,000t, thus removing the obstructions at the inland channels connecting Jiangsu Province, Zhejiang Province and Shanghai. The Hangzhou Bay Sea-Crossing Bridge has been open to traffic, so a two-hour transportation circle has taken shape among Shanghai, Hangzhou and Ningbo. The second bridge at Hangzhou Bay—the Jiaxing-Shaoxing River-crossing Road—has been completed. The Shanghai-Hangzhou-Wenzhou, the Nanjing-Hangzhou and the Hangzhou-Ningbo high speed railways have been completed. All these have greatly improved the transportation between Zhejiang and Shanghai, Jiangsu Province and have forged close economic ties.

Second, with the goal of building the Shanghai international shipping center, container trunk port and China's large bulk cargo deepwater transshipment port, Zhejiang has speeded up cooperation between the Shanghai-Ningbo-Zhoushan Port and the Wenzhou-Zhenjiang-Nanjing wharf shipping activity. Zhejiang and Shanghai have actively engaged in cooperation in the Xiaoyangshan deepwater port area which has become the deepwater port area of the Shanghai international shipping center; the integration of the Ningbo-Zhoushan Port area has been continuously promoted; the port wharf shipping cooperation among Jiangsu Province, Zhejiang Province and Shanghai has been constantly enhanced. In 2008, Hangzhou Customs signed memorandums of cooperation with Ningbo Customs, Shanghai Customs and Nanjing Customs. This shows that regional large-scale simplification of customs clearance procedures first began in China—regional customs clearance integration in the Yangtze River Delta—has covered the whole Yangtze River Delta.

Finally, enterprises have been actively encouraged to participate in the process of keeping in alignment and cooperating. With a focus on investment attraction, technical cooperation and commodity marketing, Zhejiang has adopted such means as exhibition, promotion and forums to guide enterprises to participate in economic cooperation in the Yangtze River Delta.

Under the guidance of the government's plan for adapting to the market economy, Zhejiang merchants have massively marched towards the Yangtze River Delta. According to incomplete statistics, in 2006, there were 300,000 Zhejiang merchants in Shanghai, their total investments exceeded 200 billion yuan. In late 2013, there were about 500,000 Zhejiang merchants in Shanghai; Zhejiang merchants in Shanghai ranked No. 1 among those in various provinces (autonomous regions, municipalities) in terms of enterprise scale and total investments, the proportion in Zhejiang's total investments in other provinces has accounted for more than 20% for a long time. Tremendous progress has been made in economic cooperation among Zhejiang Province, Shanghai and Jiangsu Province, greatly promoting economic prosperity in these three regions; the Yangtze River Delta city group has become one of the four largest city groups in the world.

5.3.2 *Moving Toward the West and the North to Fully Promote Regional Economic Cooperation*

1. Enhancing inter-regional strategic cooperation in resources and energy

Zhejiang Province has further engaged in strategic cooperation with other provinces, autonomous regions, municipalities in industrial transformation, energy safeguard and grain security. Since 2003, the areas of cooperation between Zhejiang Province and other provinces, autonomous regions, municipalities in grain, coal, other resources and energy have continuously increased, the cooperation mechanisms have been constantly improved and the level of cooperation has been on the rise. The leaders of the Zhejiang Provincial Party Committee and the Provincial Government have frequently led delegations to conduct exchange visits with other provinces, autonomous regions, municipalities, and a strategic relationship of cooperation has been established. Zhejiang Province has signed a number of cooperation projects involving grain, energy and industry with relevant provinces, autonomous regions, municipalities. With respect to grain, as of August, 2011, Zhejiang Province had engaged in various types of production and sales cooperation with 12 main grain-producing provinces, including Heilongjiang, Jiangxi and Shandong, and Zhejiang Province established grain production bases covering an areas of 3,050,000 mu in the main producing areas outside the province, which can supply about 1147 million kg of commodity grain. Zhejiang Province has cooperated with Shanxi, Inner Mongolia, Shaanxi and Xinjiang in the exploitation, supply and sales of coal and gas. The strategic cooperation on the above aspects has enabled Zhejiang Province to overcome the bottlenecks in energy resource supply and improve its capability for addressing grain security and has thus provided the fundamental guarantee for sound economic development.

2. Guiding enterprises to moving toward the west and the north for engaging in various types of economic cooperation

First, Zhejiang's enterprises have been organized to participate in the East-West China Cooperation & investment Trade Fair, the Harbin International Economic & Trade Fair, the Western China International Fair, the China (Chongqing) International Investment & Global Purchasing Fair and other large domestic economic and trade fairs. Zhejiang's enterprises have attended the Zhejiang-Shaanxi Entrepreneurship & Innovation Cooperation Fair, the Zhejiang-Heilongjiang Economic Cooperation Fair, the Jilin-Zhejiang Economic & Trade Cooperation Fair, the Zhejiang (Beijing) Fair on Promoting Economic Transformation and Upgrading, the Zhejiang (Guangdong) Economic Structural Adjustment Fair, the Fair on Economic Cooperation & Exchange among Zhejiang, the Reservoir Areas of the Three Gorges and at the Lower Reaches of the Jinsha River. Zhejiang Province has worked with other provinces, autonomous regions and municipalities to hold various types of exhibitions, fairs and promotion events. Zhejiang Province has organized enterprises to pay visits and engage with sister cities. Zhejiang Province has carried out relevant coordination work for other provinces, autonomous regions and municipalities to visit and attract investment in Zhejiang Province. Zhejiang Province has offered good platforms for inter-provincial cooperation, provided various kinds of information to Zhejiang's enterprises, so that Zhejiang merchants can utilize platforms to more conveniently seek investment opportunities and engage in investment cooperation.

Second, scope has been given to the role of chambers of commerce. In order to guide Zhejiang merchants to "go global" for development and to leverage the advantages of Zhejiang merchants, Zhejiang Province has established federations (chambers of commerce) of Zhejiang's enterprises outside Zhejiang Province in 29 provinces, autonomous regions and municipalities so as to carry out network-based and well-regulated work on the management, liaison and services of Zhejiang's enterprises outside Zhejiang Province. Zhejiang chambers of commerce outside Zhejiang Province have actively performed functions to provide services for local Zhejiang merchants in fellowship activities, information exchanges, cooperation and development; they safeguard the legitimate rights and interests of Zhejiang merchants, enhance exchanges between Zhejiang merchants and local governments and enterprises, give advice and make suggestions for local economic and social development, guide and coordinate the operating activities of Zhejiang merchants, and have become the important nongovernmental organizations for guiding and regularizing Zhejiang merchants in regional cooperation.

Third, Zhejiang Province has engaged in various types of inter-regional cooperation. Zhejiang merchants have been encouraged to establish energy, raw material development and primary processing bases in the areas which abound in resources; the leading agricultural enterprises have been organized to build agricultural product production bases outside Zhejiang Province.

3. Actively participating in the construction of economic cooperation zones

In regional economic cooperation, Zhejiang has attached importance to utilizing regional economic cooperation platforms and mechanisms, including the Western Taiwan Straits Economic Zone, the Silk Road Economic Belt, the Marine Silk Road Economic Belt and the Yangtze River Economic Belt, to actively engage in domestic regional economic cooperation.

First, Zhejiang Province has energetically participated in the construction of the Western Taiwan Straits Economic Zone. Local governments at various levels in Zhejiang Province have paid great attention to the establishment of the Western Taiwan Straits Economic Zone and have sought participation in its construction. In March, 2006, relevant departments of Wenzhou City, adjacent to Fujian Province, formed a group to visit Fujian Province with regard to the construction of the Western Taiwan Straits Economic Zone. Afterwards, the Office of Wenzhou City's Integration into the Western Taiwan Straits Economic Zone was officially established for studying the main themes, modes and mechanisms under which Wenzhou City integrates into the regional economic cooperation in the Western Taiwan Straits Economic Zone. In May, 2011, in order to fully leverage the advantages of Cangnan County in having close proximity to, blood ties with, the same language as, similar climate and customs with Taiwan, and to attract investment from Taiwan through the eastern areas to promote Cangnan County's economic transformation and upgrading, the People's Government of Zhejiang Province established the first Zhejiang-Taiwan economic and trade cooperation zone in Cangnan County, and included it in the management of provincial development zones. The cooperation zone has a planned area of 330 km^2, including three core areas: Longgang New City, the Lingxi New Area, the Mazhan National Taiwan Farmer Business Incubation Park. In recent years, 17 projects have been introduced and carried out, RMB 2.2 billion in capital has been introduced from Taiwan, mainly covering new and hi-tech photoelectric products, stationery, preschool education, medical care, delicate agriculture, marine trade and the Taiwan goods market. At present, the work on establishing a national Taiwan businessman investment zone in the Zhejiang-Taiwan (Cangnan) Economic & Trade Cooperation Zone has been initiated.

At the same time, a number of areas in South Zhejiang, such as Lishui, Taizhou and Quzhou, have also actively participated in building the Western Taiwan Straits Economic Zone and have enhanced economic exchanges and cooperation with Fujian, Taiwan, Guangdong and other areas.

Second, Zhejiang Province has played an active part in the construction of the Belt and Road. The national strategy of the Silk Road Economic Belt and the 21st Century Marine Silk Road put forward in 2013 and the construction of the Land Bridge project present rare opportunities for increasing the level of Zhejiang's open economy. Ningbo, Zhoushan and Wenzhou of Zhejiang Province are situated at an important point on the Marine Silk Road. Undoubtedly, the construction of the Marine Silk Road will strengthen the economic and trade ties between the coastal areas of Zhejiang Province and Southeast Asia, West Asia, Africa and Europe. In 2013, the "Yiwu-Beilun, Ningbo" sea-railway combined transport train was put into operation, which the Port of Ningbo utilized to connect the Marine Silk Road to Yiwu in Central Zhejiang Province. Although Zhejiang Province is not situated on the economic belt of the New Silk Land Road, Zhejiang merchants have also astutely taken advantage of the good opportunity. With the New Silk Land Road, Zhejiang Province has energetically promoted the construction of the Yiwu-Xinjiang-Europe (Yiwu-five Central Asian countries) international freight train. The train was first put into use in January, 2014, which marked basic completion of the great logistics channel of international railway combined transportation connecting Yiwu with Central Asia. Yiwu has the largest small commodity wholesale market in the world. As the Silk Road from the east to the west rises again, Yiwu will certainly become the new starting point of the modern silk road. Zhejiang will increase its support for the freight train, and establish a mechanism for closer economic and trade cooperation with such regions as Central Asia, Central and Eastern Europe; Zhejiang will make all-out efforts to build important pivotal points on the Silk Road Economic Belt and the Marine Silk Road and turn the freight train into a safe, convenient, all-weather green channel with a large carrying capacity. With more international container trains and sea-railway combined transport trains connecting the Eurasian regions, Central Asia and the ASEAN Free Trade Area, based on international railway container transport, Yiwu is built into the railway logistics center and is a special national station for railway containers. Traders can directly deliver commodities from Yiwu to the Central Asian countries and Europe; such convenience will further enhance the trade contacts between Zhejiang and the countries and the territories along the Silk Road Economic Belt.

Moreover, in April, 2014, the Yangtze River Economic Belt was upgraded to a national strategy. With the subsequent introduction of specific policies, the Yangtze River Economic Belt will become a large economic cooperation zone in China. The governments at various levels in Zhejiang Province and Zhejiang merchants have seized this opportunity, have actively carried out plans and participated in cooperation with a view to promoting the common development of the economy in the Yangtze River Basin Region.

4. Adopting high standards in giving assistance to the targeted areas

The Zhejiang Provincial Party Committee and the Provincial Government have attached great importance to the work on giving assistance to the targeted areas. In May, 2004, when serving as the Secretary of the Zhejiang Provincial Party Committee, Xi Jinping led delegations to visit the targeted areas to which assistance was given, including Sichuan, Chongqing and Hubei. In December, 2004, the General Office of the Zhejiang Provincial Party Committee and the General Office of the People's Government of Zhejiang Province issued *Several Opinions on Strengthening the Work of Giving Assistance to the Targeted Areas and Domestic Cooperation and Exchange*, specifying the principle of giving assistance in a government-driven, market-led and enterprise-dominated way, and the policy of combining giving assistance with developing the capability of the targeted areas to develop by themselves, placing equal emphasis on help and cooperation. According to the Opinions, the work on giving assistance to the targeted areas should be steadily promoted through exchange visits, communication, economic and trade cooperation, donations, labor service cooperation and the taking of temporary posts by cadres for exchange. Since 2003, Zhejiang has given targeted assistance to Nagqu Prefecture of Tibet and Hetian Prefecture of Xinjiang, received immigrants from the Three Gorges Reservoir Area, and made poverty alleviation efforts in Guangyuan City and Nanchong City of Sichuan Province. During the period 2005–2007, Zhejiang offered targeted assistance to three major projects, including the Zhejiang-Sichuan New Poverty Alleviation Village Project launched in coordination with the construction of the new socialist countryside, the Zhejiang-Sichuan and Zhejiang-Chongqing Economic Cooperation Project combined with industrial gradient transfer and the Zhejiang-Sichuan and Zhejiang-Chongqing Labor Training and Transfer Project for addressing labor transfer and employment.

According to the requirements of the Central Government, the Zhejiang Provincial Party Committee and the Provincial Government have made unified arrangements. Since 2007, Zhejiang has focused on giving targeted assistance to Sichuan, Tibet, Xinjiang, Haixi Prefecture of Qinghai and Chongqing's Three Gorges Reservoir Area. After rescue and disaster relief following the WenChuan earthquake in June, 2008, Zhejiang provided targeted construction assistance to Qingchuan County. In this regard, Zhejiang identified three-year targeted construction assistance goals and tasks for carrying out 211 targeted construction assistance projects and completing

6 billion yuan worth of physical construction work, with a view to fully promoting targeted construction assistance by focusing on home rebuilding, facility rebuilding, industrial rebuilding, expertise and material assistance. In September, 2010, Zhejiang Province and Sichuan Province held a symposium on assisting Sichuan and the ceremony of integrated handover of rebuilding projects. This marked the successful completion of Zhejiang Province's task for targeted assistance to Qinghai Province and Sichuan Province.

Besides Qinghai Province and Sichuan Province, Zhejiang also continued assistance to such areas as Guangyuan City and Nanchong City of Sichuan Province. Zhejiang's targeted assistance to Tibet and Xinjiang has lasted for more than a decade. In 2010, according to the new arrangements of the Central Government, Zhejiang provided targeted assistance to Aksu Prefecture of Xinjiang and Haixi Prefecture of Qinghai Province. Zhejiang Provincial Party Committee and Provincial Government attached great importance to and the governments at various levels earnestly pushed forward relevant work. In 2010, Zhejiang also assisted relevant earthquake relief work in Yushu County, Yushu Tibetan Autonomous Prefecture, Qinghai Province.

Besides targeted assistance, Zhejiang Province also took the following work as one priority in targeted assistance: stimulating enterprises to cooperate with the targeted areas for achieving a mutually beneficial and win-win outcome and common development. With the combined lever effect of projects, industries and assistance funds, Zhejiang's kind of assistance construction is vigorously promoting the economic development and social progress in the targeted areas, it has contributed to the nation's coordinated regional development, it has also created more opportunities and spaces for Zhejiang to adjust the economic structure, transform the growth mode and upgrade industries.

5.3.3 *Guiding Zhejiang Merchants to Return Home*

1. Implementing the project for making Zhejiang merchants return home

While guiding Zhejiang merchants to "go global", the Zhejiang Provincial Party Committee and the Provincial Government have given priority to the introduction of domestic investments, constantly improved the four-in-one work system of the introduction of domestic investments covering investment attraction, the return of Zhejiang merchants outside Zhejiang Province, the introduction of talents, science and technology, factors and resources. As the Zhejiang merchants outside Zhejiang Province have fully utilized local resources and markets, the scale and strength of their enterprises have greatly improved. In Zhejiang Province, after many years of robust development, both hard environment and soft environment for investment have substantially improved. Zhejiang's economic transformation and upgrading call for stimulating Zhejiang merchants to return home in order to start businesses, and the love of their hometown and relatives is a strong appeal for the Zhejiang merchants outside Zhejiang Province. In 2006, Zhejiang Province officially launched the project for stimulating the Zhejiang merchants outside Zhejiang Province to return home.

In January, 2006, the General Office of the People's Government of Zhejiang Province retransmitted the *Circular Concerning Further Strengthening the Work on Domestic Introduction*, bringing forward the project for the return of Zhejiang merchants mainly aimed at encouraging and attracting the Zhejiang merchants outside Zhejiang Province to return home in order to invest and start businesses, with a focus on guiding capital, resources, talents, information, technology and other high-quality factors to return to Zhejiang Province, strongly supporting the returning Zhejiang merchants in participating in the construction of the new socialist countryside and the Mountain-Sea Cooperation Project, so as to promote the interactive development of Zhejiang's economy and Zhejiang people's economy, and shape a new pattern of benign development featuring two-way interaction between "going global" and "bringing in". The 11th five-year plan of Zhejiang Province for domestic cooperation and exchange development more explicitly includes, in its goals, the amount and growth rate of investments made by the Zhejiang merchants outside Zhejiang Province who have returned home.

In April, 2006, Ding Lei, NetEase CEO, signed an agreement with Hangzhou National New and Hi-tech Industrial Development Zone, under which USD 38 million would be invested in building the Hangzhou R&D Base. Wenzhou's C&U Group has invested 1.72 billion yuan in its hometown. Shanghai Matsuoka Co., Ltd. has made efforts to build the Jiulongshan Provincial Resort Area covering an area of 10 km^2 in Pinghu.

As the largest, highest-level, most influential event of Zhejiang merchants in Zhejiang Province, the World Zhejiang Entrepreneurs Convention, held as from 2011, serves as an important strategic platform of the Zhejiang Provincial Party Committee and the Provincial Government for supporting Zhejiang merchants in making innovations.

2. Supporting Zhejiang merchants in starting businesses and carrying out innovations, guiding Zhejiang merchants to return home for development

As from 2008, Zhejiang's economy has entered the stage of developed industrialization, great changes have taken place in the environment of domestic and foreign economic development, the economy has shown a new normal and has entered a period of adjustment and pace-changing, and the growth rate has declined to some extent. Therefore, the significance of guiding Zhejiang merchants to return home for development has become more prominent.

First, this return home represents the necessity for addressing the severe and complicated situation and continuing to stay ahead. The instability and uncertainties in the world's economic recovery have been on the rise; the external environment for Zhejiang's economic development has become extremely severe. In China, some long-standing contradictions and short-term problems have interwoven, the problem of unbalanced, uncoordinated and unsustainable development has become more salient. Subject to more arduous reforms and developmental tasks and an increasingly fierce pattern of regional competition, the pressure on Zhejiang Province is mounting as it strives to continue to stay ahead. Supporting Zhejiang merchants in starting businesses and innovating is the inevitable way to making Zhejiang develop first and promoting Zhejiang's development in a scientific and harmonious way, ensuring that Zhejiang will continue to stay ahead nationwide.

Second, it is necessary for businessmen to return home in order to leverage Zhejiang's advantages and promote the integrative development of Zhejiang people's economy and Zhejiang's economy. More than 7.50 million Zhejiang merchants have created another "Zhejiang" in other provinces and a "Zhejiang" overseas; the total wealth created by Zhejiang merchants each year is similar to the annual GDP of Zhejiang Province; this constitutes a unique phenomenon—Zhejiang people's economy. Guiding Zhejiang merchants to return home is necessary for helping Zhejiang province achieve economic transformation and development and create new competitive advantages. Stimulating Zhejiang merchants to return home for development is a vigorous measure for boosting the integrative development of Zhejiang people's economy and Zhejiang's economy.

Finally, Zhejiang merchants are the greatest advantage of Zhejiang's economy and also the vitality and potential for Zhejiang's development. The history of Zhejiang's reform and opening up is a history of Zhejiang merchants' entrepreneurship and innovation. Zhejiang's development for more than 30 years has relied on Zhejiang merchants and private enterprises; the future creation of new developmental advantages will still depend on Zhejiang merchants and private enterprises.

Supporting Zhejiang merchants in starting businesses and innovating, and promoting Zhejiang's economic transformation and upgrading are the main goals of inciting Zhejiang merchants to return home. In late 2011, Zhejiang issued *Several Opinions on Supporting Zhejiang Merchants in Starting Businesses and Making Innovations, and Promoting Zhejiang's Development*. In early 2012, supporting Zhejiang merchants in starting businesses and innovating was identified as the No. 1 project and a landmark endeavor in Zhejiang's economic work.

Moving Zhejiang merchants through affective interaction is also an important means for calling upon Zhejiang merchants to return home. The governments at various levels in Zhejiang Province pay visits to the parents of Zhejiang merchants during the Chinese Spring Festival and invite the Zhejiang merchants outside Zhejiang Province to attend the annual sessions of the People's Congress and the People's Political Consultative Conference of Zhejiang Province as nonvoting delegates. This shows that Zhejiang Province embraces Zhejiang merchants all around the world with open arms and is looking forward to their return.

Optimizing the service environment is the key to attracting Zhejiang merchants to return home. A new round of the reform of the administrative examination and approval system is being carried out in various parts of Zhejiang province. The babysitter-type one package service which was only available for particular projects in the past has almost become the basic criterion for local authorities to guide Zhejiang merchants to return home and support Zhejiang merchants in starting businesses and making innovations.

Moreover, Zhejiang has also actively utilized the World Zhejiang Entrepreneurs Convention, the Zhejiang Merchants Hometown Tour and other major events to attract Zhejiang merchants to return home for investing.

While actively guiding Zhejiang merchants to return home for starting businesses and making innovations, Zhejiang has also energetically attracted the enterprises of other provinces, especially the enterprises with high technical content and strong strength, to invest in Zhejiang. Such areas as Hangzhou, Ningbo, Jiaxing, Shaoxing and Huzhou have become the preferred investment destinations for the enterprises of other provinces. The new and hi-tech enterprises, modern intermediary services, ecological agriculture and real estate have become the key areas for the enterprises of other provinces to invest in Zhejiang. In the fair on cooperation between Zhejiang and the enterprises managed by the Central Government held in December, 2011, Zhejiang signed 52 cooperation projects with the enterprises managed by the Central Government, with the contractual amount reaching 272 billion yuan.

5.4 Summary and Outlook

Since the reform and opening up, along with the development of both the private economy and the market economy, Zhejiang has stayed ahead nationwide in its open development of the economy. In particular, in the past ten years, Zhejiang has overcome huge difficulties and challenges from fiercer market competition, increasing pressure on resource and factor supply and the environment, the global financial crisis which broke out in 2008 and subsequent continued downturns of overseas markets and declining domestic economic growth rate, Zhejiang's open economy has reached a new stage. At present, Zhejiang has become a province with massive import and export of commodities and capital. Zhejiang has continuously ranked No. 4 nationwide in export trade volume. Zhejiang has become the region with the most cross-regional investments; it has also ranked No. 1 in China for the number and amount of overseas direct investment projects. Open development has become the main driving force for sustained and rapid development of Zhejiang's economy in more than 30 years and also the important contributor to Zhejiang's economic transformation and upgrading in more than a decade. The development of Zhejiang's open economy has also provided a relatively successful example for the open development of China's economy.

Experience shows that the development of Zhejiang's open economy is mainly attributable to the scientific strategy and policy guidance of the Zhejiang Provincial Party Committee and the Provincial Government. Since the beginning of the 21st century, given the tremendous changes in Zhejiang's economic developmental environment, the Zhejiang Provincial Party Committee and the Provincial Government have, by fully leveraging the institutional advantages of Zhejiang's private economy, the competitive advantages of industrial clusters, great advantages of mountain and marine resources, the ecological, environmental and humanistic advantages, thoroughly carried out the strategy of "going global", encouraged Zhejiang merchants to "go out of Zhejiang to develop Zhejiang", and fully pushed forward inter-regional opening up and international opening up of Zhejiang's economy. For international opening up, with the Yiwu Pilot Comprehensive International Trade Reform, Zhejiang has constantly intensified the reform of the foreign trade system, innovated the new paths and new modes for the development of foreign trade, taken the initiative in transforming the foreign trade growth mode, focused on improving the quality of the utilized foreign capital, Zhejiang has also vigorously pushed forward the exportation of Zhejiang's products, encouraged Zhejiang merchants, Zhejiang's enterprises and Zhejiang's markets to "go global" and invest overseas, stimulated Zhejiang's enterprises to take part in international labor division and collaboration in production so as to boost integration between Zhejiang's economy and the global economy. At the same time, with a focus on keeping in alignment with Shanghai and deepening cooperation in the Yangtze River Delta, Zhejiang has proactively guided Zhejiang merchants to go east and west, north and south, thus fully promoting regional economic cooperation. Furthermore, Zhejiang has taken actions to combine "going global" with "bringing in", zealously attract the enterprises of other provinces to invest in Zhejiang, support Zhejiang merchants in starting businesses and making innovations, guide Zhejiang merchants to return home for development, thus driving Zhejiang's economic transformation and upgrading.

Looking into the future, as Zhejiang's economy has ushered in the stage of developed industrialization and China's economy has entered a new normal, the constraints from the market environment and the resource factor environment will become more prominent, economic growth will further decline. Moreover, a complex and volatile international economic environment and sluggish demand will hardly change by a large margin in the long term. Zhejiang's open economy will face more challenges. This requires Zhejiang to further increase the level of the open economy; it is necessary for Zhejiang to better utilize both domestic and foreign resources and markets, guard against potential risks in the open economy, maintain all-round development of inter-regional opening up and international opening up, a relatively balanced development of export trade and import trade, coordinated development of foreign capital introduction and outward investment to better serve Zhejiang's economic transformation and upgrading.

In the future, Zhejiang should, in response to the changing trends of domestic and foreign economic environments, unceasingly enrich and optimize the opening up strategies of "going out of Zhejiang to develop Zhejiang" and "going global, bringing in"; it should also comprehensively and systematically push forward the economic system reform, strengthen innovation in the opening up mode, actively participate in the construction of the Belt and Road and the Yangtze River Economic Zone, and speed up the integration between Zhejiang's economy and the economy outside Zhejiang Province, the overseas economy; moreover, it should guide enterprises to join the global industrial chain and enjoy high added value from that chain; at the same time, it is necessary to seize the opportunities from the new industrial revolution, vigorously develop the trade in technology, intensify the introduction of high-end technologies and high-caliber talents from other provinces and foreign countries, actively guide enterprises to carry out technical innovation, accelerate the change of business forms and the innovation in the internet of manufacturing things, so that opening becomes the important driving force for Zhejiang's economic transformation and upgrading.

Chapter 6
Developing the Marine Economy and Building a Strong Marine Province

Xiaolu Wu

As Zhejiang is situated in China's coastal areas and the T-shaped Yangtze River economic belt and at the estuary of the Yangtze golden waterway, Zhejiang enjoys unique abundant marine resources and a superior advantage for its location. Zhejiang is an important province of marine resources in China's coastal areas; it abounds in such marine resources as ports, fishery, scenery, oil, tideland, energy and islands. Since ancient times, thanks to the advantage of its geographical location in the coastal area, Zhejiang has a long history of a marine economy. The traditional marine industries, including fishery, salt and shipping, began to take shape before the founding of new China. In the late 1980s, especially since the beginning of the 21st century, the successive Party Committees and governments of Zhejiang Province, have been attaching great importance to the development of the marine economy and have put forward the basic strategy of Zhejiang's development of a marine economy. After many years of continued efforts, Zhejiang has gradually marched from a large province of marine resources to a strong province with a marine economy.

6.1 The Formation and Development of the Philosophy of the Marine Economy

Zhejiang is situated in China's coastal area. Although land resources are extremely scarce, the marine resources are very abundant. Zhejiang enjoys not only the advantages of location and climate for developing a marine economy, but also the unrivalled marine resources which cannot be found in other parts of the country. In Zhejiang, such main resources as ports, fishery, tourism, oil, gas, tideland and islands are advantages which, together are unique and easily noticed.

X. Wu (✉)
Zhejiang Academy of Social Sciences, Hangzhou, China

C. Pei and J. Xu (eds.), *Chinese Dream and Practice in Zhejiang – Economy*,
Research Series on the Chinese Dream and China's Development Path,
https://doi.org/10.1007/978-981-13-7484-5_6

6.1.1 Developing the Blue Territory and Building a Large Province of Marine Economy

As early as the 1990s, the Zhejiang Provincial Party Committee and the Provincial Government paid attention to marine resources. They put forward and developed relevant plans and measures for developing a marine economy. The most typical case was the promulgation of the *Plan of Zhejiang Province for Marine Development (1993–2010)* in 1992, which indicated that Zhejiang Province officially started taking practical actions to develop the marine economy. In this period, with respect to marine development and the development of the marine economy, Zhejiang underwent two developmental stages, including "developing the blue territory and expanding new development spaces" (1993–1997) and "developing the marine industries and building a large province of marine economy" (1998–2002), thus the overall strength of the marine economy improved significantly. In 2002, the total output value of Zhejiang's marine economy was 108.27 billion yuan, accounting for 13.9% of Zhejiang's GDP; the system of a marine industrial structure dominated by marine fishery and the marine transportation industry preliminarily took shape, and the optimal pattern of the distribution of marine industries centering on Ningbo, Zhoushan, the Port of Xiangshan, Hangzhou Bay, Sanmen Bay and Leqing Bay emerged, thus laying a good foundation for all-round and rapid development of Zhejiang's marine economy.

6.1.2 Building a Strong Province of Marine Economy Through Sea and Land Interaction

6.1.2.1 The Birth and Development of the Philosophy of Building a Strong Province of Marine Economy Through Sea and Land Interaction

In late 2002, after serving as the Secretary of the Zhejiang Provincial Party Committee, based on several surveys and inspections, comrade Xi Jinping fully affirmed the important leading role of the successive Party Committees and governments of Zhejiang Province in Zhejiang's development of a marine economy, he sized up the situation to put forward the new strategy of turning Zhejiang into a strong province of marine economy and the developmental line of thought and policy of building a strong province of marine economy.

1. The establishment of the guiding principles for developing a marine economy

In the symposium on accelerating the development of a marine economy on May 16, 2003, comrade Xi Jinping brought forward the basic line of thought regarding Zhejiang's development of the marine economy and pointed out that Zhejiang's work on it was based on the following main guiding principles: (1) Giving scope to advantages: as Zhejiang Province enjoys relatively abundant resources including fishery, port, scenery, tideland and oil, there is a relatively good relevant industrial foundation, the geographical location is favorable, Zhejiang should leverage these advantages to speed up the adjustment of the structure of marine fishing and cultivation, actively integrate the port shipping sector, earnestly develop the port-centered sectors, the emerging marine industries and marine tourist sector, rationally develop tideland resources, gradually shape a number of advantageous marine industries and enhance the overall competitiveness of the marine economy. (2) Strengthening the planning: Zhejiang should act in a forward-looking, scientific and operable way to develop the master plan for the development of the marine economy and the corresponding special plans for port construction, the layout of port-centered sectors, tideland development, coastal land utilization, marine environment and marine tourism; it should, in an orderly fashion, also push forward comprehensive development of marine resources and optimize the layout of the marine economy. (3) Giving prominence to innovation: Zhejiang should intensify institutional, scientific and technological innovations and inject new vitality and driving forces into the marine economy. Zhejiang should further intensify the reform and expand the opening up. Zhejiang should speed up institutional and mechanism innovations, build a scientific and rational management system, a diversified input mechanism and a market operation mechanism to stimulate and guide the governments at various levels and various economic players to invest in the marine economy. Zhejiang should thoroughly carry out the strategy of promoting marine development through science and technology; it should accelerate the nurturing and introduction of human talents; it should energetically make innovations and progress in marine science and technology to promote the transformation from extensive marine development to intensive marine development and continuously increase the level of the development of a marine economy. (4) Coordinating development: Zhejiang should combine the development of marine industries with the protection of the marine environment; it should coordinate the development of the marine economy with the development of the land economy. Zhejiang should step up efforts to govern the sea under the rule of law, intensify the protection and construction of a marine ecological environment, more rapidly control marine pollution, make sure that resources are utilized in an intensive way and that the marine environment becomes ecological, and it should enhance the capability for achieving sustainable development of the marine economy; Zhejiang should correctly deal with the relations between the marine economy and the land economy, further adjust the industrial layout in coastal areas; it should widely boost clean production in a widespread manner, strictly control the emission of pollutants, and achieve integration between the marine economy and the land economy.

At the same time, comrade Xi Jinping called for focusing Zhejiang's development of the marine economy on the following eight fronts: the adjustment of the marine fishery structure, port construction, the development of port-centered sectors, the construction of island infrastructure, the development of marine tourism, efforts to promote marine development through science and technology, tideland reclamation and the protection and governance of the marine environment.

2. Utilization of Zhejiang's mountain and sea resource advantages for earnestly developing a marine economy

With a focus on the topics concerning Zhejiang's efforts to build a moderately prosperous society in all respects and achieve modernization in advance, the Forth Plenary Session of the 11th Party Committee of Zhejiang Province on July 10, 2003 stressed that it was necessary to thoroughly carry out the "Eight-Eight Strategies" and comprehensively put into practice the Scientific Outlook on Development. One of the major strategies consists in leveraging Zhejiang's mountain and sea resource advantages, actively developing the marine economy and turning the marine economy into a new growth point for Zhejiang's economy. Comrade Xi Jinping pointed out that it was essential to broaden horizons, transform the developmental philosophy, utilize the advances in science, technology and productive forces to cultivate the capability for developing various resources, and attach importance to abundant mountain and marine resources. He stressed that Zhejiang must further heighten the sense of both urgency and responsibility for developing the marine economy, take bolder actions, wider perspectives, higher standards and rely on the natural conditions suited to tap both mountain and marine resources, rationally develop and utilize marine and mountain resources, constantly expand the spaces for developing the marine economy, actively carry out the Mountain-Sea Cooperation Project and the project for turning the underdeveloped villages and towns into well-off ones, more quickly develop such underdeveloped areas as islands, mountainous areas, old revolutionary base areas and the areas inhabited by ethnic groups, take a path with Zhejiang's characteristics for interactive development of the marine economy and the land economy, and fruitfully work on the marine economy as a new economic growth point.

3. The establishment of the strategic goal of building a strong province of marine economy

Given that the goal of building Zhejiang into a large province of marine economy has been basically achieved, in the third meeting of Zhejiang Province on the marine economy in August, 2003, comrade Xi Jinping further expanded the basic line of thought regarding Zhejiang's development of a marine economy and put forward the strategic goal of building a strong province of marine economy. Zhejiang should conform to the new national strategy of developing a marine economy and building a strong marine country in order to govern the country better; it should take a long-term strategic perspective, fully realize the important significance of more rapidly developing a marine economy and building a strong marine province. The sea is the hope for Zhejiang's future. In order to develop Zhejiang's marine economy, it is unadvisable to merely rely on the sea and the fishery industry; it is necessary to go out of Zhejiang to develop Zhejiang, take the path of interactive development of a marine economy and a land economy, and based on maintaining Zhejiang's advantage in the development of the land economy, stress and speed up the efforts to develop a marine economy amidst a combination of and collaboration between the sea and the land, so that the marine economy becomes a new growth point for Zhejiang's economy and

Zhejiang takes the path, with Zhejiang's characteristics, of interactive development of a marine economy and a land economy.

In order to make sure that the people throughout the province fully realize the importance and urgency of developing a marine economy, in the meeting on reporting the developments in the Mountain-Sea Cooperation Project held on December 3, 2003, comrade Xi Jinping once again stressed that it was imperative to think in big-picture terms to fully realize the importance and significance of carrying out the Mountain-Sea Cooperation Project; he pointed out that only when the above project has been carried out can the regional gap be narrowed, regional coordinated development be promoted, new economic growth points be cultivated, the overall strength of Zhejiang Province constantly be improved, common prosperity be promoted and the fundamental interests of the people be realized. He also put forward the general requirement for the above project: follow the Scientific Outlook on Development to push forward the above project, move toward the goal of building a moderately prosperous society in all respects and basically achieve modernization in advance by pressing ahead with the above project, focus on optimizing the economic layout of the whole province to promote that project, and take a pragmatic approach to carrying it forward.

6.1.2.2 The Formation and Implementation of the Philosophy of Building a Strong Province of Marine Economy Through Interaction Between the Land and the Sea

Under the guidance of the basic line of thought on developing a marine economy and building a strong marine province, the consensus on earnestly developing a marine economy was built throughout the province. The Zhejiang Provincial Party Committee and the Provincial Government further identified the path for developing a marine economy: a path with Zhejiang's characteristics for interactive development of a marine economy and a land economy. In April, 2005, the People's Government of Zhejiang Province developed the *Plan for Building Zhejiang into a Strong Province of Marine Economy*, specifying the goals, main tasks, layout and framework for the development of Zhejiang's marine economy, and the policy measures for building a strong province of marine economy.

1. Building a strong province of marine economy

The overall line of thought and staged requirements for the strategic goal of building a strong province of marine economy were developed. They call for basically achieving the goal of building a strong province of marine economy by 2010 and completing the building of a strong province of marine economy in all respects by 2020.

2. Earnestly pushing forward land and sea interaction

It stresses that Zhejiang's marine economy should be developed by focusing on land and sea interaction, combining the advantages of marine resources in ports, fishery, scenery and oil with the advantages of the land economy in industry, market, capital, science and technology, talent and mechanisms, and earnestly promoting interactive development of land and marine industries, interactive distribution of productive forces, interactive construction of infrastructures, interactive protection and improvement of the ecological environment.

3. Focusing on nurturing five main advantageous industries

Full scope should be given to the combined advantages of five main resources, which are ports, fishery, scenery, oil and tideland; actions should be taken to energetically develop port transportation, port-centered industries, the marine fishing industry, the coastal tourist industry and the emerging marine industry; intensified efforts should be made to build the bases for five main industries, including storage and transportation of strategic materials, the coastal heavy chemical industry, modern marine fishing, marine ecological tourism and the emerging marine industry; the priorities and implementation plan for the development of the above five main industries were put forward.

4. Establishing three main zones of marine economy

In light of the distribution of marine resources and the characteristics of the regional coastal economy in Zhejiang, the whole province is divided into three main zones of marine economy in which Ningbo and Zhoushan constitute the main body and the coastal areas in Wenzhou, Taizhou and along Hangzhou Bay serve as two wings. In these three main zones, port cities and regional central cities are relied upon, and three major connection projects, including the Hangzhou Bay Bridge, the Zhoushan Island-Land Project and Dongtou Peninsula, serve as the bond to combine marine resources with regional advantages and achieve the interactive development of marine industries and a land economy.

5. Strengthening the protection of marine resources and marine ecology

Steps should be taken to protect and restore the marine ecological environment, carry out the Blue Sea Action Plan, intensify the comprehensive improvement, development and protection efforts at the main estuaries and important harbors throughout the province, coordinate the development and construction activities involving ports, shipping, reclamation, cultivation, tourism and port-centered industries, control sand excavation at river channels, conduct scientific river beach reclamation, properly protect the wetland, protect the marine biological resources, give priority to the implementation of the action for revitalizing offshore fishery resources, rationally develop and utilize tideland and strictly protect and rationally utilize shoreline resources and uninhabited islands.

6. The building and safeguarding of the support system for developing Zhejiang's marine economy

The innovations to institutions and mechanisms, necessary government input and policy guidance should be strengthened; full play should be given to the fundamental role of the market in resource allocation and the initiative of the whole society in participation. Measures should be taken to build a support system covering legal and policy support, scientific and technological support, fund support, the support for accelerating the construction of marine infrastructures, practical and innovation support and support for ecological protection.

With the implementation of the *Plan for Building a Strong Province of Marine Economy*, Zhejiang has embarked on the road towards a strong marine province, and the marine economy has achieved unprecedented rapid development.

First, the aggregate of the marine economy has been on the rise, while the industrial structure and layout have been gradually optimized. In 2007, the total output of the marine economy in the whole province reached 450.8 billion yuan, accounting for 8.3% of the province's GDP. Zhejiang has seen the gradual formation of a system for an industrial structure with the coordinated development of core marine industries, marine supporting industries and marine-related industries; the marine industrial structure has been constantly optimized, with the output ratio of the marine primary, secondary and tertiary industries adjusted from 18:38:44 in 2003 to 11:40:49 in 2007. In Zhejiang, the port-centered industry has rapidly risen, and the marine tertiary industry, represented by marine tourism and shipping, has boomed and become the pillar industry in Zhejiang's marine economy.

Second, great headway has been made in the core marine industries, and the advantageous industrial clusters with increasing overall competitiveness have emerged. Marine fishery, marine transportation, coastal tourism, marine shipbuilding and seawater utilization have become the advantageous marine industries in Zhejiang. In 2007, five main advantageous industries accounted for 52.3% of Zhejiang's marine economy; marine electric power, marine shipbuilding, marine biopharmaceutical and marine transportation industries grew rapidly at an average rate of 82.4%, 61.8%, 25.9% and 25.2%, respectively during the period 2005–2007.[1] Such advantageous marine industries as marine fishery, marine transportation, coastal tourism, marine shipbuilding and seawater utilization have undergone a qualitative transformation of their growth modes while achieving quantitative growth.

Moreover, the regional layout of Zhejiang's marine economy has basically formed. The three main marine economy zones in which Ningbo and Zhoushan constitute the main body and the coastal areas in Wenzhou, Taizhou and along Hangzhou Bay serve as two wings have begun to take shape. In these three main zones, port cities and regional central cities are relied upon, and three major connection projects, including the Hangzhou Bay Bridge, the Zhoushan Island-Land Project and Dongtou Peninsula, serve as the bond to meet the needs of collaboration and connection between port development, transportation and logistics facilities and the industrial chain, combine the advantages of marine resources with regional advantages and achieve interactive development of marine industries and a land economy. At the same time, under the guidance of the strategy of land and sea interaction, Zhejiang has been home to a number of industrial clusters based on land-sea interactive development which accord with resource characteristics, reflect resource advantages and have regional characteristics.

[1] Zhejiang Provincial Bureau of Statistics, A Study of the Development of the Marine Economy in Zhejiang Province. http://tjj.zj.gov.cn/art/2009/7/9/art_281_36459.html.

6.1.2.3 The Birth of the Strategy of Earnestly Developing a Marine Economy and More Rapidly Building a Strong Province of Ports and Shipping

When serving as the Secretary of the Zhejiang Provincial Party Committee, comrade Xi Jinping had always attached great importance to the construction and development of Zhejiang's port; he clearly stated that the construction of Ningbo's port would not only exert a direct impact on the process of the development of Ningbo's modernization, but it would also have a vital bearing on the development of the whole province, so it was the strategic focus of the whole province. Ningbo should, in light of the goal of building an important part of the Shanghai international shipping center, thoroughly carry out the developmental strategy of revitalizing the city through its port and promoting the development of the port through the city, take container as the developmental priority to speed up the construction of a large modern port; it should further accelerate the integration of the Ningbo-Zhoushan Port, further enhance the construction of port infrastructures, focus on a number of key projects, including a container terminal and a deepwater berth, develop modern logistics, improve the service function and canvassion system of the port, speed up the construction of the collection and distribution network and further expand the hinterland of the port. For Zhoushan, comrade Xi Jinping said, "Although currently there are difficulties, as long as its own resources are fully utilized and play is given to the advantages of fishery, the port, scenery and location advantage, and work is carried out to make the marine economy large in a deep-going way, Zhoushan can enjoy very strong late-mover advantages and is fully able to become a developed area of a marine economy. The Zhejiang Provincial Party Committee and the Provincial Government vowed to put the work on Zhoushan in a due position, support Zhoushan's development, and increase its support to actively develop Zhoushan."

Given the above strategy, the Zhejiang Provincial Party Committee and the Provincial Government focused the work relating to the development of the marine economy on port construction. In June, 2007, the 12th Party Congress of Zhejiang Province vowed to actively develop a marine economy and for the first time put forward the goal of building a strong province of port and shipping. Afterwards, relevant departments and scientific research institutions jointly conducted a survey on strengthening the development of a marine economy and building a strong province of port and shipping, carried out a feasibility study of the strategy and put into practice a relevant implementation plan. The People's Political Consultative Conference of Zhejiang Province brought forward the following strategic line of thought, tasks and measures for pushing forward the development of a marine economy: approach, plan, utilize and manage the sea in a scientific way, revitalize the sea through science and technology.

Under the guidance of the strategy and developmental line of thought, Zhejiang has energetically pushed forward the development and construction of the port, and has seen the gradual formation of a coastal port system and a modern logistics system in which the Ningbo-Zhoushan deepwater port serves as the hub, Wenzhou, Jiaxing and Taizhou constitute the backbone while small and medium-sized ports function as the supporting facilities. With an effort to break through the original one port-one city-one government mode,[2] the Port of Ningbo and the Port of Zhoushan were integrated under the principle of unified management, planning, construction and brand to achieve leapfrog development. In 2008, the Ningbo-Zhoushan Port ranked No. 8 in the world in container throughput and ranked No. 1 in the Ranking List of Comprehensive Competitiveness of Ports 2008. Therefore, the port and shipping construction in Zhejiang Province undoubtedly, based on full implementation of the Plan, further promoted rapid development of the marine economy in Zhejiang Province, thus laying the foundation for the take-off of the marine economy in Zhejiang Province.

6.1.3 Being Based on Zhejiang's Marine Economy Demonstration Areas and Taking Advantage of the National Strategy

1. Formulating the *Plan for Zhejiang's Marine Economy Development Demonstration Areas*, optimizing the layout of the development of a marine economy

In order to improve Zhejiang's strategic position in China and better promote Zhejiang's industrial structural adjustment and the transformation of its economic developmental mode, in June, 2009, the Zhejiang Provincial Party Committee and the Provincial Government, in light of Zhejiang's characteristics and advantages, chose the development of a marine economy from a number of themes, including the development of a marine economy, innovation in the private economy, international trade reform, as the theme which could be elevated to a national strategy in the future. As from October, 2009, under the leadership of the Zhejiang Provincial Party Committee and the Provincial Government with Zhao Hongzhu and Lu Zushan as the core, relevant provincial departments made plans, preparation and drafting efforts, experts held consultation and carried out a feasibility study, communication was conducted several times with such ministries as the National Development and Reform Commission, an expert group consisting of more than 20 academicians from the Chinese Academy of Engineering and more than 200 experts conducted thorough surveys and feasibility studies on 12 subjects relating to the marine economy, and finally a clear blueprint for the development of Zhejiang's marine economy took shape.

In early 2010, "accelerating the formation of large highly competitive industries including the marine economy" was included in the work report of the People's Government of Zhejiang Province for the first time. In July, 2010, the national pilot work on the development of a marine economy was officially initiated, and Zhejiang was incorporated into the national pilot areas for the development of a marine economy. In August, 2010, the People's Government of Zhejiang Province officially submitted the

---

[2]Xu Qin, Integrating Soft Resources to Improve the Competitiveness of Zhejiang's Ports, *Journal of Marine Sciences*, 2008(1).

plan of Zhejiang Province to the National Development and Reform Commission. In November, 2010, relevant ministries conducted a special survey on the development of Zhejiang's marine economy, the name of the plan was determined as the *Plan for Zhejiang's Marine Economy Development Demonstration Areas*. In the same month, the *Plan for Zhejiang's Marine Economy Development Demonstration Areas* and implementation plan were discussed and adopted by an executive meeting of the People's Government of Zhejiang Province and by the Standing Committee of the Zhejiang Provincial Party Committee.

On February 25, 2011, the State Council officially approved the *Plan for Zhejiang's Marine Economy Development Demonstration Areas*. This showed that the development of Zhejiang's marine economy was officially elevated to a national strategy and became an important part of the national marine development strategy and the regional coordinated development strategy. The *Plan for Zhejiang's Marine Economy Development Demonstration Areas* became the first plan for marine economy demonstration areas in China and also the first plan of Zhejiang Province incorporated into the national development strategy. Subsequently, the construction of the Zhoushan Archipelago New Area was officially included in the National 12th Five-Year Plan. In January, 2013, the State Council officially approved the establishment of the Zhoushan Archipelago New Area. The Zhoushan Archipelago New Area became the fourth "new area" and the first archipelago new area in China. In the same year, the National Development and Reform Commission approved the *Plan for Pilot Work on the Development of Zhejiang's Marine Economy*. Since then, the development of Zhejiang's marine economy has officially ushered in the era of a national strategy.

2. Establishing a three-in-one port and shipping logistics service system, building a strong province of port and shipping

In April, 2009, the Zhejiang Provincial Party Committee and the Provincial Government, based on "building a strong province of port and shipping" as put forward in the 12th Party Congress of Zhejiang Province, further vowed to actively promote the great development of a marine economy by focusing on building a strong province of port and shipping, and made the following basic arrangements for building Zhejiang into a strong province of port and shipping: more rapidly develop the port service industry, the logistics industry and the system of collection and distribution, expand the port-based economic hinterland in Zhejiang Province; move forward with the integration of the existing port resources, build a coastal port system with a rational structure and complete functions; strengthen the planning and management of island and shoreline resources, leaving ample spaces for future long-term development.

In order to build a strong province of port and shipping, it is imperative to improve such infrastructures as the transportation network dominated by the Ningbo-Zhoushan Port. Given this consideration, the Zhejiang Provincial Party Committee and the Provincial Government made, for the first time, the strategic arrangement of revitalizing ports through bridges, developing islands through ports and promoting the concurrent development of bridges, ports and islands. During the period of the 11th Five-Year Plan, Zhejiang completed 48.5 billion yuan of investments in ports and shipping, 3.3 times that during the period of the 10th Five-Year Plan, which ranked No. 1 nationwide, 78 deepwater berths above 10,000t were newly added. After the Wenzhou (Dongtou) Peninsula Project was completed in 2006, in May, 2008, the Hangzhou Bay Sea-Crossing Bridge with a full length of 36 km was open to traffic, greatly shortening the spatial distance between cities at the north and south wings of the Yangtze River Delta Region. In December, 2009, the Zhoushan Sea-Crossing Bridge connected Zhoushan Island with the mainland. Ningbo-Taizhou-Wenzhou Railway, the Wenzhou-Fuzhou Railway and the Shanghai-Hangzhou High-speed Railway were also open to traffic. The Beilun Phase IV Container Terminal and the Zhoushan Coal Transfer Terminal were put into operation. The first 300,000t artificial channel in China was completed and put into use. The construction of a number of major infrastructures, including Sanmen Nuclear Power, was gradually and smoothly pushed forward. In 2009, the cargo throughput of ports throughout the province exceeded 1 billion tons, hitting a new high.[3] Moreover, in order to address low economic performance amidst the rapid development of ports, in 2009, the Zhejiang Provincial Party Committee and the Provincial Government further put forward the strategic idea of building a three-in-one port and shipping logistics service system covering a bulk commodity trading platform, a collection and distribution network based on sea-land interaction and a financial and information service support system. In November, 2010, the Zhejiang Provincial Party Committee and the Provincial Government explicitly stated that the bulk commodity trading platform was the key part of the three-in-one port and shipping logistics service system, and it was necessary to follow the overall line of thought of one trading center, two service platforms, multiple trading zones and a number of storage, transportation and distribution bases to build a bulk commodity trading platform, and improve the collection and distribution network and the financial and information service system. Meanwhile, the Zhejiang Provincial Party Committee and the Provincial Government also planned the construction of the port and shipping logistics service system in the *Plan for Zhejiang's Marine Economy Development Demonstration Areas* in a systematic and detailed way by giving priority to that construction.

3. Building a modern marine industrial system, promoting the building of a strong province of marine economy

In the process of building a large marine province, especially a strong province of marine economy, Zhejiang has always highly stressed a focus on development based on land and sea interaction, and the efforts to vigorously develop the port transport industry, a port-centered industry, marine fishery, coastal tourist and emerging marine industries and build Zhejiang's complete system of a modern marine industry.

Based on "supporting and cultivating a number of strategic emerging marine industries, increasing Zhejiang's overall industrial level" as put forward in the *Plan for Zhejiang's Marine Economy Development Demonstration Areas*, the *Development Plan of Zhejiang Province for the Emerging Marine Industries* unveiled in

[3] Party History Research Office of the Zhejiang Provincial Party Committee, *Making the People Rich by Starting a Business and of Building a Strong Province through Innovation*, Zhejiang People's Publishing House, 2012, pp. 37–38.

2011 further clearly states that the future "blue economy" in Zhejiang should focus on advanced marine equipment manufacturing, marine biological medicine, the comprehensive utilization of seawater, marine clean energy, port and shipping logistics service and marine exploration and development service.

The *Several Opinions on Accelerating the Development of a Marine Economy*, issued in March, 2011, specify relevant preferential policies and support for the development of the emerging marine industries in terms of fiscal and tax preference, support in land and sea utilization, investment and financing guarantee. Zhejiang is endeavoring to develop the emerging marine industries into the pillar industries in the marine economy.

4. Establishing the Zhoushan Archipelago New Area, intensifying the development and utilization of important islands

In order to fully utilize Zhejiang's abundant island resources, in February, 2010, the Zhejiang Provincial Party Committee and the Provincial Government entrusted the Chinese Academy of Engineering to conduct strategic research on the comprehensive development of Zhejiang's coastal areas and islands, and arranged the establishment of the Zhoushan Archipelago New Area as the key strategic task in developing Zhejiang's marine economy. The *Plan for Zhejiang's Marine Economy Development Demonstration Areas*, approved by the State Council in February, 2011, officially specifies the strategy of establishing the Zhoushan Archipelago New Area. The Zhoushan Archipelago New Area was officially included in the National 12th Five-Year Plan—the Plan explicitly calls for promoting regional construction including Zhejiang's Zhoushan Archipelago New Area—and became the fourth "new area" in China, the first archipelago new area in China and the first new area focusing on a marine economy and at the level of national strategy.[4] After the Zhoushan Archipelago New Area was established, the Zhejiang Provincial Party Committee and the Provincial Government specially carried out a slew of policies for supporting the construction of the Zhoushan Archipelago New Area, with efforts centering on the construction of the Zhoushan Archipelago New Area to play an active role in seeking policy support, boosting project implementation and breaking new ground.

In recent years, Zhejiang has also actively created conditions for intensifying the development and utilization of important islands. In June, 2011, the People's Government of Zhejiang Province released the *Plan of Zhejiang Province for the Development, Utilization and Protection of Important Islands*, specifying 100 important islands within the sea areas under the jurisdiction of Zhejiang Province and stating that they would be developed in a classified way and would be utilized in an orderly

[4]The Zhoushan Archipelago New Area is covered by the existing administrative areas of Zhoushan City. Its functions are as follows: it serves as the forerunner area for the development of Zhejiang's marine economy, a comprehensive marine development experimental area, an important growth pole for the economic development in the Yangtze River Delta Region. Its developmental goals are as follows: turn it into China's bulk commodity storage, transportation and transfer processing trading center, an important marine opening gateway in East China, China's comprehensive marine and island protection and development demonstration area, China's important modern marine industrial base, China's forerunner area for coordinated land and sea development.

fashion in light of other location conditions, resource endowment and development foundation from 2011 to 2015.

Moreover, Zhejiang has also more rapidly developed and utilized uninhabited islands while intensifying the development and utilization of inhabited islands.

5. Governing the sea according to laws, strengthening the protection of marine ecology

In recent years, Zhejiang has issued 18 local environmental protection regulations, including the *Regulations of Zhejiang Province on the Prevention and Control of Environmental Pollution Caused by Solid Wastes*, the *Regulations of Zhejiang Province on the Prevention and Control of Water Pollution* and the *Regulations of Zhejiang Province on the Protection of the Marine Environment*, which have played an active role in protecting marine ecology.

6.2 From a Large Marine Province to a Strong Marine Province

6.2.1 The Marine Economy Has Rapidly Grown and Its Strength Has Continuously Increased

6.2.1.1 The Role of the Marine Economy in Zhejiang's Economy Has Been Constantly Enhanced

The aggregate of Zhejiang's marine economy has soared. In 1996, the total output value of Zhejiang's marine economy was 28,816 million yuan, accounting for 6.88% of the province's GDP; in 2002, its total output reached 108,272 million yuan, accounting for 13.53%. After serving as the Secretary of the Zhejiang Provincial Party Committee, comrade Xi Jinping inherited and developed Zhejiang's strategy for the development of the original marine economy and put forward the developmental strategy of building a strong marine province. In 2011, Zhejiang's strategy for the development of a marine economy was elevated to a national strategy, while the construction of the marine economy demonstration areas and the Zhoushan Archipelago New Area in 2013 promoted the development of Zhejiang's marine economy to a higher level. In 2013, the total output value of Zhejiang's marine economy hit 550.8 billion yuan, accounting for 14.7% of the province's GDP. The proportion of Zhejiang's marine economy in the province's national economy has been on the increase, its position has been increasingly important, and its role in driving the province's economic development forward has become very apparent.

6.2.1.2 The Position in China's Marine Economy Has Gradually Improved

In terms of regional space, China's marine economy consists of 11 coastal provinces, autonomous regions and municipalities, including Liaoning, Tianjin, Hebei, Shandong, Shanghai, Jiangsu, Zhejiang, Fujian, Guangdong, Guangxi and Hainan. Since Liaoning Province vowed to develop the marine industry for the first time and turned its attention to the sea for building a marine Liaoning in 1986, China's coastal provinces have developed respective marine development strategies and have made brilliant achievements in this regard. However, various areas are different in the natural resource they possess, the foundation of their historical development, their scientific and technological level, their social economic strength, their philosophy of the development of a marine economy and the intensity of their government support, so China's coastal areas differ greatly in the level of the development of their marine economies. Take 2013 as an example, the largest aggregate of the marine economy occurred in Guangdong Province and reached 1,250 billion yuan, while Zhejiang Province with the aggregate of the marine economy being 550.8 billion yuan, ranked No. 5 nationwide in this regard, following Shandong, Shanghai and Fujian; Zhejiang's marine economy grew by 11.1%, ranking Zhejiang No. 5 nationwide in growth rate, thus Zhejiang's marine economy was highly competitive.[5]

From the perspective of the overall development of China's marine economy, during the period 2000–2013, the total output value of Zhejiang's marine economy accounted for 14.05% (2004)—the highest proportion—and 8.34% (2001)—the lowest proportion—of the combined GDP of the 11 coastal areas in China. The proportion of Zhejiang's marine economy in China's marine economy has gradually increased since 2000—it declined slightly in 2006, but reached 10.51% in 2009 and remained at about 10% after 2009. Furthermore, during the period 2000–2013, both the growth rate of Zhejiang's marine economy and the proportion of its total output value in the GDP were higher than the nation's average levels (except 2006).

6.2.2 The Marine Industrial Structure Has Been Continuously Optimized

6.2.2.1 The Structure of the Primary, Secondary and Tertiary Marine Industries Has Been Optimized

Zhejiang's marine economy has developed rapidly. The total output value of the primary, secondary and tertiary marine industries grew from 34.6 billion yuan, 27.6

[5]Report Materials Concerning the Chinese Dream and Zhejiang's Practice (Zhejiang Province Ocean and Fisheries Bureau, 2013) and the Report of the Zhejiang Provincial Development and Reform Commission on Self-examination and Assessment during the First Stage of the Pilot Work on Zhejiang's Marine Economic Development (Zhe Fa Gai Hai Jing (2014) No. 74).

billion yuan and 5.7 billion yuan in 1998 to 37.95 billion yuan, 221.73 billion yuan and 291.12 billion yuan in 2013, respectively. As of 2013, the proportion of the primary marine industry in the total output value of Zhejiang's marine economy decreased to 6.9%. Zhejiang's tertiary marine industry has always grown rapidly and has shown a year-by-year upward trend. During the period 2001–2013, the tertiary marine industry enjoyed the largest proportion in the marine industrial structure. Compared with the tertiary industry, Zhejiang's secondary marine industry started late, but it grew gratifyingly after 2005; each of Zhejiang's secondary and tertiary marine industries basically constituted half of Zhejiang's marine economy after 2009. Therefore, Zhejiang's marine economy dynamically evolved from the primary industry to the tertiary industry and then from the tertiary industry to the secondary industry; this was consistent with the trend of industrial structural adjustment and upgrading in the marine economy; a marine industrial structure under the "tertiary, secondary and primary" mode has taken shape; the following requirement specified in the *National Plan for the Development of the Marine Undertaking* has been basically satisfied: the total output value of the marine tertiary industry makes up more than 50%.

6.2.2.2 The Emerging Marine Industries Have Developed Rapidly

The abundant marine resources and the advantage of a superior location provide a strong guarantee for the building and development of Zhejiang's marine industrial system. As the marine economy develops and the traditional industries are renovated by marine science and technology and information technology, Zhejiang's marine industries have become increasingly diverse, and a number of emerging marine industries with a high technical content and great developmental potential have emerged while the traditional marine industries have continued to developed. At present, in Zhejiang Province, an industrial system covering 13 main marine industries has taken shape, the traditional marine industries and the ever-expanding emerging marine industries have jointly supported the sustained development of Zhejiang's marine economy.

The marine economy is divided into two categories and three levels by the degree of industrial relevancy, including marine industries and marine-related industries, while marine industries can be subdivided into main marine industries and marine scientific research and educational management service industries. The main marine industries are the core industries in the marine economy, while the marine scientific research and educational management service industries are the supporting industries in the marine economy; and the marine-related industries are the peripheral industries in the marine economy. (1) Form the structural perspective, in 2011, the main marine industries, the marine scientific research and educational management service industries and marine-related industries accounted for 40.17%, 16.26% and 43.57% of the total output value of Zhejiang's marine industries, respectively; a system of industrial structure with the coordinated development of marine core industries, marine supporting industries and marine-related industries has taken shape. (2) In terms of the aggregate and growth rate, in 2011, the added value of Zhejiang's marine economy was 256 billion yuan, accounting for 56.43% of that of the whole province's marine economy—the added value of the main marine industries was 182.27 billion yuan, accounting for 40.17% of that of the whole province's marine economy. During the period 2005–2013, except for 2011, Zhejiang's main marine industries grew annually by an average of 19%, 2 percentage points higher than the average growth rate of the entire marine economy; the main marine industries have become the main driving forces for promoting the development of the marine economy in Zhejiang Province.

Zhejiang's shipbuilding industry developed rapidly as from 2004. Its average annual growth rate exceeded 40% during the period 2005–2013, 26 percentage points higher than the average annual growth rate of the main marine industries; it was one of the fastest-growing marine industries in Zhejiang during the same period. At present, it has become one of the three pillar industries in the marine economy of Zhejiang Province; Zhejiang has a long history of marine transportation. The marine transportation industry has developed well in Zhejiang; it is an important industry in the development of Zhejiang's modern marine economy. Although Zhejiang's emerging marine industries, such as the coastal tourist industry, the marine chemical industry, the marine biological medicine industry, started late, they have developed rapidly. In 2013, the emerging marine industries in Zhejiang Province accounted for more than 30% of the whole province's marine economy.[6]

6.2.2.3 The Traditional Marine Industries Have Been Continuously Transformed and Upgraded

Zhejiang's traditional marine industries mainly include the marine fishery industry, the marine salt industry and the marine aquatic product processing industry.

Although the proportion of the marine fishery industry in the marine economy of Zhejiang Province has been on the decrease in recent years, it still exceeds 1/10, the aggregate has maintained a steady growth. In 2012, the total output delivered by the marine fishery industry in Zhejiang Province was 48.5 billion yuan, 4,312,400t marine products were made in the marine fishery industry, making it steadily rank No. 4 in the nation's marine fishery industry. From the structural perspective, although the marine fishing industry remained the main part of Zhejiang's fishery industry, long-range fishing grew rapidly, the output of the long-range fishing industry rose from 160,500t in 2009 to 403,000t in 2012. Furthermore, in Zhejiang Province, efforts have been made to actively develop efficient, ecological modern fishery, help fishermen transfer to marine aquaculture, establish 88 provincial modern fishery parks and 13 aquatic stock and improved variety farms above the provincial level, with improved varieties covering 80% and the developed marine aquaculture area being about 60.53

[6]Relevant data come from The Developments in the Construction of Zhejiang's Marine Economic Development Demonstration Area, http://zjnews.zjol.com.cn/system/2014/08/11/020192318.shtml; Research Group of the Zhejiang Provincial Bureau of Statistics, A Study of the Development of Zhejiang's Marine Economy, *Statistical Science and Practice*, 2012(4).

million mu. In 2013, the quantity of marine aquaculture in Zhejiang Province was 872,000t, up 1.3% over the previous year.

Zhejiang abounds in sea salt resources and its sea salt industry has a long history. However, with the impact from the industrial structural adjustment and upgrading of Zhejiang's marine economy, the sea salt industry shrank, the salt field area, the sea salt production area, the year-end sea salt production capacity, the marine output and their proportions in the nation's total quantities declined year by year. Zhejiang's salt field area was only 2,790 hectares in 2011, down 23.41% compared with the 3,643 hectares in 2009; the production area and the sea salt production capacity decreased by 22.93% and 14.42%, respectively over 2009.

The marine aquatic product processing industry developed rapidly as from the 1990s. Since the beginning of the 21st century, Zhejiang has moved toward deep processing, fine processing of marine aquatic products and their brand improvement, and Zhejiang has broken through the restrictions on three main traditional products, including smoked products, dried products and canned products. The output of aquatic products in Zhejiang Province was 5,177,000t in 2010, up 3.8% over the previous year, accounting for 3.2% of the total output value from the whole province's marine economy.

As indicated, the degree of concentration in Zhejiang's marine industry has continuously decreased, and its dependence on the traditional industries has declined greatly; the emerging marine industries with a high technical content and great developmental potential have started to occupy the leading position; the emerging marine industries and the advantageous industries among the traditional marine industries jointly support the sustainable development of Zhejiang's marine economy—Zhejiang's marine industries are dominated by three main industries, including the marine tourist industry, the marine transport industry and the marine shipbuilding industry, laying a solid industrial foundation for building a strong marine province.

6.2.3 *The Auxiliary and Supporting Systems for the Marine Economy Have Improved*

6.2.3.1 The Marine Scientific and Technological Capability Has Improved, the Contributions from Marine Science and Technology to the Economy Have Been on the Increase

Zhejiang has carried out the strategy of revitalizing the sea through science and technology since the 1990s: (1) Zhejiang has established marine research and development centers, made breakthroughs in new and high marine technology and reserved marine talents. As of 2012, the whole province was home to 28 marine institutions of higher learning and scientific research institutions, 4 national-level marine research and development centers, 7 national demonstration bases for revitalizing the sea through science and technology, 3 national marine science parks and more than

8,300 people directly engaged in marine scientific research, and its marine scientific and technological capability constantly improved. (2) Marked effects have been produced in cultivating new and hi-tech marine enterprises and carrying out the projects for industrialization of new and high marine technologies. With the construction of provincial-level new and hi-tech marine parks, the demonstration areas (bases) for revitalizing the sea through science and technology and marine technology enterprise incubators, Zhejiang has cultivated and grown a group of new and hi-tech marine enterprises which enjoy the leading position nationwide and it has gradually nurtured a number of marine specialty industries with core competitiveness.

6.2.3.2 The Marine Infrastructure Has Continually Improved, and Construction Has Begun on the Integrated System of Transportation Networks and the Disaster Prevention and Reduction Project

Under the guidance of the Plan, breakthroughs have been made in Zhejiang's marine infrastructure: (1) Actions have been taken to further speed up the construction of transportation, electric power, water conservation and communication facilities in coastal areas and on the main islands; major projects, including th Hangzhou Bay Bridge, the Zhoushan Island-Land Project and the Wenzhou Dongtou Peninsula Project, have been completed and put into use. (2) Continued efforts have been made to promote the planning and construction of the integrated transportation network with land and sea interaction. Two accesses to the sea—the Zhoushan Island-Land Project and the Wenzhou Dongtou Peninsula—have been built to forge two important bonds for connecting the land and the sea and achieving the advantage of integration and economic interaction between the land and the sea.[7] (3) The inland corridor has been built, provincial highways and railways have been connected to the intra-provincial road network, close connections have been built among points, lines and networks, the collection and distribution capability of the whole system of the province's transportation network has improved significantly.

Furthermore, Zhejiang has also carried out the construction of the "Thousand-li Seawall Project", the standard fishing port and marine environmental monitoring system, and its marine disaster prevention capability has improved substantially.

6.2.3.3 The Soft Environment for the Marine Economy Has Been Guaranteed

First, Zhejiang has reinforced comprehensive marine management and provided institutional guarantees for the development of the marine economy. Based on earnestly carrying out the *Law of the People's Republic of China on the Administration of the*

[7]Zhou Fujun, The Interactive Development of Land and Sea Industries Demands Five Breakthroughs, *Today Sci-Tech*, 2005(11).

Use of the Sea Area, the *Law of the People's Republic of China on Marine Environmental Protection*, *Regulations of Zhejiang Province on Marine Environmental Protection*, *Measures of Zhejiang Province for* the *Administration of the Use of the Sea Area*, *Marine Function Zoning of Zhejiang Province*, *Interim Measures of Zhejiang Province for the Administration of the Collection of Fees for the Use of the Sea Area* and other laws, regulations and relevant systems, Zhejiang has completed the construction of the marine function zoning system at the provincial, municipal and county levels, developed the *Plan of Zhejiang Province for the Protection and Construction of the Marine Ecological Environment*, and attempted to comprehensively carry out the certificate for the right to sea area use and the paid use system, so unpaid, disorderly and excessive use of sea areas has been preliminarily curbed.

Second, Zhejiang has intensified marine environmental protection for ensuring the sustainable development of the marine economy. (1) The *Law of the People's Republic of China on Marine Environmental Protection* has been strictly enforced; the marine environmental assessment system for marine and coastal construction projects has been adopted; efforts have been organized to assess the marine environmental impact of a number of major construction projects, including the Hangzhou Bay Bridge. (2) The marine environmental monitoring and forecasting system and the mechanism for monitoring for early warning of a red tide emergency have been established throughout the province. (3) Great efforts have been made to carry out marine ecological environmental protection and restoration projects, actively build a number of marine natural reserves; moreover, new progress has been made in marine biodiversity protection; and Nanji Islands National Marine Natural Reserve has been included in the United Nations' Man and Biosphere Programme.

6.3 The Construction of Marine Economy Demonstration Areas and the Zhoushan Archipelago New Area

The State Council officially approved the *Plan for Zhejiang's Marine Economy Development Demonstration Areas* on February 25, 2011. The State Council approved the establishment of the Zhoushan Archipelago New Area in January, 2013; this showed that the development of Zhejiang's marine economy had been officially elevated to a national strategy and had become an important part of the national marine development strategy and regional coordinated development; it has also presented unprecedented opportunities for Zhejiang's development of the marine economy and opened a new chapter for the development of Zhejiang's marine economy and that of the regional economy as well.

6.3.1 The Construction of Marine Economy Development Demonstration Areas in Zhejiang Province

The *Plan for Zhejiang's Marine Economy Development Demonstration Areas* is the first plan for marine economy demonstration areas in China and also Zhejiang's first plan to be included in the national development strategy.

1. The important significance of the construction of marine economy demonstration areas for Zhejiang

The construction of Zhejiang's marine economy development demonstration areas is a strategic decision for implementing China's marine development strategy, improving China's strategy for the development of coastal regions, for safeguarding maritime rights and interests and national economic security; it is also a strategic choice for promoting Zhejiang's economic transformation and upgrading, cultivating new economic growth points for Zhejiang, boosting coordinated land and sea development and expanding opening up. The execution of the Plan is beneficial for Zhejiang Province to better transform from a small province of resources to a large province of resources; marine resources are comprehensively protected and rationally utilized to enhance the overall economic strength and international competitiveness of the whole province, and to achieve sustainable economic and social development in Zhejiang Province.

2. The positioning and goal of the construction of marine economy demonstration areas

The construction of Zhejiang's marine economy demonstration areas is based on Zhejiang's characteristics and advantages and serves national strategic requirements; its goal involves one center and four demonstration areas—one center is the China International Logistics Center for Bulk Commodities; the four demonstration areas are the China Marine and Island Development, Opening-up and Reform Demonstration Area, the China Modern Marine Industrial Development Demonstration Area, the China Coordinated Land-Sea Development Demonstration Area and the China Marine Ecological Civilization and Clean Energy Demonstration Area. Such a main goal needs to be achieved in two stages. The first stage (2011–2015): (1) the GDP in demonstration areas will hit 2.6 trillion yuan, accounting for 3/4 of that in the whole province; (2) the Marine GDP will be close to 700 billion yuan; science and technology will contribute more than 70%; the area of clean sea areas will exceed 15%; cargo throughput in coastal areas will reach 920 million tons; (3) The transformation and upgrading of the marine economy will produce remarkable effects, and marine science, technology and culture will stay ahead nationwide; the marine ecological environment will improve significantly; the goal of building a strong province of marine economy will be basically achieved. The second stage (2016–2020): marine GDP in the whole province will hit 1,200 billion yuan; science and technology will contribute about 80%; the added value of the emerging marine industries will account for about 35% of the marine GDP; a modern marine industrial system will take shape, the building of a strong province of marine economy will be completed in all respects.

3. The construction of marine economy demonstration areas and the marine economy development pattern of Zhejiang Province

As Zhejiang is building marine economy demonstration areas, in order to optimize the marine economy development layout, Zhejiang has determined the overall pattern of marine economy development which features one core, two wings, three circles, nine areas and multiple islands. (1) Strengthening one core—the Ningbo-Zhoushan Port sea area, islands and the cities on which it relies, building the key areas for China's participation in the international competition involving the marine economy and the strategic highland for safeguarding national economic security. (2) Elevating two wings—the circum-Hangzhou Bay and its offshore areas serve as the northern wing, while the coastal areas in Wenzhou and Taizhou and their offshore areas serve as the southern wing to create Zhejiang's marine economic industrial development belt. (3) Making three circles strong—three main coastal urban circles, including Hangzhou, Ningbo and Wenzhou, provide the main support for the transformation and upgrading of the marine economy, with efforts to intensify basic marine research, technical research and development, achieve transformation and talent cultivation, and form the important areas with the most vibrant marine economy and at a high industrial level in China's coastal areas. (4) Developing nine agglomeration areas—-focusing on building nine main industrial agglomeration areas, including Hangzhou Dajiangdong, Hangzhou Chengxi Kechuang, Ningbo Hangzhou Bay, Ningbo Meishan Logistics, the Jiaxing Modern Service Industry, Shaoxing Binhai, Zhoushan Marine, the Taizhou Bay Circular Economy, Wenzhou Oujiangkou; bringing about main carriers for transforming Zhejiang's marine economy developmental mode and cultivating new urban areas. (5) Utilizing multiple islands—focusing on pushing forward the development, utilization and protection of important islands, including Zhoushan, Daishan, Yuhuan, Dongtou, Meishan, Liuheng, Jintang, Qushan, Zhujiajian, Yangshan, Nantian, Toumen, Dachen, Daxiaomen, Nanji; building China's forerunner area for island development and opening-up.

4. Core tasks for the construction of marine economy demonstration areas

In order to carry out the plan approved by the State Council and make comprehensive arrangements for the construction of Zhejiang's marine economy development demonstration areas, in March, 2011, the Zhejiang Provincial Party Committee and the Provincial Government issued *Several Opinions on Accelerating the Development of the Marine Economy*, improving the working line of thought and the specific measures for coordinated land and sea development, developing the plan and policy opinions for carrying out the pilot work, and further specifying three core tasks for promoting the development of the marine economy. First, building a three-in-one port and shipping logistics service system covering a bulk commodity trading platform, a collection and distribution network based on sea-land interaction and a system of financial and information support; cultivating the key points for enhancing the core competitiveness for the development of Zhejiang's marine economy. Second, building Zhejiang's Zhoushan Archipelago New Area, creating the commanding height for breaking new ground in the development of Zhejiang's marine economy. Third, building a modern marine industrial system, making the underpinning point for fostering new advantages for Zhejiang's economic development in the 21st century.

5. The supporting conditions necessary for the construction of marine economy demonstration areas

In order to smoothly push forward the construction of Zhejiang's marine economy demonstration areas, the Zhejiang Provincial Party Committee and the Provincial Government vowed to build up five main supporting conditions. First, improving marine infrastructure networks. Ameliorating the integrated transportation network, the network for energy safeguarding, the network for the utilization of water resources, the high-speed information network and the network for marine disaster prevention and reduction; continuously optimizing the basic conditions for building marine economy development demonstration areas. Second, more rapidly pressing ahead with the marine scientific and technological innovation system. Deeply carrying out the strategy of revitalizing the sea through science and technology, speeding up the building of a marine scientific and technological innovation system, intensifying efforts to make breakthroughs in revitalizing the sea through science and technology and increasing special funds input. Third, accelerating the development of the marine educational undertaking and talent cultivation. Scientifically planning the layout of marine institutions of higher learning and building high-level marine higher education development platforms. Fourth, reinforcing the construction of a marine ecological civilization. Rationally utilizing and intensively developing marine resources. Fifth, increasing fiscal and tax policy support. Providing more policy support in land and sea utilization, finance and taxation, investment and financing.

6.3.2 The Construction of the Zhoushan Archipelago New Area

In January, 2013, the State Council approved Zhejiang's establishment of the Zhoushan Archipelago New Area. The construction of the Zhoushan Archipelago New Area is of important significance for building Zhejiang into a strong marine province, exploring new paths for scientific development of China's marine economy, implementing the strategy of making the country powerful through the sea and improving the overall strategy for regional development.

The Zhejiang Provincial Party Committee and the Provincial Government put forward four basic principles to ensure the developmental direction for building the Zhoushan Archipelago New Area: (1) Respecting the objective law, pursuing scientific development, correctly dealing with the relations between holistic promotion and major breakthroughs, between development utilization and ecological protection, between opening up and national defense security; continuously increasing the level of scientific development; (2) Carrying out the first-ever pilot programs, pushing ahead with open development, shaping a pattern of development and opening-up with distinctive features and prominent advantages; (3) Conducting transformation and upgrading; promoting efficient development, optimization of the marine economic structure and transformation of the developmental mode; fully improving the efficiency and performance of comprehensive marine development; upholding coordinated and interactive land-sea development, endeavoring to achieve interactive land-sea industrial development, interactive construction of infrastructures, interactive allocation of resources and factors and interactive protection of the ecological environment; (4) Putting ecology first, stressing harmonious development, attaching great importance to the protection of the marine ecological environment and the building up of a marine ecological civilization; promoting the harmonious and sustainable development of the people and the sea, making sure that the people live and work in peace and contentment and that the society is stable and orderly.

Moreover, the Zhoushan Archipelago New Area will be completed in stages according to the two-stage development goal and tasks. Eleven major guarantee systems will be set up for the construction of the new area by improving the new area management system, increasing fiscal support, expanding international opening up in an all-round way, establishing a modern marine industrial system, perfecting the marine financial support system, guaranteeing effective utilization of land, sea and shorelines, strengthening the development driven by marine scientific and technological innovations, reinforcing the construction of infrastructures, protecting the marine ecological environment and innovating the social management of islands.

6.3.3 Progress in the Construction of Zhejiang's Marine Economy Demonstration Areas and the Zhoushan Archipelago New Area[8]

1. With great attention from the Zhejiang Provincial Party Committee and the Provincial Government, promptly pushing forward and arranging for the work on the marine economy

After the State Council officially approved the *Plan for Zhejiang's Marine Economy Development Demonstration Areas*, the Zhejiang Provincial Party Committee and the Provincial Government immediately held the provincial working conference on the marine economy to arrange the work tasks relating to pilot development of the marine economy and to identify a slew of measures. In late September, 2012, Xia Baolong, the Governor of Zhejiang Province, led the main leaders from relevant provincial departments and coastal cities in conducting surveys on the "thousand-li coastline and marine economy development", arrange the in-depth studies of major measures for the development of a marine economy and develop and implement 16 special action plans. In the 13th executive meeting of the People's Government

[8]The Report of the Zhejiang Provincial Development and Reform Commission on Self-examination and Assessment at the First Stage of the Pilot Work on Zhejiang's Marine Economic Development (Zhe Fa Gai Hai Jing (2014) No. 74).

of Zhejiang Province on September 27, 2013, Li Qiang, the Governor of Zhejiang Province, assigned responsibilities and tasks relating to the next work priorities in the construction of Zhejiang's marine economy development demonstration areas and the Zhoushan Archipelago New Area, and called for finishing these tasks on schedule according to the specified quality.

2. Based on scientifically developing and effectively implementing the supporting plans, actively carrying out the pilot demonstration work in major areas and key blocks

First, the People's Government of Zhejiang Province organized relevant departments, including the Zhejiang Provincial Development and Reform Commission, to develop and issue a number of special plans, including the *Development Plan of Zhejiang Province for the Emerging Marine Industries (2010–2015)*, the *Plan of Zhejiang Province for the Development, Utilization and Protection of Important Islands* and the *Plan of Zhejiang Province for the Protection and Utilization of the Uninhabited Islands.* Second, based on the relevant tasks specified in the *Plan for Pilot Work on the Development of Zhejiang's Marine Economy*, approved by the National Development and Reform Commission, relevant coastal cities and relevant provincial departments developed and implemented six special plans on pilot work, covering the comprehensive reform of Ningbo-Zhoushan Port shipping, the reform of the Hangzhou marine scientific and technological innovation, Wenzhou's innovation and reform involving the private economy's participation in the marine economy, Jiaxing's reform involving the development of marine clean energy, Shaoxing's reform involving the development of a marine circular economy, and Taizhou's reform involving the development of a marine circular economy. Finally, the People's Government of Zhejiang Province approved the establishment of five provincial-level marine economy development experimental areas, including the Zhejiang Xiangshan Experimental area for Comprehensive Marine Development and Protection, the Zhejiang Dongtou Island Development and Protection Experimental Area, the Zhejiang Yuhuan Coordinated Island Development Experimental Area, the Zhejiang Jiaxing Coastal Coordinated Port, the Industrial and City Development Experimental Area and the Zhejiang Dachen Marine Development and Protection Demonstration Island, and a number of Zhejiang-Taiwan economic and trade cooperation zones, including Zhejiang-Taiwan (Cangnan), Zhejiang-Taiwan (Yuhuan), Zhejiang-Taiwan (Shi'pu, Xiangshan) and Zhejiang-Taiwan (Putuo, Zhoushan), gathering experience for carrying out the first-ever pilot programs in the key areas of the marine economy.

3. Making concerted efforts to propel the construction of the Zhoushan Archipelago New Area, seeking new major breakthroughs in the marine economy

The Zhejiang Provincial Party Committee and the Provincial Government identified the Zhoushan Archipelago New Area as a work priority in the development of Zhejiang's marine economy, marshaled the resources throughout the province to press ahead with the construction on various fronts and actively sought vigorous support at the national level. In April, 2011, the General Office of the People's Government of Zhejiang Province unveiled the *Three-Year (2013–2015) Action Plan for the*

Construction of Zhejiang's Zhoushan Archipelago New Area, specifying the goal of completing fixed asset investments above 300 billion yuan in the New Area within three years. Meanwhile, the Zhejiang Provincial Party Committee and the Provincial Government issued *Several Opinions on Promoting the Construction of the Zhoushan Archipelago New Area*, specifying 40 policies involving 12 aspects for supporting the construction of the New Area, while more than 10 provincial departments issued special supporting opinions according to the relevant work division plan. In July, 2011, the Zhejiang Provincial Party Committee and the Provincial Government released the *Opinions on Innovations in the Administrative System in Zhejiang's Zhoushan Archipelago New Area*, arranging and calling for completing the main work on innovations of the administrative system in the New Area by the end of September. In November, 2011, the Phase I project of the Zhoushan Port Comprehensive Bonded Zone—Zhoushan Island—passed the national-level inspection conducted by a group led by the General Administration of Customs and was put into operation at the end of the year. At the same time, the feasibility of building the Zhoushan Free Trade Port Area was actively explored, thus greatly promoting rapid growth of fixed asset investments and a marine economy in Zhoushan.

4. Redoubling efforts to cultivate the emerging marine industries, promoting the development of the modern marine industry

The Zhejiang Provincial Development and Reform Commission organized efforts to develop and subject to the approval of the People's Government of Zhejiang Province, unveiled the special implementation plans for five key areas of the emerging marine industries, including marine engineering equipment and high-end ships, desalination and the comprehensive utilization of sea water, marine medicine and biological products, marine clean energy and marine exploration and development service. In order to further optimize the development layout of Zhejiang's marine industries, in July, 2013, the Zhejiang Provincial Development and Reform Commission led relevant work to develop and carry out the *Action Plan of Zhejiang Province for the Development of the Port-centered Advanced Manufacturing Industry*. In July, the Zhejiang Provincial Development and Reform Commission (the Zhejiang Provincial Office of Marine Economy) studied and developed, and the General Office of the People's Government of Zhejiang Province officially issued, the *"822" Action Plan for Zhejiang's Marine Economy Development (2013–2017)*, stating that Zhejiang Province will, in the next five years, focus on supporting the development of eight main modern marine industries, including the marine engineering equipment and high-end shipbuilding industry, the port and shipping logistics service industry, the port-centered advanced manufacturing industry, the coastal tourist industry, the seawater desalination and comprehensive utilization industry, the marine medicine and biological product industry, the marine clean energy industry and the modern marine fishery industry; it will also focus on cultivating and building 25 marine specialty industry bases, and annually carry out about 200 major projects for the marine economy.

5. Putting into effect the construction of major projects, expanding effective investments in the marine economy

In the first half of 2011, the Zhejiang Provincial Development and Reform Commission (the Zhejiang Provincial Office of Marine Economy) organized efforts to develop, and unveiled, the *12th Five-Year Plan of Zhejiang Province for Major Construction Projects for the Development of a Marine Economy*, arranging 490 key construction projects for the marine economy in coastal and island infrastructures, a port and shipping logistics service system, the modern marine industry, marine science, education and ecological protection, with a total investment of 1,263.1 billion yuan. Each year, the Zhejiang Provincial Development and Reform Commission (the Zhejiang Provincial Office of Marine Economy) organizes efforts to develop, and unveils, the annual plan for the implementation of major construction projects for the development of the marine economy in Zhejiang; during each month of May, it organizes and carries out the monthly activity of promoting major construction projects for the marine economy throughout the province to urge coastal cities to push forward the construction of major projects; 200 billion yuan and 210 billion yuan project investments involving the marine economy were completed in 2012 and 2013, respectively. In November, 2011, the People's Government of Zhejiang Province and the State Oceanic Administration successfully held the 1st China Marine Economy Investment Fair in Ningbo, in which 106 major projects for the marine economy were signed with a total investment of 360 billion yuan. In the middle of September, 2012, the 2nd China Marine Economy Investment Fair was successfully held in Ningbo, during which 91 major projects for the marine economy were signed with a total investment of 212.7 billion yuan.

6. Actively seeking support from various policies and further developing the marine economy

Since the development of the marine economy was piloted in Zhejiang, Zhejiang has obtained support from 28 policies, involving fiscal and tax affairs, finance, land and sea utilization, opening up and industry, introduced by relevant ministries and commissions, and the People's Government of Zhejiang Province has signed the strategic cooperation agreements on supporting the construction of Zhejiang's marine economy development demonstration areas with more than 10 ministries and commissions, including the Ministry of Transportation, the State Oceanic Administration, the Ministry of Land and Resources, and the headquarters of nearly 30 financial institutions, including the Industrial and Commercial Bank of China, the Agricultural Bank of China, the Bank of China and the China Construction Bank.

At the provincial level, in March, 2011, the Zhejiang Provincial Party Committee and the Provincial Government issued *Several Opinions on Accelerating the Development of the Marine Economy*, specifying 29 policy measures involving 10 aspects for speeding up the construction of marine economy development demonstration areas. In 2013, the People's Government of Zhejiang Province increased the scale of the special funds and the support for the construction of marine economy development demonstration areas. Afterwards, relevant provincial departments and coastal cities also issued their supporting policy opinions on accelerating the development of the marine economy accordingly. The Standing Committee of the People's Congress of Zhejiang Province promulgated the *Regulations of Zhejiang Province on the Use of*

Sea Areas, stating that relevant procedures for the basic construction projects can be directly completed on the strength of the certificate for the use of sea areas. Zhoushan City set up the Sea Area and Island Use Rights Reserve (Trading) Center; Xiangshan County in Ningbo City established the Marine Resource Management Center.

6.3.4 Zhejiang's Marine Economy Has Entered the Period of Rapid Growth

1. The strength of the marine economy has increased rapidly, its ability to stimulate economic development in the whole province has improved significantly

In 2013, Zhejiang's marine GDP was 550.8 billion yuan,[9] up 62.1% compared with the 339.3 billion yuan in the base period 2009 specified in the *Plan for Zhejiang's Marine Economy Development Demonstration Areas* and the *Plan for Pilot Work on the Development of Zhejiang's Marine Economy* approved by the State, with an average annual growth rate of 12.8%. During the period 2009–2013, the proportion of Zhejiang's marine GDP in Zhejiang's GDP basically remained at about 14%, about 9% higher than the nation's GDP in the same period; the proportion of marine GDP in the national marine GDP was kept at about 10%, higher than the proportion of Zhejiang's GDP in the nation's GDP. The marine economy became an important growth pole for Zhejiang's economy. Zhejiang ranked No. 4 nationwide in the total scale of the marine economy. The marine economy became increasingly able to stimulate economic development in Zhejiang Province and its contributions to economic growth increased continuously.

2. The structure of the marine economy has been optimized continually and the modern marine industries have developed rapidly

As Zhejiang has greatly increased the aggregate of the marine economy, the structure of the primary, secondary and tertiary marine industries has been optimized constantly, with their ratio adjusted from 8:41:51 in 2009 to 6.9:40.3:52.8 in 2013; the marine industrial structure has become more rational. The advantageous marine industries have further improved—in 2013, port-centered petrochemical enterprises above the designated size throughout the province delivered 290 billion yuan in sales revenue, while the shipbuilding industry generated 88 billion yuan in total output value and the marine tourist industry realized about 300.9 billion yuan in revenue. The emerging marine industries have developed rapidly, accounting for 30% of the province's marine economy; they have made increasing contributions to economic growth.

---

[9]The Report of the Zhejiang Provincial Development and Reform Commission on Self-examination and Assessment during the First Stage of the Pilot Work on Zhejiang's Marine Economic Development (Zhe Fa Gai Hai Jing (2014) No. 74) and *China Marine Statistical Yearbook* over the years.

3. Infrastructure has been more complete and the port and shipping service capability has further improved

A number of major marine infrastructure projects have been completed and put into operation; the collection and distribution network has further improved; the efforts to build Zhejiang into a strong province of port and shipping have been accelerated. During the period 2010–2013, such major marine infrastructure projects as the Beilun Phase IV Container Terminal, the Daxie Shihua 450,000t Crude Oil Terminal, the Aoshan 300,000t Crude Oil Terminal, the Wanxiang Oil Storage and Transport Terminal, the Ningbo-Zhoushan Port 150,000t Tiaozhoumen Channel, the Zhoushan Sea-crossing Bridge and the Jiashao Bridge, were completed and put into operation; such major projects as the Wenzhou Oufei Phase I Reclamation Project, the Jiaxing River-Sea Combined Transportation Channel Renovation Project on the Hangzhou-Pinghu-Shanghai Waterway, the Zhoushan Mainland Water Diversion Phase II, the Taizhou Toumen Port Terminal were under accelerated construction; the Zhoushan Liuheng Bridge, another highway added in parallel to the Ningbo-Taizhou-Wenzhou Highway, the Zhoushan International Cruise Terminal are progressing smoothly. As of late 2013, 196 deepwater berths above 10,000t were completed throughout the province (51 of them were newly completed during the period 2010–2013), with a throughput of 890 million tons; the Ningbo-Zhoushan Port had launched 213 port container lines and had connected more than 600 ports in more than 100 countries or territories; the number of ocean-going container trunk lines able to measure the international status of a port had reached 130, ranking it No. 3 nationwide, and it became the second largest integrated port, the sixth largest container port in the world, and so its international status as a hub port was further established.

4. The marine science, technology and education undertaking has developed rapidly, its support capability has kept growing

After pilot work was carried out, relevant departments of Zhejiang Province organized efforts to develop the *Plan of Zhejiang Province for Revitalizing the Sea through Science and Technology (2011–2015)*, the *12th Five-Year Development Plan of Zhejiang Province for Marine Science and Technology*, the *Plan of Zhejiang Province for the Construction and Development of Marine Disciplines and Specialties at the Institutions of Higher Learning (2011–2015)* and the *Medium and Long-term Development Plan of Zhejiang Province for Marine Scientific and Technological Talents*. Zhejiang Province has made positive achievements in the construction of marine institutions of higher learning and marine disciplines; Zhejiang Province has completed the construction of the Changzhi New Campus of Zhejiang Ocean University, while the construction of the Zhoushan Ocean College Campus of Zhejiang University is being conducted smoothly. At present, there are 21 marine institutions of higher learning and 40 provincial key marine disciplines in Zhejiang Province. The marine scientific research platforms have gradually improved; Zhejiang Province is building a number of innovation platforms in an orderly fashion, including Zhoushan Ocean Science City, the Ningbo Biological Industrial Innovation Center of the Shanghai Institute of Materia Medica under the Chinese Academy of Sciences, the Wenzhou

Marine Science and Technology Park and Innovation Park, the Marine Scientific and Technological Innovation Park in the Shaoxing Binhai New Area.

5. Ecological environmental protection has been reinforced constantly and the marine environmental quality has improved to some extent

After pilot work was initiated, relevant departments of Zhejiang Province developed and implemented the *12th Five-Year Plan of Zhejiang Province for Ecological Environmental Protection* and other special plans, and organized efforts to take special actions for marine environmental protection, including "811", "Haidun", "Bihai" and "Hudao". In Zhejiang Province, the pollution in key areas has been reduced in a profound way; the total quantity of main pollutants entering the sea has been controlled, regional environmental pollution has been contained effectively and the environmental quality of offshore areas in the whole province has remained basically stable. The environmental monitoring and controlling capability has improved significantly. Emphasis has been placed on carrying out a number of comprehensive projects for improvement, restoration and protection, including key islands, bays and coastal zones; Zhejiang Province has been home to 13 marine natural reserves and special marine protection areas above the provincial level, 13 special aquatic resource protection areas and 11 aquatic enhancement and releasing areas.

6.4 Summary and Outlook

In 20-plus years, Zhejiang Province has transformed from a large province of marine resources to a large province of marine economy and has laid a solid foundation for the present and the building of a strong province of marine economy. Zhejiang's marine economy has become an important part of Zhejiang's economy; the emerging marine industries and port-centered industries have become the new growth points for Zhejiang's economic development; in Zhejiang Province, a harmonious developmental relationship featuring mutual complementation and mutual promotion has been established between the marine economy and the land economy, and the marine economy has effectively developed into an important driving force for Zhejiang's regional economic development. The development of Zhejiang's marine economy serves as a good example for building China into a strong marine country.

The future of the world economy hinges on the sea; the strategic spaces and strategic advantages for the future development of various countries in the world must rely on the "blue territory" to a large extent and are embodied in marine advantages. Given that the current situation and opportunities for the marine economy, the original regional strategy for the development of a marine economy under which relevant work was led by local authorities, pilot programs were first carried out by local authorities and local authorities played the dominant role, no longer work, so it is necessary to elevate the marine strategy to a national strategy so that the strategy for the development of the marine economy is planned and managed at the level of a national strategy. This is also the important reason why comrade Xi Jinping not only valued and stressed the development of the marine economy when serving as the Secretary of the Zhejiang Provincial Party Committee, but he also chose, at the right time, Zhejiang's national marine economy development demonstration area with better development of the marine economy on various fronts to pilot the national strategy for the development of the marine economy; furthermore, the new generation of state leaders with comrade Xi Jinping as the leadership core have fully realized that the Chinese Dream about making the country stronger and the people richer must be based on the future blue ocean and cannot be separated from the development and construction of the "blue territory"; moreover, the Ocean Dream is an important part of the Chinese Dream. Therefore, it is essential to summarize the experience and lessons in the development of Zhejiang's marine economy at the levels of both development of the regional marine economy and the development of the nation's marine economy, so as to better guide efforts to build Zhejiang into a strong marine province and China into a strong marine country in the future.

As a large province of marine resources in China, Zhejiang is not only the forerunner in China's development of the marine economy, but also a pilot province for China's marine economy; in particular, after Zhejiang's construction of marine economy demonstration areas was elevated to a national strategy, it has become necessary for Zhejiang to undertake the important task of exploring a new line of thought and gather new experience for the development of the nation's marine economy. The successful experience in rapid and healthy development of Zhejiang's marine economy over the years mainly includes: There should be rational planning by the top government leaders, interaction among and concerted efforts from the governments at the upper and lower levels, which constitute the precondition for promoting the development of Zhejiang's marine economy; relevant work should be carried out by proceeding from Zhejiang's characteristics and advantages, identifying the developmental goals for various stages and focusing on key tasks, which are the basic steps for pushing the development of Zhejiang's marine economy forward; it is necessary to act in a market-led way, rely on endogenous development, rationally utilize two types of resources and effectively integrate two markets, which is the strong impetus for boosting the development of Zhejiang's marine economy; the government should play the driving role, multiple measures should be taken to intensify the reform and opening up, which serves as the fundamental guarantee for the development of Zhejiang's marine economy; making breakthroughs in key fields should be effectively combined with comprehensively promoting relevant work, and it is necessary to speed up the construction of the supporting infrastructure including major marine projects, which is the main way to impel the development of Zhejiang's marine economy; rational development and utilization should be combined with marine ecological protection, and various control means, including legal, regulatory and administrative means, should be comprehensively adopted, which is the important condition for the sustainable development of Zhejiang's marine economy.

Looking into the future, the development of Zhejiang's marine economy will face many challenges and will also have major opportunities. Zhejiang must have a global vision, keep in mind the big picture and take the strategic perspective to value the development of the marine economy. It is necessary to promote institutional and mechanism reforms and innovations in an all-round way, and to further leverage the institutional advantages of the private economy; it is necessary also to continue to press ahead with land-sea interaction, integrate marine resources, scientifically plan strategy for the development of a marine economy, optimize the marine industrial structure, develop the emerging marine industries, take the construction of the Zhoushan New Area as a platform to vigorously develop the international logistics industry and marine industries, build a modern marine industrial system, revitalize the sea through science and technology, improve the marine scientific and technological innovation and marine talent cultivation mechanism and strengthen marine ecological protection to guarantee the sustainable use of marine resources.

Chapter 7 Pursuing Coordinated Urban, Rural and Regional Development

Haiyan Wen

In the process of accelerating modernization, Zhejiang is facing a salient problem—wide regional disparity. The people throughout the province cannot become well-off if the people in the underdeveloped areas do not become well-off; modernization cannot be achieved throughout the province if the underdeveloped areas are not modernized. The Zhejiang Provincial Party Committee and the Provincial Government have given overall considerations, attached importance to coordinated development and given top priority to the work regarding agriculture, rural areas, and farmers; they have taken narrowing the regional developmental gap and achieving a coordinated regional development as the core in overall coordinated development, they have actively pushed forward innovations in philosophy, policies, institutions and working methods. Attention has been paid to correctly weighing two tendencies, going beyond agriculture, rural areas and farmers to improve the work regarding agriculture, rural areas, and farmers; efforts have been made to develop agriculture, rural areas and farmers by taking actions in a coordinated way in urban and rural areas to promote a coordinated urban and rural development. An integrated urban and rural institutional framework has been preliminarily established; the whole province has entered a new stage of integrative development of urban and rural areas; Zhejiang has stayed ahead nationwide in the levels of agricultural modernization and coordinated urban and rural development; with the implementation of such projects as the Mountain-Sea Cooperation Project, the project with ten-billion in assistance and support for achieving prosperity and the project for turning the underdeveloped villages and towns into well-off ones, Zhejiang has embarked on a new path of coordinated regional development with Zhejiang's characteristics which features help and support making the local people self-reliant, develop two-way interaction and win-win cooperation; Zhejiang Province is now at the forefront nationwide in coordinated regional development.

H. Wen (✉)
Zhejiang Academy of Social Sciences, Hangzhou, China

C. Pei and J. Xu (eds.), *Chinese Dream and Practice in Zhejiang – Economy*,
Research Series on the Chinese Dream and China's Development Path,
https://doi.org/10.1007/978-981-13-7484-5_7

7.1 The Birth and Development of the Philosophy of Coordinated Urban and Rural Development

7.1.1 The Background of Giving Birth to the Philosophy of Coordinated Urban and Rural Development

1. China has generally entered the middle stage of industrialization, in which the relations between industry and agriculture, between urban and rural areas, will shift from the "first tendency" to the "second tendency"

The developmental experience of most countries in the world shows that it is a universal developmental law that industrialization is carried out by losing no time in pursuing coordinated, urban, rural, economic and social development to narrow the income gap between industry and agriculture and address the issues concerning agriculture, rural areas and farmers, and thus complete the structural transformation. According to international experience, when per capita GDP exceeds USD 1,000, a country enters the middle stage of industrialization. This stage is the most important stage in which the dual economic structure shifts to a unitary economic structure; the relations between industry and agriculture, between urban and rural areas are starting to improve. At this stage, in order to make sure that agricultural and non-agricultural industries develop on an equal footing, different countries have often proceeded from their respective national conditions and taken the corresponding measures for a balanced development; generally, they have taken industry re-feeding agriculture as the main means.

In 2003, China's per capita GDP hit USD 1,000, indicating that China generally had entered the middle stage of industrialization. At this stage, social needs are upgraded and become more diverse; social development lags behind social problems which arise amidst economic development; the pressure relating to employment and social security looms large; high economic growth is accompanied by increasing resource consumption, continuous increase in the environmental pressure and more and more institutional restrictions; there is great developmental vitality and impact from opening up and economic globalization; social contradictions become increasingly acute because the changes in social and economic relations stir the ideological and political fields. The gap between urban and rural areas, between industry and agriculture, among regions, between the rich and the poor tends to become wider and wider. With all of these factors, China's economic and social development is at a critical juncture. China is in a golden developmental period, full of hope and also a period during which incessant dangers occur and contradictions become acute. The issues concerning agriculture, rural areas and farmers have become the bottlenecks restricting China's further development. In order to properly solve the contradictions and problems of the new stage, it is essential to promptly adjust the relations between industry and agriculture, between urban and rural areas, correctly handle the contradictions between industry and agriculture, and between urban and rural areas. Therefore, the Fourth Plenary Session of the 16th Central Committee of the

Communist Party of China held that there were "two tendencies" and made the scientific judgment that China had generally entered the stage in which industry promotes agriculture and urban development stimulates rural development.

2. Coordinated urban and rural development is the objective requirement for Zhejiang in achieving a leap into the new period

In 2005, Zhejiang's per capita GDP exceeded USD 3,000, and Zhejiang entered the middle and later stages of industrialization; it became the first to have realistic conditions for shifting from the "first tendency" to the "second tendency" and establishing a mechanism under which industry promotes agriculture and urban development stimulates rural development. According to the 5th population census, Zhejiang's urbanization rate had reached 50.9%, cities had become the growth poles for the regional economy. Urbanization played an increasingly big role in promoting economic and social development, the relations between urban and rural areas, between industry and agriculture became increasingly close. Zhejiang has fully entered a new stage in which industry promotes agriculture and urban development stimulates rural development. Zhejiang is more able than other parts of the country to ensure that industry re-feeds agriculture and urban development stimulates rural development. Meanwhile, the issues concerning agriculture, rural areas and farmers and the problems amidst development have become increasingly complicated in Zhejiang, thus it is very important and urgent to establish a more rapid developmental mechanism under which industry promotes agriculture and urban development stimulates rural development.

As early as the period of the 9th Five-Year Plan, as one of the developed provinces in China, Zhejiang generally entered the middle stage of industrialization, the contradictions between industry and agriculture, between urban and rural areas and the issues concerning agriculture, rural areas and farmers surfaced first in Zhejiang. Due to the accelerated movement of population and labor, the quickened agglomeration of production factors and the faster integration of the primary, secondary and tertiary industries, the gap between industry and agriculture, the urban-rural gap and regional gap became wider and wider. The economic interests of urban and rural residents became prominently dual; it was more difficult for farmers to keep a sustained and stable increase in income. In 2003, the per capita disposable income of urban residents in the whole province was 13,180 yuan, the per capita net income of rural residents was 5,431 yuan, and the ratio of urban residents' income to rural residents' income was 2.42:1, higher than the ratio of 2.18:1 in 2000 in the early period of the 10th Five-Year Plan.[1] If some non-monetary factors in the income of urban residents, such as housing, education, medical service, social security and other social welfare, are considered, the income gap between urban and rural residents may be wider. At the same time, besides the price difference between industrial and agricultural products which has not yet been completely eliminated, the wages of rural migrant workers in cities were kept at very low levels due to the limitless supply of rural labor

[1]Zhejiang Provincial Bureau of Statistics, *Zhejiang Statistical Yearbook 2003*, China Statistics Press, 2003.

in cities and the segmentation of the dual labor markets in urban and rural areas; the urban-rural dual land system was adopted to prohibit farmers from transferring the highly scarce land to other people, the policy for using the revenue from transferring the requisitioned land to other people obviously favored urban areas, and farmers cannot fairly enjoy the income from the appreciation of the land value.

Since the beginning of the 21st century, Zhejiang Province has entered a crucial period for building a moderately prosperous society in all respects. The principal contradiction in the new period and at the new stage lies in achieving coordinated urban and rural development, promoting the construction of the new socialist countryside in an all-round way, meeting the needs of the rural people for all-round development and safeguarding the legitimate rights and interests of rural people. When serving as the Secretary of the Zhejiang Provincial Party Committee, comrade Xi Jinping pointed out that the modernization with an urban-rural dual structure was a unqualified modernization, and a moderately prosperous society with widening urban-rural gap was not a comprehensive well-off society. The Party Committees and governments at various levels should further leverage Zhejiang's advantages in coordinated urban and rural development to pursue a coordinated type of urban and rural economic and social development, gradually break through the urban-rural dual structure, constantly improve the living standard and quality of urban and rural residents, shape a pattern in which urban development stimulates rural development, industry promotes agriculture, so that integrated urban and rural development is achieved. He likened coordinated urban and rural development to the "golden key" for addressing the issues concerning agriculture, rural areas and farmers in the new period.

7.1.2 Scientific Building of the Strategic System of Zhejiang's Coordinated Urban and Rural Development

1. The Overall goal for Zhejiang's coordinated urban and rural development

In January, 2005, based on summing up Zhejiang's practice, the Zhejiang Provincial Party Committee and the Provincial Government developed and implemented the *Plan of Zhejiang Province for Achieving Coordinated Urban and Rural Development and Promoting Urban and Rural Integration*. According to the Plan, in order to achieve coordinated urban and rural development and promote urban and rural integration, it is necessary to conduct a unified economic and social plan of the urban and rural areas as a whole, break through the urban-rural dual structure and integrate the industrialization, urbanization and modernization of agriculture and the rural areas, address the issues concerning agriculture, rural areas and farmers, narrow the urban-rural gap, give full scope to the role of cities in stimulating rural development and the role of rural areas in supporting and promoting cities, so as to achieve a complementation between urban and rural areas, coordinated development and common prosperity of both areas. The Plan specifies the overall goal for Zhejiang's coordinated urban and rural development: putting the people first, carrying out the scientific outlook on fully coordinated and sustainable development, taking the improved urban and rural plan as the guide, deriving the driving force from intensifying and supporting urban and rural reforms, unswervingly pushing forward industrialization, urbanization and marketization, speeding up the modernization of agriculture and rural areas, further optimizing the spatial layout of productive forces and of the population, breaking through the urban-rural dual structure to promote a rational flow of urban and rural resources and factors, shape a new developmental pattern in which urban development stimulates rural development and rural areas promote cities, narrowing the urban-rural gap, the regional gap and the gap between industry and agriculture. By 2010, the level of rural development will have increased further, the system of coordinated urban and rural development will basically have taken shape, laying a solid foundation for further removing the urban-rural dual structure and achieving urban-rural integration.

2. Six main tasks for Zhejiang's coordinated urban and rural development

The Plan specifies the tasks for coordinated urban and rural development on six fronts.

First, ensuring coordinated urban and rural industrial development. It is necessary to accord with the trend of increasing urban-rural economic integration and interactive development of the primary, secondary and tertiary industries, holistically plan and promote urban and rural industrial development, and constantly enhance the international competitiveness of industries. It is essential to further improve the layout of urban and rural industries, shape an industrial spatial layout in which the work division between urban and rural areas is rational, the regional characteristics are distinctive, full play is given to the endowment advantages of production factors and natural resources.

Second, pursuing coordinated urban and rural development of the social programs. It is necessary to follow the requirement of coordinated economic and social development, vigorously develop the social programs involving education, science and technology, culture, health and sports, and more quickly extend the social programs to rural areas so that both urban and rural residents can share modern civilization.

Third, carrying out the coordinated construction of urban and rural infrastructures. The requirement of optimizing the layout of the productive forces and the population should be followed in order to strengthen coordinated planning and construction of urban and rural infrastructures and change the underdevelopment of the rural infrastructures.

Fourth, addressing urban and rural labor employment and social security in a coordinated way. With the aim of ensuring full employment and everyone's access to social security in the urban and rural areas, actions should be taken to promote urban-rural integration in labor employment and social security.

Fifth, engaging in the coordinated creation of urban and rural ecological environments. The requirement of building an ecological province should be considered to further intensify ecological construction and environmental protection, speed up the construction of ecological towns and villages, energetically develop an ecological economy, improve the system of disaster prevention and reduction, promote harmonious development of the people and nature.

Sixth, seeking coordinated urban and rural regional economic and social development. The requirement of coordinated regional development should be taken into account to promote the holistic development of the developed and underdeveloped areas.

3. Upholding five principles to get, as quickly as possible, the development of agriculture, rural areas and farmers onto the track of scientific development

Agriculture is the foundation for ensuring social stability and reassuring the people. The issues concerning agriculture, rural areas and farmers are always closely associated with the development of the Party and the state's cause. When serving as the Secretary of the Zhejiang Provincial Party Committee, Xi Jinping pointed out: "Zhejiang Province is currently in a crucial period for addressing the issues concerning agriculture, rural areas and farmers; it is difficult to fundamentally address these issues if we approach agriculture, rural areas and farmers by merely proceeding from agriculture, rural areas and farmers; only when we go beyond agriculture, rural areas and farmers to work on agriculture, rural areas and farmers and adopt the line of thought and the philosophy of pursuing coordinated urban and rural development can we really break through the institutional constraints on the improvement of agricultural efficiency, the increase in farmers' income and agricultural development, fundamentally overcome the difficulties in agriculture, rural areas and farmers, further emancipate and develop the rural productive forces to accelerate the modernization of agriculture and rural areas. In other words, achieving coordinated urban and rural development is the fundamental way to address the issues concerning agriculture, rural areas and farmers."[2] It is necessary to adopt the following yardstick to assess the relevant work: agriculture becomes developed, farmers are satisfied with their work, the urban-rural gap is narrowed; this would elevate urban-rural integration to a new level.

Zhejiang has vowed to uphold the following five principles to get, as quickly as possible, the development of agriculture, rural areas and farmers onto the track of scientific development.

First, valuing agriculture, rural areas and farmers from the perspective of governing for the people. It is necessary to proceed from the strategic height of governing and rejuvenating the country to firmly establish the line of thought by which the issues concerning agriculture, rural areas and farmers are fundamental to China, and always unswervingly give top priority to these issues in our Party's work.

Second, promoting the development of agriculture, rural areas and farmers by putting the people first. It is necessary to focus on the most pressing, most immediate issues that concern the rural people the most, understand well, safeguard and develop the material interests and democratic rights of farmers.

Third, developing agriculture, rural areas and farmers through coordinated urban and rural efforts. It is imperative to proceed from the overall economic and social

[2]Xi Jinping, *Zhijiang Xinyu*, Zhejiang People's Publishing House, 2007, p. 43.

development to establish a new line of thought on addressing the issues concerning agriculture, rural areas and farmers through coordinated urban and rural development, carry out the policy of making sure that industry re-feeds agriculture and cities support the rural areas.

Fourth, boosting the development of agriculture, rural areas and farmers through reform and opening up. It is necessary to press ahead with supporting urban and rural reforms, removing all institutional obstacles affecting the development of agriculture, rural areas and farmers, and establishing the mechanisms and systems conducive to eliminating the urban-rural dual structure.

Fifth, working on agriculture, rural areas and farmers in a down-to-earth manner. It is essential to emancipate the mind, seek truth from facts, keep pace with the times, understand the objective law which governs the work on agriculture, rural areas and farmers in the new period and during the new stage, and actively explore new ways of addressing the issues concerning agriculture, rural areas and farmers.

4. Taking the construction of the new socialist countryside as the strategic task for addressing the issues concerning agriculture, rural areas and farmers

Zhejiang should boost the new development of industries, build new communities, cultivate new farmers, foster new social behavior, establish new institutions to comprehensively push forward the construction of the new socialist countryside and achieve the following goals: transforming the traditional agriculture into an efficient ecological agriculture which enjoys lasting market competitiveness and one that can continuously make farmers rich; turning the traditional villages into new rural communities which can provide farmers with access to modern civilized life; nurturing the traditional farmers into becoming new-type high-caliber educated farmers who can adapt to the requirements of development based on labor division and separate operation and who are technologically and operationally advanced, shape a new pattern of urban-rural integrated development in which urban and rural areas promote each other and achieve common prosperity.[3]

7.1.3 The Expansion of the Philosophy of Coordinated Urban and Rural Development in the New Period

1. Zhejiang's coordinated urban and rural development has entered a new stage of comprehensively pushing forward integrative development of the urban and rural areas

In 2009, the per capita net income of farmers in Zhejiang Province hit 10,000 yuan, suggesting that Zhejiang's coordinated urban and rural development had entered a new stage. At the same time, the above income hitting 10,000 yuan occurred basically

[3]Xi Jinping, *Carrying out Solid Work to Stay Ahead—Lines of Thought and Practice in Promoting New Development in Zhejiang*, Party School of the CPC Central Committee Press, 2006, p. 169.

in synchronization with the following situation: the per capita GDP in Zhejiang Province exceeded USD 6,000. Structural change took place in Zhejiang's economy and society.

First, with regard to the industrial structure, the service industry has entered a period of accelerated development during which its proportion has increased year by year; the "tertiary, secondary and primary" industrial structure is more rapidly taking shape. Meanwhile, public resources available in the agricultural field have fully increased; capital and technology have replaced land and labor in an expedited way; modern agriculture has entered a period of accelerated development; the gap between industry and agriculture is expected to gradually narrow.

Second, in terms of the employment structure, as a large-scale transfer of agricultural labor force to the secondary and tertiary industries has been preliminarily completed and the system and mechanism for ensuring equal employment in urban and rural areas have been basically established; the focus on promoting employment of farmers has shifted to maintaining more stable employment of farmers.

Third, from the perspective of the urban-rural population structure, with the agglomeration development of rural industries and stable employment of the rural labor force, massive employment-based transfer of the rural labor force to non-local areas has shifted to the change of residence of the rural labor force to non-local areas, more and more farmers have become residents of cities.

Fourth, as far as the structure of social classes is concerned, with more and more people starting businesses in urban and rural areas, the increasing level of income of urban and rural residents and the growing proportion of property income of urban and rural residents, the middle-income groups will grow more rapidly.

Fifth, with respect to the structure of consumption, the increase in the level of rural consumption and the upgrading of the structure of consumption will enhance people-to-people communication between urban and rural areas, allow for the penetration of urban and rural civilization, and will narrow the urban-rural gap in lifestyle and quality of lifestyle.

These structural changes show that Zhejiang's urban-rural dual structure has been mitigated significantly, and the coordinated urban and rural development has entered a new stage of comprehensively promoting urban and rural integration.

Given the above conditions, the Zhejiang Provincial Party Committee has vowed to comprehensively increase the level of coordinated urban and rural development: First, taking comprehensively promoting the agricultural and rural work as the fundamental requirement; second, adopting the strategic path of promoting the new-type urbanization and the construction of the new countryside in a coordinated way; third, taking continuously increasing the level of farmers' income as the central task; fourth, carrying out the key measure of establishing and improving the mechanism for allocating more resources and factors to agriculture, rural areas and farmers; fifth, providing an important guarantee by deeply pushing forward the supporting institutional reforms in urban and rural areas.[4]

[4]Zhao Hongzhu, Speech in the Provincial Working Conference on Rural Areas, February 23, 2010.

2. Concurrently promoting industrialization, urbanization, IT application and agricultural modernization as well as urban-rural integration

With deepening integrative development of the urban and rural areas, the development of agriculture, rural areas and farmers in Zhejiang has faced many new situations and new problems. High costs, high risks and high constraints in agricultural production have become increasingly prominent; the growth of farmers' income has declined; the rural population is ageing, agricultural by-business and movement of educated young people to urban areas with the elderly and children left behind in rural areas have become salient; the way farmers think and their ideas, interest appeals and social classes have become diverse in rural areas; profession-based transfer of rural population has shifted to the change of residence and identity; the contradictions in the management of rural society have been on the increase; the unfavorable position of agriculture, rural areas and farmers in resource and factor allocation has not yet fundamentally changed; the systems and mechanisms leading to the unequal exchange of factors and the unbalanced allocation of public resources between urban and rural areas have not yet been fundamentally removed. Given this situation, the People's Government of Zhejiang Province put forward the overall requirement for the work on agriculture, rural areas and farmers in 2013 and a certain future period as follows: Actions should be taken to carry out the strategic arrangement of concurrently promoting industrialization, urbanization, IT application and agricultural modernization as well as urban-rural integration; the work requirement of guaranteeing supply, increasing income, making the countryside beautiful, benefiting the people through reform and promoting integration should be considered in order to more rapidly increase the level of modern agricultural development, earnestly improve the construction of a beautiful countryside, move faster to transform the way of increasing farmers' income, promote a sustained and generally rapid growth of farmers' income, make solid progress in coordinated urban and rural construction, intensify the comprehensive reform in coordinated urban and rural development and accelerate efforts to build a system of urban-rural integration.

7.2 Seeking Coordinated Urban and Rural Development and Promoting Urban-Rural Integration

7.2.1 Carrying Forward Various Reforms in Coordinated Urban and Rural Development

7.2.1.1 From First-Ever Reform of Rural Taxation and Fees in China to Comprehensive Reform in Rural Areas

1. Being the first in China to push forward the reform of rural taxation and fees

In 2001, Zhejiang put an end to the collection of agricultural special duty in 25 underdeveloped counties. In July, 2002, the Zhejiang Provincial Party Committee and the Provincial Government issued the *Circular on Comprehensively Carrying out a Reform of Rural Taxation and Fees*, stating that it would take two years to fully complete, throughout the province, the reform of rural taxation and fees focusing on making reductions, adjustments, reforms and maintaining stability, rationally sharing the burden, making transfer payment and taking supporting measures, with a view to fully stopping the collection of the special duty on agriculture in 361 underdeveloped towns. In 2005, the collection of the special duty on agriculture was stopped across the board, making this tax that had been specially imposed on farmers for several thousand years cease to exist. In the next several years, Zhejiang became the first in China to establish a special system for evaluating the farmers' burden from the departments of agricultural fee collection; it build a farmers' burden monitoring network covering the province so that the burden on the farmers would continuously decrease.[5]

2. Promoting reform of rural taxation and fees in an all-round way

In January, 2005, the People's Government of Zhejiang Province issued the *Circular on Further Intensifying the Reform of Rural Taxation and Fees*, arranging for various supporting reforms while specifying the work on fully putting an end to the collection of the agricultural tax. The Circular required continued efforts to press ahead with the reform of the town institutions, further streamline the government organs to prevent an increase in the burden on farmers. The governments at various levels have, according to the requirements of the Zhejiang Provincial Party Committee and the Provincial Government, established and improved the public finance system for urban and rural areas, gradually increased transfer payment to town governments; improved the mechanism for the guarantee of the compulsory education fund and the public service capability of grass-roots organizations.

7.2.1.2 Holistically Pushing Forward the Support for Urban and Rural Reforms, Establishing a New Mechanism for Coordinated Urban and Rural Development

1. Intensifying the reform for expanding the powers of economically strong counties

Under the principle of delegating to the lower levels the powers which can be delegated, the Zhejiang Provincial Party Committee and the Provincial Government delegated powers to the county level many times. The powers of economically strong counties were expanded three times in 1992, 1997 and 2002. In particular, in 2002, the People's Government of Zhejiang Province delegated 313 items regarding authority of economic management, originally delegated to the prefecture-level cities, to 20 counties (cities, districts), covering 12 major categories, including planning, economy and trade, foreign trade, land and resources, transportation and construction, so as to enhance the developmental vitality of the county economy. During the

[5]Gu Yikang, Shao Feng et al., *Farmers Create the Century*, Zhejiang University Press, 2009, p. 50.

period of the 11th Five-Year Plan, the fifth round of reform for expanding the powers of economically strong counties and towns was fully launched and carried out. In May, 2008, the Zhejiang Provincial Party Committee and the Provincial Government decided to pilot the comprehensive reform in Hangzhou and the comprehensive reform of coordinated urban and rural development in Jiaxing and Yiwu.

2. Intensifying the reform of the system of rural property rights

In September, 2001, the General Office of the Zhejiang Provincial Party Committee and the General Office of the People's Government of Zhejiang Province issued the *Circular on Actively and Orderly Promoting the Transfer of the Rural Land Management Rights*, calling for adopting the basic principle of being conditional, voluntary, well-regulated, under the rule of law, guidance and management, actively encouraging the adoption of various means, including subcontracting, reverse leasing and subcontracting, joint stock cooperation and leasing, to orderly push forward the transfer of the rural land management rights. The land transfer and scale management have been promoted steadily in various areas.[6]

In 2012, according to *Several Opinions on Deeply Promoting Comprehensive Coordinated Urban and Rural Reform and Actively Conducting Rural Reform Experiments* and the requirement of conducting reforms and innovations in areas and carrying out reform experiments at various points, the Zhejiang Provincial Party Committee and the Provincial Government comprehensively and deeply pressed ahead with the comprehensive coordinated urban and rural reform, solidly conducted rural reform experiments, and innovated the rural land system in an orderly fashion. The pilot compensation for cultivated land protection has been extended to one national or provincial basic farmland protection demonstration area in each city. Actions have been taken to explore and practice the mechanism for cross-cooperative replacement, paid withdrawal, and paid use of rural homesteads in an orderly manner; energetically carry out the work on rights for the use of rural homesteads and house ownership affirmation and registration as well as the issuance of relevant certificates. The pilot work on cross-cooperative replacement, paid withdrawal, and paid use of homesteads has been gradually carried out.

3. Comprehensively pushing forward innovations in the rural financial system

Given that farmers have faced difficulties in obtaining loans for a long time, based on the experience in the development of rural cooperative finance in the developed countries, Zhejiang launched a new round of rural financial system reform in 2003, with a view to building a new rural financial cooperative system according to the law of the market economy and the developmental characteristics of agriculture, rural areas and farmers. The new-type rural financial organizations have increased in quantity, scale and coverage. In 2013, Zhejiang was home to 314 small loan companies, 19 rural commercial banks, 64 village banks, 541 financing guarantee institutions, and 117 guarantee institutions above 100 million yuan; the balance of

[6]Source: The Zhejiang Provincial Department of Agriculture.

rural house mortgage loans reached 10.8 billion yuan; 1.49 million Harvest Small-Loan Cards and 23,000 Harvest Entrepreneurship Cards were issued; the Project of Convenient Payment for Farmers and the Financial Inclusion Project of rural credit cooperatives have been launched and carried out, thus basically eliminating the towns where financial services were originally unavailable.[7]

4. Continually intensifying the reform of the land requisition system, building a long-term mechanism for resettling the land-lost farmers

In response to increasingly acute contradictions in land requisition amidst accelerated urbanization, within the framework of the existing land system, Zhejiang carried out a certain reform in the agricultural land requisition system with a focus on strengthening land requisition supervision and safeguarding the land rights and interests of farmers. In December, 2002, the People's Government of Zhejiang Province issued the *Circular on Strengthening and Improving the Work on Land Requisition*, presenting clear opinions on the reform of the land requisition system.

First, Zhejiang has established the block-based composite price system for land requisition and increased the land requisition compensation standards. (1) Increasing the standard for cultivated land requisition compensation. (2) Building the block-based composite price system for land requisition in the areas of urban planning. (3) Specifying the time for paying the land requisition compensation.

Second, the basic living guarantee system for farmers whose land was requisitioned has been established. In 2003, Zhejiang established the above system. With regard to the funds for the basic living guarantee, not less than 30% of them come from the government and are withdrawn from land transfer fees, while 70% of them are from collectives and farmers. By the end of 2005, all of the counties (cities, districts) in the whole province had established the basic living guarantee system for the farmers whose land had been requisitioned, under which a guarantee is provided upon requisition.[8]

Third, multiple measures have been taken to broaden the channels for the farmers whose land was requisitioned to find jobs. (1) A quality training system has been implemented among the farmers whose land was requisitioned. Training has been provided without charge to promote employment of those farmers. (2) A system of resettling by leaving partial land has been established, under which about 10% of the requisitioned land is left to the village collective economic organizations and farmers whose land was requisitioned, and under a unified plan, farmers build a business by themselves to meet their own needs, or the village collective economic organizations manage the property to develop secondary and tertiary industries in the area. (3) Pooling of land as shares for participating in construction is permitted. The rural collective organizations are permitted to adopt various means, including pooling of land as shares, to participate in the development and construction of the profit-making hydropower and transportation projects and other projects.

---

[7] http://www.zj.stats.gov.cn.

[8] Shao Feng, *Balanced Zhejiang—New Measures for Coordinated Urban and Rural Development*, Zhejiang People's Publishing House, 2006.

5. Pioneering in launching the co-insurance operational mode of policy-based agricultural insurance

Given that the large agricultural households increased their input and were subject to increasing risks, Zhejiang pioneered in launching the co-insurance operational mode of policy-based agricultural insurance. In 7 years, from 2006 to 2013, in Zhejiang Province, the agricultural and rural housing insurance cumulatively provided 1,019.38 billion yuan in risk guarantees to 56,574,000 households; 337,000 rural households affected by disasters received 1,112 million yuan in compensation. The insurance premium paid by rural households has been on the decrease, while the degree of guarantee has been on the increase. The insurance varieties have been expanded year by year; more than 30 agricultural insurance varieties have been launched; the number of rural households covered by insurance developed from 13,800 at the initial stage to 2.11 million; the amount of risk guarantee increased from 510 million yuan to 31.9 billion yuan in 2013.[9]

7.2.2 *Giving More, Getting Less and Loosening Control to Inject Vigor, Continuously Enhancing the Self-developmental Capacity of Agriculture, Rural Areas and Farmers*

7.2.2.1 Actively Adjusting the Structure of Fiscal Expenditure, Improving the Mechanism for the Guarantee of Input for Agriculture, Rural Areas and Farmers

The People's Government of Zhejiang Province has vowed to improve the mechanism for the growth of fiscal input. Two-thirds of the increased input from finance at various levels each year is used to improve people's livelihood, especially the people's livelihood in rural areas. During the period of the 11th Five-Year Plan, Zhejiang's fiscal input in agriculture, rural areas and farmers amounted to 320.2 billion yuan, an average annual growth rate of 24.8%; the funds from the finance at various levels throughout the province grew by 16.6% in 2013.[10]

In 2013, the Zhejiang Provincial Party Committee developed *Several Opinions on More Rapidly Promoting Sustained and Generally Rapid Growth of Farmers' Income*, while relevant provincial departments worked out more than 10 supporting documents accordingly. Local authorities also introduced a series of policy documents in light of the real situation, and practically increased their policy support. In

[9]http://www.zj.stats.gov.cn.

[10]Source: the Agricultural Office of Zhejiang Province.

2013, the expenditure in agriculture, forestry and water affairs from the finances at various levels was 51,303 million yuan, up 3.49 times over 2006.[11]

7.2.2.2 Developing Efficient Ecological Agriculture, Exploring a New Path Towards the Modernization of Agriculture with Zhejiang's Characteristics

1. Making further headway in the strategic adjustment of the agricultural structure

The whole province has witnessed the gradual formation of ten main leading agricultural industries, including the vegetable, tea and aquaculture industries, and the establishment of characteristic industrial belts, industrial clusters and industrial bases above 3 million mu. In November, 2008, the Zhejiang Provincial Party Committee held a working conference to study and arrange the overall line of thought, goals and tasks for promoting the rural reform and development of the whole province under the new situation, and put forward the *Implementation Opinions on Carefully Implementing the Guiding Principles Adopted in the Third Plenary Session of the 17th Central Committee of the Communist Party of China and Accelerating Rural Reform and Development*. Afterwards, with a focus on developing efficient modern ecological agriculture, Zhejiang took modern agricultural parks and grain production function areas as the vehicles towards promoting large-scale agricultural production and making agricultural production standardized and ecological. It rapidly developed ten main leading agricultural industries with comparative advantages, and actively nurtured ten main hi-tech agricultural industries. As of 2013, 4,984 areas with the function of grain production were completed, covering an area of 310,100 ha; 446 modern agricultural parks were completed, covering an area of 116,000 ha. In 2013, the overall score of the whole province in the agricultural modernization development level was 73.22; 66.1% of the tasks under the five-year plan covering the period 2010–2015 were finished, higher than the target value—60.0%—specified for the first three years.[12]

2. Vigorously nurturing modern agricultural operators

First, more rapidly nurturing and developing the leading agricultural enterprises and large specialized agricultural households, encouraging industrial and commercial enterprises to invest in agriculture, proactively boosting the development of farmers' specialized cooperatives. In 2004, Zhejiang became the first in China to issue the *Regulations of Zhejiang Province on Farmers' Specialized Cooperatives*, increasing the organizational degree of modern agricultural development. In 2012, the *Opinions on Energetically Cultivating New-type Agricultural Operators* were introduced to overcome the difficulties concerning the ageing of agricultural laborers, agricultural by-business and land operation fragmentation. As of the end of October, 2013, there

[11]Zhejiang Provincial Bureau of Statistics, *Zhejiang Statistical Yearbook 2014*, China Statistics Press, 2014.

[12]http://www.zj.stats.gov.cn.

were 40,000 farmers' specialized cooperatives and nearly 60% of the farmers had joined specialized cooperatives in the whole province. There were more than 7,000 family farms registered with industrial and commercial administrations; the farms established through cooperation among rural households, between rural households and enterprises or among others emerged. A total of 54.2% of the rural households were driven by agricultural industrialization organizations in Zhejiang, 31 percentage points higher than the nation's figure (23.2%).

Second, thoroughly carrying out the Project for Quality Improvement of Ten Million Farmers to cultivate extra agricultural talents. As from 2006, Zhejiang adopted the policy of exempting tuition and fees for the students majoring in planting and breeding at technical secondary schools and junior colleges within the province; in 2007, this policy was extended to such specialties as horticulture, flowers, vegetables and fruit trees. A subsidy policy was introduced among the graduates from the institutions of higher learning within the province who started businesses in modern agriculture, so as to encourage more young people to take up a career in that field.

3. Being the first to build a modern agricultural service system focusing on three-in-one cooperation services

Given that rural households were small and scattered, market information was asymmetric and it was difficult to put production funds in place in Zhejiang Province. In late 2006, the Zhejiang Provincial Party Committee and the Provincial Government held a special on-the-spot meeting in Rui'an City on the basis of earnestly summarizing the experience in developing farmers' specialized cooperatives and a new-type rural cooperative economy in various areas, including the three-in-one rural cooperative associations in Rui'an City and Pinghu's Xincang Supply and Marketing Cooperative for serving agriculture. At this meeting, comrade Xi Jinping delivered an important speech, stating that the three-in-one modern agricultural service organizations were the service alliances with resource sharing, advantage complementation, complete functions and clear work divisions, which were built by supply and marketing cooperatives, credit cooperatives and farmers' specialized cooperatives with a view to reinforcing service functions, expanding service supply and improving service quality and which were supported by farmers' specialized cooperatives, supply and marketing cooperatives and credit cooperatives and guaranteed by the services and management of relevant government departments. In 2007, the Zhejiang Provincial Party Committee and the Provincial Government decided to carry out pilot work in 17 counties and cities in the province, build a three-in-one new-type rural cooperation system covering farmers' specialized cooperation, supply and marketing cooperation and credit cooperation, with a focus on providing services for the circulation and finance of farmers' specialized cooperatives.[13]

[13]Gu Yikang, Shao Feng et al., *Farmers Create the Century*, Zhejiang University Press, 2009.

7.2.2.3 More Quickly Help Farmers Find Work in Non-agricultural Fields, Broadening the Channels for Farmers to Find Jobs and Increase Their Income

1. Making the regional characteristic massive economy supported by central towns large and strong

Based on the reality that Zhejiang has fully entered a new stage in which industry promotes agriculture and urban development stimulates rural development, Zhejiang has earnestly carried out the strategy of coordinated urban and rural development, speeded up the construction of advanced manufacturing bases and urbanization, developed and grown the central cities, central towns and the characteristic massive economy to promote industrial and population agglomeration; in Zhejiang Province, 2/3 of the rural labor forces have transferred to the secondary and tertiary industries. In 2000, the People's Government of Zhejiang Province planned 136 central towns. In 2003, the opinions on rectifying small industrial areas were issued, a large number of development zones inconsistent with the overall land use plan and relevant regulations were withdrawn to further concentrate small industrial areas in industrial agglomeration zones. In 2007, the Zhejiang Provincial Party Committee and the Provincial Government issued *Several Opinions on More Rapidly Promoting the Central Town Cultivation Project*, with a view to building about 200 central towns in the whole province through government promotion, policy support, institutional innovation, market operations and turning the central towns into zones of industrial agglomeration, population concentration, areas of institutional and mechanism innovation and new countryside construction demonstration zones. In 2010, the People's Government of Zhejiang Province issued *Several Opinions on Further Accelerating the Development and Reform of Central Towns*, with the hope of cultivating central towns into strategic pivots and nodes for pushing forward the new-type urbanization and urban-rural integration.

2. Making rigorous efforts to promote the development of such industries as agritainment, processing with customer's materials and e-commerce, fully expanding the fields in which farmers can start businesses and find jobs

The advantages of natural ecological resources and labor resources in various areas have been fully leveraged to develop agritainment leisure sightseeing and tourism, processing with customer's materials, which have become the hotspots for making sure that farmers obtain employment and get rich. As from 2005, the People's Government of Zhejiang Province has held many meetings on the agritainment leisure tourism industry and has introduced relevant support policies. At the same time, the female farmers above 40 years of age and male farmers above 50 years of age who do not work outside have been fully utilized to vigorously develop the industry of processing with customer's materials in light of local conditions. In the first three quarters of 2013, the agritainment leisure tourism industry received tourists for 100 million person-times, the direct operating income and tourist shopping income reached 8.1 billion yuan and 1.8 billion yuan, up 23%, 24% and 33%, respectively over the previous period. The number of people engaged in processing with customer's materials in the underdeveloped areas hit 900,000, the paid processing charges exceeded 8 billion yuan and the per capita income in processing charges was more than 9,000 yuan. Rural e-commerce developed rapidly, Taobao Longyou Pavilion, Suichang Pavilion and Deqing Pavilion were established.[14]

3. Transforming from encouraging spontaneous transfer to stressing transfer for training reasons, comprehensively improving the employment competitiveness of rural labor forces

In 2004, the Zhejiang Provincial Party Committee and the Provincial Government launched the Project for Training Ten Million Rural People to become part of the Labor Force focusing on improving farmers' employment skills and their overall quality. Zhejiang has established a mechanism under which the government purchases training projects, schools provide training and farmers independently choose training, and it has adopted various means, including order-based training and targeted training. The vocational certificate training was further intensified as from 2007. During the period 2004–2007, 6.55 million rural people were trained throughout the province, among whom 1.87 million rural people successfully obtained transfer-based employment through training. Zhejiang has established a provincial farmer's university, 9 municipal farmer colleges and a number of county-level farmer schools; in 2013, 228,000 rural people received transfer-based employment skills training in Zhejiang (79% of them obtained transfer-based employment after training).[15]

4. Putting into practice the system of coordinated urban and rural employment

In 2001, Zhejiang became the first to reform the system of coordinated urban and rural employment. Zhejiang has developed the unified urban and rural labor resource management system, adopted the policy of ensuring equal employment for urban and rural labor forces, and established a labor market and a vocational training system covering both urban and rural areas. As from 2004, Zhejiang carried out the Project for the Improvement of the Quality of Ten Million Farmers to enhance the employment skills and entrepreneurial ability of the rural labor force; at the same time, actions have been taken to actively ameliorate the employment environment for the farmers migrating to cities, improve the urban and rural labor and social security system, utilize the market mechanism to rationally allocate urban and rural labor resources, and gradually form a unified, open, competitive, orderly integrated urban-rural labor market.

---

[14]Zhang Ruojian, An Analysis of the Situation of Zhejiang's Rural Development in 2013 and the Outlook for 2014, published in *Annual Report on Zhejiang's Development (Economy Volume)*, Zhejiang People's Publishing House, 2014.

[15]Zhang Ruojian, An Analysis of the Situation of Zhejiang's Rural Development in 2013 and the Outlook for 2014, published in *Annual Report on Zhejiang's Development (Economy Volume)*, Zhejiang People's Publishing House, 2014.

7.2.3 *Making One-Thousand-Village Demonstrations and Ten-Thousand-Village Improvement Efforts, Building a Beautiful Countryside*

1. Carrying out the One-Thousand-Village Demonstrations and Ten-Thousand-Village Improvement Projects

Given that the rural environment was dirty, disorderly and bad, villages were scattered and social programs were underdeveloped in rural areas, in 2003, the Zhejiang Provincial Party Committee and the Provincial Government decided to implement the One-Thousand-Village Demonstration and Ten-Thousand-Village Improvement Project, and called for taking five years to rectify 10,000 villages and build 1,000 of them into the demonstration villages for building a moderately prosperous society in all respects and new civilized and harmonious communities. Under the principle of being conducive to improving the living quality of farmers, inheriting historical culture and reflecting harmonious coexistence between people and nature, local authorities across the province have developed village plans and village construction plans. Efforts have been made to comprehensively improve the rural infrastructures, combine the construction of rural infrastructures, social programs and public services with village improvement and construction, and push forward a number of projects, including the Greening Demonstration Village, the 10,000-li Green Channel, the 10,000-li Clear Water Riverway, the Drinking Water for Ten Million Farmers, the Rural Broad Road, the Ecological Home for Enriching the People, the Domestic Methane for the Sewage Purification of One Million Rural Households and the Revitalizing Forests to Enrich the People. As of 2013, 27,000 administrative villages have undergone improvement efforts, accounting for 94.0% of all administrative villages. Four-hundred and fifty national ecological towns were built, ranking Zhejiang No. 1 nationwide in the number of national ecological towns.[16]

2. Carrying out the construction of a beautiful countryside

In 2010, the *Action Plan for the Construction of a Beautiful Countryside (2011–2015)* was carried out in Zhejiang. The Plan calls for building a beautiful countryside by promoting the construction of four systems, including the rural ecological habitat, the ecological environment, the ecological economy and ecological culture according to the overall requirement of ensuring scientific planning, a beautiful layout, clean and tidy villages, a beautiful environment, a better life by starting businesses to increase income, good rural conduct, a sound mind and body. The starting point lies in promoting a harmonious coexistence between the people and nature in rural areas, enhancing the living quality of farmers. Its goal is to shape the rural industrial structure, the farmers' production mode and the manner of rural consumption that is conducive to protecting the rural ecological environment and achieving sustainable development. In 2012, Zhejiang Province vowed to intensify the construction of a

[16] http://www.zj.stats.gov.cn.

beautiful countryside, and set the following goal: proceeding from traditional history, a humanistic heritage, resource endowment, topography and landform and the people's aspirations to fully build a four-level interactive construction mechanism, covering the demonstration counties, towns, excellent villages and households with clean courtyards, all for a beautiful countryside. As of 2017, all of the counties (cities, districts) across the province had reached the criteria for building advanced counties for a beautiful countryside, about 20% of the counties (cities, districts) had been cultivated into the demonstration counties for a beautiful countryside, more than 60% of towns had undergone improvement efforts, more than 10% of the administrative villages had become excellent villages or featured villages for a beautiful countryside, more than 5% of the rural households had become the households with clean courtyards for a beautiful countryside.

(1) Fully advancing the protection and utilization of historical cultural villages. The provincial on-the-spot meetings regarding the protection and utilization of historical cultural villages have been held with concerted efforts to boost village protection, restoration and utilization.
(2) Stepping up efforts to create the attractive scenery of a beautiful countryside. Actions have been taken to deeply implement the four-level mechanism for the interactive construction of a beautiful countryside, press ahead with comprehensive improvement of the village environment in a coordinated way, fully carry out the following work: renovating old residential areas, old factory areas in urban areas and the villages in cities, demolishing illegal buildings; cleaning, greening and beautifying the areas beside highways, railways, rivers and mountains; clearing river channels and cleaning the countryside; steps have been taken to fully complete the preliminary work, which include a statistical survey on the treatment of rural domestic sewage, scheme design and policy making, and a long-term cleaning mechanism for the village environment has been improved rapidly.

3. Earnestly nurturing central villages

Actions have been taken to effectively integrate such projects as comprehensive improvement of the rural land, rural house renovation, and the construction of rural community service centers, to develop a village economy, to enhance the population, the industrial carrying capacity and the integrated service function of central villages, and to initiate the cultivation and construction of 300 central villages.

4. Making coordinated efforts to promote the construction of rural infrastructures

Accelerated efforts have been made to carry forward the construction of connected rural roads, power stations, power grids, communication information, supply, marketing and circulation. As of 2013, in the whole province, every administrative village had access to the roads of a certain quality, broadcasting and post offices; electricity had been supplied to every household with the same price of electricity adopted in both urban and rural areas; rural passenger transportation had reached 93.6% of the areas; the rate of integration of urban and rural passenger transportation had reached

56.5%; the coverage rate of safe drinking water had exceeded 97.0%; rural cable TV had been available in more than 91.0% of the households. The chain convenience stores had covered 93.5% of the administrative villages; the old-age care service had covered nearly 70.0% of the incorporated villages.[17]

7.2.4 Making Progress in Rural Social Construction Focusing on Improving the People's Livelihood, Ensuring Equal Access to Public Services in Urban and Rural Areas

1. Strengthening the construction of the rural social security system, steadily increasing the level of social security

First, the system of subsistence allowances covering both urban and rural areas was established throughout the province as from 1996; in 2007, Zhejiang became the first in China to issue the provincial *Measures for Verification and Determination of the Income of Households Eligible for Subsistence Allowances*, steadily increasing the level of security for the targets of subsistence allowances. In 2007, there were 651,700 targets of subsistence allowances in urban and rural areas across the province, including 561,400 in rural areas, while the standard for monthly per capita subsistence allowances reached 149.7 yuan. In 2013, there were 623,000 targets of subsistence allowances (excluding the rural households enjoying the five guarantees) across the province, including 551,000 households in rural areas (excluding the rural households enjoying the five guarantees), while the security fund expenditure was 1.99 billion yuan. The standards for the average monthly subsistence allowances in urban and rural areas were 526 yuan and 406 yuan, up 135.9% and 214.7% over 2005, respectively, the urban-rural gap in subsistence allowances narrowed greatly.

Second, the old-age security system has been built. All farmers working at enterprises have been covered by the basic retirement insurance of the enterprises; more rural residents have been covered by social endowment insurance, the standard has been increased in an orderly fashion. In cities and counties with the highest standard, the standard reached 140 yuan/month in 2013. 2.85 million people have been covered by the basic living security for the farmers whose land has been requisitioned, the standard is 300–700 yuan/month. The information system for old-age care service has been established in 52 counties (cities, districts); various old-age care services have basically covered the urban communities and more than 70% of the rural areas.

Third, the new rural cooperative medical system has been steadily consolidated. As from 2003, in Zhejiang Province, the new rural cooperative medical system has grown out of nothing and developed from small to large, the operating mechanism and management quality have improved constantly, and the security level has gradually increased, so that the farmers who should have been covered by security were

[17] http://www.zj.stats.gov.cn.

covered. In 2013, 97.7% of the people were covered by the new rural cooperative medical system across the province; the per capita fund-raising standard and the fiscal subsidy standard were 557 yuan/year and 393 yuan/year, respectively. The ratio of settlement and reimbursement in the case of hospitalization increased to 9.2%, the reimbursement ratio within the scope of hospitalization policy reached 75%. At the same time, Zhejiang has also actively explored the integration of the new rural cooperative medical system with the basic medical insurance system for urban residents, so as to deal with urban and rural areas in a coordinated way.

Fourth, measures have been taken to establish a centralized support system for the rural people enjoying the five guarantees and the people without identification papers, a normal residence permit, and a source of income in urban areas. In 2013, in Zhejiang Province, support was provided to 37,400 rural people enjoying the five guarantees and 5,000 people without identification papers, a normal residence permit, and a source of income in urban areas. The centralized support covered 97.3% of the rural people enjoying the five guarantees and 97.7% of people without identification papers, a normal residence permit, and a source of income in urban areas, keeping it ahead nationwide. In Zhejiang Province, the standard of support for the rural people enjoying the five guarantees was an average of 8,752 yuan/man-year, while that for the people without identification papers, a normal residence permit, and a source of income in urban areas was 10,428 yuan/man-year, effectively guaranteeing the basic life of these special groups.

2. Promoting balanced development of urban and rural social programs

Zhejiang became the first in China to carry out the system for exempting tuition fees and textbook fees involving compulsory education in urban and rural areas, so that the compulsory education has become totally free; the burden on primary and middle school students across the province has been directly reduced by 1.2 billion yuan. In Zhejiang Province, 3 billion yuan have also been allocated to fully complete four projects of rural primary and middle schools and promote significant improvement in rural education. As of 2013, 15-year education had become universal at a rate of 97.9%, a project for the standardization of compulsory school education had been carried out in a thorough way, 55.0% of the primary and middle schools had been standardized.

3. Improving the rural medical and health service system, carrying out the Farmer's Health Project

The network for rural public health management and service has been steadily improved, nd a network of public health service at the county, town and village levels has taken shape. According to the requirement that 1,000–1,500 people should be covered by one community doctor in charge, a force of community doctors in charge has been established to take full responsibility for and participate in the physical examination and public health services concerning the people in the communities for which they are responsible. Physical examinations were conducted without charge among farmers once every two years beginning in 2006. As of 2013, 99 and 98% of the health clinics in towns and townships and community health service centers which had been standardized had reached the standard, the village-level medical and health services had achieved full coverage, the per capita fund of the basic public health service items had exceeded 30 yuan.

4. Earnestly carrying out the Project for the Building of a Rural Cultural Front

The construction of a rural cultural facility has been strengthened; ten projects for rural cultural construction have been fully carried out; the integrated cultural stations in towns have provided full coverage; the coverage rate of the village-level cultural activity rooms has reached 97.8%. Great efforts have been made to open such public cultural places as libraries and cultural centers to the public for free throughout the year, and the construction of rural cultural auditoriums has been initiated.

7.3 The Birth and Development of the Philosophy of Coordinated Regional Development

7.3.1 The Background of Giving Birth to the Philosophy of Coordinated Regional Development

Since the reform and opening up, Zhejiang has kept ahead nationwide in its rate of economic development; however, the development among regions within the province remains unbalanced. The gap between Zhejiang's southwestern mountainous areas, islands and the highly developed coastal areas is apparent, and the widening gap in development between the underdeveloped and developed areas has not yet been fundamentally reversed. On the one hand, the economic aggregate of the eastern coastal developed areas is large, making up a large proportion of Zhejiang's economy; this is the main embodiment of Zhejiang's comprehensive strength and regional competitiveness; the driving forces for the eastern coastal developed areas have improved continuously in structural adjustment, industrial upgrading and outward expansion; on the other hand, the economic foundation in Zhejiang's southwestern mountainous areas and Zhoushan Island is relatively weak, their capability of self-accumulation and self-development is still not high due to historical, geographical and social conditions. In 2005, the GDP in Quzhou City, Lishui City and Zhoushan City was 32,911 million yuan, 30,599 million yuan and 28,016 million yuan, accounting for 2.63%, 2.27% and 1.89% of Zhejiang's GDP of 1343785 million yuan, respectively.[18]

These areas lag behind the developed areas in economic development and their gap with the developed areas in social development, such as education and health, is wider. In 2005, the per capita net income of farmers in 28 counties in Zhejiang was 4,105 yuan, accounting for only 61.6% of Zhejiang's average level; there were

[18]Zhejiang Provincial Bureau of Statistics, *Zhejiang Statistical Yearbook 2006*, China Statistics Press, 2006.

833,000 low-income people with the per capita income lower than 1,500 yuan in Zhejiang.[19] In 2005, the per capita disposable income of urban residents and the per capita net income in rural areas were 13,006 yuan and 4,850 yuan in Quzhou City, respectively; these figures were 12,846 yuan and 3,572 yuan in Lishui City, and 15,524 yuan and 7,190 yuan in Zhoushan City.[20]

These areas enjoy unique advantages in resources and the environment, such as natural resources and land; this lays a good foundation for these areas to become the new economic growth points. At the same time, this also provides new spaces for achieving industrial transfer from the developed areas. Zhejiang's mountainous areas cover an area of about 85,800 km^2 and 53 counties and cities, they have a population of 28.14 million, accounting for 84.3, 53.5 and 51.7% of the whole province. "Zhejiang's underdeveloped areas are mostly mountainous areas, the old revolutionary base areas and the areas inhabited by ethnic groups are mainly concentrated in mountainous areas. Rationally utilizing mountainous resources to turn the undeveloped areas into the new economic growth points is the objective requirement for Zhejiang's coordinated regional development; this also represents the change of our line of thought regarding development and our major responsibility."[21]

7.3.2 *The Core of Coordinated Regional Development*

7.3.2.1 In Order to Achieve Coordinated Regional Development, Equal Emphasis Should Be Placed on Both Developed and Underdeveloped Areas

When serving as the Secretary of the Zhejiang Provincial Party Committee, Xi Jinping pointed out that narrowing the regional development gap to achieve coordinated regional development was a major historical task for Zhejiang Province during the period of the 11th Five-Year Plan. In order to complete this task, it was necessary to carry out the Scientific Outlook on Development to combine the accelerated development of the developed areas with the leapfrog development of the underdeveloped areas.[22] Speeding up the development of the developed areas is the important foundation for supporting coordinated regional development. The accelerated development of the developed areas can not only better play an important role in stimulating and leading Zhejiang's economic development, but it can also better support the underdeveloped areas in achieving leapfrog development. Promoting the leapfrog

---

[19]Shao Feng, *Balanced Zhejiang—New Measures for Coordinated Urban and Rural Development*, Zhejiang People's Publishing House, 2006, p. 322.

[20]Zhejiang Provincial Bureau of Statistics, *Zhejiang Statistical Yearbook 2006*, China Statistics Press, 2006.

[21]Xi Jinping, *Carrying out Solid Work to Stay Ahead—Line of Thought and Practice in Promoting New Development in Zhejiang*, Party School of the CPC Central Committee Press, 2006, p. 209.

[22]Xi Jinping, *Zhijiang Xinyu*, Zhejiang People's Publishing House, 2007, p. 163.

development of the underdeveloped areas is the important link for achieving coordinated regional development. The people throughout the province cannot become well-off if the people in the underdeveloped areas do not become well-off; modernization cannot be achieved throughout the province if the underdeveloped areas are not modernized. Therefore, it is essential to shore up the weaknesses—the underdeveloped areas—so that the people in various parts of the province can enjoy the achievements of economic and social development.

7.3.2.2 In Order to More Rapidly Develop the Underdeveloped Areas, It Is Imperative to Carry Out a Combination of Development, Expansion and Reduction

With increasing constraints regarding resources and factors and mounting environmental pressure, it is hard to sustain the traditional economic developmental mode mainly relying on excessive resource consumption. The development of Zhejiang's underdeveloped areas cannot be continued by merely duplicating the traditional road to industrialization; on the contrary, such development must be sustained by taking the science and technology-led, resource-conserving and ecologically friendly road to economic development. It is essential to accelerate economic development, expand the economic aggregate, reduce resource consumption, ecological damage and pollutant emissions and refrain from pursuing economic growth at the expense of the environment. Institutional, technical and management innovations should be carried out, and the quality of the labor force should be improved to help optimize the industrial structure and transform the economic growth mode; the layout of the population in the underdeveloped areas should be optimized and the conditions of the infrastructures should be improved in order to stimulate the population to move toward cities. Actions should be taken to further strengthen skill training for employment and employment guidance among the farmers in the undeveloped areas; actions should also be taken to promote cross-regional employment of the rural labor force in the undeveloped areas. Full scope should be given to the advantages of the underdeveloped areas in ecological resources and specialty industries, with great efforts made to turn the underdeveloped areas into green bases for the production of agricultural products, bases for ecological labor-intensive manufacturing, bases for the exportation of rural labor, tourist attractions and green ecological protective screens.

7.3.3 The Expansion of the Philosophy of Coordinated Regional Development in the New Period

In June, 2007, the report delivered at the 12th Party Congress of Zhejiang Province called for taking the accelerated development of the underdeveloped areas as an important part of the overall strategy of making people rich by starting a business and of building a strong province through innovation. In October, 2008, the Fourth Plenary Session of the 12th Provincial Party Committee vowed to combine the accelerated development of the underdeveloped areas with a quick transformation of the economic developmental mode, economic transformation and upgrading, in order to build a "Zhejiang in the Mountains". In 2009, Zhejiang started a new round of the Mountain-Sea Cooperation Project. According to *Several Opinions of the General Office of the People's Government of Zhejiang Province on Carrying out a New Round of the Mountain-Sea Cooperation Project*, it is necessary to focus on enhancing the driving forces, increasing the level, improving relevant mechanisms and reinforcing services, leveraging the respective advantages to deepen the cooperation between the developed and underdeveloped areas in featured advantageous industries, the construction of the new countryside, the training and employment of human resources and in social programs, so as to effectively increase the level of the industrial development in the underdeveloped areas and the income of the low-income people as well as nurture the underdeveloped areas into the new economic growth points for Zhejiang Province.

The Zhejiang Provincial Party Committee and the Provincial Government have always attached great importance to the development of the mountainous areas. In 1997, the *Plan of Zhejiang Province for the Economic Development of the Mountainous Areas (1996–2010)* was developed. Afterwards, a number of policy measures were introduced to earnestly boost the economic and social development of the mountainous areas. However, compared with the coastal areas, the mountainous areas, especially 26 underdeveloped counties (cities, districts), remain weak in their foundations for development. Since the period of the 12th Five-Year Plan, with the change of the developmental stage and the improvement of external conditions, the advantages of Zhejiang's mountainous areas in location, ecology and mechanism have become increasingly prominent. In particular, as the development of Zhejiang's marine economy has been upgraded to a national strategy, accelerating the construction of a "Zhejiang in the Mountains" is the necessity for cultivating the new economic growth points for Zhejiang Province and it is also the objective requirement for shaping a balanced regional developmental pattern in which mountains and the sea reflect each other.

According to *Several Opinions on Accelerating the Economic Development of the Mountainous Areas* issued by the Zhejiang Provincial Party Committee and the Provincial Government on July 4, 2012, Zhejiang's mountainous areas are vast in territory, they abound in natural resources and are ecologically excellent, so they are the new growth poles for speeding up economic development, and the main fields for building ecological protective screens and promoting the construction of an ecological civilization; they are important for building a modern Zhejiang which enjoys abundant materials and is culturally advanced. The basic principle for the economic development of the mountainous areas consists in putting ecology first, pursuing green development, concurrently increasing the level of economic development and improving the quality of the ecological environment in the mountainous areas; upholding agglomeration, intensive development and transformation, energetically pushing forward the transformation of the economic developmental mode in the mountainous areas; giving top priority to the people's livelihood, seeking harmonious development, continually improving the basic public services in the mountainous areas; intensifying the reform, achieving innovative development, further arousing the endogenous vitality and driving force for the development of the mountainous areas; expanding cooperation and bringing about open development, more rapidly shaping a new pattern of coordinated land-sea regional development.

7.4 Boosting the Accelerated Development of the Underdeveloped Areas

7.4.1 Building a "Zhejiang in the Mountains", Speeding up the Economic Development of the Mountainous Areas

1. Strengthening the planning and guidance of the development of the mountainous areas

Zhejiang consists of 70% mountains, 10% water and 20% farmland. The Party Committees and governments of Zhejiang Province one after another all attached great importance to the economic development of the mountainous areas, and introduced a slew of policy measures for developing those areas, especially the underdeveloped areas. In 1997, the *Plan of Zhejiang Province for the Economic Development of the Mountainous Areas (1996–2010), Several Opinions on Accelerating the Economic and Social Development of the Underdeveloped Areas, Several Opinions on Promoting the Economic and Social Development of the Underdeveloped Areas, Several Opinions on Further Accelerating Efforts to Turn the Underdeveloped Towns into the Well-off Ones* and other documents were formulated, actively pushing forward the economic and social development of the mountainous areas.

In 2012, in response to the changes in Zhejiang's economic developmental stage and external factor changes, the People's Government of Zhejiang Province developed the *Plan of Zhejiang Province for the Economic Development of the Mountainous Areas (2012–2017)*, redefining the "mountainous areas". The mountainous areas specified in the Plan are based on land where there are mountains and include a part of adjacent non-mountainous areas inherently associated with its economic and social activities. The Plan covers 53 counties (cities, districts); the land area is 85,800 km^2, the permanent resident population was about 28.14 million at the end of 2010, the GDP in 2010 was 1,140.8 billion yuan, accounting for 84.3%, 51.7% and 41.1% of the whole province, respectively.

Under the principle of pursuing agglomeration, intensive development and transformation, the Plan is designed to coordinate the development of the mountainous areas and the protection of the ecological environment, optimally form three main distinctive developmental areas, including the land-sea interactive development of

Zhejiang's eastern coastal areas, the agglomeration and intensive development of hills and basins in Zhejiang's central and northern areas and the green ecological development of Zhejiang's southwestern inland areas, and to build an ecological industrial system beneficial for leveraging resource characteristics and the advantages that the location provides as well as tapping the potential for development.

2. Building three main provincial experimental areas

According to the strategic positioning requirement of the Plan, as the experimental area for transformation development, Quzhou Mountainous Area Scientific Development Experimental Area needs to more rapidly make synchronous progress in new-type industrialization, new-type urbanization and agricultural modernization in its mountainous areas, seek ecological development that is intensive, land-sea interactive and economical and venture down a new road towards transformation development. As an experimental area for institutional innovation, the Lishui Mountainous-Area Scientific-Development Comprehensive Reform Experimental Area should make new reform breakthroughs in major fields and at key links and enhance the developmental vitality of the mountainous areas, thus providing new experience for the economic development and the reforms in institutions and in the mechanisms as well as innovations in the mountainous areas. As an inter-provincial open cooperation area, the Huzhou Inter-provincial Industrial Transfer Undertaking Demonstration Area should fully leverage the advantage of its marginal location, emancipate the mind, expand the opening up, enhance cooperation, actively draw upon the radiation effect, more quickly undertake industrial transfer, and build a new pattern of inter-provincial regional all-round opening up and cooperation.

3. Increasing fiscal support

According to the *Administrative Measures of Zhejiang Province for Special Funds and Projects for the Economic Development of the Mountainous Areas* (Zhe Cai Nong (2013) No. 607), a special fund for the economic development of the mountainous areas was arranged from the provincial finance each year during the period 2013–2017. The fund is a general transfer payment fund for special purposes; it was pooled by relevant counties (cities, districts) of the mountainous areas with a view to promoting the economic development of those areas. The fund focuses on optimizing the developmental environment of the mountainous areas, enhancing their endogenous capacity for development and developing their ecological economy; it is mainly used to support the construction of industrial platforms, the development of key blocks on the mild slopes of low mountains and hills, the development of specialty industries, scientific and technological research and development, the nurturing and introduction of human talents and ecological environmental construction.

7.4.2 *Mountain-Sea Cooperation and Land-Sea Interactive Development*

In order to stimulate gradient transfer of the industries in the developed areas to the underdeveloped areas, promote accelerated development of the underdeveloped areas, and cultivate the new economic growth points to achieve coordinated regional development across the province, in April, 2002, the General Office of the People's Government of Zhejiang Province transmitted, in the form of (2002) No. 14 Document, the *Opinions on Carrying out the Mountain-Sea Cooperation Project to Help the Underdeveloped Areas within the Province Accelerate their Development* issued by the Economic and Technological Cooperation Office of the People's Government of Zhejiang Province, kicking off the province-wide efforts to carry out the Mountain-Sea Cooperation Project and promote land-sea interactive development.

7.4.2.1 Enabling Interaction Between Government Promotion and Market Operations, with Widespread Participation of the People from Various Sectors of the Society

1. Carrying out coordinated planning with policies introduced first

After the Mountain-Sea Cooperation Project was launched in 2002, Zhejiang Province issued *Several Opinions on Accelerating the Economic and Social Development of the Underdeveloped Areas*, *Opinions on Carrying out the Mountain-Sea Cooperation Project to Help the Underdeveloped Areas within the Province Accelerate their Development*, *Several Opinions on Fully Carrying out the Mountain-Sea Cooperation Project*, *Interim Measures for the Administration of the Fiscal Discount Fund for the Mountain-Sea Cooperation Project* and other policy opinions, strengthening the government's guiding and promoting roles. Meanwhile, the Economic and Technological Cooperation Office of the People's Government of Zhejiang Province also organized efforts to develop the *Plan of Zhejiang Province for the Mountain-Sea Cooperation Project (2005–2010)* and on this basis, work out the annual implementation plan. Based on this work, Hangzhou City developed the *Measures for Resource Industry Cooperation amidst Mountain-Sea Cooperation*; Jiaxing City issued the *Opinions on the Implementation of the Mountain-Sea Cooperation Project*; Zhoushan City developed the *Measures of Zhoushan City for the Evaluation of Mountain-Sea Cooperation*; Quzhou City completed its plan for the Mountain-Sea Cooperation Project; Ningbo City actively developed a series of policy documents, including the annual plan for the implementation of the Mountain-Sea Cooperation Project, each year, with actions to build a policy guidance system led by planning, guided by an annual implementation plan and guaranteed by the evaluation of goal responsibility and strengthen the government's roles as guide and promoter.

2. Improving organizations

The People's Government of Zhejiang Province specially set up a leading group for the Mountain-Sea Cooperation Project, and made clear the targeted cooperative relationship between the developed areas, including Hangzhou, Ningbo, Wenzhou, and 65 counties (cities, districts) in the underdeveloped areas, including Quzhou, Lishui, Zhoushan. The Hangzhou Municipal Government established a resource and industrial cooperation office in Quzhou, while other cities also set up corresponding organizations, and held local meetings on the Mountain-Sea Cooperation Project to promptly get relevant information, coordinate efforts to solve problems, start bilateral interaction and comprehensive engagement. The People's Government of Zhejiang Province also established an evaluation system for the Mountain-Sea Cooperation Project and extended evaluation to municipal governments and provincial departments.

3. Building a system with a high-level platform

Since the implementation of the Mountain-Sea Cooperation Project, the Zhejiang Provincial Party Committee and the Provincial Government carried out the series of activities within the Mountain-Sea Cooperation Project by turns in the underdeveloped cities across the province ten times, while the following secretaries of provincial Party Committees and provincial governors jointly attended relevant activities, convened special meetings and delivered important speeches. Moreover, the Mountain-Sea Cooperation Project has integrated the China Yiwu International Commodities Fair, the Western China International Fair, the Industrial, Scientific & Technological Cooperation Fair and some large exhibitions in the Yangtze River Delta Region, thus extending the mountain-sea cooperation from the economic field to education, science and technology, culture, talent, labor services, information and trade, greatly enriching the connotation of the Mountain-Sea Cooperation Project and achieving full engagement and interaction between "mountains" and "the sea". In order to better adapt to the new characteristics of labor demand after industrial upgrading, provincial efforts are being made to build a number of training bases and employment bases, through which order-based training and targeted exportation are carried out to further improve the quality of the labor forces in the underdeveloped areas and transfer them better.[23]

4. Innovating the service mechanism

Zhejiang has established such long-term working mechanisms as a mechanism for attracting promotion and investment for the Mountain-Sea Cooperation Project, a project promotion supervision and inspection mechanism, a project service coordination mechanism, a system of periodic summary statistics on projects to continually reinforce the institutional guarantee for the Mountain-Sea Cooperation Project, to generate a cooperative pattern of development with interaction between the lower

[23]Source: the Economic and Technological Cooperation Office of the People's Government of Zhejiang Province, the same below.

and upper levels and concerted efforts so as to ensure the Mountain-Sea Cooperation Project is really carried out.

5. Witnessing the widespread participation of the people from various sectors of the society

With high attention from the Zhejiang Provincial Party Committee and the Provincial Government, relevant provincial departments and the Party Committees and governments of the developed areas have carried out solid work, while democratic parties, the people's organizations and the people from various sectors of the society have widely participated in this process; as a result, the mountain-sea cooperation pattern of pair-based, multi-level, multi-channel and all-round cooperation and exchange has taken shape across the province. In ten years since the implementation of the project, the transfer payment from the provincial finances for supporting the development of the underdeveloped areas amounted to 113.5 billion yuan.

6. Accelerating the construction of the mountain-sea cooperation industrial park

In order to speed up the development of the underdeveloped counties (cities, districts), including Cangnan, Wencheng and Taishun, Wenzhou City has approved and established the Lingjiang Mountain-Sea Cooperation Industrial Park as the important base for locally undertaking industrial transfer; Taizhou City has earnestly carried out the North-South Cooperation Project and established three main cooperative economic zones, including Tiantai, Xianju and Sanmen; Jinhua City has moved faster to build the Jinxi Economic Development Zone, providing the basic conditions for three underdeveloped towns in Jinxi, Tangxi, Luobu and Yangbu, to carry out mountain-sea cooperation. In the cooperation field involving specialty industries, Zhejiang Province has established 15 mountain-sea cooperation demonstration parks to transform industrial cooperation from scattered cooperation to clustered cooperation; the investment scale and return have increased year by year.

7.4.2.2 Acting in a Market-Led Way, Continuously Expanding and Intensifying the Fields of Cooperation

1. Relying on the mountain-sea cooperation platform to promote thorough integration among industries
(1) Innovating the resource and industrial cooperation mode. During the period of the 11th Five-Year Plan, the mountain-sea cooperation mode featuring resource and industrial cooperation created by Quzhou, Hangzhou, Ningbo and other cities aroused the enthusiasm of both of the sides engaged in mountain-sea cooperation. As resource and industrial cooperation has lasted for five years, such cooperation has, while promoting accelerated economic development in Quzhou, to a certain degree mitigated the contradictions between major projects in the developed areas and a shortage of urban land, and it has achieved win-win development.

(2) Further introducing large projects, especially the projects of leading industries, to the underdeveloped areas according to the requirement of accelerating transformation and upgrading. The projects of the primary, secondary and tertiary industries have been rationally introduced to the underdeveloped areas according to the requirement of making agriculture excellent, industry strong and the service industry solid. For the newly signed mountain-sea cooperation projects across the province, the ratio of funds really put into the primary, secondary and tertiary industries during the period January-March, 2013 was 6:28:66. For example, Zhoushan City gave prominence to the characteristics of the marine economy, earnestly introduced modern service industry projects, including environmental protection, logistics and tourism; with respect to the newly signed industrial cooperation projects in Zhoushan City in the first quarter, the investments in the projects of the primary, secondary and tertiary industries accounted for 84.5% of the introduced investments. Quzhou City has energetically introduced efficient agriculture, new materials and advanced equipment manufacturing, such as the ecological fish farming project of Kaihua Gulong Comprehensive Agricultural Development Co., Ltd., to promote rapid local agricultural modernization and industrialization.

(3) Combining pushing forward industrial gradient transfer with supporting innovative development of mountain-sea cooperation enterprises, propelling integrative and interactive development of industries. Based on the mountain-sea cooperation platform, various cities have widely promoted the integrative and interactive development of industries in light of local industrial characteristics and resource endowment. The developed areas should not only help the underdeveloped areas introduce projects and capital, but they should also help address the specific issues concerning technology development, market development and management operations after the completion of the project; for example, Changxing County assists Qingyuan County in carrying out the e-commerce project and in combining e-commerce with agricultural development, so that industries can promote each other and advance together; the effects are significant.

2. Combining the Mountain-Sea Cooperation Project with the construction of the new countryside

(1) Enhancing cooperation in human resource training and employment

Priority has been given to building a number of the vocational skill training bases for mountain-sea cooperation, supporting the underdeveloped areas in conducting training relating to agricultural technology and the training concerning entrepreneurial and employment skills suited to the developmental requirements of the secondary and tertiary industries, so as to continuously improve the quality of human resources in the underdeveloped areas and their ability to increase their income. In 2013, Ningbo City allocated 3.50 million yuan in a special fund to support the construction of the vocational skill training bases for mountain-sea cooperation in Zhoushan City and Lishui City. In 2014, 1.50 million was planned for the construction projects of training bases in both cities.

(2) Actively participating in the projects for the construction of the new countryside

In 2006, Hangzhou City and Quzhou City signed the agreement on the Economic Development Promotion Program for 100 Villages, under which the first 18 towns and units in Hangzhou City support the construction of the new countryside in 18 villages in Quzhou City on a paired basis. As of June, 2012, Hangzhou had carried out 136 projects for the construction of the new countryside and social programs under mountain-sea cooperation, with paid-in investments amounting to 59.82 million yuan. Songyang County and Yuyao City carried out the Mountain-Sea Cooperation Project—the Development Promotion Program for 100 Villages—beginning in 2007, continuous innovations have been made and the connotation of the work on paired assistance has been enriched, thus gratifying results have been achieved. As of 2013, Yuyao City had put in place more than 30 assistance projects for the construction of the new countryside in Songyang County, and it had earmarked more than 3.20 million yuan in assistance.

7.4.2.3 Promoting Land-Sea Interaction, Expanding the Project for Mountain-Sea Cooperation

As the development of Zhejiang's marine economy has been elevated to a national strategy, the underdeveloped inland mountainous cities and counties have "gone to the sea and ridden the waves", they have given priority to promoting land-sea interaction in expanding the Mountain-Sea Cooperation Project.

1. Setting up organizations, actively building connections

According to the spatial layout of Zhejiang's marine economy development demonstration areas, 7 cities and 47 counties (districts), including Hangzhou City, Ningbo City, Wenzhou City, Jiaxing City, Shaoxing City, Zhoushan City and Taizhou City, are included in the pilot development of Zhejiang's marine economy. However, Jinhua City, Quzhou City and Lishui City in the inland areas do not become frustrated because of that inclusion, they have actively worked with provincial departments by specially establishing the corresponding organizations, including ocean offices.

2. Fully pushing ahead with land-sea interaction and green development

(1) Giving prominence to the guiding role of major projects and interactive allocation of factors. In recent years, Quzhou City has voted down 1,345 industrial projects with a total investment of 9.3 billion yuan. In early 2013, 19 major industrial projects were signed with the agreement amount of 12.1 billion yuan, involving emerging strategic industries, including new materials, new energy, advanced equipment manufacturing, electronic information and modern logistics. Lishui City has taken pains to introduce large enterprises and great projects, and has signed cooperation agreements with the China Puda Cable Group and the Beijing Jingneng Investment Group, with a total investment of 1.49 billion yuan. The project of Zhejiang Zhoushan Jingang Investment

Co., Ltd. in Zhoushan City is the first project under the marine industry fund established by the People's Government of Zhejiang Province, with 500 million yuan put in place in the first quarter; the project plays a demonstration and guiding role in boosting the constriction of Jintang International Logistics Island and the development of Zhejiang's marine industry.

(2) Building platforms to attract investments and make promotion efforts. In late November, 2011, the 1st China Marine Economy Investment Fair, the national marine economy investment event held in China for the first time, was inaugurated in Ningbo City. Jinhua, Quzhou, Lishui and other cities also carried out various investment attraction and promotion activities. Jinhua specially held the Marine Economy & the Rise of Central Zhejiang Forum and Project-Signing Ceremony, in which 32 investment projects, including 7 foreign investment projects, were signed, with a total investment of USD 460 million, so Jinhua became the first to benefit from land-sea interaction. During the China Marine Economy Investment Fair, Quzhou signed 19 industrial investment projects with a total investment of 12.1 billion yuan, involving emerging strategic industries, including new materials, new energy, advanced equipment manufacturing, electronic information and modern logistics. The fair is the one with the highest industrial level, the highest project quality and the largest average scale of investment among the various investment attraction and promotion activities in recent years.

3. Accelerating the infrastructure construction with land-sea interaction

On December 15, 2011, the An'renpu Hub Project within the Shipping Revitalization Project of the upper and middle reaches of the Qiantang River was officially launched. As an important support project for mountain-sea cooperation, this connectivity project is the golden channel for providing Zhejiang's Quzhou, Jinhua, Hangzhou and other areas with access to rivers and the sea, and it also serves as the best bond connecting all parts of Zhejiang Province with "Zhejiang in the Mountains" and "Zhejiang in the Sea".

7.5 Summary and Outlook

The difficulties in building a moderately prosperous society in all respects and basically achieving modernization in advance lie in the underdeveloped areas, especially the underdeveloped towns. Zhejiang Province has fully leveraged the advantages of the developed areas in industry, capital, talent, science and technology to, while expanding the developmental spaces for coastal areas, actively tap the potential advantages of the underdeveloped areas, including the mountainous areas, in featured resources, factor resources and in the ecological environment; Zhejiang Province has carried out a project for turning the underdeveloped areas into well-off ones, the project with ten-billion assistance and support for achieving prosperity and the project for making low-income rural households become well-off, with a view to enhancing the endogenous developmental capacity of the underdeveloped areas and cultivating new economic growth points; Zhejiang Province has carried out the Mountain-Sea Cooperation Project, through which land-sea interaction is achieved to promote rational cross-regional flow of industries and factors and to form a pattern of development in which the developed and undeveloped areas complement each other's advantages to deliver a win-win outcome.

Zhejiang's practice in coordinated regional development proves that mutual promotion between the developed and underdeveloped areas not only reflects the philosophy of rapid and sound development, but it is also conducive to optimizing and upgrading the industrial structure and transforming the economic developmental mode across the province.

With vigorous implementation of the strategy of coordinated urban and rural development, Zhejiang has acted to ensure that new-type industrialization stimulates agricultural modernization, new-type urbanization drives industrial and population agglomeration and spurs rural labor forces to move to and work at the secondary and tertiary industries; the philosophy of modern industrial development is adopted to operate agriculture and thus push forward agricultural modernization; the system and mechanism for coordinated urban and rural development are more rapidly established to promote resource allocation in rural areas and provide rural areas with quicker access to public services, and making sure that there is a mechanism for urban and rural areas to interact with and promote each other in order to strongly promote Zhejiang's urban-rural integration.

Zhejiang's successful practice in coordinated urban and rural development fully proves that in order to promote urban-rural integration, it is essential to accord with the law of economic and social development after entry into the new stage at which industry promotes agriculture and urban development stimulates rural development; it is necessary to proceed from the removal of the urban-rural dual structure to actively experiment in establishing the equal systems in urban and rural areas and a long-term mechanism under which industry promotes agriculture and urban development stimulates rural development; it is necessary to make arousing farmers' enthusiasm about starting businesses and improving their livelihood the fundamental starting point for reform. The general process of urban-rural integration is based on industrialization and urbanization, including the gradual process in which an urban-rural gap occurs, widens and fades away; urban-rural development is not coordinated in the areas at different developmental levels and at different developmental stages of the same area. Therefore, the strategy of urban-rural integration must be made on the basis of the Scientific Outlook on Development and implemented by areas, stages and priorities according to the conditions of economic and social development in the different areas. Industrialization, urbanization, marketization, IT application, agricultural and rural modernization promote each other to achieve the common development and common prosperity of urban and rural areas.

The people throughout the province cannot become well-off if the people in the underdeveloped areas do not become well-off. If the issues concerning agriculture, rural areas and farmers cannot be fundamentally addressed, it is impossible to achieve the common prosperity of the people throughout the province and healthy economic and social development of the whole province. Zhejiang's practice best explains the Chinese Dream about making the country rich and the people strong and bringing about the great rejuvenation of the Chinese nation.

As economic development enters a new normal, the efforts to pursue coordinated urban, rural and regional development face new problems. In order to achieve the integrative development of urban and rural areas and coordinated regional development at higher levels, it is essential to focus on promoting an orderly flow of factors between urban and rural areas and among regions and enhancing the endogenous vitality of rural areas and the underdeveloped areas, to continuously innovate the system and mechanism for ensuring coordinated urban, rural and regional development, take a market-oriented approach to intensify reforms and increase input in coordinating urban and rural development, provide more policy support to the underdeveloped areas, so as to more rapidly achieve urban-rural integration at higher levels and deeper coordinated regional development.

Chapter 8
Advocating New-Type Urbanization and Promoting the Interactive Development of Urbanization and Industrialization

Haiyan Wen and Wei Mao

In the 30 years since the reform and opening up, as one of the regions with the most vibrant economic development in China, Zhejiang stayed ahead nationwide in urbanization development. Zhejiang has become No. 1 nationwide on many fronts, such as, the first farmer city, the first policy for granting registered permanent residence through the purchase of a house, the first urbanization development plan, the first urban system plan, the first plan for canceling the change from "the status of agricultural to that of non-agricultural", the first urban-rural integration plan, the first pilot work on land for social security, the first birth of the concept of new-type urbanization in China. Zhejiang has ventured down a path towards urbanization with Zhejiang's characteristics. Such great achievements in Zhejiang are attributable to continuous innovations in its philosophy of urbanization, increasing benign interaction between urbanization and industrialization and constant practice in urbanization.

8.1 The Formation and Development of the Philosophy of New-Type Urbanization

8.1.1 The Background of Giving Birth to the Philosophy of New-Type Urbanization

1. The developmental trajectory of Zhejiang's urbanization

Zhejiang really started its process of urbanization in the middle and later period of the 1980s. Since the reform and opening up, rural urbanization dominated by township enterprises, and small and medium-sized enterprises has stimulated the rise of a large

---

H. Wen (✉) · W. Mao
Zhejiang Academy of Social Sciences, Hangzhou, China

C. Pei and J. Xu (eds.), *Chinese Dream and Practice in Zhejiang – Economy*, Research Series on the Chinese Dream and China's Development Path,
https://doi.org/10.1007/978-981-13-7484-5_8

number of small towns in Zhejiang. The development of these small towns was driven mainly by private and market forces. With one product in one town and one industry in one town, small towns with Zhejiang's characteristics mushroomed. In Zhejiang Province, the number of cities under which county-level cities were established increased from 3 in 1978 to 35 at the end of 1997, the number of incorporated towns from 167 to 965, urban population from 5,251,300 to 15,744,300 and the level of urbanization went from 14.0 to 35.5%. Zhejiang's path towards urbanization of building small towns on the basis of developing small and medium-sized industries at township enterprises is consistent with the general path of the development of urbanization.[1]

As the focus of industrialization has shifted from rural industrialization to urban industrialization, Zhejiang's strategy for urbanization has gradually switched from small towns to large and medium-sized cities. The 10th Party Congress of Zhejiang Province, held in December, 1998, became the first in China to make the major strategic decision to lose no time in accelerating urbanization, and it vowed to take pushing forward urbanization as the breakthrough in a new round of Zhejiang's economic and social development. In October, 1999, the State Council approved the *Urban System Plan of Zhejiang Province (1996–2010)*, which was the first provincial urban system plan approved in China. In December, 1999, the Zhejiang Provincial Party Committee and the Provincial Government officially issued the *Urbanization Development Plan of Zhejiang Province*, making Zhejiang the first in China to unveil an urbanization blueprint and plan. In the process of promoting urbanization, Zhejiang became the first to make breakthroughs by reforming the household registration system, and it introduced a slew of supporting policies covering registered permanent residence, land, investment and financing, thus fostering a policy environment beneficial to making it possible for the population and industries to move towards the cities. In order to make central cities more capable of receiving others and to stimulate the development of their surrounding areas, Zhejiang became the first in China to conduct and complete three city group plans for the Circum-Hangzhou Bay Region, the Wenzhou-Taizhou Region, the Jinhua-Quzhou-Lishui Region and the urban system plans for counties (cities) covering the whole province.

2. Problems in Zhejiang's urbanization

During the period of the 10th Five-Year Plan, Zhejiang actively and steadily pushed forward urbanization, made remarkable progress in urban development and stayed ahead nationwide in many respects. However, from the perspective of the Scientific Outlook on Development, some deviations and mistakes occurred in Zhejiang's urbanization in this period; they are mainly reflected in the following respects.

First, the level of intensive utilization of urban land was relatively low; functions and management lagged behind; the overall carrying capacity of cities was not high; these factors imposed great constraints on Zhejiang's continued urbanization and economic development.

---

[1]Zhejiang's Experience and China's Developmental Research Group, *Zhejiang's Experience and China's Development* (Economy Volume), Social Sciences Academic Press, 2007, p. 279.

In an effort to promote urbanization, there was a preference for large cities and excessive expansion in various areas, uneconomical land utilization, "enclosure", "city construction movement", high input, high consumption, high emissions, lack of coordination, difficulty in circulation and low efficiency occurred in many areas. As city functions and management lagged behind, the overall carrying capacity of cities was not high and there were many hidden troubles in the sustainable development of cities, Zhejiang's urbanization and economic and social development were subject to two-way pressure from "congenital deficiency" and "growing pains".

Second, the urban diffusion effect was insufficient and a pattern of the coordinated development of small, medium-sized and large cities and small towns failed to effectively take shape. Many local authorities simply believed that against the background of economic globalization, enterprise development needed large cities as platforms, and urbanization should focus on developing large cities and enhancing the agglomeration function of large cities. Sufficient attention was not paid to making central cities and large cities form a well-connected whole with a rational work division. There was an insufficient function of large cities in producing a good diffusion effect and simulating the development of the surrounding areas, which not only restricted the development of large cities, but also affected their role in driving the development of small and medium-sized cities, making it difficult for small and medium-sized cities to receive small and medium-sized enterprises and the rural population. Small towns were relatively underdeveloped; there was not an effective mechanism for interactive development among cities and among towns.

Third, the differences in the level of urbanization were obvious among regions and among cities. The levels of urbanization in Zhejiang's northeastern areas and the coastal areas of Wenzhou and Taizhou—these areas were economically developed—were apparently higher than those in the western mountainous areas of Wenzhou and Taizhou and Zhejiang's southwestern mountainous areas—these areas were economically and socially underdeveloped. According to the statistical data from the fifth census conducted in 2000, the levels of urbanization in the Circum-Hangzhou Bay Region, in the Wenzhou-Taizhou Region and in the Jinhua-Quzhou-Lishui Region were 51.0%, 51.5% and 38.5%, respectively; the level of urbanization in the Jinhua-Quzhou-Lishui Region was only 75% of that in the other two regions. From the perspective of the level of economic development, in 2004, the highest per capita GDP and the lowest per capita GDP in the whole province occurred in Ningbo's urban areas and Quzhou's urban areas, being 60,361 yuan and 14,379 yuan, respectively; the latter was lower than 1/4 of the former.[2]

Fourth, the development of urbanization failed to bring about concurrent agglomeration of the rural population and urbanization was incomplete. The strategy of urbanization implemented since the late 1990s pushed forward the urbanization of the rural population, but the farmers migrating to cities were merely statistical urban residents—they worked in cities, but they only had rural registered permanent residence, they were an urban population without urban registered permanent residence. Their migration was "incomplete", they had to move back and forth between urban

[2]Zhejiang Provincial Bureau of Statistics, *Zhejiang Statistical Yearbook 2005*.

and rural areas each year. A new dual social structure occurred within cities due to the restrictions from urban barriers. As a result, there were obvious differences in housing, education, medical service, social security and other social welfares between the rural migrant workers working in cities and the urban residents.

3. The birth of the philosophy of new-type urbanization

According to the law of the development of urbanization and Zhejiang's actual conditions, the strategy of development and staged changes, in 2005, the Zhejiang Provincial Party Committee and the Provincial Government became the first in China to develop and implement the *Plan of Zhejiang Province for Seeking Coordinated Urban and Rural Development and Promoting Urban-Rural Integration*, specifying seven major measures for making sure that urban development stimulates rural development and industry promotes agriculture, enhancing interaction between urbanization and the construction of the new countryside and achieving coordinated urban and rural development. On August 8, 2006, Zhejiang held a provincial working conference on cities, in which, Xi Jinping, then Secretary of the Zhejiang Provincial Party Committee, vowed to unswervingly venture down the path towards new-type urbanization, and he gave explicit instructions about pushing forward new-type urbanization in terms of resource-conserving, being environmentally friendly, having economical and efficient development, social harmony, coordinated development of small, medium-sized and large cities and small towns and the mutual promotion and common development of urban and rural areas, with a view to getting urbanization onto the track of intensive, harmonious, coordinated and innovative development.

8.1.2 The Connotation of New-Type Urbanization

1. Combining urban development with the construction of the new countryside, going down the urbanization path of mutual promotion and common development of urban and rural areas

As different spatial economies, urban and rural areas are interdependent and inseparable. New-type urbanization calls for proceeding from coordinated urban and rural development to build a mechanism for interactive and coordinated development of urban and rural areas, so as to boost urbanization and the construction of the new countryside in an interactive way. First, it is necessary to follow the requirements of urban-rural integration to more rapidly improve urban and rural planning, actively make planning cover both urban and rural areas; move faster to build various types of infrastructure, extend urban infrastructure to rural areas, enable urban public services to cover rural areas, make sure that modern civilization spreads to rural areas. Second, it is essential to improve the capability of cities for stimulating rural development. Third, further actions should be taken to interactively press ahead with urbanization and the construction of the new countryside, build a mechanism for interactive and coordinated development of urban and rural areas more rapidly, remove the institutional barriers leading to urban and rural segmentation and steadily promote urban-rural integration.

2. Combining urban development with efforts to optimize the layout of the population and productive forces across the province, taking the urbanization path of the coordinated development of small, medium-sized and large cities and small towns

It is imperative to more rapidly build an urban system conducive to coordinated urban and rural development. On the one hand, more emphasis should be placed on giving play to the role of city groups in optimizing the layout of the population and productive forces. Quicker actions should be taken to build a number of city groups with less land use, more employment, high capability for factor aggregation and rational population distribution. It is necessary to further accelerate the development of three provincial central cities, including Hangzhou City, Ningbo City and Wenzhou City and actively cultivate regional central cities. On the other hand, it is essential to earnestly develop small, medium-sized cities and small towns, give full scope to the role of small, medium-sized cities and small towns as the strategic nodes in coordinated urban and rural development. Efforts should be made to actively push forward the rational distribution and orderly construction of villages; priority should be given to better planning and building a number of central villages capable of effectively stimulating the development of the surrounding areas and with complete supporting production and living facilities, full public services, good environmental health and urban civilization. A pattern of coordinated development of megacities, large cities, small and medium-sized cities and small towns should take shape.

3. Combining urban development with the improvement of the efficiency of resource utilization, venturing down the path of resource-conserving urbanization

It is essential to change the extensive economic growth mode, in urbanization, characterized by high input, high consumption, high emissions, lack of coordination, difficulty in circulation and low efficiency; place equal emphasis on both development and saving, put saving first, focus on improving the efficiency of resource utilization, give priority to the economical use of land, intensify the reform involving the market-oriented allocation of land resources, effectively overcome the difficulty—where does land come from? Actions are taken to work on comprehensive energy-saving in the cities, strengthen the comprehensive utilization of resources and accelerate the building of resource-conserving cities.

4. Combining urban development with environmental protection and ecological construction, undertaking the environmentally-friendly path towards urbanization

On the one hand, urban planning and construction should take into full account the capacity of the ecological environment for carrying out urban development, coordinate the environmental interdependence between cities and regions and combine urban development with environmental protection and ecological construction. On the other hand, it is necessary to foster the philosophy of putting the environment first and undertaking the environmentally-friendly path towards urbanization in urban development. Steps should be taken to build and improve an urban ecological balance system, earnestly develop a circular economy, actively advocate the environmentally-friendly consumption mode, constantly develop a circular economy, energetically uphold the environmentally-friendly consumption mode, make continued efforts to nurture an environmentally-friendly cultural atmosphere so that cities become the first choice for practicing environmentally-friendly measures.

5. Combining urban development with the transformation of the growth mode, undertaking a path towards urbanization that is economical and efficient

In order to achieve the intensive development of the urban economy, emphasis must be placed on optimizing the industrial structure to promote urban development. It is essential to focus on developing the manufacturing industry with high added value, speeding up the development of the modern service industry so that economic growth no longer mainly relies on industry and instead is interactively driven by industry and the service sectors. It is necessary to aggregate innovation factors, activate innovation resources, transform innovation achievements, improve the capability for independent innovation, and ensure that economic growth mainly depends on scientific and technological advances and human capital rather than on the input of capital and material factors.

6. Combining urban development with the building of a harmonious society, undertaking a path towards urbanization that is socially harmonious

It is imperative to carry out urban and rural institutional reforms to orderly push forward the transfer and transformation of the rural population, and establish a mechanism for smooth social mobility. An active employment policy should be adopted to increase the level of employment of the whole society; social programs involving culture, education, medical service, health and social security need to be developed rapidly so as to build the basic public service system covering the whole population, optimize the allocation of public resources, promote equal access to the basic public services, establish a rational interest coordination mechanism, a safe social security mechanism and an effective mechanism for addressing contradictions. With the comprehensive governance of public order, actions should be taken to crack down on various illegal criminal activities according to laws to safeguard social security and create a harmonious social environment. Measures should be taken to make sure that everyone shares the achievements in urban development.

8.1.3 The Focus of New-Type Urbanization

1. Stimulating urbanization through new-type urbanization

With a focus on increasing the industrial level and developing the service economy, continued efforts should be made to enhance the competiveness of the urban economy and the capability of cities for driving rural development forward. "It is necessary to combine the service industry with the construction of the advanced manufacturing bases to promote the development of the modern service sectors closely associated with production, including logistics, finance, intermediary, software and information, better serve the construction of the advanced manufacturing bases."[3] With efforts to boost the interactive development of industrial and service sectors, IT application is enabled to stimulate the development of the advanced manufacturing industry and the modern service industry; scientific and technological innovations, cultural creative work is carried out to drive forward the development of the urban economy, thus promoting the transformation and upgrading of the province's economy.

2. Giving prominence to the core role of the urban economic circle in driving development forward, taking the city group as the main form for boosting urbanization

According to the guiding principles adopted in the 16th CPC National Congress and the Third Plenary Session of the 16th CPC Central Committee and the requirements of the Scientific Outlook on Development, the Zhejiang Provincial Party Committee and the Provincial Government have planned and built the industrial belt and city group around Hangzhou Bay. With respect to the pattern of development, one zone, one belt and two networks have been planned. One zone means the advanced manufacturing agglomeration zone focusing on nurturing five main industrial clusters, including electronic information, modern pharmaceuticals, petrochemicals, textiles, clothing industries, and six growing industrial clusters. One belt means the belt of the urban sprawl which is dominated by two main urban economic circles, Hangzhou and Ningbo, and joins other cities to form an orderly regional urban system with functional complementation and a rational layout. Two networks mean the green ecological network consisting of green open space, a green corridor and various protected areas, and the network of modern infrastructure made up of transportation, logistics, information, water supply and drainage, energy supply and environmental protection facilities. In light of Zhejiang's reality, the Zhejiang Provincial Party Committee and the Provincial Government have put forward the overall line of thought and basic pattern of generally pushing forward relevant work in four regions, including the circum-Hangzhou Bay region, the Wenzhou-Taizhou coastal region, Zhejiang's central region and Zhejiang's southwestern underdeveloped region.

3. Improving the systems and mechanisms for coordinated urban and rural development

Zhejiang should break through the original management mode under which there is segmentation between urban and rural areas, it should transform the mindset, innovate the management mode and management methods, with a focus on shaping a new pattern in which urban and rural areas interact with each other and advance in tandem. The reform of the household registration system should be intensified, and a unified urban-rural population registration system should be gradually established.

---

[3]Xi Jinping, Cultivating and Growing the Service Industry into the Main Industrial Driving Force, *Zhijiang Xinyu*, Zhejiang People's Publishing House, 2007, p. 120.

Actions should be taken to intensify the reform of the employment and social security system and build an integrated urban-rural employment system, and give an equal opportunity for development to farmers. Steps should be taken to actively explore and solve the problems in social security concerning rural migrant workers. The reform of the land requisition system should be intensified and the mechanism of rational compensation for the farmers whose land has been requisitioned should be improved to practically safeguard the legitimate rights and interests of those farmers. Actions should be taken to gradually increase public finance's coverage of rural areas, intensify fiscal transfer payment, and supply more public goods and public services to rural areas.

8.1.4 The Development of the Philosophy of New-Type Urbanization

1. Achievements from and problems in the strategy of new-type urbanization

During the period of the 11th Five-Year Plan, Zhejiang carefully carried out the Scientific Outlook on Development and fully implemented the strategy of new-type urbanization; the level of urbanization of the whole province steadily increased, it reached 61.6% in 2010, 12 percentage points higher than the nation's average level; Zhejiang stayed ahead nationwide regarding the level of urbanization. The spatial layout of urban and rural areas was further optimized. Urban functions were enhanced significantly. The level of coordinated urban and rural development increased noticeably.

Although Zhejiang made tremendous achievements in urbanization during the period of the 11th Five-Year Plan, many problems still existed; for example, urbanization was unbalanced, there was pseudo-urbanization, urbanization layout was irrational and the land destined for urban construction was insufficient.

2. The overall requirement and principles for Zhejiang's efforts to expand new-type urbanization

The *Plan of Zhejiang Province for Expanding New-type Urbanization* and the *12th Five-Year Plan of Zhejiang Province for the Development of New-type Urbanization*, unveiled in 2012, specify the overall requirements and basic principles for Zhejiang's efforts to promote new-type urbanization during the period of the 12th Five-Year Plan.

(1) The overall requirements. Holding high the great banner of socialism with Chinese characteristics, taking the Deng Xiaoping Theory and the Important Thought of Three Represents as the guide, comprehensively carrying out the Scientific Outlook on Development, thoroughly implementing the "Eight-Eight Strategies" and the overall strategy of making the people rich by starting a business and of building a strong province through innovation, focusing on the urbanization of the population, deriving the driving force from coordinated

urban and rural institutional reforms, taking the city group and the metropolitan area as the main forms to make cities more capable of gathering high-end factors and developing high-end industries, of creating a livable environment and improving the quality of life, and of driving urban development forward, carrying forward coordinated development of new-type urbanization, new-type industrialization and agricultural modernization, thus accelerating the formation of a new pattern of urban-rural integration.

(2) Principles and orientation. Upholding six basic principles, including coordinated development, intensive development, green development, interactive development, harmonious development and innovative development. The developmental orientation for thoroughly promoting new-type urbanization: First, building a modern new-type urban system more quickly; second, speeding up the construction and development of city groups and metropolitan areas; third, accelerating the development of regional central cities, quickening the development of central towns and the cultivation of small cities; fourth, speeding up the construction of the new socialist countryside focusing on central villages.

3. Accelerating the construction of smart cities

With rapid development and in-depth application of new-generation information technology, city smartness represents the important trend and basic characteristic of urban development in today's world as well as the new mode of modern urban development. In order to accord with that trend, the People's Government of Zhejiang Province has vowed to accelerate the construction of smart cities and take 3–5 years to embark on a smart city construction path with Zhejiang's characteristics, so as to play an active role in making substantial progress in speeding up economic transformation and upgrading, innovating social management and transforming the developmental mode.[4] In 2012, Zhejiang officially launched demonstration and pilot construction of smart cities and chose Hangzhou, Ningbo, Jiaxing, Shaoxing, Taizhou and Lishui as the first batch of pilot cities; as of 2013, Zhejiang had launched demonstration and pilot projects for the construction of 20 smart cities across the province, covering smart health, smart tourism, smart home and smart transportation.

4. Planning new-type urbanization at a high starting point

Since Zhejiang became the first in China to venture down a new-type urbanization path in 2006, Zhejiang's urbanization rate has increased steadily at an average annual rate of 1.1 percentage points; as of 2013, it reached 64%. According to the arrangements made during the central working conference on urbanization, the nation's target urbanization rate is 60% by 2020, which means that Zhejiang achieved that target six years in advance. Zhejiang needs to plan the work on new-type urbanization at a high starting point.

[4]The General Office of the People's Government of Zhejiang Province, *The Circular Concerning Pilot Work on the Construction of Smart Cities* (Zhe Zheng Ban Fa (2011) No. 107).

8.2 Interactive Development of New-Type Urbanization and New-Type Industrialization

8.2.1 Knowledge-Focused Industrial Development and Urbanization

1. Achieving intensive development of the economy, optimizing the urban structure

In early 2004, the Zhejiang Provincial Party Committee and the Provincial Government put forward a mechanism of reverse transmitted pressure because resource and environmental factors restrict development, and stressed that Zhejiang should seek the greatest economic and social development at the lowest resource and environmental price, protect its resources and the environment at the lowest social and economic cost, undertake an economic developmental path that is science and technology-led, resource-conserving and ecologically-friendly. During the provincial economic working conference held in late 2004, Xi Jinping, then Secretary of the Zhejiang Provincial Party Committee, stressed that Zhejiang must be determined to adopt the line of thought which states that "vacating the cage to change birds", the spirit of "achieving the rebirth of the phoenix amidst fire" and "born of fire" to more rapidly transform the economic growth mode, so that the good "birds" which "eat less, lay more eggs and fly far" can lead Zhejiang's economy.[5] Afterwards, the successive Party Committees and governments of Zhejiang Province unremittingly carried out the strategy of "vacating the cage to change birds". In 2013, Zhejiang shut down 18,000 low-end out-dated enterprises and workshops, phased out 1,029 high energy-consuming and heavily polluting enterprises, put into use 96,000 mu of idle construction land, and urged 1,658 enterprises in 18 key industries, including iron and steel, cement and papermaking, to phase out the out-dated production capacity, thus greatly optimizing the structure of the urban spaces.

2. Accelerating the building of a large brand province, improving urban competitiveness

According to Xi Jinping, "achieving the rebirth of the phoenix amidst fire" means that Zhejiang should, with great courage, get rid of its dependence on extensive growth, vigorously improve the capability for independent innovation, move faster to build a strong province of science and technology and a large brand province, take pains to turn manufacturing into creation, OEM into brand creation, and make industries and enterprises "born of fire" and "born again".[6] As indicated, strengthening brand building and actively creating famous brands is the important path for enterprises to undertake in order to "achieve the rebirth of the phoenix amidst fire". In 2013, the Zhejiang Provincial Party Committee and th Provincial Government made decisions

---

[5]2005 Classic Zhejiang—Zhejiang's Economy "Vacated the Cage to Change Birds" in a Year, *Zhejiang Daily*, December 20, 2005.

[6]Xi Jinping, Taking the Scientific Developmental Path to Move towards Building a Moderately Prosperous Society in All Respects, *People's Daily*, March 3, 2006, p. 8.

and arrangements about the projects of "vacating the cage to change birds", replacing the people with machines, optimizing space to save land, expanding the market through e-commerce, nurturing well-known enterprises, famous products and eminent experts, with all-out efforts to push forward these projects. In 2014, during the provincial meeting on promoting the projects of nurturing well-known enterprises, famous products and eminent experts, Zhejiang officially initiated pilot cultivation of the first 38 enterprises, including Wahaha, Wanxiang and Transfar, with respect to nurturing well-known enterprises, famous products and eminent experts.

3. Enhancing independent innovation and the quality of urbanization

Since the reform and opening up, Zhejiang has gradually developed an industrial structure with the following characteristics: light, small, private and processing; while pushing forward Zhejiang's regional economic development, this industrial structure has inevitably caused the following problems—low, small, scattered, weak—in the development of Zhejiang's economy: the industrial level is low, the scale of the enterprises is small, productive forces are distributed in a scattered manner and the capability for independent innovation is low.[7] In order to overcome the low capability for independent innovation of Zhejiang's economy, during the provincial conference on independent innovation in March, 2006, the Zhejiang Provincial Party Committee and the Provincial Government vowed to take 15 years to build Zhejiang into an innovative province and basically complete the building of a strong province of science and technology. In May, 2013, the *Decision of the Zhejiang Provincial Party Committee on Comprehensively Implementing the Strategy of Innovation-driven Development and Accelerating the Building of an Innovative Province* was deliberated and adopted during the Third Plenary (Enlarged) Session of the 13th Party Committee of Zhejiang Province. After many years of unremitting efforts, Zhejiang's new and hi-tech industries have developed tremendously. In the first half of 2014, the added value of Zhejiang's emerging strategic industries reached 139.5 billion yuan, up 7.8%, being 0.8 percentage points higher than the growth rate of the GDP in the same period.

8.2.2 Industrially Ecological Development and Urbanization

1. Energy and resource saving

For many years, given Zhejiang's reality that the territory is small and resources are available in small quantities, the Zhejiang Provincial Party Committee and the Provincial Government attached great importance to resource saving. In June, 2005, the Zhejiang Provincial Party Committee and the Provincial Government held the provincial working conference on the circular economy and set up a leading working group led by Xi Jinping, then Secretary of the Zhejiang Provincial Party Committee,

[7]Guo Zhanheng, The Basic Line of Thought Regarding Zhejiang's Transformation and Upgrading during the 12th Five-Year Plan Period, *Zhejiang Economy*, 2009(23).

and in the charge of Lu Zushan, then Governor of Zhejiang Province. In August, 2005, the *Plan of Zhejiang Province for the Development of the Circular Economy* was unveiled; the Plan states, "accelerating the development of the circular economy is of important significance for mitigating the resource and environmental bottlenecks, transforming the developmental mode and building an ecological civilization". Since 2006, local governments have earnestly followed the requirements specified in the *Work Program on the "991" Action Plan of Zhejiang Province for the Development of the Circular Economy* to actively develop nine key fields of the circular economy, adopt nine groups of means and each year carry out about 100 major projects for the circular economy.[8] In 2008, Zhejiang also carried out ten major projects for energy conservation and the reduction of consumption, changed the energy conservation and consumption reduction means from technology to a combination of structure, technology and management. Besides energy conservation, Zhejiang also paid great attention to saving water. As from October 1, 2007, Zhejiang officially carried out the *Measures of Zhejiang Province for Water Conservation*, specifying the measures for managing, promoting and adjusting water-conservation. In 2013, the Fourth Plenary Session of the 13th Party Committee of Zhejiang Province made a major decision about treating sewage, controlling flooding, discharging the accumulated water, guaranteeing water supply and saving water, in which water conservation was specified.

2. Control of environmental pollution

The best way to control pollution lies in reducing it. In 2007, Zhejiang issued the *Circular Concerning Further Strengthening the Reduction of the Discharge of Pollutants*, calling for assigning the discharge reduction tasks to various industries, major pollutant discharging units and major pollution control projects. In 2008, Zhejiang developed the *Implementation Measures of Zhejiang Province for the Evaluation of Total Reduction in the Discharge of Main Pollutants*, taking the result of the evaluation of total reduction of the discharge of main pollutants as the important basis for comprehensive evaluation of the leading body and leading cadres from the governments of the cities divided into districts, and stating that the accountability system and the one-vote veto system would be adopted.[9]

Besides pollutants discharge reduction, Zhejiang's work on pollution control can be summarized as water treatment, haze treatment and soil improvement. In 2004, the People's Government of Zhejiang Province took an environmental pollution control action focusing on 8 major water systems and 11 key provincial areas under environmental protection supervision throughout the province (the "811 Environmental Improvement Action").[10] In November, 2013, the Fourth Plenary Session of the 13th Party Committee of Zhejiang Province vowed to treat sewage, control flooding, discharge the accumulated water, guarantee water supply and save water. For the improvement of the air, Zhejiang issued the *Regulations of Zhejiang Province on Air*

[8]Shen Manhong, From Green Zhejiang to Ecological Zhejiang, *Zhejiang Daily*, May 25, 2012.

[9]Shen Manhong, From Green Zhejiang to Ecological Zhejiang, *Zhejiang Daily*, May 25, 2012.

[10]Zhejiang: 811 Environmental Improvement Action Won the First Battle, *China Economic Times*, December 24, 2007.

Pollution Control in 2003, the *Clean Air Action Plan of Zhejiang Province* in 2010 and the *Measures of Zhejiang Province for the Evaluation of Ambient Air Quality Management (Trial)* in 2013; in 2014, it unveiled the *Air Pollution Control Action Plan of Zhejiang Province (2013–2017)* which is more specific, stricter and more operable, calling for reducing the concentration of fine particulate matter (PM2.5) throughout the province by more than 20% by 2017 from the concentration registered in 2012. For soil pollution control, according to the *Regulations of Zhejiang Province on Environmental Control of Solid Waste Pollution*, the system for the restoration of the polluted soil became effective as from June 1, 2006. In July, 2006, the People's Government of Zhejiang Province decided that the competent departments for agriculture above the county level should build and improve a network for the monitoring of soil fertility and fertilizer application. In July, 2011, Zhejiang unveiled the *Clean Soil Action Plan of Zhejiang Province*. According to the Action Plan, by 2015, in Zhejiang Province, a relatively complete working mechanism for soil pollution control will have been established, a legal system for soil pollution control will have become basically complete, a soil environment monitoring network will basically have covered the whole province, the soil pollution in the areas dedicated to the production of the main agricultural products will be controlled effectively, major potential safety hazards in soil environment will have been basically eliminated.

3. Ecological safety guarantee

In 2004, Zhejiang carried out some practical work on the ecological compensation mechanism.[11] In 2005, the People's Government of Zhejiang Province issued *Several Opinions on Further Improving the Ecological Compensation Mechanism*, further making the ecological compensation mechanism institutionalized and well-regulated. In 2012, the first trans-provincial mechanism for ecological compensation in river basins in China—the Ecological Compensation Mechanism for Xin'an River Basin—was launched. According to the regulations concerning the ecological compensation mechanism for river basins, when Anhui in the upstream section provides water with a quality that is above the basic standard, Zhejiang in the downstream section should compensate Anhui; when the quality of the water from Anhui is lower than the basic standard, Anhui should compensate Zhejiang. Regarding emission trading, as early as 2005, emission trading was launched in Xiuzhou District, Jiaxing City, Zhejiang Province. In 2009, as Zhejiang was included in the first batch of pilot provinces for emission trading in China, the Zhejiang Emission Trading Center was established and pilot paid use and trading of emission rights was officially initiated in Zhejiang. Afterwards, Zhejiang issued a number of relevant regulations and policy documents, including the *Interim Measures of Zhejiang Province for Pilot Work on Pilot Paid Use and Trading of Emission Rights*. As of the first half of 2014, pilot work had begun in 68 counties (districts) in 11 cities divided into districts, 9,573 paid uses of emission rights had occurred, 1,725 million yuan of paid use fees had been paid, emission trading was conducted 3,863 times, with a trading amount of

[11] Zhejiang Explored the Establishment of the Ecological Compensation Mechanism, People's Daily Online, June 24, 2004.

773 million yuan. In order to address water shortage in some areas, Zhejiang has also piloted water rights trading.

8.3 The Practice of New-Type Urbanization

8.3.1 The Construction of Four Main Metropolitan Areas

8.3.1.1 The Construction of the Hangzhou Metropolitan Area

In early 2002, the Hangzhou Municipal Party Committee and the Municipal Government made a major strategic decision about urbanization—building a metropolis, making a new paradise. In 2002, when inspecting and surveying Hangzhou, Xi Jinping stressed that it was necessary to give prominence to key points, push forward relevant work across the board to improve the overall quality of the economy and speed up urbanization. In 2013, the Hangzhou Municipal Government set up a leading group of Hangzhou City for promoting new-type urbanization, with a view to actively boosting new-type urbanization and accelerating urban-rural integration.

1. Taking the Dajiangdong Industrial Agglomeration Area as the main carrier for building the provincial high-end manufacturing center

In order to make Hangzhou leap from the "West Lake Era" to the "Qiantang River Era", in 2002, the Hangzhou Municipal Party Committee and the Municipal Government initiated the construction of a large industrial zone—the Hangzhou Xiaoshan Jiangdong Industrial Zone—in the reclamation area in the northeastern part of Xiaoshan District. In 2006, the National Development and Reform Commission announced that the Hangzhou Jiangdong Industrial Park had officially passed the examination and verification of a provincial development zone. In late 2008, Jiangdong Bridge connecting Hangzhou's Xiasha with Xiaoshan was officially opened to traffic, so the connection between the Jiangdong Industrial Zone and Hangzhou's main urban areas has become increasingly close. In 2009, Hangzhou further vowed to plan and build the Dajiangdong New Area in a coordinated way to achieve Dajiangdong regional integration. In May, 2009, the expert review meeting on the *Strategic Plan of Hangzhou City for the Development of the Dajiangdong New Area* was held. In August, 2010, the Zhejiang Provincial Development and Reform Commission conducted surveys and a feasibility study on the *Developmental Plan for the Hangzhou Dajiangdong Industrial Agglomeration Area*; in late 2010, the Plan was approved by the People's Government of Zhejiang Province. According to the Plan, the Dajiangdong Industrial Agglomeration Area is generally positioned as follows: focusing on developing the advanced manufacturing industry, the strategic emerging industries, the modern service industry and the airport industry; reinforcing the modern industrial functions, the integrated service functions, the high-end urban functions, the first-class ecological functions; becoming a provincial industry-led, high-quality modern industrial agglomeration demonstration area which puts ecology first and provides full services. In October, 2012, the Management Committee of the Hangzhou Dajiangdong Industrial Agglomeration Area was inaugurated. The Dajiangdong Party Working Committee was set up in April, 2014; it shares one office with the original Dajiangdong Management Committee while keeping separate identities, and it is an agency assigned by the Hangzhou Municipal Party Committee and the Municipal Government to perform relevant functions at a local level. In August, 2014, major adjustments were made in the system of Hangzhou's Dajiangdong, the management bodies of such original function zones as Jiangdong, Linjiang and Qianjin were removed, while the administrative areas in five sub-districts in Xiaoshan District, including Hezhuang, Yipeng, Xinwan, Linjiang and Qianjin, and other areas within the scope of the Dajiangdong plan would be managed by the Dajiangdong Party Working Committee and the Management Committee. At present, the Dajiangdong Agglomeration Area has been home to major full vehicle projects including Changan Ford and Dongfeng Yulong, and a 100 billion yuan automobile industry chain. In the future, in the Dajiangdong Industrial Agglomeration Area, actions will be taken to vigorously develop high technology manufacturing, focus on major equipment manufacturing and car making, actively develop strategic emerging industries, including new energy, new materials, information technology, biotechnology, energy conservation and environmental protection, and turn the Dajiangdong Industrial Agglomeration Area into the high-end manufacturing center in Zhejiang Province, even of the Yangtze River Delta Region.

2. Taking the Future Sci-Tech City (the Overseas High-level Talents Innovation Park) and the Qingshan Lake Sci-Tech City (the Provincial Technical Innovation Park) as the main carriers for making the provincial innovation center

In 2005, construction began on the Cangqian New and Hi-tech Industrial Block, designed to fully develop new and hi-tech industries in Yuhang District. In 2007, Yuhang District expanded the Cangqian New and Hi-tech Industrial Block as the Yuhang Innovation Base—Ecological Technology Island – characterized by higher education, new and hi-tech industries and high-level housing. In 2009, the Central Government initiated the implementation of the Recruitment Program of Global Experts and the construction of an overseas high-level talent innovation and incubation base. Zhejiang decided to centrally build the Zhejiang Overseas High-level Talents Innovation Park in Yuhang District, Hangzhou City. In July, 2010, the Overseas High-level Talents Innovation Park was officially inaugurated at the Yuhang Innovation Base. In December, 2011, the Overseas High-level Talents Innovation Park was further upgraded to a Future Sci-Tech City, one of the four major talent bases built by the enterprises managed by the Central Government. On January 2, 2012, the Zhejiang Hangzhou Future Sci-Tech City was officially inaugurated, 6 hi-tech projects, including the Medical Center of Zhejiang University, were also launched. In December, 2012, construction began on 8 major projects, including Sunking Technology and DragonSoft, in Hangzhou Future Sci-Tech City, covering an area of 324 mu, with a total investment of 4.3 billion yuan. In 2013, the Future Sci-Tech City (the Overseas High-level Talents Innovation Park) was designated as a National Intellectual Property Demonstration City Expansion Area; this was another national title granted to the Future Sci-Tech City, following such titles as the Hangzhou National Information Industry Base Expansion Area, the National E-commerce Pilot City Expansion Area and the China Service Outsourcing Base Demonstration City Expansion Area.[12]

Qingshan Lake Sci-Tech City serves as an important vehicle for implementing the strategy of making the people rich by starting a business and of building a strong province through innovation developed by the Zhejiang Provincial Party Committee and the Provincial Government. In 2009, construction officially began on the Lin'an Qingshan Lake Sci-Tech City. In the same year, Zhao Hongzhu, then Secretary of the Zhejiang Provincial Party Committee, Lu Zushan, then Governor of Zhejiang Province, and other leaders surveyed the Qingshan Lake Sci-Tech City and vowed to turn Qingshan Lake Sci-Tech City into an important vehicle for building a strong innovative province, and make it become an internationally advanced, domestically first-class scientific and technological resource agglomeration area. In December, 2010, construction officially began on the first 8 scientific research institutions in Qingshan Lake Sci-Tech City. In February, 2011, construction began on the urban complex of Qingshan Lake Sci-Tech City, covering an area of about 1,200 mu and with the planned building area of 1.40 million m^2. In 2012, the Science Technology Department of Zhejiang Province released the science, technology, talent, innovation and entrepreneurship policy of Qingshan Lake Sci-Tech City. According to the policy, the Science Technology Department of Zhejiang Province and Hangzhou City would allocate 100 million yuan in a special fund each year to introduce large institutions, well-known universities, research and development institutions, while Lin'an City would also provide multiple fund subsidies. In 2014, a three-year action plan was carried out in Qingshan Lake Sci-Tech City, with a focus on taking the great breakthrough action of introducing the strong and outstanding ones, the supporting great breakthrough action for improvement and the great breakthrough action for environmental improvement, and pushing forward the industrial quality improvement project, the reform and innovation project and the new area co-construction project.

3. Taking Hangzhou CBD and Qianjiang Century City as the main vehicles for building a provincial business center

On July 1, 2001, construction began on the Hangzhou Grand Theatre, which marked the official launch of the construction of Hangzhou CBD. In February, 2002, Hangzhou CBD saw the complete launch of the construction of infrastructure dominated by two east-west roads, nine north-south roads and two major water systems. Construction began on such projects as the Hangzhou International Convention Center, the Civic Center, Qianjiang International Times Square, the Zhejiang Fortune & Finance Center, CapitaLand Raffles City, the Oceanwide International Center, the

[12]The Science and Technology Bureau of Yuhang District, Hangzhou Future Sci-Tech City Was Designated as a National Intellectual Property Demonstration City Expansion Area, January 2, 2014.

Ping An Financial Center and they were completed. In 2014, full-swing construction began on the Phase II project of Hangzhou CBD, mainly including Qianjiang Financial City, Sibao, the Qibao Unit, the Jingfang Sanbao Unit and Fisherman's Wharf. In 2003, the approval of the controlled plan for Qianjiang Century City indicated that the development and construction of Qianjiang Century City had substantively been launched; as of 2013, it had introduced such headquarters projects as the Jiangning Building, the Zhejiang Private Enterprise Development Building, the Hangzhou International Office Center, the Agricultural Building, and the Zhejiang Chamber of Commerce Building.

8.3.1.2 The Construction of Ningbo Metropolitan Area

1. Speeding up the integration of the Ningbo-Zhoushan Port

In January, 2004, the Ningbo Port Authority, the Zhoushan Port Authority and Hong Kong Ning Shing (Holdings) Co., Ltd. signed a letter of intent for a joint venture on the Jintang Island Dapukou Container Terminal Project, which marked the launch of cooperation on the integration of the Ningbo-Zhoushan Port. In May, 2005, when surveying Ningbo and Zhoushan, Lu Zushan, then Deputy Secretary of the Zhejiang Provincial Party Committee and then Governor of Zhejiang Province, stressed that it was essential to further deepen understanding, strengthen leadership, unify the planning, integrate the resources, carry out orderly development and accelerate the integration of the Ningbo-Zhoushan Port. Xi Jinping, then Secretary of the Zhejiang Provincial Party Committee, pointed out that the port was the only resource advantage for Zhejiang to keep a foothold in the world and participate in international competition, it was urgent to make it large, strong and outstanding. In July, 2005, the People's Government of Zhejiang Province set up a leading group for the integration of the Ningbo-Zhoushan Port, thus such integration entered the stage of substantive operations. In 2009, the *Master Plan for the Ningbo-Zhoushan Port*, unveiled after the integration, was officially approved by the Ministry of Transportation and the People's Government of Zhejiang Province. The *Global Port Development Report (2013)*, officially released by the Shanghai International Shipping Institute on March 10, 2014, shows that the Ningbo-Zhoushan Port ranked No. 1 worldwide; its cargo throughput was 809.78 million tons in 2013.

2. Accelerating the development of a port-centered industrial cluster

After the Ningbo-Hangzhou Bay Sea-Crossing Bridge Project was determined, the tideland on the south bank was first included, by Cixi City, into the strategic layout for embracing the "bridge economy". In November, 2011, the construction project of the Hangzhou Bay New Zone was officially launched. In October, 2004, the Management Committee of the Hangzhou Bay New Zone was officially inaugurated. In 2010, the Hangzhou Bay New Zone became the demonstration base for the Ningbo smart city. In 2013, two major cultural leisure vacation projects—MGM, Huaqiang—and ten major projects, including the Geely powertrain and the Geely-Volvo China Design and Test Center, were signed and construction began on them. In February, 2008, the Ningbo Meishan Bonded Port Area was established with the approval of the State Council and became the 5th bonded port area in China. As from July 1, 2011, the Ningbo Meishan Bonded Port Area was fully opened to carry on bonded business. On December 28, 2013, the customs office of the Ningbo Meishan Bonded Port Area was officially put into operation.

8.3.1.3 The Construction of Wenzhou Metropolitan Area

1. Vigorously enhancing the capacity and functions of core areas

Within three districts of Wenzhou City, after readjustments during the period 2000–2003, at present, there is a core metropolitan area consisting of Lucheng, Longwan, Ouhai, Oujiangkou, Dongtou and Oujiang North Bank including Shangtang. In April, 2011, according to the master plan of a metropolitan area, with a focus on "1650", the division of core urban areas, including Lucheng District, was adjusted in Wenzhou. Since 2011, actions have been taken to commence the construction of the Binjiang Business District Financial Agglomeration Area, the Binhai Commercial Core Area and other projects. In 2013, Wenzhou saw the completion of a core administrative block in Ouhai New City, the business block Phase I, the Zhanqian commercial and trade area, the headquarters economy park, the ATL Mall, the financial agglomeration area and other projects.

2. Speeding up the construction of the Oujiangkou Industrial Agglomeration Area and the new area

In the 1970s, the Wenzhou Municipal Party Committee and the Municipal Government envisioned the construction of the Wenzhou shoal project. In June, 2002, the Zhejiang Provincial Ocean and Fisheries Bureau organized efforts to review the report on the feasibility study regarding the use of the sea area in the Wenzhou shoal Phase I project, and confirmed that the use of the sea area in the Wenzhou shoal project complied with the requirements of Zhejiang Province and Wenzhou City for large-scale marine function zoning. In 2006, as Lingni North Dike was completed and opened to traffic, and the tideland reclamation project was further promoted, the plan for building a new industrial zone in the west area of the peninsula project was put on the agenda. After many years of construction, in October, 2010, the Oujiangkou Industrial Agglomeration Area officially became one of the 14 industrial agglomeration areas in Zhejiang. According to the *Developmental Plan of Wenzhou City for the Oujiangkou Industrial Agglomeration Area*, the structure of the developmental space of the industrial agglomeration area features one core, two axes and eight subareas. In March, 2011, the Oujiangkou New Area Development and Construction Management Committee of Wenzhou City was officially inaugurated, the master plan for the Oujiangkou New Area was included in the urban master plan of Wenzhou City, the overall functional structure of the new area, which features one axis and multiple corridors, two cores and multiple points, three subareas and two sides, was determined. In August, 2012, construction began on 14 key industrial and major supporting projects in the Oujiangkou New Area; in December, construction began on17 major projects. In December, 2013, construction began on ten major projects in the Oujiangkou New Area, including a new area hospital and a development building.

8.3.1.4 The Construction of Jinhua-Yiwu Metropolitan Area

1. Accelerating the construction of the Jinhua Emerging Industry Agglomeration Area

For many years, the Jinhua Emerging Industry Agglomeration Area was dedicated to developing strategic emerging industries, including new energy automobiles, electronic information and new materials. In early 2011, the *The Plan for the Development of the Jinhua Emerging Industry Agglomeration Area* was officially approved by the People's Government of Zhejiang Province, stating that the agglomeration area focuses on cultivating strategic emerging industries and thus stimulating the transformation and upgrading of the traditional industries. In September, 2011, the Management Committee of the Jinhua Emerging Industry Agglomeration Area was inaugurated. In August, 2012, the Jinhua Municipal Party Committee and the Municipal Government issued *Several Opinions on Accelerating the Construction of the Jinhua Emerging Industry Agglomeration Area*, specifying the supporting policies covering land guarantee, fiscal and tax affairs, investment and financing reform, environmental capacity allocation and helping to attract investments and construction in the agglomeration area. As of August, 2012, 2.31 billion yuan of major infrastructure investments and 10.57 billion yuan of major industrial project investments were completed; and 165 enterprises and projects were newly introduced in several major parks involved in the Jinhua Emerging Industry Agglomeration Area.

2. Pushing forward the Reform of Yiwu Pilot Comprehensive International Trade

In 2011, the Reform of Yiwu Pilot Comprehensive International Trade was fully initiated. Its specific goal is as follows: by 2020, improving Yiwu's strategic position in international trade, turning Yiwu into the demonstration area for the transformation of the foreign trade developmental mode, an important base for stimulating industrial transformation and upgrading, the world's leading international small commodity trade center and a well-known international commercial and trade city suitable for doing business in, living in and traveling to. In August, 2011, the Zhejiang Administration for Industry and Commerce and Yiwu City signed the *Framework Agreement for Cooperation on the Joint Construction of the Reform of Pilot Comprehensive International Trade*. In October, 2011, in order to support the Reform of Yiwu Pilot Comprehensive International Trade, the Zhejiang Provincial Department of Commerce issued *Ten Opinions on Accelerating the Work on the Reform of Yiwu Pilot Comprehensive International Trade*, and signed the *Framework Agreement on Jointly Promoting the Reform of Pilot Comprehensive International Trade* with Yiwu. In August, 2012, the Zhejiang Provincial Department of Construction and

Yiwu signed *Ten Cooperation Agreements on Jointly Promoting the Reform of Pilot Comprehensive International Trade*. In January, 2014, the General Administration of Customs, the Ministry of Finance, the State Administration of Taxation, the State Administration of Foreign Exchange jointly issued a relevant document to approve the establishment of Yiwu Bonded Logistics Center (Type B); in March, 2014, eight ministries, including the National Development and Reform Commission, the Ministry of Finance and the Ministry of Commerce, jointly issued a relevant document to approve the building of the second group of 30 cities, including Yiwu City, into national e-commerce demonstration cities.

8.3.2 The Optimization of the Urban System

1. Pushing forward the strategy of main functional areas

Spatial structure epitomizes regional economic and social activities in regional space and is also the result of the interaction among regions. The 11th Five-Year Plan, deliberated and approved in the Fourth Session of the 10th People's Congress of Zhejiang Province in 2006, specifies the guiding opinions on the main scope, main tasks and policy orientation of four types of main functional areas in Zhejiang Province. In 2013, the *Plan of Zhejiang Province for the Main Functional Areas* was officially unveiled, stating that by 2020, the provincial overall pattern of land space development featuring three belts, four zones and two screens will basically have taken shape; the ratio of urban land, industrial land, agricultural land and ecological land in the whole province will become more rational. In April, 2004, six counties of Zhejiang Province, including Kaihua, were included in the national list of areas for pilot construction and demonstration of main functions. In May, 2014, Li Qiang, then Governor of Zhejiang Province, chaired the symposium on Zhejiang's implementation of the strategy of main functional areas, and required relevant departments to conduct in-depth surveys and studies, and adopt new philosophies and lines of thought, pragmatic policy measures to thoroughly carry out the strategy of main functional areas.

2. Pressing ahead with urban-rural integration in a coordinated way

In 2004, Xi Jinping, then Secretary of Zhejiang Province, set the goal of seeking coordinated urban and rural development and promoting urban-rural integration in Zhejiang Province: by 2010, basically removing the urban-rural dual structure, significantly narrowing the urban-rural gap, shaping a pattern of coordinated urban and rural development; by 2020, basically realizing urban-rural integration in sync with basically achieving modernization in advance. He also stressed that it was necessary to thoroughly carry out the One-Thousand-Village Demonstration and Ten-Thousand-Village Improvement Project as the powerful means for promoting urban-rural integration. In January, 2005, the Zhejiang Provincial Party Committee and the Provincial Government issued the *Plan of Zhejiang Province for Seeking*

Coordinated Urban and Rural Development and Promoting Urban-Rural Integration, focusing the tasks for promoting urban-rural integration on coordinated urban and rural industrial development, coordinated development of urban and rural social programs, coordinated construction of urban and rural infrastructures, coordinated urban and rural labor employment and social security, coordinated construction of urban and rural ecological environments and coordinated regional economic and social development. In April, 2008, Zhejiang designated Jiaxing City and Yiwu City as the province's pilot areas for comprehensive reform for coordinated urban and rural development. In 2010, Zhejiang vowed to build a beautiful countryside and especially developed the *Action Plan of Zhejiang Province for Building a Beautiful Countryside (2011–2015)*. In 2011, Zhejiang put forward nine reform measures to intensify the reform of the system for urban-rural integration, including the intensification of the reform of the agricultural operational system, innovating the system of agricultural technology research, development and popularization, intensifying the reform of the rural collective construction land system, innovating the rural social management system, intensifying the reform of the rural financial system, building a farmer entrepreneurial service system, intensifying the reform of the household registration system, deepening the reform of the rural property rights system and the reform of the public service system.

3. Boosting the coordinated development of small, medium-sized and large cities and small towns

Since the 11th Party Congress of Zhejiang Province, Zhejiang has continued to speed up the construction of three main central cities, Hangzhou, Ningbo and Wenzhou, actively support the efforts to make regional central cities large and strong, move faster to cultivate three main city groups, the Circum-Hangzhou Bay Region, the Wenzhou-Taizhou coastal region and Zhejiang's central region. Actions have been taken to encourage more counties to develop into medium-sized cities with complete functions and give full scope to the important role of the county economy in coordinated urban and rural development. The development of small towns is an important part of urbanization. Zhejiang piloted a comprehensive reform of small towns in 1995. In 2005, 11 towns in Zhejiang Province were included in the first batch of national pilot small towns for development and reform. In 2008, 14 towns in Zhejiang Province were included in the second batch of national pilot small towns for development and reform; there were a total of 25 pilot small towns in Zhejiang, ranking Zhejiang No. 1 nationwide for the number of pilot small towns. In 2012, 16 towns in Zhejiang Province were included in the third batch of national pilot small towns for development and reform. In 2014, 11 ministries and commissions, including the National Development and Reform Commission, the Ministry of Finance, the Ministry of Land and Resources and the Ministry of Housing and Urban-Rural Development, jointly carried out pilot comprehensive work on national new-type urbanization. In October, 2014, the News Office of the People's Government of Zhejiang Province announced, on its official microblog "Zhejiang Release", that Ningbo City, Jiaxing City, Yiwu City and Longgang Town were included in the national pilot list of new-type urbanization.

8.3.3 The Construction of Smart Cities

1. Developing the Internet of Things (IoT) industry

The IoT industry started early, its industrial foundation was solid and its technical strength was powerful in Zhejiang Province, but the industry is still generally at the initial stage. In 2009, Zhejiang initiated the standardization of the logistics industry; as a result, logistics enterprises can utilize the unified information platform to build the IoT for information interconnection and sharing, so as to reduce logistics costs and improve the efficiency of total production. In March, 2010, Zhejiang set up a group for developing the plan for the IoT and planned to turn Zhejiang into a national IoT industrial base, and build an IoT industry cluster with Hangzhou as the core and Jiaxing and Wenzhou's Yueqing as two wings. In October, 2010, the People's Government of Zhejiang Province specially developed a plan for the development of the IoT industry. In September, 2011, the Zhejiang Association for the IoT Industry was established. In March, 2013, with the adoption of the platform of a credit "black box" system, in coordination with the previously completed GPS monitoring platform, the first IoT for engineering safety supervision was officially completed in Zhejiang. In 2014, the Chu Cang Kuai Jie E-commerce Park, the first e-commerce IoT industry service base, was launched in the Binjiang New and Hi-tech Development Zone in Hangzhou City.

2. Spurring the development of cloud computing

In November, 2010, the National Development and Reform Commission and the Ministry of Industry and Information Technology officially decided to carry out pilot and demonstration work on cloud computing innovation and development in Beijing, Shanghai, Shenzhen, Hangzhou and Wuxi. In December, 2010, the West Lake District Cloud Computing Service Platform, the first cloud computing service platform in Zhejiang, jointly built by the Electronic Information Management Committee of West Lake District and IBM, was officially launched. On September 22, 2011, the Shaoxing Didang Calling Center of Zhejiang Mobile was officially put into operation, which indicated that the world's largest cloud computing calling center deployed by Zhejiang Branch was officially put into commercial use. On October 19, 2012, the China Cloud Computing Application Alliance was officially established in Hangzhou, its office is located in Hangzhou; nearly 120 enterprises, including Shanghai Shanda, Beijing Cloud Base, Shenzhen PowerLeader and Sungood Technology, have become members of this Alliance. In January, 2013, the Watone Cloud Data Center, the first cloud computing industry park in Zhejiang, was put into operation. On June 25, 2014, Li Qiang, then Governor of Zhejiang Province, announced that Zhejiang Government Affairs Service Online was officially launched; netizens can use this Government Affairs Supermarket to visit government departments like going shopping at Taobao, about 60,000 items subject to examination and approval by municipal and county governments can be dealt with online, with payment made through Alipay .

3. Expanding big data applications

In March, 2013, the first smart big data test base for electric power in China was completed in Haiyan, through which the big data system is used to analyze the data regarding daily electricity charges on enterprises and accurately judge whether the electric power consumption at enterprises is rational and the electricity charge is normal, thus turning the originally meaningless data into a magic weapon for analyzing the daily production at enterprises. In December, 2013, under the policy guidance of the Zhejiang Provincial Economic and Information Commission, AdTime worked with manufacturers, users and research institutions in the big data technology application field in Zhejiang, including Hangzhou H3C, the Zhejiang Branch of China Telecom, Zheshang Securities, Zhejiang University, the Bank of Hangzhou and other enterprises and public institutions, to establish the Zhejiang Big Data Application Industry Alliance.

8.4 Summary and Outlook

For many years, Zhejiang has, in light of the stage of its economic and social development and the changes in resources and the environment, become the first to put forward the strategy of new-type urbanization, actively and steadily pushed forward urbanization, basically shaped a pattern of interactive development of new-type urbanization and new-type industrialization and promoted intensive utilization of resources. An urban structure of harmonious development of the small, medium-sized and large cities has preliminarily taken shape, the status and role of the central cities in the regional economy have improved constantly, new-type urbanization has served as an important driving force for Zhejiang's economic transformation and upgrading. In 2013, the urbanization rate of Zhejiang Province reached 64% in terms of permanent resident population, 10.3 percentage points higher than the nation's average level, making Zhejiang remain ahead nationwide.[13] Zhejiang's path towards urbanization in more than 30 years, especially regarding new-type urbanization practice in the past 10 years, has provided beneficial reference for China in its promotion of new-type urbanization.

As shown by Zhejiang's experience in new-type urbanization, Zhejiang has placed emphasis on pushing forward interactive development of new-type urbanization and new-type industrialization, Zhejiang has pressed ahead with knowledge-focused industrial development and industrially ecological development to stimulate urban IT applications and environmental optimization and to promote the development of the urban economy. Meanwhile, Zhejiang has paid attention to optimizing the urban system, and has pushed forward the coordinated development of small, medium-sized and large cities by building main functional areas. Great efforts have been made to propel the construction of four main metropolitan areas, and enhance the capability of the central cities for driving ahead with regional economic development. Actions

[13]http://www.zj.stats.gov.cn.

have been taken to support the development of the central towns and promote urban-rural integration in a coordinated way. Various solutions have been adopted to develop the Internet, boost the development of cloud computing and expand big data, so as to more rapidly build smart cities and effectively promote economic transformation and upgrading.

Of course, Zhejiang's urbanization has also been accompanied by some inadequacies; for example, the intensive utilization of land is at a relatively low level in some cities; many cities lag behind in function and management, their overall carrying capacity is not high; the diffusion effect of cities is not sufficient, it is still necessary to enhance the capability of cities for driving forward the development of the surrounding areas, especially of the rural economy, the urban system still needs to be optimized; the levels of urbanization are greatly different among regions and among cities; in particular, the level of urbanization of Zhejiang's southwestern areas still needs to be increased; urbanization does not synchronize with the agglomeration of the rural population, urbanization is incomplete to some extent. For the future trend, with massive agglomeration of urban populations and the popularization of cars, the land, resource and environmental constraints on Zhejiang's urbanization will become increasingly severe, and the environmental problems, including those concerning air and water resources, will become more striking. Therefore, it is necessary for Zhejiang to continuously innovate its path towards and mechanism for urbanization.

In the future, as Zhejiang advances in new-type urbanization, it is essential to further enable harmonious interaction between industrialization and urbanization, undertake an environmentally friendly and resource-intensive urbanization path, enhance urban IT applications and optimal urban ecological construction, make sure that it and industrial IT applications, industrially ecological development interact and promote each other; it is necessary to give prominence to the role of cities, especially small and medium-sized cities and central towns, in stimulating rural development and build a mechanism for the mutual promotion and common development of urban and rural areas; actions should be taken to earnestly promote the construction of metropolitan areas and regional central cities, accelerate the development of city groups along the Shanghai-Hangzhou-Ningbo Highway and the Wenzhou-Taizhou Highway; at the same time, importance should be attached to the coordinated development of small, medium-sized and large cities and small towns and the optimization of the urban structure; the development of small cities and central towns should be supported; moreover, it is necessary to persevere in the fundamental goal of putting the people first to promote people-oriented urbanization, the reforms of the rural land system and the household registration system, provide an institutional guarantee and resource and factor support for pushing forward Zhejiang's new-type urbanization. Only in this way can Zhejiang's path towards new-type urbanization become wider and China's new-type urbanization be better promoted.

Chapter 9
The Experience and Inspiration from Zhejiang's Economic Transformation and Development

Zhigang Huang and Xiahui Liu

As indicated by the 30-year course of Zhejiang's reform and opening up, the pioneering work carried out by the Zhejiang Provincial Party Committee and the Provincial Government at different stages was immeasurably important for building a prosperous Zhejiang. The great development of township enterprises and specialized markets in the 1980s was conducive to rapidly promoting Zhejiang's urbanization and industrialization. Since the beginning of the 21st century, the "Eight-Eight Strategies" put forward by the 11th Party Committee of Zhejiang Province and the strategy of making the people rich by starting a business and of building a strong province through innovation—that strategy continues and expands the "Eight-Eight Strategies"—initiated the efforts to adjust Zhejiang's economic structure and promote its transformation, elevating Zhejiang's transformation of the economic developmental mode to a new level. Zhejiang has ranked No. 1 nationwide for 13 consecutive years in the per capita disposable income of urban residents; this undoubtedly suggests that Zhejiang has entered a new stage of economic transformation and upgrading and coordinated development. With solid work done to stay ahead, Zhejiang carried through one blueprint to pursue development over 10 years; obviously, the experience and inspiration from Zhejiang's developmental practice in this process are great treasures for China as China is undergoing comprehensive economic transformation and upgrading. The previous chapters of this book provide a systematic analysis of institutional reform, open economy and new-type urbanization, while this chapter will, on this basis, fully summarize the basic characteristics of and experience from the 10-year-long development of Zhejiang's economic transformation.

Z. Huang (✉) · X. Liu
Chinese Academy of Social Sciences, Beijing, China

C. Pei and J. Xu (eds.), *Chinese Dream and Practice in Zhejiang – Economy*, Research Series on the Chinese Dream and China's Development Path,
https://doi.org/10.1007/978-981-13-7484-5_9

9.1 An Analysis of the Basic Characteristics of the Development of Zhejiang's Economic Transformation

9.1.1 Based on the First Mover Advantage of the Private Economy, Relying on Institutional Innovation to Deeply Promote the Market-Oriented Reform, Provide a Strong Impetus to and a Solid Guarantee for the Development of Economic Transformation

The factors well-positioned to make Zhejiang stay ahead nationwide are its developed private economy, the market-oriented systems and mechanisms which Zhejiang became the first to build up. When the state-owned economy played the dominant role, such first-mover advantages represented the greatest characteristic of Zhejiang's economy. After the socialist market economy was established, making the private economy better, large and strong and expanding the market-oriented systems and mechanisms were the key to ensuring that Zhejiang's economy would continue to maintain its advantages and stay ahead. As stated by comrade Xi Jinping, one of the important reasons why Zhejiang has developed from a province with fewer resources into an economically large province since the reform and opening up is the rapid development of its private economy. Thus the "Eight-Eight Strategies", put forward by Xi Jinping in 2003, give top priority to further leveraging Zhejiang's advantages of institutions and mechanisms to earnestly promote a pattern in which the public ownership remains the mainstay and the economy with different types of ownership develops side by side.

Although institutional innovations are reflected at many levels, the fundamental factor is ownership, which is the cornerstone in the economic system. Only when a complete ownership structure is built can spaces be really released for multi-level institutional innovation. In this regard, when serving as the Secretary of Zhejiang Province, comrade Xi Jinping put forward four important philosophies for invigorating the state-owned economy: First, fully finishing the reform of state-owned and urban collective enterprises which focuses on reforming the property rights system and transforming employees' labor relations; improving the mechanism for distribution incentives within enterprises; strengthening the management of enterprises; further improving the corporate governance structure; establishing the systems of modern enterprises. Second, building and improving a state-owned assets administration system under which powers are commensurate with obligations and responsibilities at the provincial and municipal levels, and in which assets administration is combined with the administration of personnel and affairs. Third, quickening the strategic adjustment in the layout of th state-owned economy, making the state-owned economy better and stronger. Combining the reform of the state-owned enterprises with actions designed to promote the integration of enterprises and increase their vitality; providing classified guidance for the existing state-owned enterprises, developing and growing a number of state-owned enterprises, optimizing and organizing a group of state-owned enterprises and shutting down and phasing out some state-owned enterprises. More rapidly nurturing a number of large internationally-competitive enterprises and conglomerates in the key fields and advantageous industries. Fourth, boldly investigating various ways to realize a state-owned economy. Providing foreign and private capital with more access, actively developing a mixed ownership economy.[1]

In order to realize these four philosophies, it is essential to show perseverance on the following five fronts: first, conducting asset reorganization and structural adjustment to further optimize the layout and structure of the state-owned assets, nurture a number of internationally-competitive large enterprises and conglomerates, improve the overall quality of the provincial state-owned enterprises, preserve and increase the value of the state-owned assets, and give prominence to development and full scope to the leading role of the state-owned economy. Second, seeking truth from facts, making bold experimentation, focusing on the key links in reform, breaking through the institutional bottlenecks; making breakthroughs in diversifying the owners of property rights, improving the corporate governance structure and building up a state-owned assets administration system; earnestly developing a mixed ownership economy, actively exploring various effective ways to realize public ownership. Carefully working out reform schemes, proactively and steadily pushing forward various reforms. Third, in an effort to promote reform, it is essential to consider the specific conditions of enterprises and provide classified guidance, adopt different restructuring means for different types of enterprises, proceed from reality to take active exploratory and practical actions and introduce various effective means to promote the restructuring of state-owned enterprises. Fourth, putting the people first, earnestly safeguarding the rights and interests of employees, properly dealing with the relations among reform, development and stability, placing equal emphasis on the intensity of reform, its speed and the extent to which employees can endure reform and steadily pushing forward reform under the condition of maintaining stability. Fifth, performing well-regulated operations and strictly preventing the loss of state-owned assets by working on the following three key links: making the whole process well-regulated, carrying it out in a fully open way and receiving oversight from the whole society.

The optimization of the state-owned economy has really opened the way to removing the barriers hindering the development of the private economy and expanding its developmental spaces and fields. In 2004, Xi Jinping put forward the following requirements for the development of Zhejiang's private economy: further emancipating the mind, taking bold practical actions, more quickly promoting innovations in system, science, technology and management; fully making the private economy more scientifically and technologically advanced, larger, more intensive and international; constantly enhancing the overall strength and international competitiveness of the private economy; maintaining the leading position of Zhejiang's private econ-

[1]Xi Jinping, Remaining Steadfast on Two Fronts, Creating New Advantages for Zhejiang in Developing the Economy with Different Types of Ownership, *Economic Times*, March 15, 2003.

omy nationwide; he also pointed out that in order to achieve a new leap in the private economy, it is essential to press ahead with five transformations and make five improvements (as shown in the "Introduction" to this book).

9.1.2 Taking Park Construction as the Vehicle, Building a Modern Industrial System and a Modern Industrial Cluster by "Achieving the Rebirth of the Phoenix Amidst Fire" and "Vacating the Cage to Change Birds" on the Basis of Massive Economy

The famous massive economy is undoubtedly a regional economic form which possesses Zhejiang's characteristics to the greatest extent; it has also become the hallmark of Zhejiang's economy to a certain degree. It is the massive economy spontaneously generated by non-governmental forces amidst market competition in a self-reliant and market-oriented way and by constantly breaking through administrative barriers; it has made sure that Zhejiang's economy would win the first mover advantage in the market-oriented institutional breakthrough; it has promoted great development of the rural household industry and rural industrialization and has opened the door to prosperity for Zhejiang's rural areas. However, with the advancement of the times, the massive economy, grown out of villages and households and once reputed for being fast, flexible and swift, has started to show disadvantages: low, small and scattered. Increasing difficulties in sustainable development have loomed large in those clusters of small and medium-sized enterprises mainly engaged in the traditional industries and characterized by a relatively low grade of products, low level of capability for technical innovation, high consumption, heavy pollution, low added value, less industrial relevancy and low ability to stimulate the development of others. Therefore, the massive economy has entered a new model—the industrial park—which is an organizational form capable of optimizing the layout of enterprise development and promoting economic transformation and upgrading.

With the change in the form of agglomerations, the substantive development of enterprises and industries has changed accordingly. In this regard, the philosophy of "two birds", put forward by Xi Jinping, then Secretary of the Zhejiang Provincial Party Committee, in late 2004, captures exactly the essence—in order to create glory again, Zhejiang must proceed from the Scientific Outlook on Development to transform the economic developmental mode and better raise the "two birds": "achieving the rebirth of the phoenix amidst fire" and "vacating the cage to change birds"; in other words, resources are limited, but the people's desire is unlimited. Only when Zhejiang achieves the rebirth of the phoenix amidst fire can Zhejiang be born again.

According to the philosophy of "achieving the rebirth of the phoenix amidst fire" and "vacating the cage to change birds", the development of Zhejiang's economic transformation should be pursued by building a modern industrial system and a modern industrial cluster; it is supported by independent innovation, while the focus of the development of transformation is the transformation and upgrading of the industrial economy. The prominent manifestation of that transformation and upgrading is that they are achieved through the construction of large platforms, large industries, large projects and large enterprises.

As shown above, Zhejiang takes park construction as the vehicle for building a modern industrial system and a modern industrial cluster on the basis of a massive economy; this is an important characteristic of Zhejiang's economic development and transformation—serving as the pillar and playing the supporting role.

9.1.3 Based on the Developed Specialized Markets, Placing Equal Emphasis on Opening-up and Cooperation, Combining "Going Global" with "Bringing in", Expanding Both Domestic and Foreign Markets, "Going Out of Zhejiang to Develop Zhejiang"

Zhejiang's specialized markets and massive economy are like two wheels of a vehicle and two wings of a bird; this is also an important mark of an economy with Zhejiang's characteristics. Specialized markets deliver the small commodities produced by the massive economy to the households within and outside Zhejiang Province, at home and abroad, thus small commodities get access to big markets, small enterprises engage in extensive cooperation, small capital gathers on a large scale. Thanks to actions taken to first develop various types of commodity markets characterized by specialized markets and promote the continuous improvement of Zhejiang's market system and the rapid development of its massive economy, Zhejiang is hailed as a large province of markets; as a large province of markets, it serves as the bridge; Zhejiang has leaped from a small province of resources to an economically large province.

Being hailed as a large province of markets is attributable to "going out of Zhejiang to develop Zhejiang"—an important characteristic of Zhejiang's economy. This characteristic results from the following subjective and objective factors. Subjectively, this is associated with Zhejiang's profound cultural traditions—facilitating trade to benefit industry, placing equal emphasis on righteousness and benefit, etc.—embodied in the following respects: Zhejiang's people have always attached importance to the tradition of going into business and developing a market, they enjoy excellent quality—advocating learning, being bold to make breakthroughs, being smart, diligent, pragmatic, they help each other. As Zhejiang's people are flexible, hard-working and adventurous, they highly adapt themselves to the realistic environment, and dare to make breakthroughs and innovations. Objectively, Zhejiang is a small province of resources, in particular, Zhejiang lacks the resources necessary for industrialization, so both ends of commodity production exist outside the province—its commodity production mainly relies on the resources and markets outside the province. Both factors make it necessary for Zhejiang to adopt a unique mode: "going out of Zhejiang to develop Zhejiang".

Obviously, Xi Jinping, then Secretary of the Zhejiang Provincial Party Committee, fully realized and practiced this important characteristic of Zhejiang's economic development. For example, comrade Xi Jinping held that the driving force behind Zhejiang's economic development since the reform and opening up mainly came from local private economy, it was a kind of endogenous development. However, under an open economic system, endogenous development was not closed development, it should be combined with opening up and outward expansion. Being based on Zhejiang did not mean being confined to Zhejiang; instead, actions should be taken to actively integrate into the national and global economic systems and better utilize both domestic and foreign markets, the resources outside the province and the country, promote a rational flow and optimal allocation of resources and factors; this was beneficial for Zhejiang in breaking through the bottlenecks and constraints in the supply of factors such as resources, environment and technology to enhance industrial competitiveness and push forward economic transformation and upgrading, so that Zhejiang's economy could better keep a foothold in and develop Zhejiang. In late 2002, based on surveying the economic development in Zhejiang and the Yangtze River Delta soon after serving as the Secretary of the Zhejiang Provincial Party Committee, Xi Jinping put forward the strategy of connecting Shanghai on the north. In early 2003, he decided to actively keep in alignment with Shanghai and energetically engage in cooperation and exchange with the Yangtze River Delta, and identified this decision as one of the decisions in the "Eight-Eight Strategies". Thanks to this decision, Xi Jinping, then Secretary of the Zhejiang Provincial Party Committee, and Lu Zushan, then Governor of Zhejiang Province, led a delegation of officials from the Zhejiang Provincial Party Committee and the Provincial Government to visit Shanghai and Jiangsu, jointly explore the way of "government-led, market-driven interactive development" of the Yangtze River Delta; they separately signed the *Agreement on Further Promoting Shanghai-Zhejiang Economic Cooperation and Development* and the *Agreement on Economic and Technical Cooperation and Exchange between Zhejiang Province and Jiangsu Province*; *Several Opinions on Actively Keeping in Alignment with Shanghai and Energetically Engaging in Cooperation and Exchange with the Yangtze River Delta* were issued, stating that according to the overall requirements of modestly learning, actively keeping in alignment and sincerely cooperating to achieve a win-win outcome, Zhejiang would proactively engage in cooperation and exchange with the Yangtze River Delta in constructing infrastructures including transportation, building advanced manufacturing bases, developing ecological, high-quality and efficient agriculture, further utilizing foreign capital and developing tourism resources and markets; and in the scientific and technological, educational, cultural and talent aspects, so as to promote economic integration in the Yangtze River Delta and further increase the level of Zhejiang's inter-regional opening-up and international opening.

As Xi Jinping, then Secretary of the Zhejiang Provincial Party Committee, fully affirmed and actively pushed ahead with "going out of Zhejiang to develop Zhejiang"—an important characteristic of Zhejiang's economy; "going out of Zhejiang to develop Zhejiang" has become increasingly amazing, and with the intensification of opening-up and cooperation, equal emphasis on "bringing in" and "going global", and the adoption of the strategy of stimulating industrial development through trade and promoting production by marketing, Zhejiang has carried through one blueprint in its development and leaped to a new level, at the level of the open economy. The 12th Party Congress of Zhejiang Province in 2011 vowed to expand its developmental spaces by adopting the line of thought of "going out of Zhejiang to develop Zhejiang" and maintaining a good momentum of development. The Second Plenary Session of the 12th Party Committee of Zhejiang Province stressed, "in order to fully push forward entrepreneurship and innovation, it is essential to fully utilize both domestic and foreign markets and the resources at home and abroad." Therefore, "going out of Zhejiang to develop Zhejiang" has become an important part of Zhejiang's current overall strategy of making the people rich by starting business and of building a strong province through innovation and was also a strategic move for expanding Zhejiang's spaces for entrepreneurship and innovation.

9.1.4 Carrying Forward the Tradition That the Government Respects the Market, Making First-Ever Breakthroughs in Building an Efficient, Highly Capable, Public Service-Oriented Government Which Actively Plays Its Due Role

When the planned economy was dominant, the Government of Zhejiang, with a high capability, actively took proper actions, respected the law of the market, relaxed control to develop the private economy, and became the first to make institutional breakthroughs; this was crucial for Zhejiang in gaining the first-mover advantage in economic development. During economic transformation, the Zhejiang Provincial Party Committee and the Provincial Government continued to carry forward the tradition of respecting the market, actively transformed functions, and in the capacity of servant rather than wealth creator, provided various types of market players with the basic pubic services involving protecting property rights, spurring competition, regulating the market order and encouraging entrepreneurship and innovation, etc.; it reduced or restrained the power of governments at various levels in resource allocation, improved the mechanism for market-oriented formation of resource and factor prices, energetically pushing forward market-oriented reform of public utilities, provided the institutional and mechanism guarantee for Zhejiang's economic transformation and development, thus building the image of an efficient, highly capable, public service-oriented government which actively plays its due role.

In fact, Zhejiang's developed private economy, advantageous systems and mechanisms and its overwhelming development since the reform and opening up have proved the high capability and active role of the Government of Zhejiang. These facts are certainly associated with the cultural tradition of the region, open-minded government officials and the great efforts made by Zhejiang's people with the courage to make breakthroughs and innovations. However, they are, to some extent, related to the following scenario: two disadvantages in Zhejiang at the initial stage forced the Government of Zhejiang to first take actions in improving services. These two disadvantages are as follows: First, Zhejiang has a large population with less land and a shortage of resources; second, Zhejiang is located at the coastal frontier, less state investments were made in Zhejiang during the period of a planned economy, and state-owned enterprises and the industrial foundation were relatively weak in Zhejiang. Given these disadvantages, the people in various parts of Zhejiang had to develop the economy by leveraging advantages and bypassing disadvantages, starting from small private enterprises and small commodities to carry out an arduous business endeavor; as a result, with an efficient market-oriented allocation of resources, a massive economy and specialized markets dominated by the private economy emerged, a large number of private entrepreneurs survived severe market tests, giving birth to a prosperous Zhejiang. Apparently, the disadvantage of a shortage of resources motivated Zhejiang's people to blaze new trails in a pioneering spirit; the disadvantage that state-owned enterprises were available in small quantities was turned into an advantage after 1978—the integration of government administration with enterprises was less severe, this provided a large space for development for the private economy. Zhejiang's government funds were allocated more to supply public goods and public services accordingly. Thus in Zhejiang, both government and non-governmental acts broke through institutional constraints.

History has provided an opportunity for the Government of Zhejiang to become highly capable and play an active role, so in the period of the development of economic transformation, the Government of Zhejiang had to leverage this advantage and rely on breakthroughs to continue staying ahead with a high capability and great efforts. This is because currently the institutional gap across the country has gradually narrowed, there is a continued decrease in the advantages of Zhejiang, as a reform forerunner, in the market mechanism and the space available for local governments to introduce preferential policies for the development of the local market economy; in order to maintain Zhejiang's advantages in economic development, it is absolutely necessary for Zhejiang to make new breakthroughs in governmental acts. After all, a great barrier to China's economic development came from the government itself. If the government relentlessly sought its own interests, it would lose the long-term and extensive interest in the whole society; however, if the government gave priority to the interests of the society and the people in words and deeds, provided convenience to the private economy and ensured a smooth operation of the market economy, not only could sufficient sources of taxes be guaranteed, but also the whole region could become prosperous.

For the above considerations, during the period of the 10th Five-Year Plan, comrade Xi Jinping, then Secretary of the Zhejiang Provincial Party Committee, made arrangements according to the relations between two hands—the government and the market—in light of Zhejiang's characteristics, greatly prompting Zhejiang to stay ahead in the transformation of government functions. As stated by comrade Xi Jinping, only one hand—the government—worked under the planned economic system, so prominence should be given to the other hand—the market—and play should be given to the fundamental role of the market in resource allocation during the initial stage of reform. With the intensification of the reform, it is necessary to transform governmental functions to make sure that the government only performs functions in economic regulations, market supervision, social management and public services, that it builds a service-oriented, limited government under the rule of law, better leverages, regulates and coordinates the "two hands". When the reform has been gradually promoted to a certain extent, the "two hands" should work in the following way: with regard to economic and social regulations, the market regulates the economy more, while the government strengthens social management and public service functions; in terms of economic operations, the market regulates the economic activities in the micro fields, while the government makes the rules of game and exercises macro control; with respect to fairness and efficiency, the market activates efficiency, while the government pays more attention to fairness; when it comes to urban and rural development, urban development relies more on market operations, while the government performs more functions in rural development. This entails a process, but the reform must be constantly intensified in this direction.

As shown, indisputably, an efficient, highly capable government which respects the market, can make first-ever breakthroughs and play an active role, and this represents a basic characteristic of the development of Zhejiang's economic transformation.

9.1.5 Seeking Coordinated Urban, Rural, Regional Development and Engaging in Mountain-Sea Collaboration to Promote Urban-Rural Integration and New-Type Urbanization, Social Harmony and to Achieve Common Prosperity

The holistic work on pushing forward coordinated urban, rural and regional integration and new-type urbanization is a comprehensive systemic project; it involves coordinated development of multiple relations, such as the relations between urbanization and the construction of the new countryside, among small, medium-sized, large cities and small towns, between urbanization and industrialization, between urbanization and agricultural modernization, between the developed and underdeveloped areas; it needs an overall arrangement and plan; it aims at promoting the harmonious social development of the whole province and common prosperity of various areas and residents. In this regard, Zhejiang has once again stayed ahead nationwide and become the first to make and implement a plan for urban-rural integration.

The plan for urban-rural integration is designed to incorporate both urban and rural areas into an organic whole for coordinated and harmonious development—one end connects the issues concerning agriculture, rural areas and farmers and the leapfrog development of the underdeveloped areas, the other ends connects the industrialization and urbanization of the developed areas to boost their rapid and sound development and better leverage the driving and guiding role of the developed areas. As stated by Xi Jinping, then Secretary of the Zhejiang Provincial Party Committee, in order to narrow the regional developmental gap and achieve coordinated regional development, it is essential to carry out the Scientific Outlook on Development and place emphasis on both ends and combine the efforts to promote rapid and sound development of the developed areas with the leapfrog development of the underdeveloped areas. "The fundamental way to narrow the regional developmental gap and achieve coordinated regional development lies in accelerating the development of the developed areas and promoting the leapfrog development of the underdeveloped areas; this is the core of coordinated development."[2]

For the issues concerning agriculture, rural areas and farmers, in the opinion of comrade Xi Jinping, only when Zhejiang goes beyond agriculture, rural areas and farmers to develop agriculture, rural areas and farmers and adopts the line of thought and philosophy of coordinated urban and rural development can Zhejiang break through the institutional constraints on improving agricultural performance, increasing farmers' income and developing the agriculture, fundamentally overcome the difficulties concerning agriculture, rural areas and farmers, further emancipate and develop rural productive forces and quicken the modernization of agriculture and the rural areas. In other words, achieving coordinated urban and rural development is the fundamental way to address the issues concerning agriculture, rural areas and farmers.[3] He also compared achieving coordinated urban and rural development to the "golden key" to addressing the issues concerning agriculture, rural areas and farmers in the new period. At the same time, comrade Xi Jinping believed that actions should also be taken to speed up the construction of the new countryside, and pointed out that the construction of the new socialist countryside should bring about a new countryside which is prosperous, better-off, democratic, culturally advanced and harmonious, reflects the requirements of the Scientific Outlook on Development, the developmental level of a society which is moderately prosperous in all respects, and the developmental trend of urban-rural integration as well as the substantive characteristics of socialism. Zhejiang should boost a new development of its industries, build new communities, nurture new farmers, foster new social conduct, establish new institutions to comprehensively push forward the construction of a new socialist countryside and achieve the following goals: transforming traditional agriculture into efficient ecological agriculture which enjoys lasting market competitiveness and can continuously make farmers rich, turning the traditional villages into new rural communities which can provide farmers with access to the modern civilized life and nurturing the traditional farmers into new-type high-caliber educated farmers who can adapt to the requirement of development based on labor division and separate operationing and know technology and operations, shape a new pattern

[2] Xi Jinping, Carrying out Solid Work to Stay Ahead—the Line of Thought and Practice in Promoting New Development in Zhejiang, Party School of the CPC Central Committee Press, 2006, p. 202.

[3] Xi Jinping, *Zhijiang Xinyu*, Zhejiang People's Publishing House, 2007, p. 43.

of urban-rural integrated development in which urban and rural areas promote each other and achieve common prosperity.[4]

For the development of the developed and underdeveloped areas, Xi Jinping, then Secretary of the Zhejiang Provincial Party Committee, held that Zhejiang's underdeveloped areas must leap over some stages of traditional industrialization and seek new development from the high points of economical, clean and safe production. The economic aggregate of the developed areas is large and makes up a high proportion of the province's economy; it epitomizes Zhejiang's overall strength and regional competitiveness. Likewise, the goal of the developed areas is to achieve rapid and sound development. Such a way can better leverage the important role of stimulating and leading the province's economic development, better support the leapfrog development of the underdeveloped areas, so as to promote the coordinated regional development of the whole province.[5] In this regard, comrade Xi Jinping, according to the requirements of coordinated regional development, prompted Zhejiang to carry out three major projects, which were the Mountain-Sea Cooperation Project, the project for turning the underdeveloped villages and towns into well-off ones and the project with ten-billion assistance and support for achieving prosperity, to fully leverage the comparative advantages of the underdeveloped areas, increase the support for the underdeveloped areas, earnestly develop the primary, secondary and tertiary industries suited to the characteristics of the underdeveloped areas, turn Zhejiang's underdeveloped areas into bases for the production of green agricultural products, tourist attractions and green ecological protective screens.

With painstaking efforts made by comrade Xi Jinping to promote coordinated urban and rural development and urban-rural integration, and the implementation of the philosophy of "carrying through one blueprint to seek development" by the successive Party Committees and governments of Zhejiang Province in the past 10–20 years, Zhejiang's coordinated urban and rural development and province-wide coordinated development have increasingly demonstrated Zhejiang's striking characteristics; the issues concerning agriculture, rural areas and farmers have been effectively addressed; great progress has been made in the construction of the new countryside; the relations between the coastal developed areas and the underdeveloped areas have been developed in a coordinated way; the interactive development of small, medium-sized, large cities and small towns, urbanization and industrialization, industrialization and agricultural modernization has exhibited a new pattern; there is a great impetus for promoting benign interaction between Zhejiang's urban and rural areas, narrowing the urban-rural gap, the industry-agriculture gap and the regional gap, achieving coordinated development of the whole province and common prosperity of various classes, thus making Zhejiang stay ahead nationwide. This also gives expression to an indispensable important characteristic: during the development of its economic transformation, Zhejiang has sought coordinated urban and rural development, coordinated regional development, carried out mountain-sea cooperation

[4]Xi Jinping, Carrying out Solid Work to Stay Ahead—the Line of Thought and Practice in Promoting New Development in Zhejiang, Party School of the CPC Central Committee Press, 2006, p. 169.

[5]Xi Jinping, *Zhijiang Xinyu*, Zhejiang People's Publishing House, 2007, p. 163.

and promoted urban-rural integration and new-type urbanization to enhance social harmony and achieve common prosperity.

9.1.6 Enabling Land-Sea Interaction, Earnestly Developing the Marine Economy, Fostering a New Growth Point for Economic Development

Unlike the massive economy and specialized markets familiar to everyone which have Zhejiang's characteristics and reflect the basic economic characteristics of the Zhejiang Model, Zhejiang's marine economy did not stand out conspicuously until the 21st century. Although previously it was not part of the Zhejiang Model, it will certainly become a characteristic of Zhejiang's economic development. This is because Zhejiang enjoys unique marine resources and an advantage for its location, it is natural for Zhejiang to leverage the comparative advantage of resource endowment; this is the reason why the marine economy becomes a basic economic characteristic of the development of Zhejiang's economic transformation.

Zhejiang has been considered as a small province of resources for a long time; however, if marine resources are included, such a situation will improve. Zhejiang's land area is only 101,800 km^2, while its sea area is 2.6 times its land area; Zhejiang enjoys extraordinarily abundant and unique marine resources, including sea areas, islands, ports, fisheries, tourism, oil and gas. Its coastline and island shoreline reach 6696 km^2; there are 2878 islands covering an area of more than 500 m^2 and 222,700 km^2 of offshore fishing grounds, ranking Zhejiang No. 1 nationwide. There are 761 km shoreline resources suitable for development under the usual conditions, including 506 km of deepwater shoreline which can be planned for building berths above 10,000t, accounting for more than 30.7% of the nation's total quantity; there are nearly 4 million mu of tideland resources, accounting for about 13% of the nation's total quantity, while sea areas and islands also abound in new marine energy and marine tourist resources. As indicated, Zhejiang, with a shortage of land resources, is really a large marine province. Furthermore, situated in China's coastal areas, the T-shaped economic belt of the Yangtze River and at the estuary of the Yangtze River golden waterway, Zhejiang also enjoys a unique advantage for its location. Obviously, as Zhejiang develops the marine economy and conducts land-sea interaction, Zhejiang can break through the bottlenecks in land resources, and will certainly make it become a new economic growth point and generate new spaces for Zhejiang's economic and social development.

In this connection, after serving as the Secretary of Zhejiang Province, based on on-the-spot surveys and inspections, comrade Xi Jinping affirmed the great efforts made by the previous Party Committees and governments of Zhejiang Province in developing the marine economy, and many times proceeded from multiple fronts in major meetings held by the Zhejiang Provincial Party Committee and the Provincial Government, to stress that it was necessary to develop Zhejiang's marine economy and turn Zhejiang into a strong province of marine economy. In the symposium on accelerating the development of the marine economy on May 16, 2003, comrade Xi Jinping made public for the first time his basic attitude about Zhejiang's development of the marine economy, the specific plan and four main guiding principles for that development, eight priorities and key points in the future development of Zhejiang's marine economy, thus promoting Zhejiang's development of the marine economy to a new stage. The four main guiding principles are as follows: first, leveraging Zhejiang's advantages—these advantages include the following: Zhejiang abounds in resources, including fishery, its port, the scenery, tideland and oil, the relevant industrial foundation is relatively good, the location conditions are favorable—and speeding up adjustment of the marine fishing and cultivation structure, actively integrating the port shipping sector, vigorously developing the port-centered sectors, the emerging marine industries and marine tourist sector, rationally developing tideland resources, making breakthroughs in the development of marine biological resources and that of gas and oil in the East China Sea, gradually shaping a number of advantageous marine industries and enhancing the overall competitiveness of the marine economy. Second, acting in a forward-looking, scientific and operable way to develop the master plan for the development of the marine economy and the corresponding special plans for port construction, the layout of port-centered sectors, tideland development, coastal land utilization, marine environment and marine tourism; orderly pushing forward the comprehensive development of marine resources and optimizing the layout of the marine economy. Third, giving prominence to innovation, intensifying institutional, scientific and technological innovations, injecting new vitality and driving forces into the marine economy. Further intensifying the reform and expanding the opening-up, speeding up innovations in the institutions and mechanisms, building a scientific and rational management system, a diversified input mechanism and a mechanism of market operations to stimulate and guide the governments at various levels and various economic players to invest in the marine economy. Thoroughly carrying out the strategy of promoting marine development through science and technology; accelerating the nurturing and introduction of talents; energetically making innovations and progress in marine science and technology to promote transformation from extensive marine development to intensive marine development and continuously increasing the level of development of the marine economy. Fourth, combining the development of marine industries with the protection of the marine environment; coordinating the development of the marine economy with the development of the land economy. Stepping up efforts to govern the sea under the rule of law, intensifying the protection and construction of the marine ecological environment, more rapidly controlling marine pollution, making sure that resources are utilized in an intensive way and the marine environment becomes ecological, and that sustainable development of the marine economy is achieved; correctly dealing with the relations between the marine economy and the land economy, further adjusting the industrial layout in coastal areas; widely boosting clean production, strictly controlling the emission of pollutants, and achieving integration between the marine economy and the land economy. The priorities for and key points in the future development of Zhejiang's marine economy are the adjustment of the marine fishery structure, the construction of the port, the development of port-centered industries, the construction of island infrastructures, the development of marine tourism, science and technology-based marine development, tideland reclamation and the protection and governance of the marine environment.

On this basis, during the third meeting of Zhejiang Province on the marine economy on August 18, 2003, comrade Xi Jinping officially put forward the strategic goal of building a strong province of marine economy, and designated it as an important part of the "Eight-Eight Strategies". He stressed that in order to develop Zhejiang's marine economy, it was unadvisable to merely rely on the sea and the fishery industry, it was necessary to go out of Zhejiang to develop Zhejiang, venture down the path of interactive development of the marine economy and the land economy, make the marine economy become a new growth point for Zhejiang's economy, embark on the path, with Zhejiang's characteristics, of interactive development of the marine economy and the land economy. He also took actual steps to actively push forward the Mountain-Sea Cooperation Project; support Zhoushan's development, proactively develop Zhoushan's late-mover advantage; fully carry out the developmental strategy of revitalizing the city through the port and promoting the development of the port through the city. As we know, after serving as the Secretary of the Zhejiang Provincial Party Committee, comrade Xi Jinping not only inherited and developed the original strategy for the development of the marine economy of Zhejiang Province, but he also put forward and pushed forward the developmental strategy of making mountain-sea interaction possible and of building a strong marine province, thus making solid progress in the development of Zhejiang's marine economy. Under the philosophy of "carrying through one blueprint to seek development", the marine economy has become an important part of Zhejiang's current strategy of making the people rich by starting a business and of building a strong province through innovation. The strategy for the development of a marine economy of Zhejiang Province was upgraded to a national strategy in 2011 and the State Council approved the establishment of the Zhoushan Archipelago New Area in 2013, thus boosting the development of Zhejiang's marine economy to a new level.

With great impetus from the "Eight-Eight Strategies" put forward by comrade Xi Jinping and Zhejiang's current strategic arrangement of making the people rich by starting a business and of building a strong province through innovation, encouraging achievements have been made in the development of Zhejiang's marine economy: for example, the total output value of Zhejiang's marine economy soared from 108,272 million yuan in 2002 to 495.8 billion yuan in 2012, the proportion of the marine economy in Zhejiang's GDP increased to 14.3%, the average annual growth rate reached 16.43%, so the marine economy made up an increasing proportion in Zhejiang's GDP and its status became more and more important; the marine economy played an obvious role in stimulating Zhejiang's economic development. At present, with the historic opportunity from the national strategy for Zhejiang's marine economy, along Zhejiang's coastline, a large number of major infrastructure and industrial projects have been rapidly launched and completed; modern new port cities and international trade port islands have emerged; a large port-based industrial belt with a length of about a hundred kilometers has rapidly risen; new enterprise groups, new industrial clusters and new industrial agglomeration areas are more quickly taking shape. Undoubtedly, a new economic growth point is in the making in Zhejiang and this brings new hope for the development of Zhejiang's transformation.

9.2 Summary of Experience from the Development of Zhejiang's Economic Transformation

9.2.1 Institutional Transition

The first and foremost experience from Zhejiang's practice is that after Zhejiang's economic development entered the transformation stage, Zhejiang pressed ahead with institutional transition, placed more emphasis on relying upon institutional innovation to consolidate and expand the first-mover advantage of the private economy, used it as a strong impetus and solid guarantee for the development of economic transformation. Under the guidance of the four main philosophies concerning the reform of Zhejiang's state-owned economy put forward by comrade Xi Jinping and the perseverance on five fronts as well as the strategic line of thought of five transformations and five improvements in the development of the private economy, Zhejiang's practice is mainly reflected in unremitting efforts in the following three respects: First, constantly optimizing the layout and structure of the state-owned economy, diversifying the property rights of state-owned and collective enterprises; increasing the concentration of state-owned capital in key fields, important industries and advantageous enterprises, giving full scope to the leading role of the state-owned economy; second, unceasingly breaking through the institutional barriers to the development of the private economy, establishing the status of private enterprises as market players, promoting a new leap of the private economy; third, earnestly pushing forward the mixed ownership economy in which state-owned, collective and non-public capital become each other's shareholder and develop side by side. The proportion of the added value from Zhejiang's non-public economy in Zhejiang's GDP hit 71.5% in 2007. As indicated, early on, Zhejiang saw the formation of a good pattern with local characteristics, in which the economies with different types of ownership compete with each other and develop side by side, and Zhejiang became the first to carry out the fundamental reform for improving the structure of ownership; this certainly produces an important demonstration effect on the nation's economic development.

To be specific, first, at the level of the state-owned economy. With the goal of establishing the system of modern property rights, the reform of state-owned enterprises focusing on diversifying the owners of and investors in property rights has been carried out, actions have been taken to increase the concentration of state-owned capital in key fields, important industries and advantageous enterprises and optimize the layout of the state-owned economy. In practice, the enterprises in a good operational state and with strong core competitiveness have continued to be controlled by state-owned capital; where the administrative units have been holistically restructured into companies but still operate under the existing system, the restructuring of their subsidiaries has been intensified, large enterprises and conglomerates have been nurtured; with regard to the enterprises whose competitive advantages have not been obvious in competitive industries and which have difficulties in operation and been subject to high risks, these enterprises have been restructured, the proportion of state-owned shareholding has been greatly reduced, even state-owned capital has fully withdrawn from these enterprises. With reform, the state-owned economy maintains a strong control over the national economy and serves as the pioneer of the emerging industries, the innovator of cutting-edge technology, the guardian of key fields, the constructer of the basic sector, the supporter of small and medium-sized enterprises.

Second, at the level of small and medium-sized private enterprises. An important reason why Zhejiang's private enterprises always maintain the leading position nationwide is that these small and medium-sized enterprises can occupy the commanding height in technology and the market through continuous innovation. In order to maintain this tradition, Zhejiang has specially established a number of technical service centers for small and medium-sized enterprises and regional specialty industries, with a view to providing technical and talent support for the technical innovations of enterprises. In addition, in order to implement the growth plan of small and medium-sized enterprises, Zhejiang has also promoted the construction of the socialized service system for small and medium-sized enterprises. Moreover, in order to guarantee a stable institutional transition, capital combination has been achieved to make private enterprises large and strong, and some high-quality enterprises have forged strong alliances to integrate their advantages and enhance their strength. In this process, private enterprises have become the main body in Zhejiang's enterprise shareholding reform, which is a prominent bright spot. During the shareholding reform of private enterprises and research institutions, state-owned strategic investors have been introduced, even private enterprises have been listed overseas to seek financing, while these actions represent new breakthroughs. Therefore, Zhejiang's private enterprises have gradually changed from mere profit-seekers in the capital market to the constructers of Zhejiang's economy, from the system and mechanism-savvy gamers to the active participants in system-building, from those passively adapting to macro regulation to the practitioners in transitional development.

Finally, the institutional reforms at other levels, including reforms in investment and financing, financial, fiscal and tax systems for promoting the development of the private economy. For the financial affairs, actions have been taken to promote the construction of small loan companies, establish the bidding and tendering system for the main promoters of small loan companies, build connections between enterprises and banks, put into practice stock right pledge loans, carry out pilot work on small loan companies and village banks, improve a risk compensation mechanism for loans involving small and medium-sized enterprises, and take differentiated credit policy measures. For fiscal and tax affairs, relevant policies have been adopted to review charges to reduce the burden on private enterprises, clear and cancel enterprise-related administrative and institutional fees, reduce and exempt the small and micro enterprises in difficulties from relevant taxes and dues if they satisfy the requirements of transformation and upgrading, permit the enterprises in difficulties to postpone the payment of charges relating to endowment insurance, unemployment insurance, medical insurance, work-related injury insurance and maternity insurance, reduce the rates of basic medical insurance for urban workers, unemployment insurance, work-related injury insurance and maternity insurance, provide social insurance subsidies, job subsidies and the subsidies for on-the-job training of employees. For investment and financing, emphasis has been placed on removing the barriers to private capital investment, introducing major public resource type projects to private capital, carrying out pilot credit financing support for small and medium-sized enterprises in government procurement, guiding small and medium-sized enterprises to directly engage with domestic and foreign investment and financial institutions, stimulating Zhejiang's small and medium-sized enterprises to go global together, developing a slew of measures for making private lending well-regulated and supporting private capital to participate in local financial reform, thus turning Zhejiang into the forerunner of investment and financing for small and medium-sized enterprises and the highland for private capital investment. In order to optimize the environment for the development of the private economy, on the one hand, Zhejiang has fully carried out the 36 measures of the State Council for the non-public economy, built the mechanisms for guaranteeing equal footing in market access, tax administration, fee standards, financial loans and sector services, and accordingly developed 32 opinions of Zhejiang Province on the non-public economy, specifying new measures, which inspire private enterprises, for relaxing the control over market access, increasing fiscal, tax and financial support, pushing forward the non-public economy, and more quickly adjusting the economic structure and transforming the growth mode; on the other hand, Zhejiang has actively experimented with institutional innovations in the reform of the mechanism for the market-oriented allocation of such factors as capital and land, the reform involving the prices of resource products and the reform of the local financial system. Thanks to these measures, Zhejiang can maintain institutional advantages at a higher level and the leading position of the private economy nationwide for a long time.

9.2.2 Independent Innovation

Under the guidance of the philosophy of "two birds", the development of Zhejiang's economic transformation has mainly proceeded from building a modern industrial system and a modern industrial cluster, while the focus of the development of transformation is the transformation and upgrading of the industrial economy. Specifically, from the perspective of the primary, secondary and tertiary industries, the building of a modern industrial system consists in developing efficient ecological agriculture, the advanced manufacturing industry and the modern service industry, and creating a circular economy and undertaking a new-type industrial path. For industrial economic transformation, first, the upgrading of the traditional industries is conducted by replacing the portion with high consumption, heavy pollution and low added value with the industries with low consumption, low pollution and high added value; second, great efforts are made to develop the manufacturing industry and new and hi-tech industries, and advanced manufacturing technologies are used to upgrade the manufacturing industry, thus helping transform from "Made in Zhejiang" to "Created in Zhejiang", driven by technical innovation; third, actions are taken to earnestly develop the strategic emerging industries, support the development of various types of technology enterprise incubators, new and high-tech industrial bases, major high technology industrialization projects and new and hi-tech enterprises with core technology, making them a strategic choice for promoting economic transformation and upgrading. A modern industrial system is built by taking park construction as the vehicle to developing a modern industrial cluster. For the formation of industrial clusters, besides the transformation and upgrading of the traditional massive economy, Zhejiang has also guided small and medium-sized enterprises to become the specialized, precision, special and novel ones and turned them into industrial clusters; Zhejiang has also consciously nurtured and developed a group of major backbone enterprises with prominent main business, advanced processes and equipment, high innovation capability, high international competiveness and brand advantages and a number of industrial parks and development zones with outstanding regional brands; as a result, modern industrial clusters and advanced manufacturing bases have emerged.

The building of a modern industrial system and modern industrial clusters ultimately relies on independent innovation. Independent innovation is the foundation for realizing Zhejiang's philosophies of "achieving the rebirth of the phoenix amidst fire" and "vacating the cage to change birds" and also the most central supporting force for building a modern industrial system and modern industrial clusters; it is also the guarantee for the straightforward realization of Zhejiang's economic transformation, so Zhejiang's practice and experience in improving the capability for independent innovation deserve attention.

For an understanding of independent innovation, Zhejiang has always positioned enterprises as the core force for driving innovation forward; with the adoption of a strategy of intellectual property, a strategy of standardization and one of brands, Zhejiang has turned innovation into the core of the competitiveness of enterprises and regional industries, and leveraged innovation as support to build the core competitiveness of small and medium-sized enterprises to help upgrade the massive economy of the traditional industries dominated by small and medium-sized enterprises and establish modern industrial clusters. In this regard, in the provincial meeting on independent innovation in 2006, Xi Jinping, then Secretary of the Zhejiang Provincial Party Committee, pointed out that Zhejiang had entered an important period of transforming from investment-driven development to innovation-driven development, and more quickly enhancing the capability for independent innovation to build an innovative province and a strong province of science and technology was particularly important given the new requirement of carrying out the Scientific Outlook on Development and building a harmonious society, the new goal of building a moderately prosperous society in all respects and continuing to stay ahead nationwide as well as the new task of building a resource-conserving and environmentally friendly society.

Meanwhile, Xi Jinping provided six points to guide the work on accelerating efforts to build Zhejiang into an innovative province: first, cultivating and carrying forward Zhejiang's spirit of keeping pace with the times, further arousing the innovative and creative vitality of the whole society, following the trend of the times to nurture and carry forward the spirit of "seeking truth, being pragmatic, honest, harmonious and open-minded, forging ahead", developing the culture of innovation with Zhejiang's characteristics, laying the most extensive and solid social and humanistic foundation for independent innovation. Second, doing something in some areas but refraining from acting in other areas, making key breakthroughs and achieving leapfrog development, giving priority to developing energy, mountain and sea resources, conserving the water resource and environmental protection technologies; speeding up the development of the high technology industries, including electronic information, biological medicine, new materials and advanced equipment manufacturing, obtaining the proprietary intellectual property rights of core technologies to make breakthroughs in enhancing the competitiveness of Zhejiang's industries; accelerating the application of information technology, biotechnology, new material technology and other technologies in traditional industry and agriculture, comprehensively increasing the technical level of traditional industries, actively developing efficient ecological agriculture; organizing efforts to carry out the projects of 8 major scientific and technological innovations,[6] screening out several strategic products or key generic technologies as major special projects, concentrating resources to make breakthroughs in these projects, with a view to achieving leapfrog development. Third, focusing on strengthening the status of enterprises as main players, moving faster to promote the construction of the system of regional innovation, making enterprises become the decision-makers, investors, interest sharers and risk bearers in technical innovation; building a market-oriented, enterprise-dominated open regional innovation system with cooperation among industries, universities and research institutions, relying on large enterprises and conglomerates to encourage and support enterprises to actively seek intellectual support from scientific research institutions and the institutions of higher learning, engaging in cooperation among industries, universities and research institutions, establishing enterprise engineering centers and technical centers with a relatively high capability for research and development. Supporting the technical innovation activities of small and medium-sized enterprises, focusing on improving various types of enterprise incubators, cultivating a number of small and medium-sized hi-tech enterprises with a high capability for innovation and growth potential. Accelerating efforts to develop various types of intermediary scientific and technological service bodies for serving enterprises, promoting knowledge flow and technology transfer among enterprises, among enterprises and the institutions of higher learning and scientific research institutions. Fourth, combining independent innovation with brand strategy, promoting the building of a large province of brands. Adopting the brand strategy to stimulate independent innovation, propelling

---

[6]The high and new technology industry, the traditional manufacturing industry, equipment manufacturing, modern agriculture, environmental resources, marine development, health and safety, IT application in the service industry.

independent innovation to support the brand strategy, focusing on developing the system of brand cultivation and improving the enterprises' capability for brand creation, building a number of internationally competitive well-known brands with proprietary intellectual property rights. Actively carrying out the strategy of intellectual property and standardization, making technologies patented, patents standardized and standards international. Fifth, upholding reform, innovation and open integration, striving to gather and allocate innovation factors in an open-minded and market-oriented way, pushing forward scientific and technological progress and innovation, establishing and improving a technical innovation mechanism and a modern system of intellectual property. Intensifying the reform of the system of scientific research, encouraging the development of private scientific research institutions and making a number of major scientific research institutions large and strong. Giving full scope to the fundamental role of the market in allocating scientific and technological resources and better addressing the disconnection between science, technology and the economy. Making good use of resources for innovation by allocating them nationwide, even worldwide. Actively integrating the existing technologies, pushing forward integrated innovation, encouraging enterprises to really assimilate and further innovate foreign advanced technologies while introducing them. Sixth, putting the people first to build an innovative talent force with a rational structure, good quality and high strength. Comprehensively carrying out the strategy of building a strong province through talents; accelerating efforts to push forward the Million and Ten-Million Scientific and Technological Innovation Talent Project and the Leading Innovative Talent Program. Improving the mechanism for talent incentives, better carrying out and improving the policy for including technical factors in distribution and increasing the scientific and technological rewards to fully arouse the enthusiasm and creativity of innovative talents and scientific and technological personnel.

In this regard, Zhejiang has established a number of systems and mechanisms for promoting independent innovation to improve the environment for scientific and technological progress and innovation; for example, intensifying the reform of the system of scientific and technological management, adjusting the system of scientific and technological programs to shape a four-in-one work layout covering the environment, talents, platforms and projects; pressing ahead with brand strategy; establishing the independent innovation policy to put into practice the regular meeting system; enhancing the publicity and training of the policy of innovation, fostering a social environment for encouraging independent innovation, guiding various parties to take part in innovative practice, gathering innovation factors to enterprises; enabling industrial integration, promoting the interactive development of the manufacturing industry and the service industry; achieving industrial extension, making enterprises extend from processing and manufacturing to both ends—research, development, design and brand marketing; putting in place IT applications, taking enterprise IT application projects as a means, promoting the integration of information technology with the industry and economy and adopting other means to enhance the capability for independent innovation. Based on innovation, Zhejiang has initiated the process of entrepreneurial and innovation integration; actions are taken to make the people rich by starting a business and to build a strong province through innovation; starting a business is the foundation for making the people rich, while innovation is the source for building a strong province.

In practice, the strategic measure of enhancing the capability for independent innovation is embodied in promoting the construction of large platforms, large industries, large projects and large enterprises, while that construction develops and deepens the "Eight-Eight Strategies".

Large platforms mean industrial parks which serve as the forerunners for economic transformation and upgrading and enjoy the resource agglomeration advantage; such industrial parks include the Hangzhou Dajiangdong New Area, the Linjiang Industrial Park, the Jiangdong Industrial Park, the Airport Economic Zone and the Qianjin Industrial Park; these fast-rising large platforms for economic development provide large stages for industrial transformation and upgrading. Large industries proceed on three fronts: First, transforming the traditional massive economy, developing the transformation and upgrading plans for 11 industries including textile, light industry, building material and nonferrous metals, in coordination with a number of the national revitalization and adjustment plans for major industries; second, focusing on leading and cultivating the massive economy in new technology, new energy, new materials, a circular economy, high-end manufacturing and business model innovation, so as to drive the transformation and upgrading of the traditional massive economy; third, nurturing and developing the strategic emerging industries, determining the developmental plans for nine major strategic emerging industries, including biology, the Internet of Things, new energy, new materials, high-end equipment, energy conservation and environmental protection, emerging marine industries and the new energy automobile and nuclear power-related industry; pushing forward the construction of new-type technical innovation platforms, establishing new-type industrial bases. However, both large platforms and large industries must be reflected in large projects, while the implementation of major action plans for project construction plays the supporting and indispensable role in them. In this connection, Zhejiang has actively carried out the construction plans for the government-led investment projects and industrial projects, and has proactively worked on introducing large projects; Zhejiang has, according to the requirement of attracting the large investors, introducing the strong investors and choosing the excellent investors, unveiled a number of major projects designed to attract external investments; Zhejiang has fully leveraged the advantages that its private capital is ample and its private economy is developed, with actions taken to encourage private investment and make sure that the investments of private enterprises basically cover various fields of the national economy and that the non-state-owned economy becomes the main investment force in the manufacturing field. With the impetus from large projects, a number of forerunners have stood out in the massive economy. Finally, Zhejiang has placed emphasis on cultivating the leading and backbone enterprises in various industries, made them become the leaders in transformation and upgrading, and carried out the building of large enterprises. With the adoption of preferential policies involving capital guarantee, land supply, technical innovation, tax reduction and exemption, project application and talent support, a number of backbone enterprises have rapidly risen, stimulating the development of the corresponding industries; the enterprises which were once at the "grassroots level" have grown into giants in Zhejiang's economic transformation and upgrading and have become the key factors in improving the competiveness of industries and the regional economy.

Moreover, further noteworthy practical experience in the development of Zhejiang's economic transformation is the role of ecological environmental protection in forcing the transformation of the economic developmental mode. In this respect, Zhejiang is a province of foresight. More than ten years ago, comrade Xi Jinping, then Secretary of Zhejiang Province, put forward the famous scientific philosophy that "lucid water and lush mountains are gold and silver mountains" and held that the ecological environment was the foundation for economic and social development; he adopted the dialectical relationship between lucid water, lush mountains and the "gold and silver mountains" to illustrate the construction of Zhejiang as an ecological province (as shown in the "Introduction" to this book). Guided by the line of thought of "two mountains" in which the ecological environment forces the transformation of the economic developmental mode, the successive Party Committees and governments of Zhejiang Province carried through one blueprint to seek development; in particular, in recent years, the Zhejiang Provincial Party Committee has worked on renovating old residential areas, old factory areas in urban areas and the villages in cities, demolishing illegal buildings, treating sewage, controlling floods, discharging the accumulated water, guaranteeing a water supply and saving water, while such work has elevated the pioneering move that ecological construction forces transformation and upgrading to a new level. This practical experience highly deserves to be drawn upon in China's current economic development.

9.2.3 *Going Out of Zhejiang to Develop Zhejiang*

"Going out of Zhejiang to develop Zhejiang" is an important characteristic of Zhejiang's economic development; it has greatly contributed to Zhejiang's economic development. This characteristic has not only brought about a large province of markets, but also with a large province of markets as a bridge, it turned Zhejiang from a small province of resources into a large economic province. Thus the following practical experience gained by Zhejiang through its developed private economy is indeed useful for other provinces, autonomous regions and municipalities across the country: Zhejiang has spared no effort in allocating resources nationwide, even worldwide, developing its market, expanding economic development spaces and fields, it has "gone out of Zhejiang to develop Zhejiang".

Specifically, the practical experience of pushing forward opening up and cooperation on the basis of specialized markets and "going out of Zhejiang to develop Zhejiang" can be illustrated at four levels: First, the traditional specialized markets were adjusted. As from the 1990s, information technology developed rapidly, in particular, new-type retail forms and online transactions, which incorporated information technology, including chain stores, stockrooms and supermarkets, emerged and spread; they greatly reduced transaction costs and posed more risks to the development of the traditional specialized markets, making them subject to new tests. Therefore, according to the requirement of the modernization of circulation, Zhejiang started to innovate the transaction mode and functions of specialized markets, develop modern circulation forms, including chain operations, logistics distribution and e-commerce, expand spaces for the development of the market, and carry out online transactions, substantially reducing transaction costs and gradually changing the tangible market into an intangible market. At the same time, Zhejiang also actively adopted the trade mode of combining exhibition with the market to increase market influence.

Second, Zhejiang extended from commodity exportation to the following scenario: capital and enterprises "went global". Internally, Zhejiang integrated into the Yangtze River Delta Region led by Shanghai to push forward the construction of special mechanisms for cooperation across the Yangtze River Delta Region; it fully kept in line with and participated in the construction of the Western Taiwan Straits Economic Zone; it participated in China's western development, the rise of Central China and the revitalization of the old industrial bases, including Northeastern China; it explored and established the mode of strategic inter-provincial cooperation with the provinces in Western China and Central China, including "exchanging investments for resources" and "joint development of coal and electricity"; for example, in March, 2006, when meeting with entrepreneur representatives from Jiangxi and Zhejiang, Xi Jinping, then Secretary of the Zhejiang Provincial Party Committee, said that the government engaged with Zhejiang merchants with outward investments by thinking in light of circumstances, expecting successful cooperation, actively promoting relevant work, providing services, making policies and building platforms; engaging in regional economic exchange and cooperation was not only the inevitable requirement of Zhejiang's development, our political responsibility, but also a smart choice for Zhejiang's enterprises. At the same time, Zhejiang also actively enhanced cooperation and exchange with Hong Kong, Macao and Taiwan; besides efforts to improve the competiveness of export commodities, Zhejiang also supported enterprises in setting up overseas marketing networks, increasing overseas investments and conducting cross-border mergers and acquisitions; it encouraged enterprises to establish overseas marketing headquarters, exclusive shops, trade representative offices or production bases, industrial parks, economic and trade cooperation zones in the developed countries and emerging markets; this prompted Zhejiang's key commodity markets to build submarkets, product distribution centers and self-owned marketing networks overseas, so that Zhejiang's enterprises gradually transformed from mere suppliers to distributors and brand owners.

Third, while guiding commodities, capital and enterprises to "go global", Zhejiang also carried out the "bringing in" project, constantly improved the four-in-one domestic introduction work system covering the attraction of investments, the return of Zhejiang merchants to other provinces, the introduction of talents, science and technology and the introduction of factors and resources. Zhejiang established the mechanisms of attracting foreign investment through private enterprises, foreign-funded enterprises, thus attracting intellectuals through capital; Zhejiang followed the requirements of "attracting the large investors, introducing the strong investors and choosing the excellent investors, placing equal emphasis on quantity and quality, attracting both capital and intellectuals" to guide and encourage foreign investments to be made in the high-end manufacturing industry, the high and new technology industry, the modern service industry and in the new energy, energy conservation and environmental protection industries; Zhejiang strictly restricted high energy-consuming enterprises, heavily polluting enterprises and highly resource-focused product enterprises; it launched and implemented the project for making Zhejiang merchants in other provinces return home, held the World Zhejiang Entrepreneurs Convention, encouraged Zhejiang merchants to expand development spaces in a wider scope, absorb high-quality factors, enhance competitiveness, which greatly motivated Zhejiang merchants to return home to start businesses.

Finally, Zhejiang intensified inter-regional opening up, international opening up and cooperation, placed equal emphasis on "bringing in" and "going global", stimulated industrial development through trade, promoted production through marketing, increased the role of "going out of Zhejiang to develop Zhejiang" in driving the development of the surrounding areas; Zhejiang also actively implemented the brand strategy in market development and derived strong impetus from brand building for Zhejiang to improve its market connotation, upgrade commodities and enhance market competitiveness. This is because with the increasing scale of operations of Zhejiang's market players, the corporatization of operators and the brand-focused operation of commodities represented an important developmental trend, and developing and revitalizing cities through brands gradually became a consensus on Zhejiang's economic development. With the adoption of the brand-focused path towards development and the development of the sole distributor, the sole agent and exclusive sales, brand-focused and exclusive sales markets rapidly rose, greatly upgrading Zhejiang's commodity markets. While establishing and improving the mechanism of fostering, developing and protecting the brands of its export products, Zhejiang also pushed forward the brand construction of export bases, extending the brand effect from enterprise brands to regional brands, markedly improving the international competitiveness of Zhejiang's massive economy, the bargaining power, pricing ability and risk resistance capacity of Zhejiang's commodities on the international market.

As indicated, Zhejiang can successfully "go out of Zhejiang to develop Zhejiang" because there is the following fundamental guarantee: based on the developed specialized markets, pushing forward opening up and cooperation, placing equal emphasis on "bringing in" and "going global", developing the market and allocating resources nationwide, even worldwide, expanding economic development spaces and fields, optimizing the structure of opening up, improving the quality of opening up, building a new pattern of opening up which is all-round, wide-ranging and multi-level, upholding inter-regional opening up and international opening up to increase the level of the open economy.

9.2.4 The Government Is Highly Capable and Plays an Active Role

Since reform and opening up, with high capability and an active role, the Government of Zhejiang has always respected the law of the market and has taken first-ever actions to break through institutional constraints. How have the Zhejiang Provincial Party Committee and the Provincial Government inherited and carried forward such a tradition during economic transformation to transform from an economic construction-oriented government into a public service-oriented government, improved the government's social and public administration function, removed the barriers to and provided protection for the development of the market economy, promoted the revolution in government efficiency and accelerated the transformation of government functions? What is the practical experience of Zhejiang in staying ahead and doing solid work? It is summarized mainly in six aspects.

First, the Government of Zhejiang became the first to carry out the reform of the administrative management system and early on it launched the reform of the administrative examination and approval system; Zhejiang has become one of the provinces with the smallest number of items subject to provincial administrative examination and approval nationwide, it innovated the examination and approval system and mode. For example, with regard to investments, Zhejiang has piloted the private investment project registration system and replaced the project initiation examination and approval system with the project registration system; in terms of market access, Zhejiang has piloted the before-licensing examination and approval notification and commitment system for enterprise registration; with respect to the examination and approval mode, Zhejiang has launched the online examination and approval system and it has built a new online examination and approval system characterized by one-network connectivity, localized application, joint handling, real-time supervision and a fully open process; it has adopted a joint examination and approval operation mechanism and has carried out administrative examination and approval in a unified, integrated, holistic, synchronous and transparent way.

Second, Zhejiang has reformed the investment system and the planning system, pushed forward the system of assessment, disclosure and agent-based construction of government-invested projects, carried out the major project tracking service responsibility system and audit system, and it has built the interactive examination and approval system covering projects, land and environmental protection, the evaluation system involving the land supply rate and the proportion of projects whose construction has begun.

Third, Zhejiang has improved the public finance system and optimized the fiscal expenditure structure, and has used more than 2/3 of the increment in fiscal expenditure to address the people's livelihood. Zhejiang has intensified the reform of the management system with separation between revenue and expenditure, built a fiscal management mode under which all income is put into one "cage", all budget becomes balanced on one "board" and all expenditure comes from one "opening"; it has fully carried out the systems of departmental budget, centralized payment at the national treasury and government procurement and established the well-regulated departmental budget system involving the governments at the provincial, municipal and county levels. Zhejiang has also propelled the reform of the civil service card and official business vehicle systems and fully piloted case-by-case fiscal incentives and subsidies for village-level programs for public good.

Fourth, Zhejiang has intensified the reform involving the management system under which counties are directly under the management of the provincial government, it has delegated powers to the departments at lower levels, introduced the fiscal policy of guaranteeing the balance of financial revenue and expenditure in the current year, ensured the fulfillment of government duties and tasks, linking provincial subsidies and incentives with the growth of local fiscal revenue, under the fiscal system of tax revenue sharing; Zhejiang has speeded up the development of the county economy, pushed ahead with the reform for expanding the powers of strong towns, granted the economic and social management authority, as it is basically the same as the county-level one, to the pilot towns cultivated to become small cities, and the corresponding economic and social management authority to other central towns.

Fifth, Zhejiang promoted the reform involving open decision-making and sunshine operation of powers. For example, Hangzhou City incorporated eight categories of items having a bearing on the interests of the people, such as major policies, legislation and reform, into open decision-making, and pioneered in the system of attending the government's executive meeting as nonvoting delegates, and open decision-making at the municipal government and the governments of 13 districts and counties (county-level cities). Such reform measures granted China the innovation award for local governments. Furthermore, Hangzhou City, with respect to administrative matters, established a mechanism for sunshine operation of powers, developed the flow chart of power operations, cleared and regulated the power matters of departments; received and handled applications online, addressed feedback and accepted supervision online, with open operations during the whole process.

Sixth, Zhejiang has pushed forward the participatory budgeting reform, made the public budget transparent and democratic, involved the people in government budgeting, with the possibility for the draft budget to be examined and revised by the people's congress, in order to more rationally distribute budget funds, effectively expand the people's participation, and strengthen supervision over budget execution to make government expenditure more efficient. At the same time, such reform measures won China the innovation award for local governments.

It was hard to reform the government itself in China for a long time and there is still a long way to go for the Government of Zhejiang to build a perfect public service-oriented government; however, guided by the philosophy of the coordinated operation of "two hands"—the government and the market—as emphasized by comrade Xi Jinping, the functional reform of the Government of Zhejiang has not deviated from that fundamental direction. Evidently, it has made painstaking efforts to constantly seek breakthroughs amidst difficulties and has made much progress. Of course, in order to make substantial progress in the reform of the system of administrative management, a fundamental leap needs to be achieved and more first-ever breakthroughs should be made in building a government under the rule of law, a responsible government, a public service-oriented government and a clean government.

9.2.5 *Coordinated Urban and Rural Development*

As an essential important characteristic of Zhejiang's economy during the development of transformation, coordinated urban and rural development and urban-rural integration constitute a major systematic project which involves two fronts and needs to be promoted in a three-dimensionally interactive and holistic way. The practical experience of Zhejiang in staying ahead in this respect deserves to be drawn upon by other provinces, autonomous regions and municipalities across the country.

As coordinated urban and rural development and urban-rural integration involve the coordinated development of multiple relations, such as those between urbanization and the construction of the new countryside, industrialization and agricultural modernization, urbanization and industrialization, small, medium-sized, large cities and small towns and between the developed areas and the underdeveloped ones; it is unnecessary and impossible to provide details about the practice. Only the framework of the overall layout and plan is summarized to reflect the hierarchy and key points of this integrated systematic project.

For the multiple relations involved in coordinated urban and rural development, first, it is necessary to overcome the dual structure which severely hinders China's economic development. Therefore, the top priority in coordinated urban and rural development lies in breaking through the dual urban-rural structure, continuously improving the living standard and quality of urban and rural residents, achieving urban-rural integration in which urban development stimulates rural development and industrial development promotes agricultural development. Thus the first priority consists in combining urban development with the construction of the new countryside and undertaking the path towards urbanization characterized by mutual promotion and common development of urban and rural areas. This calls for working on the following aspects: (1) urbanization should be conducted by seeking healthy development, undertaking a path towards urbanization that is intensive, economical, efficient, resource-conserving and environmentally friendly, thus increasing the quality and intensity of stimulating rural development by urban development; (2) it is essential to extend urban infrastructure to rural areas, make urban public services cover rural areas, spread urban civilization to rural areas, establish a long-term mechanism under which urban development stimulates rural development and industrial development promotes rural development; (3) it is necessary to optimize the spatial layout of productive forces and the population, break through the dual urban-rural structure, promote the rational flow of urban and rural resources and factors, shape a pattern of development in which urban development stimulates rural development and rural development promotes urban development; (4) it is imperative to more quickly transfer rural labor forces, build new rural communities and the new countryside. In summary, actions should be taken to seek integrated and coordinated development of urban and rural areas in infrastructure construction, labor employment, social security, ecological environmental construction, social programs and industrial development, to promote benign interaction between urban and rural areas, narrow the urban-rural gap, the industry-agriculture gap and the regional gap in order to achieve coordinated development and common prosperity.

Second, Zhejiang has attached importance to the coordinated development of small, medium-sized, large cities and small towns. This covers two fronts: (1) carrying out the construction among small, medium-sized, large cities—building the Hangzhou-Ningbo-Wenzhou metropolitan economic circle and the city groups in Zhejiang's central region, strengthening the leading position of three major central cities, which are Hangzhou, Ningbo and Wenzhou, in the provincial urban system to ensure coordinated development of cities; (2) cultivating and developing central towns to make them become the nodes connecting urban and rural areas and the important vehicles for prospering rural areas, serving agriculture and gathering farmers together. The successful construction of central towns determines the smooth transformation of central towns into the hubs for coordinated urban and rural development and urban-rural integration, while taking the cultivation of central towns as the vehicle and relying on economic development to cultivate small towns is the greatest characteristic of the development of Zhejiang's small towns. Central towns are important because they serve as the transitional areas between city groups and rural areas and they also aggregate Zhejiang's massive economy; most of the small towns have been home to specialty industries, such as the Tongxiang woollen sweater industrial cluster, the Cixi home appliances industrial cluster, the Zhuji socks industrial cluster, the Haining leather industrial cluster, the Shengzhou necktie industrial cluster, the Yongkang hardware industrial cluster and the Yueqing low-voltage apparatus industrial cluster; they have enjoyed a certain dominant position nationwide, and even worldwide, they have the conditions for achieving coordinated development of the secondary and tertiary industries, of making towns strong through industries and revitalizing towns through the tertiary industry, and they also serve as the important vehicles for enabling the flow of rural labor forces and the rational flow of urban and rural resources and factors. Therefore, central towns are the strategic nodes for stimulating and promoting urban-rural integration and also the hubs for coordinating the relations among urbanization, industrialization and agricultural modernization.

Finally, Zhejiang has achieved the coordinated economic development of the coastal developed areas and the underdeveloped areas. With the implementation of the Mountain-Sea Cooperation Project, the project for turning the underdeveloped villages and towns into well-off ones and the project with ten-billion assistance and support for achieving prosperity, Zhejiang has promoted the common prosperity of regions and residents. The project for turning the underdeveloped villages and towns into well-off ones aims at stimulating the farmers on high and remote mountains to descend from the mountains and migrate to other areas, transferring these farmers to other sectors and jobs, more quickly helping them shed their poverty. The Mountain-Sea Cooperation Project centers on project cooperation and focuses on industrial gradient transfer and the rational allocation of factors to enable multi-channel, multi-mode, multi-level and all-round regional economic cooperation and exchanges in a government-led, enterprise-dominated, market-oriented, mutually beneficial and win-win way, to transfer the labor-intensive industries in the developed areas to the underdeveloped areas, to introduce the surplus labor from the underdeveloped areas to the developed areas and to promote the coordinated development and common prosperity of the coastal developed areas and such underdeveloped areas as Zhejiang's southwestern mountainous areas and islands. In this regard, comrade Xi Jinping made a well-targeted remark in 2005 by stressing that the Mountain-Sea Cooperation Project should be carried out under the following principles: (1) proceeding from coordinated regional development to make the choice of paths towards development for the underdeveloped areas; it was unadvisable to indiscriminately copy the traditional path towards industrialization adopted in the developed areas to the underdeveloped areas; instead, it was essential to follow the requirements of the Scientific Outlook on Development to concentrate cooperation on optimizing the industrial structure and promoting the transformation of the economic growth mode, and on boosting innovations in system, technology and management, enhancing labor quality, achieving intensive utilization of resources and improving the quality of the ecological environment. The underdeveloped areas should be developed by carrying out a combination of development, expansion and reduction—accelerating economic development and expanding the economic aggregate; development should also include reducing resource consumption, ecological damage and pollutant emissions, promoting technical progress and improving labor quality, gathering the population in cities and boosting the outward transfer of the population; (2) enabling all-round cooperation between the developed areas and the underdeveloped areas to intensify relevant work in a well-targeted way, shore up the weaknesses in the underdeveloped areas, so that the people in various parts of the province enjoy the achievements of economic and social development; (3) focusing on optimizing the economic layout of the whole province to push forward the Mountain-Sea Cooperation Project, firmly complying with the regional strategy for development of the whole province to do something in some areas but refrain from acting in other areas. Giving full considerations to the gap between the location conditions and resource endowment of the underdeveloped areas, adapting measures for local conditions and providing classified guidance. In the underdeveloped areas in the islands, relying on the marine resource advantages to carry out economic cooperation activities in port development, port-centered industries, marine fishery, the coastal tourist industry and the emerging marine industries to make the marine economy large and strong. In the coastal underdeveloped areas with better locations, actively creating conditions to undertake industrial transfer from the developed areas, enhance their capability for self-development. In the underdeveloped areas within the ecological function areas, especially at the source of river basins, always giving priority to protecting the ecological environment, and vigorously developing the ecological economy while helping farmers descend from the mountains to overcome poverty. Moreover, specially transferring rural labor in the underdeveloped areas.

In the above large systematic project for Zhejiang's coordinated urban and rural development and urban-rural integration, the most noteworthy aspect is the practical experience of Zhejiang in the construction of central towns. This is because that construction is the most crucial, most important and most unique part and is decisive for achieving success.

According to the *Developmental Plan of Zhejiang Province for Central Towns (2006–2020)* issued by Zhejiang in 2007, 200 towns, which are economically powerful, enjoy excellent locations and great development potential, can effectively undertake the functions and tasks from large and medium-sized cities and stimulate the development of the surrounding villages and towns, are planned as provincial central towns for aggregating the population and industries and as the hubs for interaction among counties, central towns and central villages. In order to better build central towns, Zhejiang has adjusted the administrative division of central towns, expanded the developmental spaces for central towns, made sure that the average regional area of central towns is apparently higher than the average area of the incorporated towns across the province, increased the scope of stimulating the development of the surrounding areas as far as possible and enhanced the ability to drive others' development forward. In order to make central towns large and strong, Zhejiang has developed supporting policies covering the provincial, municipal and county levels, and has customized relevant vigorous policies for central towns with respect to increasing the proportions of retuned fees and charges and the shared fiscal revenue, expanding the management authority, building the financing platforms, intensifying industrial support and other input; Zhejiang has established a special fund for supporting central towns, while the governments at the provincial, municipal, county (county-level city, district) levels have also introduced policy measures concerning household registration, land system, administrative management and the law enforcement system, injecting reform impetus and fresh vitality for the construction and development of central towns. Meanwhile, the corresponding actions have been taken to increase the administrative level and treatment of central towns, develop central towns into small cities with a high management level, high aggregation capability and complete service functions, and carry out scientific planning, pilot cultivation, industrial agglomeration, public investment and institutional reform to establish special funds for pilot towns in infrastructure, social programs, industrial functional areas, technical innovation and talent agglomeration service platforms, a public service platform and innovations in institutions and mechanisms; turn them into county centers or sub-centers with distinctive industrial characteristics, a good ecological environment, advanced social programs and complete functions and facilities; transform, upgrade and develop a number of extra-large towns into small cities, and make pilot towns leap from towns to cities.

In recent years, Zhejiang has made remarkable achievements in nurturing central towns, it has built industrial development platforms, nurtured and grown the advantageous industries of central towns, concentrated production factors and advantageous industries in central towns, thus Zhejiang has greatly promoted benign interaction between urban construction and the development of the new countryside, significantly made sure that urban construction and the development of the new countryside promoted each other and advanced side by side. At present, Zhejiang's central towns have increasingly stimulated the construction of the new countryside; undoubtedly, they have become the important vehicles for helping to prosper rural areas, serving agriculture and farmers in Zhejiang; they have served as the important supporting points for the county economy and the strategic nodes for achieving urban-rural integration.

9.2.6 The Marine Economy

As a large marine province and the first marine economy demonstration area in China, given the rare growth spaces and developmental opportunities, Zhejiang has naturally made all-out and active efforts to seek development. After the marine economy became an important part of Zhejiang's "Eight-Eight Strategies" and the strategy for making the people rich by starting a business and for building a strong province through innovation, in order to implement the marine strategy, Zhejiang established an interactive land-sea developmental path with its own characteristics—achieving interactive industrial development, an interactive arrangement of productive forces, interactive construction of infrastructure and interactive protection and governance of the ecological environment; Zhejiang identified five major advantageous industries—developing the port shipping industry, new-type port-centered industry, modern marine fishery, the coastal ecological tourist industry and the emerging marine industry; with respect to the driving force for development, Zhejiang adopted the strategy of revitalizing the sea through science and technology to promote transformation from extensive marine development to intensive marine development, intensifying the attraction of investments in the marine economy and strengthening the construction of the government-guided and market-led diversified input mechanism and the market-oriented operational mechanism.

The State Council officially approved the *Plan for Zhejiang's Marine Economy Development Demonstration Areas* on February 25, 2011; this shows that the development of Zhejiang's marine economy was officially elevated to a national strategy and became an important part of China's first plan for marine economy demonstration areas, a national strategy for marine development and a coordinated strategy for regional development; this also suggests that the development of Zhejiang's marine economy had entered a new stage. According to the Plan, the construction of Zhejiang's marine economy development demonstration areas features one center and four demonstration areas—one center means that it is the China International Logistics Center for Bulk Commodities; four demonstration areas are China Marine and Island Development, the Opening-up and Reform Demonstration Area, the China Modern Marine Industrial Development Demonstration Area, the China Coordinated Land-Sea Development Demonstration Area and the China Marine Ecological Civilization and Clean Energy Demonstration Area. Obviously, the efforts made by Zhejiang, as the first marine economy demonstration area in China, to push forward the development of the marine economy undoubtedly produce great reference value and a demonstration effect for the development of the marine economy in other coastal provinces, autonomous regions and municipalities.

First, Zhejiang has made a huge development arrangement for the development of the marine economy and has put forward the overall pattern for the development of the marine economy which features one core, two wings, three circles, nine areas and multiple islands (as shown in Chapter Five of this book). Such an enormous spatial layout almost incorporates 47 counties (county-level cities, districts) in 7 cities, including Hangzhou, Ningbo, Wenzhou, Jiaxing, Shaoxing, Zhoushan and Taizhou, into the scope of the development of the marine economy; it covers the "excellent resources" of the whole province and really gives expression to land-sea interaction.

Second, Zhejiang has built a three-in-one port and shipping logistics service system to make a strong province of port and shipping—developing the port service industry, the logistics industry and the collection and distribution system, expanding the hinterland of Zhejiang's port economy, integrating the existing port resources, building a coastal port system with a rational structure and complete functions, strengthening the planning and management of islands and coastline resources, but leaving a sufficient amount of space for future long-term development. For example, Zhejiang has carried out the primary task of enhancing the construction of such infrastructure as a transport network dominated by the Ningbo-Zhoushan Port, with a view to improving the conditions of port transportation and the collection and distribution network, so that ports obtain support from land hinterland, and the marine economy can connect with land hinterland. Furthermore, in order to expand the functions of the coastal port service and extend the industrial chain and the supporting port collection and distribution system, the financial service system and the information platform, Zhejiang has developed the strategic vision of building a three-in-one port and shipping logistics service system covering a bulk commodity trading platform, an interactive land-sea collection and distribution network and a financial and information service support system.

Third, Zhejiang has built a modern marine industrial system. With a focus on land-sea interaction, actions have been taken to develop the port and shipping, the port-centered industries, marine fishery, the coastal tourist industry and the emerging marine industry, so that the modern marine industrial system becomes more perfect; Zhejiang has focused its future "blue economy" on strategic emerging industries and fields, including advanced marine equipment manufacturing, marine biomedicine, comprehensive sea water utilization, marine clean energy, port and shipping logistics service and marine exploration and development service, with great efforts to develop them into the pillar industries in Zhejiang's marine economy. Therefore, Zhejiang has preliminarily formed a pattern for the development of the marine economy in which the Ningbo-Zhoushan Port serves as the center and the area around Hangzhou Bay and the coastal area in Wenzhou and Taizhou constitute two wings, while the long coastal belt is becoming the main axis in the layout of productive forces across the province.

Fourth, Zhejiang has developed and utilized important islands and built the Zhoushan Archipelago New Area. As Zhejiang abounds in islands, island development is a unique advantage of Zhejiang's marine economy. Zhoushan is the first archipelago new area and the first new area focusing on a marine economy and that is defined at the level of a national strategy in China; at present, it has been positioned as the forerunner in the development of Zhejiang's marine economy, the experimental area for comprehensive marine development and the important growth pole for the economic development of the Yangtze River Delta Region; it is growing into China's bulk commodity storage, transportation, transfer processing trading center, an important marine opening gateway in the eastern region and China's important modern marine industry base. In order to develop important islands, in light of location conditions, resource endowment and development foundation, Zhejiang has classified 100 important islands into the islands for comprehensive utilization, port logistics islands, port-centered industrial islands, clean energy islands, coastal tourist islands, modern fishery islands, marine scientific education islands and marine ecological islands; these islands are utilized in an orderly fashion through classified development to achieve differentiated and characteristic development. For example, Jintang Island is positioned as a modern port logistics island and a port-centered industrial island; Yanwa Island has been developed into a tourist island, hailed as the "Bali in the East China Sea"; other islands, including "Fodao" Mount Putuo, "Nidao" Xiushan Island, "Xiadao" Taohua Island, "Diaodao" Baisha Island, are emerging as theme islands with the connotation of marine culture.

9.3 The Chinese Dream and Inspirations from Zhejiang's Economic Development

Since the reform and opening up, Zhejiang has always stayed ahead nationwide in China's economic development; since the beginning of the 21st century, Zhejiang has become the first to enter the stage of development of economic transformation. The practical experience in the development of transformation gained by Zhejiang under the guidance of the "Eight-Eight Strategies" and the strategy of making the people rich by starting a business and of building a strong province through innovation—this strategy continues and expands the "Eight-Eight Strategies"—is an invaluable treasure for China as China is undergoing economic transformation; in particular, the self-reliant path towards economic development with local characteristics adds charm to its transformation path. Therefore, the practical experience from Zhejiang's transformation path and policy of "carrying through one blueprint to seek development" in more than ten years more convincingly explains the economic dream and the Chinese Dream, and provides more realistic inspirations.

Inspiration One: Common Prosperity

The greatest characteristic of Zhejiang's economy is the developed private economy. In Zhejiang, there are numerous small and medium-sized enterprises, a large number of people start businesses, and Zhejiang has been the first to initiate rural industrialization; this means that Zhejiang has a huge middle-income population and numerous farmers have moved from Zhejiang's agricultural fields; this also suggests that Zhejiang's achievements in economic development are mainly shared by the people. On the Chinese Mainland, no province, autonomous region and municipality are better than Zhejiang in making the wealth shared by the people. The growing private economy, the ever-increasing small and medium-sized enterprise groups and the sharing of the wealth by the people constitute the solid foundation for achieving common prosperity.

Since China initiated the construction of the socialist market economic system in 1992, great progress has been made in the private economy nationwide, but Zhejiang can still constantly expand the first-mover advantage of its private economy; this is certainly associated with the tradition of being keen on starting businesses and doing business, but this is more closely associated with the developments of its state-owned economy and government acts. As the proportion of the state-owned economy was not large in Zhejiang, on the one hand, the integration of government administration with enterprises was not too severe; on the other hand, it provided a large space for the expansion of the private economy, and reduced the barriers to the sound operation of the market mechanism, it was easier for government funds and acts to focus on public goods and public services. Therefore, a developed private economy, a limited state-owned economy and its rational layout as well as the public service-oriented government acts are the preconditions for making it possible for the wealth to be shared by the people and they are the foundation for achieving common prosperity.

Of course, a developed private economy, advantageous systems and mechanisms do not mean that common prosperity is bound to be achieved. The Western developed countries have experienced the historical period during which the market economy was developed but the wealth gap was huge. Thus the "visible hand"—the government—must play the role of regulating the distribution of social wealth. Obviously, the systematic projects of coordinated urban and rural development, urban-rural integration and the holistic promotion of new-type urbanization, first promoted by the Government of Zhejiang, embody precisely the active and correct functions fully performed by the government as the "visible hand". These large systematic projects have paved the broad road for Zhejiang, with the wealth shared by the people, to achieve coordinated development and common prosperity as these projects are designed to break through the dual urban-rural structure, constantly improve the living standard and quality of urban and rural residents, make sure that urban development stimulates rural development and industrial development promotes rural development and promote benign interaction between urban and rural areas, narrow the urban-rural gap, the industry-agriculture gap and the regional gap. At the same time, with the implementation of three major projects for promoting the coordinated economic development of the coastal developed areas and the underdeveloped areas, including the Mountain-Sea Cooperation Project, the project for turning the underdeveloped villages and towns into well-off ones and the project with ten-billion assistance and support for achieving prosperity, Zhejiang has further enhanced multi-channel, multi-mode and multi-level economic cooperation and exchange between the developed areas and the underdeveloped areas, it has intensified transfer payment, and thus it is more possible for Zhejiang to achieve common prosperity. As indicated, making up for market failure and correctly performing the functions of the government as the "visible hand" is also an indispensable factor for achieving common prosperity.

Although Zhejiang is still on the way towards economic development, the road to common prosperity is definitely certain. Therefore, with regard to the Chinese Dream, there is the following inspiration: In order to achieve common prosperity, it is essential to steadfastly develop and grow the private economy and take it as the strong impetus and solid guarantee for economic development and maintain a limited and rational proportion of the state-owned economy. At the same time, it is necessary to fully leverage the functions of the government as the "visible hand" in regulating unbalanced economic and social development and the redistribution of social wealth, push forward cooperation and exchange between the developed areas and the underdeveloped areas, and further the rational flow of social wealth between the rich and the poor.

Inspiration Two: Independent Innovation and Strong Economic Competitiveness

Independent innovation is the foundation for realizing Zhejiang's philosophy of "achieving the rebirth of the phoenix amidst fire" and "vacating the cage to change birds"; it is also the guarantee for Zhejiang's successful economic transformation and upgrading. During the development of transformation, Zhejiang intends to actively develop the equipment manufacturing industry and the high and new technology industries, and carry out independent innovation and adopt the advanced manufacturing technology to upgrade the manufacturing industry, so as to transform from "Made in Zhejiang" to "Created in Zhejiang" with technical innovation as the new impetus. The innovation-driven development is pursued mainly by enterprises.

Undeniably, it is absolutely correct for Zhejiang to define enterprises as the main executors of independent innovation; however, it must be stressed that the real innovators are mainly small and medium-sized enterprises. Thc kcy to regarding small and medium-sized enterprises as the main innovators is that they can continuously focus on a special field, and subject to great competitive pressure, they must innovate, otherwise, their survival and development will be threatened. This is because innovation results from continued painstaking efforts in a special production field and major innovation does not suddenly pop up, while small and medium-sized enterprises often focus on the production in special fields. The Growth Enterprise Market in the capital market mainly serves as the platform for financing the innovations made by small and medium-sized enterprises; many well-known large enterprises in the world, whether technology enterprises or traditional enterprises, are the result of the gradual expansion of small and medium-sized enterprises amidst innovation. In the global competitiveness ranking of economies, such countries and territories as Northern European countries and Switzerland have stayed ahead for a long time thanks to the high capability for innovation of small and medium-sized enterprises. For example, in Finland, which ranked No. 1 in global competitiveness for three consecutive years, except for the agricultural field, there were 263,000 companies in 2008, 99.7% of them were small and medium-sized enterprises with the number of employees below 250; 93% of Finnish enterprises were micro enterprises with the number of employees below 10.[7] Numerous small and medium-sized enterprises with cutting-edge patented technologies make up an important part of Finland's economy, while even Nokia, once a large enterprise, has been supplied with different technologies and parts by small enterprises with the world's leading technologies in an all-round way. Therefore, small and medium-sized enterprises are the sources of independent innovation and the development of cutting-edge technology.

Moreover, small and medium-sized enterprises can become main innovators because of the form of their economic organization—industrial cluster. Industrial cluster is a new concept in the theory of the new economics of competition developed by Michael E. Porter. In his book *Clusters and the New Economics of Competition*, Michael E. Porter defines it as follows: Clusters are geographic concentrations of interconnected companies and institutions in a particular field. Clusters encompass an array of linked industries and other entities important to competition. They include, for example, suppliers of specialized inputs such as components, machinery, and services, and providers of specialized infrastructure. Clusters also often extend downstream to channels and customers and laterally to manufacturers of complementary products and to companies in industries related by skills, technologies, or common inputs. Finally, many clusters include governmental and other institutions—such as universities, standards-setting agencies, think tanks, vocational training providers, and trade associations–that provide specialized training, education, information, research, and technical support.[8] As shown by this long definition, industrial clusters stress that many enterprises engaged in cooperation based on due division of labor in a particular industry, and the institutions and organizations related to them aggregate within a certain region through an intertwined network relationship. Apparently, industrial clusters mainly consist of many small and medium-sized enterprises; both fierce competition and close cooperation occur among them, the resulting operational mechanism which motivates innovation naturally gives birth to their high economic competitiveness. Michael E. Porter even elevated the economic competitiveness shown by industrial clusters to the level of the national competitive advantage; he pointed out that the national competitive advantage was reflected in industrial clusters rather than comparative advantage, while industrial clusters were the main sources of the national competitive advantage. The economic competition between countries was manly embodied in the competition among industrial clusters, while the main characteristic of industrial clusters was cost reduction and continued improvement of the innovation capability resulting from a long-term stable competitive-cooperative relationship among enterprises.[9]

As shown, the vehicles of independent innovation and strong economic competitiveness consist in numerous small and medium-sized enterprises, while those of

[7]Ye Huijue, Behind Finland Pavilion: Clustered Rise of Small and Medium-sized Innovative Enterprises, *21st Century Business Herald*, August 9, 2010.

[8]Chen Liuqin, The Agglomeration Trend of Industrial Development—Industrial Clustering, http://www.chinavalue.net/Finance/Article/2006-1-26/19308.html.

[9]You Zhenlai, Liu Yingzong, A Review of Western Theories of Industrial Clusters, *Journal of Northwest Agriculture & Forestry University* (Social Science Edition), 2008(3).

small and medium-sized enterprises linked by a competitive-cooperative relationship lie in industrial clusters, so developing industrial clusters is an important measure for achieving independent innovation and obtaining strong economic competitiveness. Although Zhejiang's massive economy is still far from becoming industrial clusters of that kind, Zhejiang is working on building industrial parks, promoting the upgrading of the massive economy and making modern industrial clusters, making it possible to achieve independent innovation and strong economic competitiveness in the future. Therefore, when it comes to the Chinese Dream, there is the following inspiration: In order to achieve independent innovation and obtain strong economic competitiveness, the government must sincerely, substantively provide vigorous support to small and medium-sized enterprises, rationally guide them to aggregate, and offer various services to shape really competitive industrial clusters.

Inspiration Three: A Public Service-oriented Government and a Big Open Market

As shown above, the government's roles are all-around: if the government did not relax control and provide support, Zhejiang's private economy could not develop; if the government did not promote relevant work and offer support, it would be impossible to conduct independent innovation, evolve from "Made in Zhejiang" to "Created in Zhejiang", transform and upgrade the massive economy, or build modern industrial clusters; if the government did not push forward opening-up and cooperation, it would be hard to place equal emphasis on "bringing in" and "going global", "going out of Zhejiang to develop Zhejiang"; coordinated urban and rural development, coordinated development, land-sea interaction and the development of the marine economy have more directly resulted from the government's efforts at planning and implementation. Therefore, in China, the government is not only an important and indispensable force, but also the crucial and pivotal force having a direct bearing on success.

In China, discussions about the government entail many considerations. Overall, at present, the operation of China's economy is still led by the government, and administrative intervention remains pervasive; it is hard to deny this fact. The three-in-one system covering the government, state-owned enterprises and state-owned banks guarantees smooth government-led economic operations. The ability of Zhejiang's private economy to gradually develop is attributable to the following factors: the number of state-owned enterprises was small, the proportion of the state-owned economy was low and the three-in-one chain as the core link was weakened at the initial stage of reform and opening up, while it was natural for government acts to favor the private economy and be willing to open up the market. The small number of state-owned enterprises and the low proportion of the state-owned economy mean that the market was monopolized just at a small proportion and by weak forces, and there was less resistance for specialized markets to stand out. Therefore, the orientation of the government's acts is of great significance for correctly leveraging its functions. At present, correct orientation is certainly the building of a public service-oriented government; this requires the government to advance or retreat in a well-founded way, transform from an economic construction-oriented one to a market service-oriented one, gradually narrow the extent and scope of direct participation in the market, remove administrative intervention in market operation, change from the market dominator to the market server, from the leading actor in economic operations to a supporting actor, or shift from the one on the stage to the one behind the scene. The Chinese Government's acts of going beyond, refraining from performing its due economic functions or performing undue economic functions epitomize the government's failure to advance or retreat in a well-founded way. Relatively, the Zhejiang Provincial Party Committee and the Provincial Government can be considered to have stayed ahead in this regard; Zhejiang is hailed as a large province of markets thanks to great efforts from the government.

A large province of markets is of great significance for Zhejiang's economic development; it serves as the bridge for developing a small province of resources into a large economic province. At present, the Government of Zhejiang is pushing forward inter-regional opening-up, international opening-up, regional cooperation and exchange through multiple channels in various ways, combining "bringing in" with "going global", optimizing the open structure and improving the quality of opening-up. The efforts to build a large all-round, wide-ranging, multi-level open market pattern certainly produce a great positive effect on developing a large province of markets into a strong province of markets, while the formation of a strong province of markets means the birth of an economically strong province. Such countries and territories as Northern European countries and Switzerland have less abundant resources, a small population and a small geographical area, but their products are crucial in global high-end markets, so they are powerful countries of markets and economically powerful countries, as evidenced by the fact that they have stayed ahead in global economic competitiveness for a long time. As shown above, with respect to the Chinese Dream, there is the following inspiration: At present, China falls short of resources and energy and faces the crisis of shortage, while that crisis can be addressed by nurturing a large open market, further developing markets, allocating resources and expanding spaces worldwide, utilizing technologies and capital to obtain resources and energy, transforming China from a large country of markets to a powerful country of markets, from a large economic country to an economically powerful country. For building a public service-oriented government, there is this inspiration: It is necessary to reduce the number of state-owned enterprises and the proportion of the state-owned economy to keep them within a limited and a rational scope, prompt them to leave the fields where there is competition with the private economy, and weaken the functions of the three-in-one chain to leave the spaces for growing small and medium-sized enterprises; at the same time, the government should actively guide and serve the building of a benign competitive-cooperative relationship among private enterprises, build industrial clusters governed by an endogenous innovation mechanism and create the conditions for turning enterprises into the main executors of independent innovation.

Inspiration Four: The Marine Economy and a Powerful Marine Country

According to the report delivered at the 18th CPC National Congress, China will improve its ability to develop marine resources, develop the marine economy, protect the marine ecological environment, resolutely safeguard national marine rights and interests and build a powerful marine country. Thus the significance of developing the marine economy is not limited to the economic level and involves the levels of national rights and interests, even that of a powerful country.

China is a large land country with land territory covering an area of 9.60 million km^2; people know little about the fact that China has a coastline that is 18,000 km long and 200-sea-mile-long exclusive economic zones, China ranks No. 4, No. 5 and No. 10 worldwide in coastline length, the area of continental shelf and the area of exclusive economic zones, respectively, so China is really a large marine country. Zhejiang is a small province of resources, but it is actually a large marine province; Zhejiang ranks No. 1 nationwide in coastline, island shoreline, the number of relatively large islands and the area of offshore fishing grounds; it is highly logical that Zhejiang should become the first marine economy demonstration area in China. Zhejiang's development of the marine economy is not only of great significance for itself, but it is also conducive to exploring a path towards the development of a marine economy for China. The marine economy is a new growth point for both Zhejiang's and China's economic development; Zhejiang needs to utilize marine resources; likewise, it is urgent for China to develop marine resources; Zhejiang's plan for the overall pattern of development for the marine economy serves as the template for the plans of other coastal provinces, autonomous regions and municipalities; Zhejiang's marine strategy for land-sea interactive development, the building of a modern marine industrial system and the three-in-one port and shipping logistics service system also produce a demonstration effect. Therefore, Zhejiang is considered as the forerunner to bringing China to the century of the ocean and turning China into a powerful marine country; Zhejiang's practical experience and success or failure in developing the marine economy introduce important inspirations to China.

History proves that going with the ocean brings about prosperity, while going against the ocean leads to decline. History also proves that if there is no strong marine power, it is impossible to effectively withstand marine threats, guarantee access to the sea, and utilize the marine resources jointly inherited by mankind in the open sea and international sea bed. The 21st century is a century of the ocean; if China fails to become a powerful marine country during this historical period, China cannot become a world power, while making the people rich and the country powerful is the tireless pursuit and common aspiration of the Chinese people, so building a powerful marine country is certainly the inevitable choice for realizing the Chinese Dream of the great rejuvenation of the Chinese nation and an important part of the Chinese Dream of building a powerful marine country.

A powerful marine country is defined as a marine country with a developed marine economy, advanced marine science and technology, a powerful navy, capability for scientific and efficient ocean management, a complete marine legal system, a healthy marine ecological system, a sustainable marine resource environment, a strong marine awareness and unique marine culture soft power.[10] As shown, developing the marine economy is the first step on the path of building a powerful marine

[10]Cao Wenzhen, The Strategy of a Powerful Marine Country and the Chinese Dream, *China Ocean News*, July 21, 2014.

country and the foundation for realizing a powerful marine country; in other words, a country needs to become a powerful country of marine economy before it can become a powerful marine country. Obviously, this historical task of exploration has been first imposed on Zhejiang's people, it is arduous and the mission is glorious. Second, a powerful marine country should also be a powerful country of marine science and technology; in other words, marine science and technology leads the world, a galaxy of marine high-tech talents emerge, the capability for marine scientific and technological innovation and research and development remains ahead worldwide; this is an important hallmark of a powerful marine country. This is because only when the developed marine science and technology is relied upon can a powerful navy be built and can a mighty integrated marine force dominated by the navy be established, can China's sea rights be safeguarded, can a marine defense system under a complete safeguarding mechanism be built, and can China smoothly join the ranks of marine military powers and ultimately a powerful country measured by overall marine strength—a complete and well-rounded powerful marine country. Therefore, developing the marine economy and building a powerful marine country on the basis of this development is essential for China to achieve sustainable development and become a world power.

Given the relationship between the marine economy and a powerful marine country, as Zhejiang has been the first to undertake the heavy task of developing the marine economy, Zhejiang will certainly assume the responsibility and mission for being the first to carry out marine scientific and technological innovation, research and development, leading China to become a powerful country of marine science and technology. In fact, this also suggests that Zhejiang must and is bound to become a strong force for driving China to realize the dream of a powerful marine country. Thus Zhejiang's success in developing the marine economy will certainly bring experience and be a demonstration effect to the marine economy in other coastal provinces, autonomous regions and municipalities across the country. There is a long way to go for Zhejiang in the 21st century to help realize the Chinese Dream.

Postscript

According to the overall arrangement and survey plan for the major program "The Chinese Dream and Zhejiang's Practice" jointly carried out by Zhejiang Provincial Party Committee and the Chinese Academy of Social Sciences, the Research Group of "The Chinese Dream and Zhejiang's Practice·Economy Volume" consists of relevant personnel from the Institute of Economics under the Chinese Academy of Social Sciences and the Institute of Regional Economy under the Zhejiang Academy of Social Sciences, etc. In the Research Group, Pei Changhong, Director, research fellow of the Institute of Economics under the Chinese Academy of Social Sciences, serves as leader, while Xu Jianfeng, Director, research fellow of the Institute of Regional Economy under the Zhejiang Academy of Social Sciences, serves as deputy leader. The Research Group first designed the outline of this book, solicited opinions from experts and scholars within and outside Zhejiang, conducted several revisions and feasibility studies. Afterwards, the members of the Research Group communicated with each other many times to determine the division of the work and its contents. The members of the Research Group carefully studied relevant works of comrade Xi Jinping, consulted a great deal of relevant materials from the Zhejiang Provincial Party Committee, the Provincial Government, relevant departments and local authorities, conducted on-the-spot surveys in Hangzhou, Wenzhou, Ningbo and other areas, listened to the remarks made by relevant departments, and visited enterprises to obtain a large quantity of first-hand material, thus laying a good foundation for research on the subject.

The Chinese Dream and Zhejiang's Practice·Economy Volume is the result of the active participation of and joint research by more than 10 experts and scholars within and outside Zhejiang, concerted efforts, repeated modification, and several changes made by participants. In this Volume, Pei Changhong and Xu Jianfeng serve as the editor in chief and associate editor, they are responsible for the design of chapters and sections, final compilation and editing, while comrade Yang Jianjiang from the Zhejiang Academy of Social Sciences has conducted a lot of research and much work on coordinating the meetings.

C. Pei and J. Xu (eds.), *Chinese Dream and Practice in Zhejiang – Economy*,
Research Series on the Chinese Dream and China's Development Path,
https://doi.org/10.1007/978-981-13-7484-5

The writers of the Economy Volume include:
Chapter 1, Xu Jianfeng (Zhejiang Academy of Social Sciences);
Chapter 2, Xiang Feng (Zhejiang Academy of Social Sciences);
Chapter 3, Guo Ying (Zhejiang Academy of Social Sciences);
Chapter 4, Guo Ying (Zhejiang Academy of Social Sciences);
Chapter 5, Xu Jianfeng (Zhejiang Academy of Social Sciences);
Chapter 6, Wu Xiaolu (Zhejiang Academy of Social Sciences);
Chapter 7, Wen Haiyan (Zhejiang Academy of Social Sciences);
Chapter 8, Wen Haiyan, Mao Wei (Zhejiang Academy of Social Sciences);
Chapter 9, Huang Zhigang, Liu Xiahui (Chinese Academy of Social Sciences).

A heartfelt thank-you goes to the Chinese Academy of Social Sciences and the Publicity Department of the CPC of the Zhejiang Provincial Committee for extensive guidance and support! A further thank-you goes to the Zhejiang Provincial Development and Reform Commission, the Zhejiang Provincial Economic and Information Commission, the Zhejiang Provincial Department of Commerce, the Zhejiang Provincial Department of Science and Technology, the Zhejiang Provincial Bureau of Statistics, the Zhejiang Provincial Agricultural Office, the Zhejiang Provincial Economic and Technological Cooperation Office, the Zhejiang Provincial Ocean and Fisheries Bureau, the Zhejiang Administration for Industry and Commerce, the Zhejiang Federation of Industry and Commerce and other provincial departments, as well as Party Committees, governments and relevant departments of Hangzhou, Wenzhou and Ningbo City for their great assistance! Finally, a thank-you must be expressed to the experts and scholars from the Party School of the Zhejiang Provincial Party Committee, the Policy Research Office of the Zhejiang Provincial Party Committee, the Policy Research Office of the People's Government of Zhejiang Province, the Research Office of the Zhejiang Provincial People's Political Consultative Conference, the Party History Office of the Zhejiang Provincial Party Committee, Zhejiang University, Zhejiang University of Technology, Zhejiang Gongshang University, Zhejiang University of Finance & Economics, etc. for their valuable opinions! Much needs to be improved due to the tight schedule and heavy task; criticisms and corrections from leaders, experts and scholars are highly appreciated!

Research Group of *The Chinese Dream and Zhejiang's Practice (Economy Volume).*
December 10, 2014.

MIX
Papier aus verantwortungsvollen Quellen
Paper from responsible sources
FSC® C105338

If you have any concerns about our products,
you can contact us on
ProductSafety@springernature.com

In case Publisher is established outside the EU,
the EU authorized representative is:
Springer Nature Customer Service Center GmbH
Europaplatz 3, 69115 Heidelberg, Germany

Printed by Libri Plureos GmbH
in Hamburg, Germany